T0344801

Achieving Investment Excellence

The Frank J. Fabozzi Series

Handbook of Finance: Volume I: Financial Markets and Instruments edited by Frank J. Fabozzi

Handbook of Finance: Volume II: Financial Management and Asset Management edited by Frank J. Fabozzi

Handbook of Finance: Volume III: Valuation, Financial Modeling, and Quantitative Tools edited by Frank J. Fabozzi

Finance: Capital Markets, Financial Management, and Investment Management by Frank J. Fabozzi and Pamela Peterson-Drake

Active Private Equity Real Estate Strategy edited by David J. Lynn

Foundations and Applications of the Time Value of Money by Pamela Peterson-Drake and Frank J. Fabozzi

Leveraged Finance: Concepts, Methods, and Trading of High-Yield Bonds, Loans, and Derivatives by Stephen Antczak, Douglas Lucas, and Frank J. Fabozzi

Modern Financial Systems: Theory and Applications by Edwin Neave

Institutional Investment Management: Equity and Bond Portfolio Strategies and Applications by Frank J. Fabozzi

Robust Equity Portfolio Management + Website by Woo Chang Kim, Jang Ho Kim, and Frank J. Fabozzi

Quantitative Financial Risk Management: Theory and Practice by Constantin Zopounidis and Emilios Galariotis

Portfolio Construction and Analytics by Dessislava A. Pachamanova Frank J. Fabozzi

Achieving Investment Excellence: A Practical Guide for Trustees of Pension Funds, Endowments and Foundations by Kees Koedijk, Alfred Slager, and Jaap van Dam

Achieving Investment Excellence

A Practical Guide for Trustees of Pension Funds, Endowments and Foundations

KEES KOEDIJK
ALFRED SLAGER
JAAP VAN DAM

WILEY

Library of Congress Cataloging-in-Publication Data

Names: Koedijk, Kees, author. | Slager, Alfred, 1967- author. | Dam, Jaap van, 1961- author.
Title: Achieving investment excellence : a practical guide for trustees of pension funds, endowments and foundations / Kees Koedijk, Alfred Slager, Jaap van Dam.
Description: Chichester, West Sussex, United Kingdom ; Hoboko, NJ : Wiley, 2019. | Includes bibliographical references and index. |
Identifiers: LCCN 2018043877 (print) | LCCN 2018058407 (ebook) | ISBN 9781119437697 (Adobe PDF) | ISBN 9781119437727 (ePub) | ISBN 9781119437659 (hardcover)
Subjects: LCSH: Pension trusts. | Endowments. | Portfolio management.
Classification: LCC HD7105.4 (ebook) | LCC HD7105.4 .K64 2019 (print) | DDC 332.67/253—dc23
LC record available at https://lccn.loc.gov/2018043877

Contents

About the Authors

Kees Koedijk is a professor of Financial Management at TIAS Business School and Tilburg University, the Netherlands. He has won several national and international awards for his research on sustainable development. He has published extensively on finance, responsible investment and pension management. During the last 10 years he has served at several investment committees of asset institutions and acted as consultant to international pension funds. Kees Koedijk is a co-editor of the *Journal of International Money and Finance*, and is on the editorial board of the *Journal of Portfolio Management*. In 2010, Kees Koedijk published the book *Investment Beliefs* together with Alfred Slager. Many funds across the globe have since then adopted the framework on investment beliefs that was developed in the book.

During his career, Kees Koedijk has also acted as a serial entrepreneur in financial services. Together with Piet Eichholtz (Maastricht University), he founded the company Global Property Research (GPR) in Amsterdam in 1994, which produces leading indexes for real estate securities worldwide. GPR is now part of Van Lanschot Kempen. In 2004 he co-founded the company, Finance Ideas, with Piet Eichholtz and Thomas Heijdendael. Finance Ideas is a financial advisory firm, which originally specialized in social real estate but increasingly acts as strategic consultant and partner to institutional investors.

Alfred Slager is an economist, trustee, and advisor who has worked and published widely on issues to help pension fund boards with their strategy and investment management. He is professor at TIAS Business School, Tilburg University, and a trustee at the Dutch pension fund for general practitioners, SPH.

He has performed many different roles, generally bridging academic finance and practical investing. Starting out as a portfolio manager in 1995, he spent 15 years as research analyst, investment strategist, and chief investment officer at different pension funds and investment management firms, earning his PhD cum laude in 2005. Over the years, Alfred has advised many institutional investors on investment strategy and investment governance. He has written several books, including *Investment Beliefs* together with Kees Koedijk, as well as on the internationalization strategies of banks and the effectiveness of investment committees, and has acted as editor of a book on the best practices in pension investments. Alfred serves on several investment committees and supervisory boards of pension funds, as well as on the board of the Dutch CFA Society VBA Netherlands.

Jaap van Dam is the Principal Director of Investment Strategy at PGGM in The Netherlands. He is chairman of the European chapter of The 300 Club, whose mission is to raise awareness about the potential impact of current market thinking and behaviors, and of the Dutch Association of Investors for Sustainable Development (VBDO). He holds a Master's Degree in Finance from Erasmus University in Rotterdam, the Netherlands. Jaap's career in investment management spans more than three decades. His lifelong ambition is to improve investment management by integrating academic insights into practice and by asking academia for help in solving practical investment challenges.

Jaap has performed many roles within the field, ranging from fundamental and quantitative analysis to external manager selection and portfolio construction. He joined PGGM in 2005 as Head of Internal Equity Management. In 2006 he was appointed Chief Strategist. Notably, within PGGM he was responsible for developing PFZW's new investment framework and Investment Strategy 2020. Jaap is a member of ICPM's research committee and the International Advisory Board of EDHEC.

Acknowledgments

This book did not materialize overnight; a succession of articles, presentations, and papers have shaped our thinking over the years, inspired by first-hand experience, sharing dilemmas and insights with trustees, investment managers and regulators.

Sharing numerous discussions and experiences with trustees, acquired when giving courses, serving on pension funds' boards or assisting boards advisory projects on strategies, we were regularly struck by how much the investment profession has evolved in the past 40 years. Portfolio techniques have evolved; risk management too, supported by an ever-increasing need and supply of information. One thing is clear though: new texts and insights that keep up with the changing markets and role of trustees are needed, integrating the new insights in portfolio management with investment governance in such a way that trustees and board keep on excelling.

Our minds were first opened to the importance of boards and governance by Roger Urwin and Gordon Clark. Their thinking formed and still forms a great source of inspiration. Roger very much likes to refer to the importance of "the soft stuff" of leadership and governance, which is so often overlooked in investing. In addition, Keith Ambachtsheer with his ongoing plea for the importance of strong pension fund governance has been a source of wisdom for us. Among other people that should be mentioned here is Ashby Monk, with whom Jaap had a conversation on the importance of trust that had a long-lasting impression on him. At PGGM and PFZW, important people for the development of his thinking have been Jean Frijns, as wise a board member as you'll ever see; Florent Vlak, the chair of the PFZW Investment Committee; and Else Bos, who made the connection between PGGM and the small group of inspiring best practice global asset owners.

Another source of inspiration for Alfred was serving as a trustee on the board of the pension fund for the general practitioners (SPH), where the board creates and fosters an environment to be the best they can for their participants, continuously raising the standards in investment governance to meet that goal. The importance of the "soft stuff" pragmatically could be seen at work in an energetic environment, which helped shape thinking on the role of boards and board room dynamics in this book.

We have benefited from numerous discussions with trustees giving courses or serving on pension funds' boards and investment committees, helping us to shape the ideas into the applicable frameworks that the reader finds throughout the book. We were also fortunate to discuss our research and ideas at several seminars and conferences. In particular, the International Centre for Pension Management (ICPM) provided a stimulating platform to discuss our ideas with the top professionals in the pension sector.

We would like to thank the many individuals who played important roles in producing this book. Charles Ellis inspired us to think long and hard about what the essence is within investment management from the perspective of a trustee. Sung Cheng Chih, Frank Fabozzi, Eduard van Gelderen, Knut Kjaer, Steve Lydenderg, Kasper Rozsbach and Jaco van der Walt reviewed the document and provided, despite their hectic time schedules, invaluable advice to make the book more relevant to trustees' needs.

Many board members, trustees and practitioners in the field have, without knowing it, inspired us with their insights and knowledge on investment governance, and have made a valuable contribution in keeping our ideas practical. A special mention goes to Marcel Andringa, Bart Bos, Wouter van Eechoud, David Iverson, Anne Gram, Jacco Heemskerk, Rob Heerkens, Jeroen van der Hoek, Fieke van der Lecq, Lionel Martellini, Jan Bertus Molenkamp, David Neal, Jan Overmeer, Jeroen Schreurs and Martijn Vos.

Peta Baxter and Caroline Studdert molded the draft into a readable and accessible book, while Nicole Rijnen and Corine Schriks helped us manage the project. We thank Samantha Hermans and Rubin Mehlhorn, who provided skillful research assistance. A special mention goes to Ruben Uijting who not only provided high quality research assistance, but also instilled sorely needed project management discipline, asked the critical questions at the right time, and prevented us from drifting off from time to time. Any pension fund aiming at achieving excellence should be glad to have him on board.

A final thank you goes to the editorial services of Wiley for their support of the book's copyediting needs.

Foreword

As CEO of one of the largest U.S. pension plans, I have become a humble admirer of board members who take on the weighty responsibility of governing the pension investments on behalf of current and future beneficiaries.

Board members face an onslaught of challenges when they land a trustee role: They often are highly trained professionals, but often in fields unrelated or distantly related to investment management. They are faced with complex and often technical investment decisions, and they have to quickly come up to speed while evaluating vast amounts of data or converging viewpoints.

To support and assist board members facing such challenges, my most trustworthy solutions have been education, structured dialogue and adequate time for meaningful debate. My board and staff invest a significant amount of time together in study and discussion to ensure we're on the same shared journey towards a good long-term pension outcome for our fund and its beneficiaries; the emphasis here is long term.

As a pension fund with fiduciary obligations that span generations of public workers, we have very long-term obligations. We are necessarily interested in building an investment solution that will generate solid, risk-adjusted returns over time. Our board members must arm themselves with fortitude and enough resiliency to maintain proper perspective amid an overwhelming array of short-term distractions. Decision makers at pension funds must frequently cope with a low return environment, high volatility and constant shifts in industry offerings—all while remaining committed to a mission of building real investment value over the long term. My objective has always been to build a steadfast, mission-driven institution that focuses on investing for the long term.

So how do we encourage institutional investors, money managers and our portfolio companies to take a longer view? I am convinced that success starts at the board level—the front end of the investment value chain.

When board members are well educated and fully engaged, they are better equipped to pursue the long-term success of a pension plan. Ask any airplane pilot how they respond to an emergency situation, and they inevitably talk about how "the training took over their actions." Similarly, board members must train themselves to recognize short term trade-offs, but act in terms of multiple, long market cycles. They must understand how to put today's fleeting issues into a global context with an appropriate time horizon. When faced with adversity, they must know the difference between responding and reacting. Today boards are not only challenged by a tough investing environment, but with increased desires by stakeholders who wish to use the influence of investment capital to support various societal agendas. At times, it's all too easy to allow others' missions to consume or conflict with the investment mission of a pension fund. Balancing fiduciary and societal interests is an ever-present reality for today's pension fund trustee.

To maintain such balance, a firm set of investment beliefs can help a board establish its "North Star." This allows the board to stay on course so the fund adds value for pensioners and society over time. Boards also must be clear on delegation—empowering talented investment professionals to achieve their best for the pension plan, while exercising appropriate oversight and avoiding micro-management. Knowing when to guide, listen or to follow is essential; knowing how to challenge or support those same investment professionals are vital board skills that in my experience can be cultivated. When it works well, this leads to a healthy board dynamic, a strong staff and a mutually beneficial relationship.

During the last two decades, the Washington State Investment Board has established strong investment beliefs, clear rules around delegation and reshaped its board agendas to focus much more heavily on education, strategy and risk discussions. In short, our board is focused less on transactions and short-term market movements, and more on strategy and long-term positioning of funds. Our board embraces dedicated time for education and structured dialogue, including debate around new practical research and academic insights. Our board members also are willing to engage in self-reflection, analysis of decision making practices, and maintenance of healthy board room dynamics.

This focus on education and debate has proven valuable enough to earn a spot as a permanent feature of our strategic planning process. We explicitly recognize that all of our success rests on the foundation of a "skillful board," therefore our board sets goals for its own development each year, all of which brings me to the purpose of this foreword.

Thus far, there has not been a high-level source for systematically educating board members on their challenges of their duties. Most of the investment literature is either too superficial or too specialized. *Achieving Investment Excellence* spans the relevant fields. It is both comprehensive and an accessible primer for trustees, something that's been missing in trustee education. It doesn't bog down in technical jargon or fall victim to over-simplification; it is thoughtfully designed to help board members to gain valuable, pragmatic perspective while equipping board members to keep asking the right questions. I believe it will help board members to do their best work when faced with demanding responsibilities. I'm quite sure it will lead to better conversations in many boardrooms.

I fully intend to use *Achieving Investment Excellence* for my own trustee onboarding, helping new trustees to hit the ground running. And for my experienced trustees, I envision there will be new insights they will gain to enhance their skills. Bottom line, the authors have succeeded in providing boards with practical tools to help achieve the best possible governance for their participants.

Theresa J. Whitmarsh

If you are reading this book, you are almost certainly a trustee or board member. Or perhaps you are considering becoming one. Maybe you are an adviser looking for tips on how trustees think about the complex issues you advise on, or you are a board member of a pension fund, endowment or foundation. Irrespective of your level of expertise and profession in the industry, why should you read this book, and which problems are we attempting to solve here? More importantly, how should you use this book and apply it to your own practice for the benefit of your fund and its long-term performance?

The basic premise of this book is that trustees have a crucial role to play in the long-term success of pension funds and other long-horizon asset owner organizations: sovereign wealth funds, endowments and foundations. Trustees are able to make to a real and meaningful difference when it comes to sustainable pensions for millions of pensioners in the coming decades. For a trustee this may be a powerful, but at the same time scary, idea. In the past decade, the very low interest rates have dramatically increased the cost of meeting future pension payouts, beyond all expectations. The time that you allocate and the level of knowledge that you need to demonstrate have probably increased disproportionately over the years as a consequence of the increased regulation. The stakes for your personal reputation are higher than ever. You understand the importance of doing this job well. You are aware that you matter for the thousands and millions of future pensioners who depend on your choices for their future retirement. As a trustee you have both a large responsibility and a large opportunity regarding the investments you oversee. Given that you are at the beginning of the investment chain it is imperative to understand what contributes to investment success and what detracts from it. This matters all the more because the margin of error is steadily narrowing. Consider, for instance, that in the year 2000, trustees would have expected equities to earn 10% per year, whereas today, they would be more than happy to expect half as much.

It is easy to get lost in the complex landscape of investing. Understanding and overseeing what really matters is key. This book benefits anyone who is seeking to ask the right questions in the boardroom, and is looking for a guide that will help them in setting the agenda in ways that allow for effective and relevant decision-making. This book is also intended as a potent counterbalance to the highly skilled management of the investment organizations that trustees face. Above all, this book contributes in a very pragmatic way, as we review and consolidate years of academic research and case studies on day-to-day implementation, translating these into inspiring examples and actionable alternatives that are of practical use to trustees worldwide. We systematically integrate the important perspectives into the five parts of this book. In Chapter 14, all perspectives are brought together in a way that assists trustees in determining where they stand right now, and what is needed to move to the next level in the pursuit of investment excellence. Reading this chapter first will help you to read the book in a more goal-oriented manner.

As a trustee, having oversight and pushing the right buttons is difficult. We have come to this conclusion based on years of extensive practical and academic experience, in combination with our own research and the ample available evidence. We are fairly confident in saying that there is a lot to be gained from learning how to do this correctly. We feel that trustees should take an active role in this process on behalf of the beneficiaries they represent.

Trustees are often highly competent individuals who are relatively new to the situation in which they have to govern a pension organization. It can take quite some time before they grasp the task in its entirety, appreciate its complexity and fully understand what really matters and what does not. Trustees are more often than not in the process of "learning on the job," which creates a risk of them only having a partial understanding of the issues at hand. Such a risk is manageable and may even be tolerable when financial markets are calm and the political environment is stable. Unfortunately, at this time, the opposite is true. We are witnessing abrupt and profound shifts in the political and technological landscape; and given generally low solvency, the margin of error is small. This book aims to bring the reader up to speed fast. Moreover, we hope it will stimulate a structured conversation within the fund, where views can be shared and exchanged in order to assess the current state of the fund, and possibilities to improve it can be determined.

We argue that there is a substantial governance "bonus" to be harvested. We believe that by transforming any weak pension organization into to an excellent one, additional annual long-term return gains of 1%–2% can be achieved.[1] Of course, the potential gain depends to a large extent on the starting situation of the plan. Exhibit I.1 below specifies a number of sources of higher returns, splitting them in two parts: avoiding negative contributions to returns and intensifying the use of positive contributions.

The potential gains of moving up on the scale of excellence depicted in the table above are crude and will differ from fund to fund. This table zooms in only on the financial side of things, but there also are other issues at hand that may drive success: How do you cope with environmental, social and governance (ESG) matters? What is your policy on climate change? We are witnessing a shift in the expectations of beneficiaries and other stakeholders. Not having a sound answer to these questions or hiding behind a narrow definition of fiduciary duty may come at a high cost in terms of the license to operate the fund.

Quite a few of the sources of improvement are accessible to almost all funds, regardless of their size. They all require well-applied knowledge and understanding from the board of trustees and investment committee. Essentially, the message here is to plug any leaks and avoid avoidable mistakes. Some of the sources are scale-dependent and depend on the availability of a "proprietary" investment organization that can, for example, harvest the risk premia available in illiquid assets in a cost-effective way. To a large extent, in both cases the board and the board investment committee play crucial

Avoid Negative Contributions	Order of Magnitude	Discussed in Chapter
Lower total cost of implementation	0.5%	9
Avoid behavioral traps (manager turnover, selling after the fact)	0.5%	5 & 14
Weed out negative contributions (e.g., active management, TAA)	0.3%	4 & 7
Insourcing	0.3%	12

Add Positive Contributions	Order of Magnitude	Discussed in Chapter
Disciplined rebalancing	0.3%	8
Add illiquid investments	0.5%	8
Diversification	0.2%	4 & 8

EXHIBIT I.1 Bonus to be harvested when moving up from mediocre to excellent on the scale of excellence.

roles in driving the fund into the direction of excellence—or vice versa. Therefore, the quality, knowledge and, most of all, drive of boards matter—a lot.

Doing 1–2% better is a considerable amount in a world in which expected returns for well-diversified portfolios are somewhere in the range of 3–6% in nominal terms. We estimate that harvesting 80% of this bonus requires only a limited amount of work once you understand the drivers and put in place the right groundwork. For example, it involves getting your beliefs right and making sure that they are consistently translated into the investment process. It involves designing an investment process that helps to achieve your fund's goals and tackling the main known governance issues. We believe that there are five activities that together can create "excellent investing;" we discuss them at a later point in time. We feel these are the roughly the same for every fund, even though pension funds come in all shapes and sizes. Our experience is that the same issues pop up around the globe. As the answers to these common issues may vary slightly due to cultural or regulatory circumstances, we will address such differences in size and structures (and their consequences) wherever necessary and appropriate.

The central message throughout this book is that the board is key in achieving long-term investment excellence. The board, however, is not the party managing the investments, but the party that is meant to be in charge of the design, strategy, monitoring, and improvement of the "machine" that delivers the output. This requires a specific set of perspectives, which we summarize as the right altitude, the right distance, and the right horizon. *Altitude*: Does the board look at the total fund setup and its outcomes from a helicopter view? Can it achieve a critical distance towards itself? *Horizon*: Has the board organized itself in such a way that it can look forward and backward at least over a 5–10 year perspective? Can it do so even if that time span is longer than the individual's timespan as a member of the board? And *distance*: Is the board able to maintain the right distance from the execution of the investment management—is it close enough to be able to fully carry out its responsibility, yet not so close that it is taking operational decisions that should be taken by the executive?

Excellent pension funds strike the right balance between altitude, distance and horizon. They do not get caught up in the vast forest of investment strategies, nor do they get drowned by oceans of financial data. They are not distracted by mathematics and investment industry jargon. Often, too much attention is paid to the (sometimes highly technical) detailed investment side (i.e. doing things right), while important issues remain unanswered (i.e. doing the right things). Excellent pension funds and especially their trustees, therefore, know when and how to take the fiduciary perspective in managing the investment organization, while at the same time making sure that they are a partner in the investment process, where all stakeholders depend on each other for sustainable results. In other words, transforming from good to great requires a board that is not only keen on staying the course but is, perhaps more importantly, very much attuned to learning, adapting and reflecting on its own behavior.

In order to balance the attention of the board between doing the right things and doing things right, we introduce the "excellence loop" presented in Exhibit I.2: the left part is the strategic, design, "doing the right things" loop; whereas the right part is the much faster implementation and the "doing the things right" feedback loop. The connection between the loops deserves a lot of attention: often this is the point where serious challenges can arise in terms of delegation and principal–agent issues.

In this respect, our aim is to help trustees in identifying activities that need to be carried out in order to develop a good pension fund and, if their ambition reaches

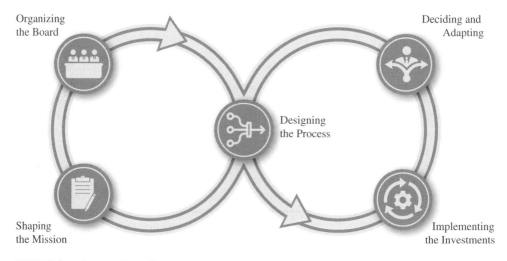

Organizing the Board

Deciding and Adapting

Designing the Process

Shaping the Mission

Implementing the Investments

EXHIBIT I.2   The excellence loop.

higher (which in our opinion it should), what is needed to develop an excellent pension fund. While drawing on our own experiences and research as well as that of generations of trustees and investment professionals, we offer trustees a practical "how to" guide in grasping the fundamentals of creating and operating a pension organization successfully.

Our goal is to provide insight into the key activities for building long-term excellence in investing. We combine "hard" investment thinking, for example about the design and implementation of the investment process, with "softer" elements, such as the organization of the investment committee or the self-reflection of the board. In doing so, we maintain an unbiased attitude towards the practical and academic evidence on what does and does not work in investment management. While overwhelming evidence already exists about the various ways we make decisions and about the sense and lack of sense of investment strategies, we also observe a growing body of evidence and literature that shows us how we can actually organize this in a good way. Unfortunately, trustees often enough ignore such evidence or are simply not aware that it exists. We trust that this book offers them powerful and compelling tools and knowledge.

We believe that pension funds and their beneficiaries may expect trustees and boards who are intrinsically motivated to move towards excellence. Therefore, we will almost never look at regulatory requirements or at the role of the regulator, which we see as a setter of minimum standards, not as a motivator to move towards excellence.

To summarize, this book will support the trustee at three levels. First, we outline the five key dimensions that drive long-term investment success. As a trustee, you know how the investment process is organized. But do you also know why the investment process is organized the way it is? Is it indeed the best way to achieve the pension fund's goals, and does it reflect the (right) risks in the pension plan? These are all obvious, but nevertheless crucial, questions that we will help you pose and formulate. You will see which assumptions matter, so that next time you don't simply go through the motions in a board or investment committee, but instead can immediately get to the questions that matter. Secondly, the book offers sound and practical advice that is built on both academic work and broad real-world experience. What might work in practice does not always have a sound theoretical basis, and vice versa. Consider, for instance, that the integration of sustainability in the investment process started long before academic evidence even supported such a move. Conversely, academic research has in turn produced many studies on new types of portfolio construction, such as factor investing for example, which may not (yet) have been (fully) embraced by the industry. The wise and successful trustee therefore would do well to be pragmatic in determining what exactly strengthens the investment process, rather than upending it. Finally, this book provides the trustee with the necessary insights to become a better decision maker while putting the ideas and concepts into practice. Boardroom dynamics are complex, as is making investment decisions today that will have an impact in decades to come. The challenge is to incorporate the insights whilst acknowledging that people and their interactions are crucial to the very success of their mandates. Here too, we choose a hands-on and evidence-based approach, recognizing that as a trustee, you are thrown in at the deep end, confronted with the acute challenges and complexities of an existing situation.

LEVELS OF EXCELLENCE: ASSESSING AND IMPROVING YOUR PRACTICE

Every chapter in the book ends with a short list of self-reflection questions. You can use these to position yourself and the fund and help identify any points for improvement. In each chapter, you can assess your fund on the four levels explained below: "weak," "sufficient," "strong," or "excellent." In addition, you can build a list of issues to reflect on and issues to act on. This allows trustees to develop and test their own individual views on the main concepts treated in the book. The underlying logic of the four levels has a strong analogy with typical "maturity level" thinking. Think of *weak* as reactive, ad hoc, coincidental, individual, local, dogmatic and rigid. And think of *excellent* as proactive, planned, systematic, collective, holistic, learning and adaptive. A more detailed description of the different practices is given in Exhibit I.3. Looking at the cases we have studied, we also feel that being open and transparent in general correlates with higher levels of excellence.

Becoming excellent is difficult but armed with examples and logic we feel it is achievable. However, it asks a lot. It also requires at least a certain scale; we would argue $5 billion or more: this is a size which makes it possible to have a serious governance budget, invest in the proprietary knowledge, and thereby enormously reduce the dependence on external advice and asset management. In practice, if a fund has a smaller size than this, by realizing strong practice it does a good job, and will probably be a lot better than the average peer, because there will be spillage going on. It takes strength to be disciplined.

Practice level	Description
Weak Practice	Attention needed. Missing parts in design or implementation. Reactive and ad hoc way of operating, often depending on a few people who happen to be around.
Sufficient Practice	Design, decision-making and or implementation are thought out and documented. The fund complies fully with regulatory requirements. Key processes work well and are independent of specific people.
Strong Practice	Design, decision and implementation are sound and well founded. Comparable pension funds are taking a comparable approach. The board might be aware of the development and research behind it, but has not developed these insights itself. Serious evaluation and improvement are part of the regular process.
Excellent Practice	The fund aims to be best-practice or even to shape the best practice on a continual basis, not one-off but in a permanent way. The choice, design or implementation are recognized by peers as leading and serve as examples. Sometimes, this will mean going into uncharted territory, but always on the back of sound reasoning, well-founded beliefs and adequate skills. Learning and adapting are fully integrated in the processes.

EXHIBIT I.3 Levels of practice.

Strong practice is known territory: you can get there by studying theory and evidence and learning from relevant peers. Excellence requires something more: the guts, trust, vision, and quality to move beyond charted territory. Strong practice takes time to develop and be embedded within regulation, the standard courses for trustees and other bodies of knowledge.

Sufficient practice is: keeping up with the existing design, decision and/or implementation to fit within the regulatory framework of the pension fund. This model suits pension funds that have a highly standardized and easy to implement pension—and investment framework—just fine.

Certainly, all levels of practice do develop over time. Even to simply stay in the same place, you must learn, change and adapt: the body of knowledge develops, the regulator develops, the available product and "investment ecosystem" develop, the external environment develops.

We previously mentioned that there are five activities towards excellence. These are: (i) Understanding the Role of Pension Funds, Shaping the Mission; (ii) Designing the Process; (iii) Implementing the Investments; (iv) Organizing the Board; (v) Learning, Adapting and Improving.

Correspondingly, this book consists of five parts, each covering one of the five key activities:

- Part I, "Pension Funds: Understanding the Role, Shaping the Mission," has an introductory character, it provides a crash course into what trustees need to know in order to play their role well. This activity lays the foundations for the pension fund, defines purpose and translates purpose into strategy. What is the role of the fund, what are the roles and responsibilities of the board? Who are you and what do you want to achieve for your participants? This consists of having clarity about your purpose—why you exist for your participants, what the added value is that trustees want to highlight. Purpose, mission and strategy translate into achievable goals, such as the pension deal that you are you offering.

- Part II, "Designing the Process," takes a strategic approach to the design of the investment function and investment organization that is needed for the strategy to be implemented. This part starts with creating a common language for trustees when investment is concerned. We review the key investment concepts that trustees need and will be used throughout the book. Next, we focus on investment beliefs or principles that drive the differentiating choices in the investment process. Then, we delve into the investment management process, the process by which the fund intends to achieve its returns. A number of "investment models" have emerged in recent decades, taking different approaches to the investment function and role of pension funds. We identify the main models and discuss what trustees need to consider when consciously choosing one of these models and making it their own.

- Part III, "Implementing the Investments," focuses on the effective execution and implementation, from the perspective of a trustee. This part of the process is fully delegated. Execution builds on portfolio construction, implementation and feedback, monitoring and evaluation. The execution translates the objectives into investment outcomes. There will always be leakage between implementation and plan, but this should be minimized. For boards and investment committees, execution predominantly translates into: how do you organize the investment process in such a way that the different steps build on each other's insights; and how do you make sure that the results are continuously evaluated, where the art is to separate random short-term noise from results that affect the fund's long-term goals? The questions of the right distance, altitude and horizon are crucial here: if the board is short sighted and obsessed with detail, it will choke the investment organization. If the distance is too large, the tail—the investors—will wag the dog—the fund. Based on our research, we highlight the choices that trustees spend most of their time on in their role.

■ Part IV, "Organizing the Board." This part focuses on the oversight and governance of the investment process, designing, steering, and overseeing the realization of the mission of the pension fund. In the earlier activities, the emphasis was on relatively hard and objective matters: strategy, process, and implementation. The present activity is performed by boards and committees consisting of individuals with different backgrounds, skill sets, and mental makeups. To turn these into a well-performing orchestra, both in peacetime and in wartime, is an enormous task. So, in this activity the harder to pinpoint human factor plays the main role. How will the board organize itself to realize purpose and mission? What are the board's key tasks; what does it delegate to whom? What should the board be aware of, and organize beforehand when setting up investment committees and executive offices to support their tasks? And what are valuable insights in dealing with the investment management organization?

■ Part V, "Learning, Adapting and Improving," revisits the role of trustees and delves into learning and adapting. This activity focuses its attention on boardroom dynamics. What does it take to make a good decision? What special challenges does a board have when it is supported with complex decision tools such as Asset Liability Management (ALM)? Is the board aware of the special role advisors have, and how they can influence decision-making? Finally, it requires a down-to-earth board to take all the necessary steps in implementing the elements required to achieve investment excellence. It asks for an exceptional board that holds on to its strategy and beliefs and when financial markets come under stress, while at the same time keeping an open mind to adapt insights as new research and developments in the industry come to light that require the board to adjust its principles.

HOW TO USE THE BOOK

The book is mainly aimed at trustees of pension funds, endowments and foundations. Accordingly, it often directly addresses trustees. However, its contents are also very suitable for upper level undergraduate and MBA audiences that have an interest in institutional investments and investment governance. Let us have a look at how this book can be relevant to such a diverse audience of readers.

■ *Trustee.* As a trustee, you can utilize this book to acquire knowledge on the drivers of investment excellence. You will gain valuable insights into methods of assessing and improving the quality of your fund's investments.

- *Fiduciary manager, outsourced chief investment officer (OCIO).* As a fiduciary manager or OCIO, you are in a unique position to be able to help boards to go on a conscious path of improvement. At the same time, you will reap the benefits in the form of an improved conversation with the board that may have positive consequences for quality and the outcomes of the fund at hand.
- *Asset manager.* As an asset manager, you will develop an improved insight into what really matters to trustees. Such enhanced understanding of the asset owner's perspective subsequently allows you to effectively design and continuously improve your (tailor-made) services to this group of clients.
- *Regulator.* As a regulator or government official, you will be able to accumulate the knowledge and theory needed to advance your understanding and judgment of the key issues that are relevant to pension funds within a political and regulatory context. You will be able to better grasp and comprehend the effects and impact of regulation on pension funds, recognize its potential barriers, and identify ways in which it can facilitate the industry.
- *Student in finance and investment.* As a student, you will be looking for additional reading material that complements your traditional textbooks by providing a rich and practical context to them. Our book offers such enrichment of the theoretical perspectives as we present real-life examples, as well as actionable models and concepts that can be implemented in practice.

In the book, special features have been integrated with the purpose of encouraging readers' interaction with, and application of, the text, and to assist them in effectively absorbing the material. For instance, self-reflection questions that allow readers to share and extend the main concepts presented within their own organization, thereby encouraging effective debate. We have concentrated the self-reflection questions in the last chapter of the book in order to allow trustees to collectively create a map of where the fund is and how it can go to the next level.

CHAPTERS OF THE BOOK

PART I: PENSION FUNDS: UNDERSTANDING THE ROLE, SHAPING THE MISSION

Part I provides a crash course into what trustees need to know in order to play their role well. It lays out the role, purpose and resulting strategy of a pension fund. It can be read selectively, either as a refresher or in order to build an understanding of the role of pension funds, or the fiduciary duty of trustees, for instance.

Chapter 1: The Role of Pension Funds, and the Role of Boards

The core of this introductory chapter is to understand the role of pension funds and the board of trustees. Why do large collective organizations (still) exist in a world where the global financial order and system are transforming at such a breakneck pace and with such profound impact on the structure and configuration of institutions? What part do they play within this context, and what is their actual function? Furthermore, we also investigate the role of trustees. As a trustee, you are a board member as well as a fiduciary. You have a specific role and an important task to fulfil that brings about several unique and serious responsibilities. We take a broad perspective on how trustees effectively define the goals of the pension fund, set policy, organize the investment process, and monitor and adjust choices in order to adapt to any changing circumstances.

Chapter 2: Developing Purpose, Mission, Vision and Goals

One of the key responsibilities of the board is to develop, implement and foster mission, goals and strategy. Investment organizations (should) have a purpose, made explicit in their missions and their goals. The design of the investment organization and process is rooted in beliefs, principles and theories on the basis of which organizations formulate their strategic course in order to stay ahead of important developments and capitalize on opportunities that may present themselves. Without such comprehensive frameworks, pension organizations will soon find it difficult to navigate through a world that is characterized by rapid and profound changes in demographics and socioeconomic trends, where disruptive innovations pose a threat to the overall continuity, and where increasingly volatile returns put the entire industry under heavy public scrutiny.

In this chapter, trustees will learn how to develop an effective mission and set of goals, partly by learning from other pension funds. We offer guidance on how to translate vision and mission into practical but powerful goals. In turn, these are translated into concrete return objectives and a risk appetite, formulated as a risk appetite statement. Combined, all of these aspects will help govern and steer the investment function and organization.

PART II: DESIGNING THE PROCESS

Part II takes a strategic approach to the design of the investment function and investment organization that is needed for the strategy. This part starts with creating a common language for trustees where investments and risk management are concerned. We review the key concepts that will be used throughout the book and identify common pitfalls. Next, we focus on how the investment function is organized, and identify the organizational values and beliefs that drive the differentiating choices in the investment process. A number of "investment models" have emerged in recent decades, taking different approaches to the investment function and role of pension funds. We identify the main models and discuss what trustees need to consider when consciously choosing one of these models and making it their own.

Chapter 3: Grasping the Investment Essentials

The day-to-day implementation of investments may seem bewildering and complex. However, the key concepts of investment theory are actually not as obscure as one may think. For a trustee to become relatively fluent in investment terminology, it requires them to get comfortable with roughly 10 building blocks. From the perspective of the trustee, we will discuss concepts such as efficient markets, expected return, risk, diversification, the use of benchmarks, and so forth.

We cover those topics and questions that we know will come up frequently in board meetings. By distinguishing between "big picture" and "detail" concepts we rank their importance. So, after having read this chapter you will be able to have meaningful conversations about investing with, for example, the people who represent the investment organizations that you and your fund deal with.

Chapter 4: Investment Beliefs as Guiding Tools

Observed from a distance, most pension funds and their investment processes look alike. What sets them apart from each other, however, are their underlying choices and decisions. These can differ quite fundamentally and completely change the entire structure and fabric of the pension organization. It is imperative that such underlying choices are identified and articulated for the purpose and benefit of the design and implementation of the investment management process. We delve further into the "beliefs" behind many of such fundamental choices and discuss how these should be viewed and put to use.

Beliefs can and will differ widely among the various funds and investment organizations. They are part of the fund's DNA and say something about the nature and character of the board and its stakeholders. Beliefs are not rigid or cast in stone, rather they tend to evolve and grow over time. Some beliefs have proven to be crucial for those choices that determine success or failure. Some beliefs are more important than others, and some are backed by more evidence than others. We identify those investments beliefs that are likely to have a strong effect on the fund's results. In our analysis, we ask ourselves whether a belief is practically applicable, and whether it makes sense in light of the state of today's finance and investments. Subsequently, we present practical examples and case studies, and demonstrate how trustees and institutions can use these investment beliefs and strategies to enhance their competitive edge.

Chapter 5: Designing the Investment Management Process

We take a detailed look at the investment process, translating the mission, vision, goals, and beliefs into actual investment choices and investments. The portfolio management process is an integrated combination of steps that need to be taken in a consistent and coherent manner in order to create and maintain an appropriate portfolio (i.e. a combination of assets) that meets the clients' stated goals.

The portfolio management process consists of three consecutive steps: planning, execution, and feedback. In the planning step, investment objectives and policies are formulated, capital market expectations are defined, and strategic asset allocations are established. In the implementation and execution phase, the portfolio manager constructs the portfolio. In the feedback step, the manager subsequently monitors and evaluates the portfolio and compares this with the initial plan. Any changes that the feedback may suggest must be examined carefully to ensure that they represent long-term motives and considerations. For each such step, we identify the role of the trustee in setting the policy, monitoring or accountability. The next chapters then elaborate on the main components of the investment management process.

Chapter 6: Organizing the Investment Function

Chapter 6 takes a strategic perspective to the investment management process and identifies five investment approaches models that currently dominate the pension fund industry worldwide. Boards may not necessarily be aware of this, but usually they have been given the advice to incorporate one of these main investment approaches. Its adoption includes a predefined set of assumptions, means of implementation, and requirements for governance. This chapter therefore integrates the insights of the previous chapters and illustrates the five dominant models by looking at their fundamentally different choices in: (i) mission, goals and beliefs; (ii) the investment process; and (iii) the investment organization. We identify the prerequisites, criteria and challenges that trustees would have to address when adopting one of those models.

PART III: IMPLEMENTING THE INVESTMENTS

Part III focuses on the execution, from the perspective of a trustee. Based on our research, we highlight the choices that trustees spend most of their time on in their role. One chapter focuses on the main choices and assumptions leading to the strategic asset strategy and allocation. In a chapter that discusses implementation, we focus on what really matters and is known. Finally, we expand on the monitoring and feedback: an important but not so well understood part of the investment cycle.

Chapter 7: Implementing the Investment Strategy

Implementation is the process that puts the pension fund's plans and strategies into action in order to achieve its goals and objectives. This chapter takes a closer look at how the fund's strategic plan should address the essential aspects of implementation that will ultimately determine the success (or failure) of an investment strategy. For example, we discuss how resources need to be assessed effectively and how objectives need to be quantified on a more granular level, in order to combine these into a flexible plan.

Moreover, the plan should also explain how the fund intends to diversify across opportunities and how it aims to manage the risk of failure in meeting minimum required returns (determined by way of scenario analysis in relation to the fund's defined risk appetite). As risk management forms such an integral and essential part of the entire implementation of the investment process, this chapter considers the most important factors affecting implementation. These include, for instance, the way the investment value chain is designed (are investment choices integrated or disaggregated), the way selection of mandates is organized, and the decision whether to manage all, or only parts, internally or externally (a decision which has enormous consequences for cost and flexibility).

Chapter 8: Building the Investment Portfolio

In portfolio construction, the actual synthesis of fund objectives and capital market expectations of relevant asset classes (i.e. equities, bonds, etc.) takes place, ultimately resulting in the fund's asset allocation. The chapter considers the fact that trustees have a wide range of choices to make at this stage of the design process, including asset allocation and diversification. Although this may sound like a rather mechanical process, in fact it is not. In addition to matters of diversification, the chapter continues with a discussion on supplemental considerations for trustees, which are relevant in constructing portfolios. For instance, we discuss active versus passive portfolio construction and demonstrate that the decision on which to choose should follow from the beliefs that are adopted. We further identify and elaborate on the grey zones that exist, so that trustees can really acquire a broad understanding that will help them rely on their own judgment when confronted with complex issues that require informed decision-making.

Chapter 9: Monitoring and Evaluation

Suboptimal (inefficient) governance of pension funds comes at a significant cost and is thus one of the biggest concerns for board members and those involved in the actual execution of the investments. In this respect, the monitoring function is one of the least thought-out components in the investment management process. This chapter discusses different monitoring "models" that will assist in determining how to effectively organize all of this, and enabling the trustee to differentiate between short- and long-term feedback, as well as distinguish skill from luck. As feedback loops tend to be long in financial markets, a poorly designed investment process may very well lead to good outcomes in a short-term horizon (i.e. by "luck"), whereas a well-thought-out process can lead to lousy outcomes. Clearly, the monitoring and feedback process should be carefully designed in a way that not only includes the outcomes of the process but, more importantly, also considers the quality of the process itself, so that (collective) learning is valid and can lead to improvement.

PART IV: ORGANIZING THE BOARD

Part IV looks at the organization of the pension fund. The board is supported by staff, committees, and in a number of cases is also the owner of the investment management organization. We look at the roles and responsibilities of these actors, as well as how they interact.

Chapter 10: Becoming an Effective Board

The primary role of the board is defining the goals, organizing the investment process, and monitoring and (re)adjusting choices in order to adapt to any changing circumstances. This may seem straightforward, but in reality it seldom is. This chapter reviews why this is the case and revisits the fiduciary responsibilities of the board.

We then translate these findings into the strategic design of the investment management organization and its decision-making process.

Subsequently, we analyze the board's function and role in more detail, by looking at its composition, its focus, and the key roles that individual board members need to fulfil in order to encourage balanced board discussions. Finally, we discuss the role of the chairperson in further detail. How can the chairperson give shape to discussions and debate; what sort of agenda should they set; and what tools do they have at their disposal to create informed discussions and reach clear decisions that are executable and can be monitored effectively?

Chapter 11: Establishing the Investment Committee

The board is highly dependent on the investment committee and the executive office. It is therefore imperative that the board has articulated how they (should) work together. We highlight the position of the investment committee in more detail. In some cases, the committee fulfils a highly proactive role on basis of the executive mandate that is entrusted to the committee in making investment decisions on behalf of the fund. In other instances, the duties and responsibilities of the committee may be restricted to a purely advisory role, requiring its members only to meet a few times per year. We discuss in which cases each of these types of investment committees serves the specific goals and investment process of a particular fund best. Correspondingly, we examine the composition of the investment committee and discuss how its members and the committee's external advisors can operate and collaborate in an effective way. To this end, we also identify the potential pitfalls for external advisors. The chapter concludes with a review of the investment committee's agenda, the role of its chairperson, and the interplay between the committee and the board.

Chapter 12: Managing the Investment Management Organization

In this chapter, we turn our attention to the investment management organization. We begin with a discussion on the different types of investment management organizations, ranging from fully outsourced to fully insourced. We discuss implementation issues regarding the investment organization that currently dominate an industry-wide debate among trustees. "Alignment of interests" is such an example of a highly debated issue, because the interaction between the investment committee (representing the interest of the fund) and the investment management organization is regarded as probably the most important factor in creating investment success. It pertains to the very core of their relationship, involving multiple complex dimensions that need to be well understood and properly managed. We argue that any solution will, to a certain degree, bring alignment of interest problems as the difference between the asset owner and the asset manager is simply too large in terms of size, responsibilities, and potential earnings.

PART V: LEARNING, ADAPTING AND IMPROVING

Part V revisits the role of trustees. How can trustees improve decision-making, handle complex choices, and actually diagnose and improve the investment quality of the fund in cooperation with the other people and stakeholders that matter in the context of the fund? The reader will be provided with a set of concrete tools, instruments and real-life examples.

Chapter 13: Learning to Decide and to Take Advice

This chapter covers what is required from a board to make decisions. The profession of a trustee is hard work that involves the development of an appropriate strategic agenda fitting the fund's mission, goals and objectives. It requires careful and thorough preparation, while maintaining ongoing dialogue within the board in order to facilitate successful decision-making. In this chapter, we analyze what exactly is required for a board to actually make a good investment decision. Indeed, trustees have to make decisions all the time, ranging from trivial investment decisions (e.g. changes in investment restrictions) to decisions that have a substantial impact on the entire organization (e.g. asset allocation strategy, de-risking during crises, firing the fiduciary manager). Some boards may delay and hold off decisions by endlessly searching for more information, while others may invite external advisors to offer their recommendations. Whatever the procedure of decision-making, trustees are expected to solicit and pursue "proper advice" because failure to comply often means that a trustee will be directly (and personally) accountable to the relevant regulator. Pension funds may therefore choose to turn to an independent financial advisor, an investment consultant or the fund's own actuary for proper financial advice. In this respect, Chapter 13 also elaborates on how trustees can make sure that the internal or external advisor indeed will act in the interest of the board and will continue to provide the trustee with support, instead of taking over his or her role.

Chapter 14: Achieving Investment Excellence

Whereas in previous chapters the book confronted managers and trustees with thought-provoking questions, this chapter provides the trustees a practical instrument with which they are able to assess their fund's status in terms of achieving sustainable investment excellence. Chapter 14 equips the trustee with the necessary intelligence and practical tools that will allow the board to transform into a perpetual "learning board."

SELF-REFLECTION QUESTIONS

This chapter provides the reader with self-reflections questions that can be used to perform a self-assessment. What is the level of practice of your fund? How well are you doing? Did you think of all the steps in a process? The chapter presents useful questions to conduct a self-assessment and serves as a reminder of important questions that nobody has asked you, nor have you asked yourself. Trustees often implicitly take processes or steps for granted; it is helpful to make these steps or processes explicit. Furthermore, this chapter serves as guiding tool for those who want to read specific sections of the book; the questions help to find the relevant sections for those readers who wish to read this book in a specific order.

ENDNOTE

1. See Ambachtsheer et al. (2006, 2007) and Clark and Urwin (2007) on the potential bonus of better governance. Willis Towers Watson (2017) identifies building blocks of value creation via long-horizon investing, providing evidence of a sizeable net long-term premium of 0.5–1.5% per annum.

One

Pension Funds: Understanding the Role, Shaping the Mission

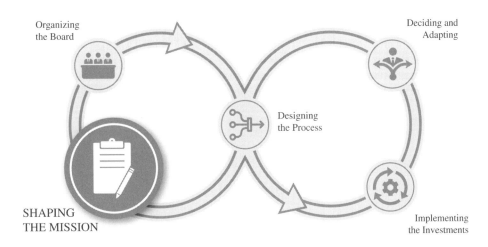

Organizing
the Board

Deciding and
Adapting

Designing
the Process

SHAPING
THE MISSION

Implementing
the Investments

The basic question considered in Part I is the role and purpose of a pension fund, both in a generic and in a specific sense. This will be useful later in the book, as investing is the means for realizing the pension fund's purpose. We will also home in on the role of the board and its members. This is important, because throughout the book we will return time and time again to the critical role of the board in creating investment excellence. Fiduciary duty is important here, but there is also more; steering the fund strategically through a changing societal context, for example. Then we will move on to specific questions: How can you formulate a mission, a vision, and a strategy? How do you move towards your vision?

In this first part of the book we find ourselves firmly in the slow-moving, strategic part of the organizational loop. This is the part where the board sets the scene. Because in daily life, boards tend to spend a lot of time on the immediate issues at hand, it is not always easy to see this strategic layer.

Part I Topics Include:
- The role of a pension fund, and the roles of a board and its trustees;
- The meaning of fiduciary duty;
- How to formulate the mission, vision, and strategy of a pension fund;
- The importance of explicitly stating the strategic foundation of a fund in order to avoid confusion later on in the process.

After reading Part I, you should be able to state with confidence: This is the reason for the existence of my fund and this is what it does to realize its objective, given the current context. If this is not totally clear to—and shared by— everybody involved, there is still work to be done!

CONTRIBUTION OF THIS PART TO INVESTMENT EXCELLENCE

Part I gives insight into the role and responsibilities of the board and establishes the idea that the board can make or break investment excellence. By shifting the attention from ad hoc and sometimes reactive decision-making to formulating the mission and the strategy for the fund, it helps the board to look further ahead. This makes it possible to move systematically and in a controlled way towards the achieving the mission, while at the same time taking into account the changing environment in which the fund operates. Operating in the way, decision-making will be more proactive and the fund will be much more in control of its future path.

CHAPTER 1

The Role of Pension Funds, and the Role of Boards

Key Take Aways

- Pension funds help people with their retirement provisions. They are entities that specialize in making long-term decisions. Trustees have the overall responsibility of formulating the policy of the fund, and of ensuring the required quality of implementation of the policy.

- Trustees can have three different roles, which involve different—and sometimes conflicting—responsibilities: the role of fiduciary, the role of employer, and the role of shareholder.

- A guiding light for making informed decisions and policy is fiduciary duty: behaving responsibly with other people's money. For investments, this comes down to prudent investing. It is important to reflect on this and to become familiar with fiduciary duties.

- Trustees delegate. Delegation is a balancing act between the added value of specialization and the agency cost of lengthening the investment chain. How can a board make sure that the agency issues are minimized?

- It is important to understand the motives of stakeholders of the pension fund; they can have societal, political and/or financial motives. Ignoring the motives involved is usually detrimental for the participants' interests.

In this chapter, we focus on the pension fund and its board of trustees. The primary role of the board is defining the goals of the pension fund, setting policy, organizing the investment process, and monitoring and adjusting choices in order to adapt to any changing circumstances. Boards can be a complex and diverse combination of lay people in the field of finance, as well as people with a professional background in finance or investing. The board is the key determinant of the success of a pension fund.

In a recent review of how boards have developed over time, Ambachtsheer[1] states that "while there is some evidence of improvement of pension organizations [. . .], the finding is that the major concerns about how board members are selected and trained, about the effectiveness of board oversight processes, and about the ability to attract and retain key executive and professional skills remain. Much remains to be done to materially raise the effectiveness of the governance function in pension organizations."

A malfunctioning board can have a considerable negative impact on the pension fund. The malfunction can have many causes, from failing to understand the crucial role of the board to appointees lacking the skills needed to be effective board members. This chapter outlines the very first step a board should undertake in order to be well functioning: understanding its roles and responsibilities, thus forming the framework for all other steps and decisions required in the investment process and governance. Understanding these roles, however, requires background knowledge on what it actually is that a pension fund does. To this end, we start with a short overview of pension funds, why they exist, and what their roles are. Our view is that these roles and responsibilities—give or take a few cultural and regulatory differences—have clear commonalities around the world. Following this, we discuss the characteristics of a pension plan, which defines who pays what (premiums), who receives what (pensions), and, crucially, who holds which risk.

Zooming in on the role of the board, we consider a trustee's responsibilities from three angles: the duties as a fiduciary, the duties as a board member and the duties as a shareholder of an investment organization. An important question is how to balance these roles. Because delegation is an important board task, we discuss delegation and agency issues that arise as a result of delegation. The chapter concludes with a section on understanding and managing different stakeholders.

THE ROLE OF PENSION FUNDS

As the baby boom generation started to retire in the first decade of the twenty-first century, the amount of capital needed to provide for future income increased. In 2017,[2] global wealth was $280 trillion. This is about four times the global gross domestic product (GDP), which totaled $75 trillion in 2015. Pension funds in the 22 most important pension countries managed $36.4 trillion at the end of 2016, amounting on average to 62% of their local GDP.[3] Thus, pension funds are significant players in the world's economy. A pension fund is an institution set up to accumulate assets in order to pay retirement obligations. It thus provides the means for individuals to accumulate savings over their working life so as to finance their consumption needs in retirement, either by means of a lump sum or by provision of an annuity. To a large extent—often 75% or more—the benefits are paid out of investment returns. This means that pension funds are important investors and sources of potential long-term capital to parties such as corporations, governments and sometimes households.[4]

In many countries the pension system consists of three pillars: a state pension, the supplementary company pensions, and the private individual pension products that each person can arrange for themselves.

First pillar pensions are a basic pension provided to all citizens by the local government of many countries around the world. This requires (tax) payments throughout the citizen's working life in order to qualify for the benefits upon retirement. A basic state pension is a "contribution-based" benefit, and depends on an individual's contribution history. Examples are National Insurance in the UK, or Social Security in the US.

The second pillar consists of the company pension schemes, as well as pension schemes for occupations and industries. This book focuses on these second pillar pensions, but its insights and lessons are easily applicable for the other types of pension schemes as well. The basis for setting up a second pillar pension fund is the pension plan, i.e. a plan that determines the funding, accrual and payout of benefits; detailing the rights and obligations of members and sponsors.[5] Pension funds then administer the pension plan.

The third pillar is formed by individual pension products, such as an annuity insurance or via a tax-efficient blocked savings account. These are mainly used by the self-employed and employees in sectors without a collective pension scheme. However, these products can be serviced or offered by pension organization, where the boards have similar fiduciary duties to second pillar pension plans.

Each pension plan has certain key elements. These include[6]:

- A pension agreement that describes the pension benefit structure and guides day-to-day operations;
- A trust fund, foundation or other form of organization, independent from the sponsor, to hold the plan's assets and the administration of pension benefits. The trust is legally and financially independent from the companies;
- A record-keeping system to track the flow of money going to and from the retirement plan;
- Documents to provide plan information both to the employees participating in the plan, and to the government;
- At times, a number of officials with discretion over the plan; these are the plan's fiduciaries.

For a trustee, the main concern is to ensure that the members' retirement obligations will be properly funded and protected. The trustee's role is to make sure that pensions are paid not only now, but also in the future. These obligations stretch out over a long period. Understanding the longevity of the obligations provides a starting point for trustees in getting to know the fund. Taking a brief look back in time, in 1889, German Chancellor Otto von Bismarck introduced the first pension for workers aged over 70, at a time when the average life expectancy of a Prussian civil servant was 45. In 1908, when the British Prime Minister Lloyd George secured a payment of 5 shillings a week for underprivileged workers who had reached 70, Britons, and especially those who were poor, were lucky to survive much beyond 50. By 1935, when the United States set up its Social Security system, the official pension age was 65, just 3 years more than the lifespan of the average American worker.[7] Pension plans, especially state-sponsored plans, were thus set up for the few people with long lifespans. Today, retirement is for everyone. In some European countries, retirement lasts for more than a quarter of a century on average. In the United States, the official pension age is 66, but the average American retires at 64 and can then expect to live for another 16 years. This puts into perspective the responsibilities of a pension fund.

Ensuring financially sustainable retirement benefits is a global challenge. With a population that is living longer, payout periods are extended. Governments, plan sponsors and industry are constantly challenged to make informed decisions that will meet both the retired, and the working population's needs.

When workers are covered by collective bargaining agreements, pensions, insurance and health benefits are key items of negotiation between management and labor. This has been important in the United States and the United Kingdom, as well as in the Netherlands, Germany, Sweden and Switzerland. For employers, who are concerned with managing their human resources, offering participation in a pension scheme has traditionally been a means of locking in older skilled workers while stabilizing labor turnover in competitive labor markets.[8] However, with the introduction of new technology and flexible labor contracts the traditional organization of labor markets is changing rapidly, and this is altering the view employers have of the role of pension schemes. Nevertheless, in many cases the employer still provides for, or facilitates access to, a form of pension scheme.

The pension scheme itself is an arrangement for providing employees with an income during retirement, when they are no longer earning a steady income from employment. Retirement plans often require both the employer and employee to contribute money to a fund during their employment in order to receive predefined benefits upon retirement. This is a tax-deferred savings vehicle that allows for the tax-free accumulation of a fund for later use as retirement income. Funding can be provided from external sources, such as labor unions or government agencies, or via self-funded schemes.

Pension schemes operate under a high level of scrutiny from the government, lawmakers, regulators and participants. Plans must continually balance the needs of sponsors and of members. The plan's design needs to be optimized to ensure employees are getting the most cost-effective plan with the best possible benefit package. The investment choices play a large role in defining both the cost and the expected benefits of a pension fund. With low risk investments such as high-grade government bonds, the outcome over time will be relatively low, but certain, resulting in high premiums and/or low benefits. With high-risk investments, returns over time may be expected to be higher, which lowers the premium and raises the expected benefits, but at the same time makes the outcomes more uncertain, at least in the short term. Someone in the fund must decide on this risk/return trade-off, and come to an agreement with all of the stakeholders concerned as to how the risk is allocated between the company, pensioners, pension fund and active members. Sometimes, but less and less so, this will be the employer or the sponsor, sometimes it will be the beneficiaries, sometimes the premium payers, and often a combination of these. At the same time, the fund must ensure that the plan meets tax and regulatory guidelines, as well as manage costs.

THE PENSION TRIANGLE

When setting up and managing the pension scheme, there is a triangular relationship between the employee, the employer and the pension provider. The basic principle of this relationship is that pensions are a part of the terms and conditions of employment. Within this triangle, we can observe the following relationships:

- The relationship between the employer and the employee, who have jointly entered into a pension agreement or a pension plan;

- The relationship between the employer and an external pension provider, the pension fund, to whom the administration of the pension agreement is outsourced on the basis of an administration agreement;
- The relationship between the pension fund and the employee, as a result of the outsourcing of the administration of the pension agreement. The pension fund provides the employee with the pension scheme as well as agreed-upon information and services.

The pension scheme is drafted by the pension administrator in accordance with the pension and administration agreement. The pension scheme is organized around three institutional choices,[9] as shown by Exhibit 1.1. First, there is a formal separation between sponsors' interests and the interests of the plan's beneficiaries. Second, a legal regime of trusteeships exists to protect the interests of the beneficiaries. Third, the management and investment of fund assets is delegated to expertise, either within the fund or externally.

Pension schemes tend to be semi-autonomous financial institutions, and, as the number of assets increases, they are increasingly viewed as such by regulators. In general, the pension triangle tends to be at its most complex in the case of Defined Benefit (DB) schemes. In that case, legal regulations require current funding of the plans to meet expected future liabilities, where sponsors' interests and the plan's beneficiaries' interests might not coincide, and where there even may be significant differences between the interests of older and younger beneficiaries, for example. In a DB scheme, the focus is on collective funding and how the employer will bridge the gap in funding. The participant of the DB scheme builds up a claim in pension payouts that do not depend, or depend only in part, on the investment returns and financial health of the pension fund. The participant is a consumer; payments are more or less clear when entering the scheme, a (nominal) pension policy provides regular cash payments from the predetermined retirement age onwards. The promised payouts are liabilities of the pension fund and do not vary with the financial health of the fund.[10]

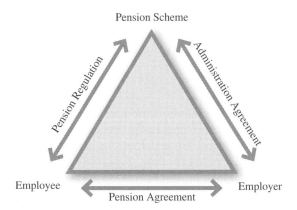

EXHIBIT 1.1 The pension triangle: relationship between employee, employer and scheme.

The majority of the risks and responsibilities in a Defined Contribution (DC) arrangement are with the participant rather than the employer. The participant is a co-investor rather than a customer. Payments to the participant are not clear when entering the scheme and fully depend on the investment return. With DC governance, trustees have to focus on individual financial planning and help participants consider areas such as when to retire, what level of benefits to retire on, what is the tolerance to risk and, if applicable for the specific pension market, what sort of annuity the participant should buy. DC schemes are by definition fully funded and are by design managed with the aim of maximizing the investment return and the accumulated value of the plan's participants' contributions within the agreed risk appetite. Here, the formal separation between sponsors, such as employers, and beneficiaries is virtually complete, simplifying the complexity of the pension triangle considerably.

With a DB scheme, the investment governance and strategy is set over a number of years to ensure full funding and realization of indexation goals. If full funding is not feasible, the valuation will show any shortfalls in funding and recovery plans can be put in place and reviewed accordingly.

DC schemes are, on the other hand, by definition fully funded and show no shortfall in funding. DC schemes rely on regularly monitoring and reassessing members' attitude to risk and appetite for engaging in the investment process; the combination of these members' choices determines the investment strategy.[11]

DUTIES OF TRUSTEES

While many trustees understand that they are appointed trustees of the interests of the beneficiaries, they may be less aware of just what their fiduciary duties include. Until a few years ago, there was little need to scrutinize the list of fiduciary obligations of trustees. But things are changing. For one thing, in the past decade investment returns have fallen behind compared to previous decades, periods where strong investment returns were the norm and participants did not complain. Participants are increasingly asking tougher questions, as are regulators. As pension funds have grown in size in the last decade through consolidation, the number of parties involved and the complexity of strategies have increased, requiring trustees to manage these parties proactively to contain costs. Pension funds are also expected to grow further, transforming them into heavyweight financial institutions and yet further increasing the need to explicate roles and responsibilities.

A trustee is a named fiduciary to whom the administration of the pensions, the management and the investment of the fund assets in the pension scheme are delegated by the sponsors and the beneficiaries. While definitions of fiduciaries vary, a practical one is any organization named as a plan sponsor, or person named as a trustee. Investment advisors (who are paid fees) and plan administrators are so-called "deemed" fiduciaries, which include any persons who exercise any discretionary authority or control in management or administration of the plan or its assets. This comprises fiduciary managers, who can exercise considerable discretionary authority, as well as the underlying asset manager. This also includes the staff or executive office of a pension fund. Depending on how the board of trustees organizes the support function, it either heavily influences the choices in management and/or administration in the plan through policymaking; or, alternatively, the board delegates discretionary authority or control over the implementation and monitoring of board policy to the staff or executive office.

The role of the trustee depends among others on the type of governance of the pension scheme is. In an overview study by the Organisation for Economic Co-operation and Development (OECD), two types of pension funds are identified, institutional and contractual.[12] There is an institutional type, where the fund is an independent entity with legal personality and capacity, and hence it has its own internal governing board. Examples include pension foundations and associations in countries such as Denmark, Finland, Hungary, Italy, Japan, Norway, Poland, the Netherlands, Switzerland, as well as Austria and Germany. In most of these countries pension funds have a single governing board, whose members are typically chosen by sponsoring employers and employees (or their representatives). In some countries, like Germany and the Netherlands, there is a dual-board structure. In Germany, there is a supervisory board that is responsible for selecting and monitoring the management board, which in turn is responsible for all strategic decisions.

On the other hand, a contractual-type pension fund consists of a segregated pool of assets without legal personality and capacity that is governed by a separate entity, typically a financial institution such as a bank, an insurance company, or a pension fund management company. The governing body of a fund set up in the contractual form is usually the board of directors of the management entity, although in some countries some key responsibilities are shared with a separate oversight committee. Examples of contractual-type pension funds are to be found in the Czech Republic, Mexico, Portugal, Slovakia, Turkey, and the open funds in Italy and Poland.

Trustees have characteristics of both the institutional and the contractual type. Under the trust form it is the trustees who legally own the pension fund assets. Trustees must administer the trust assets in the sole interest of the plan participants, who are the beneficiaries from the investment of those assets according to the trust deed. While this feature of trusts is similar to that of foundations, the trustees are not legally part of the trust. Indeed, in Australia or Ireland a trustee may be of the corporate type that makes the pension fund resemble a contractual arrangement.

The United States has an additional feature as the governing body may be the plan sponsor, the trustee, or/and some third party. ERISA (Employee Retirement Income Security Act of 1974) requires single company pension plans to have one or more named fiduciaries who have authority to control and manage the pension plan, including its investments. The sponsoring employer and the trustee are always named fiduciaries but it is possible for the trustee to be devoid of any major fiduciary responsibility, following instead another named fiduciary (e.g. a plan committee). In addition, asset managers, financial advisors, and other persons and entities that exercise some discretion over the fund's assets are considered functional fiduciaries, all of whom have some legal responsibility for the pension fund.

The formal documentation of the pension plan should provide answers to questions with respect to who has the responsibilities and discretion for the plan administration and investment of the assets, and specifically the role and responsibilities of the trustees.

In general, as long as they are acting in their professional capacities,[13] accountants, attorneys, actuaries, and other consultants are not identified as fiduciaries. These individuals do not ordinarily exercise discretion and control over the plan. However, they may become fiduciaries if they are formally hired to take on any of the responsibilities identified above, and to exercise discretion and control over the plan. A situation that trustees must avoid at all times is one where these professional advisors are not formally hired, but in practice take on the responsibilities or influence the board in a decisive way.

The fiduciary role is the trustee's most important role, but seldom the only one, as he or she combines several roles on the board. In many countries, the members of the board of trustees are also employers and board members. The board of trustees can own the executive office or staff organization, as well as the pension delivery organization(s). These forms of organization can make sense from the point of view of the fiduciary duty—they create the framework for the execution of duties in the participants' best interests, lowering costs, and helping with the monitoring—but alongside the fiduciary duty, they also create the additional responsibilities of an employer and shareholder. Below, we discuss the following three roles of trustees: fiduciary responsibilities related to running the pension scheme; employer responsibilities for setting up a staffed office or other entity to support the trustees; and finally shareholder responsibilities when the trustees set up an investment management organization that is partly or wholly owned by the pension fund and that executes part or whole of the pension plan. These roles are visualized by Exhibit 1.2.

Responsibility as a Fiduciary

Acknowledging the role of trustees leads to the next step, that is, understanding how to comply with the fiduciary responsibilities. A good starting point is ERISA, the Employee Retirement Income Security Act of 1974, a federal law in the United States that impacts fiduciary responsibilities related to qualified retirement plans. Under ERISA, regardless

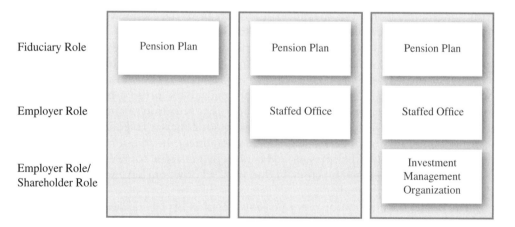

Fiduciary Role	Pension Plan	Pension Plan	Pension Plan
Employer Role		Staffed Office	Staffed Office
Employer Role/ Shareholder Role			Investment Management Organization

EXHIBIT 1.2   The different roles of trustees in a pension plan.

of the size of the pension scheme or pension fund assets, all fiduciaries have responsibilities and are subject to standards of conduct because they are acting on behalf of participants in a retirement plan and their beneficiaries.[14] These responsibilities include:

- Acting solely in the interest of the plan's participants and their beneficiaries and with the exclusive purpose of providing benefits for them and avoiding conflicts of interest;
- Carrying out their duties prudently; thus ensuring that the plan offers a diversified investment approach that minimizes the risk of long-term losses. The investment approach is designed to cover the scheme's technical provisions to ensure funds are invested in a manner appropriate to the nature and duration of the expected future retirement benefits payable under the scheme. Diversification means avoiding excessive reliance on any particular asset, issuer or group of undertakings in order to avoid accumulations of risk in the portfolio as a whole;
- Following the plan documents;
- Paying only reasonable plan expenses. The fiduciary knows what they are paying in terms of total plan expenses and how these costs compare to the market. It is not necessary to have the lowest costs;
- Monitoring investments—implementing a continuous program for the evaluation of the pension funds' investment managers for consistency of style, performance against set goals and benchmarks, and changes in their organization;
- Avoiding prohibited transactions—a fiduciary must not engage the fund in transactions that are prohibited or represent a potential conflict of interest.

These standards are more or less generally accepted in many countries, while being adapted to suit local purposes. Depending on the jurisdiction, different issues are accentuated or raised. For example, in the UK, pension legislation focuses on liquidity. Trustees are required to exercise their investment powers in a manner "calculated to ensure the security, quality, liquidity and profitability of the portfolio as a whole."[15] Additionally, pension fund assets should consist predominantly of investments admitted to trading on regulated markets. Other (unregulated, illiquid) investments must be kept at a prudent level.[16]

Delegation and Agency Relationships An alternative approach to understanding the responsibilities of trustees is to realize that they are entrusted with managing several layers of principal–agent relationships, which are the consequence of delegation of administration and management of investment activities.[17] The pension fund has the ownership (on behalf of the beneficiaries or savers) of the assets and acts as principal, but delegates the management of the assets to specialized asset managers, the agents. Therefore, the trustees are the agents of the plan's participants who have delegated their pension problem to the pension fund; and financial service providers are the trustees' agents because parts of the investment problem are delegated to them.[18]

The term "agent" refers to a key concept in economic theory: whenever a "principal" decides to delegate or outsource a task to somebody else (the "agent"), agency issues will arise: how can one be certain that the agent acts on behalf of the principal, and not in its own interests? Perfect alignment between principal and agent is practically unattainable. In each decision to delegate, the pros (e.g. specialized knowledge, cost efficiency, less time consumption) should be carefully weighed against the cons (e.g. agency costs, such as monitoring costs, contract costs and intensified risk management).

Because it is impossible to recruit perfect agents, trustees need to carefully design and monitor agency relationships. Two problems that will need to be resolved[19] can arise in agency relationships. The first is the agency problem that arises when (i) the desires or goals of the principal and agent conflict and (ii) it is difficult or expensive for the principal to verify what the agent is actually doing. The problem here is that the principal cannot verify that the agent has behaved appropriately. This is also referred to as information asymmetry. This problem is increased when the feedback loop between decision and outcome is long, which is usually the case with pensions and investments.

The second is the problem of risk sharing that arises when the principal and agent have different attitudes towards risk. The problem here is that the principal and the agent may prefer different actions because of the different risk preferences.

Such problems arise in part due to information asymmetry between the principal and the agent (the agent having superior information); this makes it difficult for the principal to monitor the agent's actions or assess the motivation of the decisions that it takes on the principal's behalf. In addition, the principal and the agent may have different interests. For example, consider a case in which the principal, the board of the pension fund, is investing to meet its liabilities in the long term, while the agent, an investment manager, is paid and retained or fired on the basis of short-term performance.

For many pension fund trustees, delegation is the predominant strategy. The most obvious way to handle potential agency issues is in the form of contracts governing the relationship between the principal and the agent. The question is then how to determine the most efficient contract governing the principal–agent relationship for the delegation of responsibilities, given basic assumptions about people (e.g. their self-interest, limits to rationality, risk aversion), organizations (e.g. conflicting goals among members), and information (e.g. information as a commodity that can be purchased).[20] Sometimes, not delegating or keeping activities nearby is the best possible way to minimize agency costs.

Boards should identify the main agency relationships in advance, allowing them to design and manage the relationship more proactively. Exhibit 1.3 shows five typical agency relationships that a trustee has to consider and manage:

Delegation involves layering of agency relationships. A participant in a DC plan is simultaneously involved in at least five principal–agent relationships:

1. The relationship between the beneficiary and the sponsoring company;
2. The relationship between the sponsor and the investment consultant;
3. The relationship between the consultant and the asset management company (that wins the investment mandate);
4. The relationship between the sponsor and the asset managers, whose products are part of the chosen menu;
5. The relationship between the asset manager and the individual portfolio manager, who makes the actual investment decisions.

Conflicts of interest can arise between any of the relationships in the chain outlined in Exhibit 1.3. While these issues are not new to the pensions industry, increasing

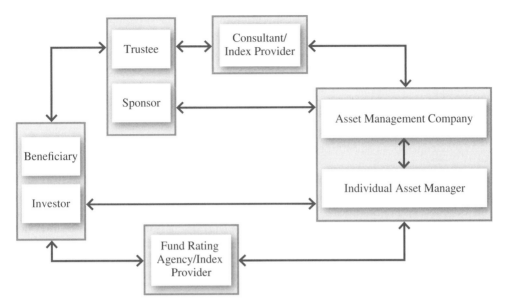

EXHIBIT 1.3   The different layers of agency relationships for a pension fund.[21]

investment complexity and the fallout from the global financial crisis have focused more attention on managing conflicts and improving the alignment between investors and the agents to whom they delegate.

As the number and complexity of agency relationships increase, so does the likelihood of conflicts of interest between investors and their agents. As a consequence, investment decisions can differ across funds, in part due to differing numbers and combinations of agency relationships. For example, investments chosen by DC pension funds can differ substantially from those in DB plans, given that the former choices are made by households investing on their own, while the latter are guided by pension fund trustees acting for the pension fund's beneficiaries as a group. In addition, investment decisions by individual customers might further be influenced by the advice of investment firms' sales networks, which may have certain incentives to sell or recommend particular products.

These differences in agency relationships may also imply differences in optimal contractual relationships. Optimal (compensation) contract design for delegated portfolio managers is a thoroughly researched topic. The results of this research have not been wholly conclusive. The basic conclusion is that contract design is highly sensitive to the specifics of individual agency problems. Various strategies have evolved over the years to manage these agency problems, usually involving some combination of the following components:[22]

- A profit sharing rule (i.e. a fee structure), to align incentives in terms of returns;
- Making returns comparable by measuring relative performance against a benchmark, to monitor performance and risk;

- Checks on risk-taking, such as maximum allowable tracking error, reporting requirements and constraints on available investment choices;
- Employing consultants who regularly act as intermediaries between trustees and service providers to evaluate the value and performance of agency relationships in accordance with industry benchmarks;
- Using competing financial service providers for the same functions, thus using competition to discipline costs and achieve service quality;
- Building trust relationships between privileged service providers, thereby sharing knowledge about the supply and demand of services.

Trustees employ a combination of the above-mentioned components to deal with agency problems. The weightings differ, depending on the board's assessment of costs and benefits, and sometimes also depending on which component might be more in vogue given the political environment and societal discussions. Effective boards not only have an eye for effective mitigation of agency costs, but they are also sensitive to potential negative externalities that may arise due to such issues.

Responsibilities as a Board Member

In the line of fiduciary duty, the trustee adopts the role of a board member to fulfill the fiduciary duties he or she has undertaken on behalf of the participants. The board, or board of directors, is the body within the pension fund that directs the fund on behalf of the beneficiaries.

The board of directors, as a unified body, takes on the responsibility on behalf of the beneficiaries of collecting, managing, administering and paying out (future) pension entitlements. The board firstly has a legal remit of formulating policies to fulfill these responsibilities. The main duties of the governing board of an occupational pension plan should normally be enshrined in the relevant legislation. The pension plan or fund statutes will include these duties and make them more specific to the fund's situation.[23]

The central responsibility of any pension fund board should be to set out a clear mission for the fund, including specific measurable objectives (e.g. indexation ambition, funding levels, return targets, etc.); to define a strategy for meeting those objectives (e.g. selecting a broad asset allocation, choosing between internal and external management, etc.); and to monitor the fund's success (and that of its staff and external managers) in achieving those objectives. This will be discussed in Chapter 3. The board also needs to consider suitable governance structures for implementing its long-term strategy and consider, for example, how the investment function and staffing should be designed, implemented, monitored and remunerated. The pension fund board has to manage five tasks; these will be further explained in the chapters of this book.[24] These tasks are:

1. Policy formulation and foresight: developing a long-term perspective; the fund's mission;
2. Strategic thinking: translation of the mission into strategy;
3. Design of governance, organization of the pension scheme: pension administration, investment advice and record-keeping;

4. Supervision of management: monitoring the execution and progress of the pension scheme;
5. Accountability: reporting on results to stakeholders, evaluating strategy and readjusting when necessary.

Responsibilities as a Shareholder

Alongside their fiduciary role, the board of trustees is often also an employer. They can own the executive office or staff organization, as well as the pension delivery organization(s). These organizations make perfect sense from the point of view of fiduciary duties; they create the framework for the execution of such duties in the best interests of beneficiaries, lowering costs, and helping with the monitoring. But they also create a separate set of responsibilities: those of a director. One option is for the board to appoint a director to manage the pension delivery organization, operating outside the board. Another approach for a number of jurisdictions would be to set up a single-tier board, where the executive directors on the board manage the pension delivery organization, and the non-executive directors monitor, review and guide the strategy of the fund. The OECD Principles of Corporate Governance provide guidance on the responsibilities of directors; these principles are presented in Appendix "OECD Principles".

Many of these responsibilities as a shareholder overlap with the fiduciary duties that are discussed in this chapter and the key tasks of a board discussed in Chapter 10. However, new elements are ensuring a formal and transparent board nomination and election process; monitoring and managing potential conflicts of interest of management, board members and shareholders—including misuse of corporate assets and abuses in related party transactions; and ensuring the integrity of the corporation's accounting and financial reporting systems, including the independent audit.

Balancing the Three Roles

The challenge is to balance the three responsibilities—fiduciary, board member, and shareholder—when they exist within one pension fund board. Much of the interaction between the three roles is sensible and supports an alignment of goals. If trustees are the employers of the staff and executive office, then developing a professional human resources role and treating employees with trust creates the right culture to help trustees to get the best support and follow-up in their decision-making. A more difficult situation, however, arises when the pension fund is the sole owner of a pension delivery organization, and also has a shareholder role to consider. What should be done when, for example, on the one hand, trustees push for cost-effective solutions in the investments carried out by their pension delivery organization, compelling it to reduce costs and/or margins, while on the other hand, they demand decent shareholder returns from the same organization? Here it becomes visible that the different hats the trustee has to wear may lead to difficult dilemmas and even conflicted interests, especially if the board has not acknowledged these different roles. A common approach is to prioritize these roles and discuss them separately. For example, the board first decides on the investment policy. In a subsequent shareholder meeting, the board of the investment organization discusses the consequences for the organization, as well as the changes that should be made to realize the goals of the investment policy.

UNDERSTANDING AND MANAGING YOUR STAKEHOLDERS

It is important to understand the role of the stakeholders and the environment in which pension funds operate. The pension fund operates on behalf of its members or owners. It also operates in a broader environment with a number of stakeholders such as regulators, politicians, non-governmental organizations (NGOs) and the press. On the investment side, it operates in financial markets as part of a long chain that includes a large number of agents such as asset managers, investment funds and consultants.

Understanding the stakeholders and their potential roles is the key issue here. More important for a trustee is to comprehend when and how these actors are in sync with the trustee's requirements and desires, as well as when there might be a potential clash. To help the reader understand some of the possible stakeholders, we will review the following agents: the government, the regulator, the financial market and NGOs.

Government

The government has a crucial role to play. It decides on how pension provisions are organized within the country, sometimes described as the "pillar discussion." In addition, it decides on how the contributions, investment returns and pension payouts are taxed. But it also has a broader set of goals. For example, it may wish for pension funds to invest in the home country, for instance in infrastructure. Alternatively, it may want to stimulate the stream of investments towards a more sustainable future. Often, the thinking of the government reflects the thinking in broad layers of society. Because ultimately it is the government that to a large extent defines the license to operate for pension funds, it pays off to understand this stakeholder and maintain a constructive dialogue with it, either directly or through industry bodies.

Regulator

Public regulation and supervision of pension activities are the two most powerful instruments any jurisdiction has for shaping the market. Their role is to impart socially desirable qualities to the ways and means by which commercial institutions are operated. Regulation is about setting standards and is closely tied to lawmaking—and thus is also exposed to political and market pressures.

Pension regulations have a number of objectives. They seek to promote efficient administration of work-based pension schemes, and to improve confidence in such pensions by protecting the benefits of scheme members. To meet these objectives, pension regulators increasingly employ a risk-focused approach, concentrating their resources on schemes that pose the greatest risk to the security of members' benefits.

A crucial element of this risk-focused approach is that a capital sum or buffer is determined, based on the scheme's investment risks and liabilities, which pension funds are required to hold by regulation.

Supervision, in contrast to regulation, is only peripherally involved in standard-setting activities, at a very basic, pragmatic level—if at all. Its main focus is the enforcement of regulatory requirements for pension funds and the pension sector. Hence it is closer to the technical side of the business and is focused more on the micro dimension than on the macro dimension. The supervisor promotes high standards of scheme administration and works to ensure that those involved in running pension schemes have the necessary skills and knowledge.

To ensure supervisory objectivity, it is generally recommended that supervisory operations be independent of political, governmental and industry interference. Despite those fundamental differences between regulation and supervision, in practice they are similar to plants and animals; they depend on each other. Regulation without an enforcement mechanism is simply powerless. Supervision, on the other hand, requires a legal framework for its operation, which is mainly provided by regulation. Because it is at the forefront of the market and in daily contact with market institutions, supervision is well positioned to provide important alert signals and inputs for the regulatory process. The better the professional quality of supervisory institutions, the better the chances of an adequate regulatory focus and regulatory standards. At the same time, supervisory institutions set the limits of the regulatory framework, as they define the applicability and feasibility of the standards to be met both by the entities supervised, and by the supervisory system.

In the aftermath of the global financial crisis, we are faced with increased regulation of the finance and insurance industry and an expansion in the regulatory culture. One only has to think of the wave of recently introduced or debated standards on solvency, corporate governance, fit and proper internal controls, transparency, financial conglomerates, insurance groups, financial reporting, etc. to notice this. In addition, regulatory standards have been expanded to cover previously largely unregulated activities—intermediation, reinsurance and personal claims advisors. Correspondingly, self-regulation is increasingly marginalized.

Financial Markets

Pension funds operate in the realm of financial markets. If a trustee joins a board, they become part of an ecosystem of organizations and structures. Some of these might help the pension fund, but not fully understanding their motives might also give the impression that you, as a trustee, are not pulling your weight. After all, a pension fund sits on considerable sums of money, and has a large industry and many mouths to feed.

In a financial market, securities are sold and resold. The means to realize this exchange is the asset price—the valuation of a security based on supply and demand. There is no such thing as a single financial market. There are innumerable financial markets, catering for different regions and securities. Insiders sometimes describe financial markets as living organisms. They can be positive, giddy or ecstatic. In reality, markets are no such thing, but investors trading on the markets can be. Similarly, financial markets are simply platforms that register sales and purchases. The financial markets have migrated considerably over the last decades, and continue to do so, with several implications.

Throughout the 1990s, it became increasingly difficult for even the largest plans to maintain internal fund management functions. The salaries, bonuses, options, and career prospects for internal managers have in general not kept pace with those offered by leading investment banks. Moreover, given the increasing importance of recurrent investments in computer systems, the scale economies of the largest service providers have driven many funds to outsource the provision of necessary financial services.

The market for pension-related financial services is quite distinct and varies from country to country. The Dutch, for example, have developed hybrid financial service conglomerates, intimately linked to pension fund sponsors. Boards of directors overlap with one another, with many of the largest funds acting both as consumers and suppliers of financial services. Custodial services, insurances, and investment manage ment services can be found in Dutch pension fund related companies. Nevertheless, perhaps more than any other continental country, the Dutch have sought to purchase expert advice and advanced financial products from London and Wall Street firms. For the German and Swiss funds, by contrast, long-term relationships with banks and related actuarial firms have dominated the provision of pension fund management services. Thus, until very recently, the market for financial services in many European countries was an internal market either between directly related "firms," or between long-term partners with substantial cross-representation on boards of management. This stands in contrast with the disintermediated market for services characterizing the Anglo-American world.[25],[26]

Non-Governmental Organizations

NGOs are typically not-for-profit organizations that focus on a limited number of societal goals. They exert influence on pension funds by way of trustee and trustee composition, as well as with publicity. Without a clear vision, purpose and strategy supported by the participants and known to the stakeholders, a pension fund can be confronted with the danger of regulatory capture to the benefit of specific interest groups within the insurance industry; or outside of it to the benefit of competitors, customers, suppliers, etc. Certain large funds will be targeted by NGOs, for example to invest tobacco-free or fossil free, as seen in recent cases. Similarly to governments, NGOs often give voice to important current issues in society. Therefore, it is important to listen to them, to be open to their message and to have an open dialogue with them. But, taking this a step further, the message of some NGOs might give the board guidance to the way the fund could or should adapt or invest in the future.

ENDNOTES

1. See Ambachtsheer (2016, p. 80).
2. See Credit Suisse Research Institute, Zurich (2017). Global Wealth Report.
3. See Willis Towers Watson (2017). Global Pension Assets Study.

4. See Davies (2000).
5. Definitions based on Davis and Steil (2004, p. 450).
6. See Department of Labor Employee Benefits Security Administration, U.S. (2017).
7. See the 'The End of Retirement' in The Economist (2009): 'Demography means virtually all of us will have to work longer. That need not be a bad thing'.
8. See Clark (2000).
9. See also Clark (2000).
10. See Merton (1995) for a formal distinction between customer and investor.
11. See for example Clark and Urwin (2010), Stewart and Yermo (2008), or PTL (2013) "Distinguishing Features of DC Governance" for discussion on the governance of DC Schemes and the differences between DB and DC. Available at: http://www.oecd.org/finance/private-pensions/34722818.pdf and http://ptluk.com/files/2013/11/DC-Grid1.pdf respectively.
12. Discussion on contractual and institutional type taken from Stewart and Yermo (2008).
13. See for example Sych and Metzger (2014).
14. See Department of Labor Employee Benefits Security Administration, U.S. (2017).
15. See The Law Commission (2014, Response 14.29).
16. See The Law Commission (2014, p. 65).
17. See Ambachtsheer and Ezra (1998).
18. See Clark (2000).
19. See Eisenhardt (1989).
20. See also Eisenhardt (1989).
21. Committee on the Global Financial System (2003, p. 1–69).
22. See Clark (2000).
23. See Stewart and Yermo (2008).
24. Adapted from Stewart and Yermo (2008), cited in Garratt (2010).
25. See Dufey (1998).
26. See Edwards and Fischer (1996).

Case Study—GEPF

THE DUAL MANDATE DILEMMA

Background

The Government Employees Pension Fund (GEPF) was launched by the Mandela government in May 1996.[1] At the moment, it is the largest fund in Africa. Its assets under management are more than R1.67 trillion in March 2017, which is about $150 billion (depending on exchange rates).[2] It employs a liability-driven approach to maximize returns and minimize risks relative to liabilities.[3] The fund was set up for government employees in South Africa and has more than 1.2 million active members and in excess of 400,000 pensioners and beneficiaries.

The board, appointed for a four-year term as prescribed by law, consists of 16 trustees, led by an elected chairperson and vice-chairperson. As GEPF is committed to building a better society, it plays an important role in "driving the corporate sector towards adopting sustainable business practices that generate long-term financial rewards and have a positive impact on South Africa."[4] GEPF has created the GEPF's Development Investment Policy, which has adopted a four-pillar approach to developmental investing:

1. Investment in economic infrastructure;
2. Social infrastructure;
3. Sustainability projects; and
4. Enterprise development projects.

"Many of these developmental projects are located in areas where poverty is high and GEPF believes these investments will go a long way towards creating jobs, alleviating poverty, increasing economic participation of impoverished communities, and assisting and supporting with skills development and skills transfer."[5] GEPF's objective is to be a sustainable fund for the entire South African society.

Challenge

As one of the most unequal countries in the world, South Africa faces enormous challenges. In a situation of extreme disparities between wealth and poverty and between black and white, the pension policy adopted for workers in the public sector is remarkable. The effectiveness of social policy very much depends on the extent to which it reduces the disparities and tackles poverty. Specifically, for GEPF it means it has to make trade-offs between developmental considerations and investment returns. This has to do with the fact that there are "stakeholders who look at GEPF as if it's a development finance institution or a charity," while others see GEPF as in the "business of paying pensions to South African civil servants upon retirement." In other words, the challenge of a dual mandate emerges for GEPF.

Ninety percent of GEPF's assets are invested in South Africa: "any constraints on South Africa's economic growth will have a similar impact on the fund." GEPF cannot invest more in international assets due to the legislation of the fund. The ministry of finance guarantees the benefits of the GEPF members and, in turn, their asset allocation process is carried out in close consultation with the government. That GEPF cannot invest much outside of South Africa might restrict the ability to grow of the fund. In addition, a result is that the outcomes of the fund are highly dependent on the economic well-being of the country. Of the remaining 10%, 5% is allocated to the rest of the African continent and 5% beyond Africa, to international bonds and equities. As a consequence, due to its high concentration in the domestic stock market, GEPF has a high stake in almost all the companies on the Johannesburg Stock Exchange. This also means that GEPF does not have "what you might call the luxury of selecting companies that are strong on environmental, social and governance (ESG) criteria or divesting from those that don't." So, compared to other pension funds, divestment is really a last resort.

Process

GEPF is not kept awake at night because it has a large allocation in South Africa. The fund expects that South Africa has an enormous growth potential. For example, GEPF invests in education loans. The fund argues that these provide a diversifying benefit and increase the future potential of the country's output because of the high unemployment rate. The fund is adamant about the consumption of the continent's one billion people, because many of them grow into the middle class. It strongly believes that Africa has a huge long-term earnings potential. GEPF has created a 15-year outlook and aims to provide funds for partnerships across Africa, aiming to benefit from the believed potential.

GEPF is as big as one third of South Africa's GDP (gross domestic product). With 90% of its assets invested in the country, it means that a lot of infrastructure, consumption needs, or any other kind of activity are related to the investments of the fund. GEPF recognizes it has an enormous impact on the economy and society of South Africa, stating: "It is critical that the manner in which we invest somehow benefits the economy and benefits the GEPF."

To deal with the ESG investing in South Africa challenge, GEPF and its investment management organization PIC have developed an ESG matrix. This matrix is used to analyze the top 100 companies on the Johannesburg stock exchange. "GEPF and PIC expect to see some interesting changes at Johannesburg Stock Exchange during the coming years with regards to the JSE ESG strategy to assist both issuers and investors from an ESG data disclosure and performance viewpoint." And to tackle the challenge of having to make trade-offs between ESG considerations and returns, the

GEPF's Development Investment Policy promotes investment across the four pillars mentioned in the background section.

The outcome

By investing via the four developmental investing pillars, GEPF is expected to obtain "long-term returns for the GEPF's members and pensioners, as well as for the broader South African economy." GEPF has already addressed issues which have a transformational social and environmental impact: it has invested in education, healthcare facilities, housing, enterprise development, and funding of renewable energy projects. By investing in such projects, GEPF was also able to create a lot of new jobs. "Anything that you care to see when you arrive in South Africa—whether you arrive at the airport, whether you drive on the roads, whether you buy food in the shops, or whether you stay in a hotel—we own a piece of it."[6] Therefore, it is crucial that when GEPF invests, it invests in a way that benefits the economy and benefits GEPF itself. "GEPF is effectively a third of South Africa's GDP so what we think is that if the country does not do well then the fund will not do well because we own a slice of the economy," says John Oliphant, the former principal executive officer of GEPF. Furthermore, GEPF has the potential to exert effective influence on corporate policies and practices.[7] That also means that active trading in shares of companies in which the fund is so heavily invested would result in significant price movements, and could thus be self-defeating. Therefore GEPF invests passively.

Lessons for Achieving Investment Excellence

- A dual mandate asks for strong governance as it is always hard to find and keep the right balance between the two objectives and avoid achieving one at the cost of another.
- Considerable focus on a single country leads to concentration risk and suboptimal international diversification.
- A large size of a fund can be a handicap and limits the degrees of freedom a fund has. This will come at a cost. Funds have to strike a balance between being able to move their assets without having a large market impact and their wish for having influence and impact with their investments.

ENDNOTES

1. See http://gepf.gov.za/index.php/about_us/article/who-is-gepf.
2. See Saklatvala (2014).
3. See article by Worldbank "Governance and Investment of Public Pension Assets."
4. See England and Cotterill (2016).
5. See Riley (2012).
6. See Riley (2012).
7. See Viviers (2013).

CHAPTER 2

Developing Purpose, Mission, Vision, and Goals

Key Take Aways

- A pension fund should have a purpose, a mission, a vision, and strategic goals that are developed and maintained by the board. These provide answers to questions such as: Why do we exist? What would we like to achieve and how will we achieve this?

- Purpose is based on a unique combination of the functions of pension funds. It is important to understand these functions in order to stipulate the best way to fulfill your fund's purpose and make explicit how to best add value for the fund's participants.

- Formulating the mission of the fund requires both the knowledge of what the purpose of the fund is, and making sure that the mission is in line with its participants.

- Articulating your values and vision helps to forge consistency within the fund and the investment organization, by defining a clear path to reach your strategic goals.

This chapter focuses on the strategy development process for the pension fund on whose behalf investments are made. Defining a purpose and a mission, as well as explicating the values that matter are instrumental processes in shaping the investments that achieve the mission of the fund. What are the participants' needs, both in the short and the long run? How can the investments fulfil those needs? And if the participants' needs change, can the fund still provide added value, or is there a tendency to keep on going just because the organization exists? Is the mission broader than the purely financial interest of the beneficiaries? Does it include collective or societal goals? Trustees should have shared answers for these questions in the form of a mission statement before they move on to formulating strategic goals and using these to design the investment function.

A board that has taken the time to develop a strategic plan will be able to provide its pension fund and participants with direction and focus. A pension fund that does not have a clearly defined and implemented strategy will find that it is time and time again simply reacting in the face of financial, economic and regulatory developments; the organization will be trying to deal with unanticipated pressures as they arise, and will also be at a competitive disadvantage. Strategy development requires the board to carry out and take ownership of the following six steps to enable its effective implementation. Specifically, the board must:

1. Define the *purpose* of the pension fund—why do we exist?
2. Define the *mission*—in general, how do we realize the purpose; what is our ambition?
3. Define the *vision*—what do we aspire to become and achieve in the next 5–10 years?
4. Make explicit the *values* that the fund holds.
5. Define the pension fund's strategic *goals*—how do we go from where we currently are to where we want to go?
6. Facilitate and monitor the *implementation strategy*—develop a set of actions, measures and plans to achieve the formulated goals.

Exhibit 2.1 visualizes the six aforementioned steps of the strategy development process. One of the key messages of this chapter is that the way in which a fund invests may, and probably will, be influenced by its mission, vision and strategic goals. We will explore the formulation of purpose, mission, vision, and strategic objectives of the fund, as well as discuss how values are an integral part of the purpose and mission, and how they are vital for formulating the right strategic objectives. The main message is how the board can get the fund from where it is at the moment, to the place it wants it to be. Another key point is that defining and maintaining the purpose, mission, goals and strategy are important functions of the governing board—functions that cannot be delegated to staff or consultants.

An integral part of defining the mission and purpose is getting to grips with the actual activities of the fund. When quizzed, chances are that trustees will intuitively

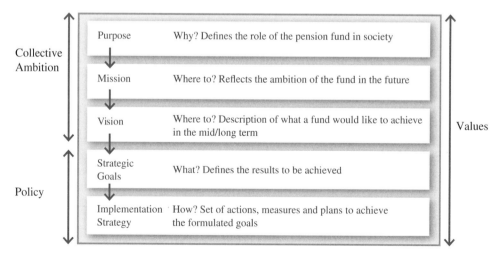

EXHIBIT 2.1   The strategy development process.

mention administration of pensions and investment of assets as the core of what constitutes a pension fund. While this is not wrong, it is also a narrow focus, and it helps for trustees to take a broader view. Understanding the generic *functions* of a pension fund will aid trustees in formulating its mission and strategy. For this reason, we have added a subsection to this chapter that considers these functions.

Values influence the mission, vision and strategy of a fund in a marked way, especially when investments are concerned. A pension fund has a specific DNA, which is related to its purpose and may reflect the industry it works for. For example, the pension fund for the Dutch airline KLM has a very different idea about the nature of risk from the typical investment professional—which is a reflection of what risk means in the airline industry. Another example is the Dutch health care pension fund PFZW, which does not invest in tobacco-related companies.

In order to be able to formulate effective strategic goals, the fund needs to understand where it currently stands and which forces will shape the future. This can be aided by carrying out a SWOT analysis to identify current Strengths & Weaknesses, and Opportunities & Threats from the external world. More information about this can be found in the Appendix.

THE FUNCTIONS OF A PENSION FUND

Developing a purpose and a mission requires in-depth knowledge of the true added value of pension fund organizations. After all, while it is true that consumers need pensions, it is not necessarily the case that they need pension funds. So, the question the board must ask itself is: What are the fund's key functions, those that matter most to the participants, and which add so much value that it makes sense to make those the basis for formulating the fund's purpose?

The activities of pension funds have changed and are still changing so rapidly that it is crucial to recognize and define the basic functions that remain stable, as opposed to the specific forms and organizations that will change with time and technology.[1] The basic functions of a pension fund are:

- *Pooling of contributions* to reduce costs and gain access to more investable assets;
- *Transforming assets* in terms of risk, duration, denomination in order to earn risk premiums, and making sure that the level of investment risk is aligned with the participants' goals and risk appetite;
- *Managing risk*, to ensure that the fund invests in rewarded risks, and that unrewarded risks are mitigated or diversified;
- Acting as a delegated monitor on behalf of the members to make sure that the financial parties and transactions live up to their promise;
- Acting as a delegated monitor to support and *guide the participants' financial choices*;
- *Transforming markets* by helping savings and investments come together in an economy, creating financial returns as well as positive side effects.

The first function of a pension fund is pooling, which is one of its fundamental characteristics. In investment, economies of scale are advantageous: you pay less for the management and the running of a fund. A fund can thus afford more professional advice and gain access to a wider range of more specialized investment opportunities. Finally, pooling helps diversify participants' risks by widening the exposure to different assets and strategies. Pooling of funds from individuals provides a mechanism to facilitate large-scale indivisible undertakings, as well as the subdivision of shares in enterprises to facilitate diversification.

Pooling also provides access to new investment opportunities, improving the return/risk trade-off over time. Although costs have fallen in recent decades, transactions costs in securities markets, the bid–ask spread, and the minimum size of some investments still make it difficult for individuals to diversify optimally through direct securities holdings. One reason for this is that there are economies of scale in large transactions, partly based on the fixed costs involved. This means that individual investors do not have access to a wide range of investments, such as private equity, real estate, and infrastructure. Generally, the risk incurred if diversification is insufficient is not compensated by higher returns, because such risk can be diversified when one has the resources to do so.[2] Historically, this meant that individuals either took excessive risks or were obliged to hold lower-yielding assets such as bank deposits. Pension funds can offer the opportunity to invest in large denomination and indivisible assets such as property, which are unavailable to small investors. Furthermore, they have the clout to negotiate lower transactions costs and custodial fees. Professional asset management costs are also shared among many participants and, as a consequence, are markedly reduced. The direct participation costs of acquiring information and knowledge needed to invest in a range of assets also decrease. In addition, the costs of undertaking complex risk trading and risk management are reduced (although the costs of monitoring the asset manager remain). All in all, pooling can help to maximize the pensions by making processes more efficient.

The second function of pension funds is transforming assets in terms of risk, duration or currency to earn risk premiums, while ensuring that the amount of investment risk is aligned with participants' goals and risk appetite.

Transforming assets is also a crucial function of a pension organization. Essentially, the board of a pension fund is entrusted with the task of transforming today's premiums into pension wealth and payouts in future decades. The consequences of these differing timescale requirements are resolved by *asset transformation*: the pension organization issues financial claims that in the future can be cashed in as pension payouts, which are more appealing to savers than holding on to the premiums or saving themselves. Pension funds must keep these pension contracts on their balance sheets until they expire: the contracts are generally non-marketable.

Any asset transformation can be unbundled into a combination of one or more of the following types of transformation: maturity, liquidity, denomination or country, and currency. Maturity transformation has the most far-reaching consequences for a pension fund and is usually defined as the asset-liability management (ALM) process. In macroeconomic terms, the maturity transformation relates to the difference in holding period preference between firms and individuals. An individual has compelling reasons not to offer their total amount of excess savings to firms. For example, they can have a precautionary motive for holding more money than required for current transactions in case of unforeseen events. In the case of a pension fund, the board has a responsibility to make sure that the assets are not underinvested, and carry the amount of risk that is in line with the longer-term ambition and associated risk appetite.

The third function of a pension fund is managing risk. It is plausible that, if a pension fund plans to transform risks, it only agrees to this if it expects to be rewarded. But the purchase of financial instruments for risk transformation, or entering into future financial commitments, can create unintended side effects. Investments in another country may carry a currency risk, as well as a country risk. A pension fund can opt to avoid unnecessary risk-taking, to share risks with participants, to transfer risks to other participants in the financial markets, or to absorb and direct the risk within the organization. Avoiding unnecessary risks requires good due diligence standards and/or portfolio diversification.[3] For starters, a level of risk that is inconsistent with the desired characteristics or features of the fund needs to be avoided.

A pension fund can also shift the risks to other participants in the financial markets. For example, a pension fund that deals with payouts in the future is exposed to changes in interest rates. The risk can then be mitigated by means of derivatives such as interest rate swaps. If a pension fund gains no clear advantage from taking this risk, or if it is unable to absorb the risk, then this is an obvious step. Finally, the risks that the fund needs or wants to absorb remain. Participants with a customized pension scheme might have such specificity in their risks that the contract cannot easily be traded or sold to other market participants, and is therefore kept and managed on the balance sheet of the pension fund. One example is longevity risk. Investment risk can also be shared between different generations of participants to even out the peaks and troughs in investment returns and stabilize the pension outcomes of the participants.

The fourth function of a pension fund is being a delegated monitor in the financial markets on behalf of its participants. One problem that is faced by the individual participant paying pension premiums is the high cost of information collection. After the purchase of securities, participants need the progress of their investments to be monitored in a timely and comprehensive fashion. Failure to monitor their investments exposes them to agency costs, that is, the risk that the firm's owner or managers will take actions contrary to the promises made at the start or as stipulated in the covenants or agreements. This is especially relevant when the manager, as party to the financial transaction, has information the saver does not, or when one is an agent of the other, and when control and enforcement of contracts is costly.

One could view a pension fund as an information-sharing coalition and a delegated monitor who act on the depositor's behalf.[4] Once the premiums are invested, further activities of the investments should be monitored, to at least ensure loan redemption. Any individual saver would have to devote a considerable amount of time and money in order to collect sufficient information to assess what the firm was undertaking, and would be better off if such monitoring were delegated and the transaction costs shared. The pension fund is the logical choice for delegation since it has more information than individuals about the firm invested in and can also put its experiences with other investments to good use. The pension fund can thus become an expert in the production of information, enabling it to sort out superior, rewarded risk from bad, unrewarded risk.

The fifth function is being a delegated monitor for the participants' financial choices. Anyone holding the responsibility for a pension scheme knows that employees need help. The responsibility for retirement funding is increasingly shifting either in part or almost entirely from the employer to the worker. Seeing that many employees may not be prepared for this undertaking, well-intentioned efforts to educate them have been under way. Plan sponsors and retirement plan service providers alike have spent vast amounts of time and money on participant education programs. As the literature shows, the rational capacity for making complex financial decisions about pensions, among other matters, is limited. Where this ends, people increasingly rely on mental shortcuts (or heuristics, as behavioral economists have called them). Unfortunately, this process leads to suboptimal retirement planning. A pension fund can act as a delegated monitor for the participants' financial choices, making them aware of when financial choices should be made, and providing information on how to make them. Depending on the board's or the regulator's vision, fiduciary duty could be extended to include helping participants to avoid behavioral biases, and promoting optimal choices.

Finally, the sixth function of a pension fund is to be a market participant. Pension funds have become sizeable players in the financial markets, a development that Peter Drucker signaled in the 1970s: they form large investment pools that can exercise influence on companies.[5] From a macroeconomic viewpoint, a pension fund has a crucial role to play in transforming the savings of individuals into investments by companies, which in turn keeps the economy growing. Pension funds are financial intermediaries, similar to banks and insurance companies. Financial intermediaries bring together those economic agents with surplus funds who want to lend (invest), and those with a shortage of funds who want to borrow. In doing so, they offer the benefits of maturity and risk transformation. Financial intermediaries enjoy a related cost advantage in offering financial services, which not only enables them to make profit, but also raises the overall efficiency of the economy. As financial intermediaries, pension funds thus play a role in matching savings and investments in an efficient way, supporting the long-term welfare of the economy. In matching savings and investments, pension funds can target specific markets: they can select markets that are not functioning well, or they can create new ones. The former are markets where, for example, there is a lot of demand, but few suppliers. A pension fund could be well positioned to enter such a market due to its long-term horizon, increasing the supply/demand ratio in the sector and improving price-setting behavior.

All pension funds' purposes are, in one way or another, based on these functions. However, the focus and weighting differs widely, depending on the background of the industry the pension fund works in, the culture of its participants, and the culture of the board.

PURPOSE

A fundamental question for anyone becoming a trustee of a pension fund is: What is the purpose of the organization? This can be followed up by questions such as: Why is it here? What is its reason for being? What must it do to stay relevant?[6]

The answer to the first question may seem obvious—to make returns on investments in order to be able to pay out the promised pensions in decades to come. However, in these competitive times, this answer is not good enough. Earning investment returns is a necessary condition: without positive returns, a pension fund dwindles away and becomes insolvent over time. But this condition is not sufficient. Over time, pension funds have changed dramatically. In Western European countries, where they have increased enormously in size following decades of growth, funds are now being terminated, changed in scope, or merged with other funds. Sponsor covenants change, participants change and, by definition, pensions' needs therefore also change.

An integral part of defining purpose is thus getting to grips with what a pension fund actually does. Having a wider focus than simply administering pensions and investing assets will help with defining the purpose. The US pension provider TIAA, whose purpose is "to be the #1 provider of lifetime financial security for those who serve others"[7] focuses on the delegated monitoring function, helping and assisting participants with information asymmetry. For the Norwegian Fund, the purpose is to "work to safeguard and build financial wealth for future generations."[8] This suggests a strong role for asset transformation and risk management—as well as for market transformation, given that future generations are named as the beneficiaries of its purpose. For another US provider, CalPERS, the purpose is to be "a trusted leader respected by our members and stakeholders for our integrity, innovation, and service." Here, too, the delegated monitoring role is emphasized. In other words, understanding the function of a particular pension fund helps a board to formulate its purpose.

MISSION

There is a subtle difference between mission and purpose that trustees need to be aware of.[9] A purpose is the fundamental reason for an organization's existence, an answer to the "why" question. A well-stated purpose is timeless, conceptual, and guiding in nature. Purposes are not a marketing slogan, nor should be made so. A mission is quite different. It is by definition achievable—to reach a certain target within a certain timeframe given specific resources. It is an answer to the "where to" question; or in what way you will fulfill the purpose. The board, working with its participants, has to define a mission to which all the members of the organization can commit. What might such a mission look like? We've chosen four examples:

- The London Pension Fund Authority's mission is "to provide an excellent cost-effective pensions service to meet the needs of our different customers."[10]
- The South African Government Employees Fund's mission is "to ensure the sustainability of the fund; the efficient delivery of benefits; whilst empowering our beneficiaries through effective communication."[11]
- TIAA's mission, "unchanged since 1918, is to serve those who serve others. Focusing primarily on institutions and individuals in the academic, medical, cultural, research and governmental communities, we offer solutions that help provide lifetime financial security and wellbeing on the best terms practicable, consistent with our nonprofit heritage."[12]

- The Second AP Fund's mission is to maximize the long-term return on pension assets under management.[13]

Each of these missions has one or more elements making it possible to create tangible and strategic goals, whether in terms of the needs of the customers, the sustainability of the fund or—the most straightforward goal—the maximization of long-term returns. The task of the board of trustees is to position the organization in a robust way for different future environments—political, economic, environmental, and social—and with the slim resources available, to set up systems for monitoring trends and changes on a regular basis. Gathering and analyzing information related to future environments enables the board to develop informed decisions about future strategies.

An important element for trustees to consider in formulating the mission is whether they view their participants as investors or clients/customers. This distinction matters, because it guides the choices down the line: will the organization be modelled along the lines of a mutual fund, or more like an insurance company? Financial services such as life insurance and retirement annuities usually involve payments to the customer of specified amounts of money, contingent on the passage of time and events. The promised future services are liabilities of the firm, both economically and in an accounting sense. Since investors in the firm also hold its liabilities, the distinction between customers and investors is not always so clear. Merton[14] argues that a distinction can be made:

- *Customers* who hold the intermediary's liabilities are characterized by their strong preference for the payoffs on their contracts being as insensitive as possible to the fortunes of the intermediary itself. Thus, a life insurance policy provides beneficiaries with a specified cash payment in the event of the insured party's death; a (nominal) pension policy provides regular cash payments from the predetermined retirement age onwards;
- By contrast, *investors* in the liabilities issued by an intermediary (e.g. its stocks, bonds, or mutual funds) understand that their returns may be affected by profits and losses. Their function is to allow the intermediary to better serve its customers by shifting the burden of risk-bearing and resource commitment from customers to investors. The investors expect to be compensated for this service with an appropriate return.

Formulating the mission of the fund requires knowledge of what the purpose of the fund is, as well as how the participants are viewed, so that the mission can be in line with them.

VALUES

Values are what support the purpose and mission, shape the culture, and reflect what the pension organization values. Values form the core of the identity of a fund. They can play an important role in binding the beneficiaries together and in the attraction of personnel. Pension leaders love to talk about values. They put them on the website, frame them, and proudly espouse them in media interviews. The notion of values has become so pervasive that it's hard to find any board that doesn't tout their importance.[15] Formulating values makes sense for the pension fund on an organizational level, dealing with participants, and dealing with financial markets.

On an organizational level, boards that make the effort to articulate the values that are core to the participants and the pension fund can deal with potential inconsistencies that may arise at an early stage and in an open way. When pension funds articulate their values, many of them will probably share many of these. But chances are that when a combination of values stands out, or a particular value is accentuated, the board and organization has spent time considering this, helping the pension fund to differentiate itself from peers or competitors, often not just in product qualities, but also in cultural features.

When dealing with the pension fund's participants/customers, making values explicit matters. Values form the basis for the pension product, for example the way in which or the intensity with which environmental, social and governance (ESG) is integrated into the pension fund. In addition, defining values helps the pension fund align with its financial stakeholders: what sort of organizations and people would they like to be associated with, and what would they really like to avoid?

Pension funds almost always already have a set of values, even if they are not explicit. Therefore, it is important to discover these. Management author Jim Collins discusses the idea that organizational values cannot be "set" but should rather be unearthed.[16] In other words, it would be a mistake to pick core values out of thin air and try to fit them into an organization. The average pension fund wants to "put the participant first," or "be perceived as an organization with high integrity." Formulating or adopting such statements without internalizing them may seem to be a short cut but it carries a long-term risk. A participant or employee could confront the boards with the values—especially if there is a disappointing outcome that is the result of explicit or implicit non-adherence to these same values by the board. And that is exactly what values are for: shaping the behavior of the fund. In this sense, values without consequences are not values at all.

Core values are neither "one size fits all" nor "best practices" in the pension industry. But you can hold the same core values as your competitors, as long as they are authentic to your organization, staff and participants. We have discussed why core values are important, as well as some strategies for defining core values. Below are several core values that have been developed by Government Pension Fund Global (GPFG)[17] (the Norway fund):

Excellence. We always strive to deliver: We are committed to a high degree of professionalism. Our investment philosophy based on diversification and specialization leads us to use various investment styles and strategies in a focused and consistent manner. Accuracy and thoroughness are at the core of our business culture;

Integrity. We do the right thing: As individuals, we stand for honesty, integrity and loyalty. Recognizing the importance of reputation, we keep a modest profile as representatives of our organization. We have a culture characterized by openness, tolerance and accountability;

Innovation. We encourage new ideas: In order to succeed we are willing to take risks and we have a corporate culture that embraces change. We encourage different approaches and views. Creativity and flexibility are vital for developing new investment opportunities and adapting to changing market environments;

Team spirit. We work together as one team: As colleagues, we respect and support each other. We believe that cooperation and interaction creates a strong organization. We never underestimate the value of enthusiasm and a good sense of humor.

When a pension fund is in the process of defining its values, it has to overcome some challenges. It has to consider multiple sets of values, e.g. the values within the organization of the board, of participants, and of the investors; and determine whether there is tension between them and how this can be solved.

Participants share a set of values depending on the nature and homogeneity of the workforce. For several sectors, the unearthing of values is a straightforward process. Participants working in the healthcare sector are almost bound to share a desire to improve people's health and would like to see this reflected in the values of the fund. Similarly, participants in the metal sector's pension scheme find their working conditions important, and a teacher's pension fund would probably name values that embed the prospect of education and equal opportunities. Theoretically, the values of the fund should reflect those of participants. The board on the other hand needs to consider additional values:

- It has to consider that the participant base might well be too diverse to distill common values, in which case the board has to settle for the greatest common denominator;
- The board can interpret its fiduciary duty more broadly and is therefore inclined to incorporate values like paternalism: listening very closely to the participants' needs and wishes but resisting the temptation to follow up on all of them;
- As already discussed, some boards of trustees are also responsible for the pension delivery organization and have intimate knowledge of the values that exist there. There can be quite a discrepancy between what the investors feel is a good way of investing and the values of the members. This often leads to tension, for example when integrating ESG into the investment process. It is important to understand and tackle this tension.

Conceptually, the board's challenge can be pictured in Exhibit 2.2. The challenge is to manage the degree of overlap in a transparent way. The task of the board is to act in the best interests of the participants, but a situation may arise in which the participants feel that the board does not consider their values sufficiently. For example, it may be that participants have a very critical attitude towards investing in fossil fuel companies even

Too Aligned   Aligned   Disaligned

Board   Participants

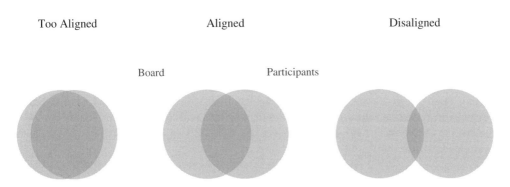

EXHIBIT 2.2   The different levels of alignment between board and participants.

though it could be in their best interests. This will lead to tension, which is not easily relieved. Other examples of "productive tension" could be the remuneration of the investment management organization, or the choice of publicly visible and controversial investments. The pursuit of ESG goals and investments that have little bearing on the characteristics and concerns of the participants is an example of too little alignment.

Formulating a set of values leads to two follow-up questions that need to be considered: do they really guide choices; and what can the board do to make them credible and felt throughout the organization?

Values should guide choice, and at times this choice has a cost. In an article in the *Harvard Business Review*, management expert Patrick Lencioni writes, "If you're not willing to accept the pain real values incur, don't bother going to the trouble of formulating a values statement."[18] When values are formulated, the follow-up question could therefore be: "What do these values cost you?" This cost could be monetary or non-monetary, but more importantly, it implies that you have to be explicit about them. This has for example been the center of a debate ever since the late 1990s when funds focused on formulating values around participants and the community. From the 1990s onwards, trustees had begun integrating the value of socially responsible investing into the investment process. The difficult question was whether this value was something that could and should be framed as a choice that cost something. In this case, the choice of financial instruments is determined by the values that participants have—for example, would they agree with their pensions being invested in the weapons industry? Some funds framed it as an investment trade-off: would customers prefer an investment strategy that excluded certain investments and on paper led to a potentially suboptimal investment result, versus an optimal trade-off that would include some investments that disagreed with the customer's values?

VISION

The vision clarifies how, given the current situation and any future changes, the fund aims to become or remain fit for purpose in the future. A good vision should be stretched, but realistic: if it is too far from the current position of the fund, the people involved will lose faith and the vision will not be realized. There are two dimensions involved when formulating a vision. First, the amount of time you allow yourself to realize the vision. A good rolling horizon is 5–10 years. You need a certain horizon to be able to change in a strategic way, but on the other hand, who can or wants to look further than 10 years ahead? Second, the level of aspiration. In terms of this book, your vision could be that you want to increase your level of investment excellence over the course of the next five years. Normally, people will enjoy such aspirations as long as they are attainable.

STRATEGIC GOALS

The next step in the strategic formulation process requires the board to identify the performance targets for the clearly stated objectives. Strategy has many definitions, but generally involves setting goals, determining actions to achieve these goals, and mobilizing resources to execute the actions. A strategy describes how the means can be used to achieve the ends. Strategy can be planned (intended) or can be observed as a pattern of activity (emergent) as the organization adapts to its environment or competes. Intended objectives may include market position or position relative to the competition, quality of financial pension product, improved customer services, corporate expansion of the pension delivery organization, advances in technology, and increasing assets under management.

In order to ensure success, strategic objectives must be communicated to all the pension fund's employees and stakeholders. All members of the organization must be made aware of their role in the process and how their efforts contribute to meeting the organization's objectives. Additionally, members of the organization should have their own set of objectives and performance targets for their individual roles. When formulating strategic goals with one's sights on investing, we could differentiate between:

- *Investment and financial goals.* Along the lines of improving long-term pension and health benefit sustainability;
- *Organizational goals.* How to foster a high performance, risk-intelligent, cost-effective organization that adapts; how to maintain its strengths and address its weaknesses;
- *Collective goals.* There are many important collective goals for pension funds, such as good regulation, good corporate governance and disclosure, which will only be realized by collective action. These are goals to enhance the long-term efficiency and effectiveness of the pension fund and financial markets. Engaging in these activities is a choice that pension funds must make. The size of the fund, its ability to influence outcomes with the management of investments, and the pressure from stakeholders (government or lobby groups) determine the fund's ability to engage in these kinds of activities. We suggest that if possible it is worth contributing, to avoid becoming a free-rider, which may be a cost-efficient position, but also a mentally impoverished one to be in.

The full scope of the strategic goals of a pension fund is much wider, but this is beyond the scope of this book. Examples of this scope include how to communicate to participants, or how to apply the newest technology in fund administration, etc. We encourage trustees to delve deeper into this matter. Understanding a fund's function and purpose lays the foundation for the mission. By making your values and vision explicit, you enable an easier and more efficient path to realize your strategic goals, all in order to fulfil the fund's purpose.

ENDNOTES

1. See Merton (1995).
2. See Sirri and Tufano (1995).
3. See Allen and Santomero (1997).
4. See Saunders (1994, p. 54).
5. See Drucker (1976/1995).
6. See Garratt (2010, p. 98).
7. See TIAA Code of Business Conduct (2014).
8. See NBIM's Mission and Values (2017).
9. See also Garratt (2010).
10. See LPFA's Strategic Policy Statement (2013).
11. See GEPF's Vision and Values (2014).
12. See TIAA-CREF's Code of Business Conduct (2014).
13. See AP2's Mission (2018).
14. See Merton (1995).
15. See Collins (1996).
16. See also Collins (1996).
17. See NBIM's Mission and Values (2017).
18. See Lencioni (2002).

Two

Designing the Process

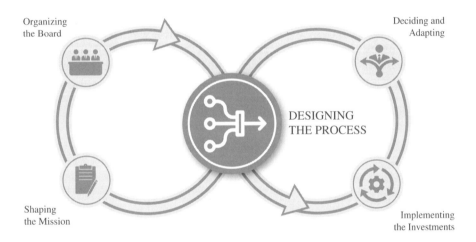

Organizing
the Board

Deciding and
Adapting

DESIGNING
THE PROCESS

Shaping
the Mission

Implementing
the Investments

As a trustee, you are responsible for devising an investment strategy that will secure your members' pension in the decades to come. This does not mean deciding on whether to buy specific stocks and bonds; that is the investment manager's task. The board's task is to provide the structure necessary to produce the investment outcomes sought by the fund, within the defined boundaries. There are three key ingredients for this structure: a set of sound investment beliefs, a clear investment process and an appropriate investment organization. In Part II, we connect the fund and board domains with the investment domain. Part II builds on the foundation of Part I but can be read separately.

Part II Topics Include:
- Key concepts in investing, enabling an understanding of the most important concepts;
- Recognizing how portfolio construction builds on risk premiums, also here distinguishing the key building blocks from the add-ons;

- Investment beliefs and how to think about and use them in the investment process;
- The structure and key building blocks of the investment management process;
- Different ways of organizing the investment management process—their pros, cons and the way they fit in with beliefs—and the nature of the investment challenges facing the fund.

CONTRIBUTION OF THIS PART TO INVESTMENT EXCELLENCE

Part II directs attention to the things that lay the groundwork when it comes to designing the investments. This groundwork is often taken for granted, or as part of the standard investment body of knowledge, but it is hard to overestimate its significance. Small changes in interpretation or implicit assumptions on investment choices have significant effects on long-term results. Once established, it will be hard to change. In terms of excellence, it pays off to offer a lot of attention to the design. By having a shared understanding of what matters most in investing and working from deeply felt investment beliefs, a fund will remove a lot of noise from the table when it comes to execution. By carefully thinking about the investment process and the investment model, the most important drivers of the long-term outcome of the fund will be determined, including the important question of the level of delegation to staff or investment managers. Therefore, the contribution to excellence of this part is that it pays to invest time and governance budget to the design or redesign of the fund.

CHAPTER 3

Grasping the Investment Essentials

Key Take Aways

- It is important for a trustee to understand the key investment concepts and what subject matter actually is at hand. Or, to use driving language terms as an example: Are we talking about the brakes or about the interior lighting? Are we talking strategic risks or implementation risk?

- Applying measures and numbers to concepts can often create a misleading illusion of accuracy (spurious accuracy). Investing is typically a coarse kind of problem. When looking ahead, we need to understand that investing is about doing things approximately right, in a robust way.

- Investors should be able to use clear language to communicate about this aspect. However, not many can. Some may even have the tendency to hide behind technical language: the "smoke and mirrors" syndrome. Having a shared understanding of investment concepts is crucial for a board of trustees.

- There often is some confusion between concepts and measures. For instance, volatility is one of many measures of risk, but it is not risk itself.

Trustees often use words such as "investing," "risk" and "return" among themselves, or during conversations with asset managers; and these words are also used throughout the investment policy, monitoring report, and evaluation of investments. However, not having a shared definition of such words may lead to confusion. As we have noted, because in pension investing trustees are looking at many layers of the investment process, it is easy to confuse these levels. Are we, at one extreme, looking at portfolio design (effectiveness, or "Are we doing the right thing?"), or at the other extreme, are we looking at the quality of the implementation of the portfolio (efficiency, or "Are we doing things the right way?")? Before any meaningful policy development of the investment goals or process can be initiated, we need to develop a shared understanding of the basic concepts of investing and risk management. In order to have a shared understanding of these basic concepts, it is very important to collectively understand the investment essentials and make sure that these are shared throughout the organization.

The aim of pension investments is to generate the returns (after cost) needed in the future to pay the promised pensions on a specified time horizon and with acceptable risk. It seeks to achieve this by constructing a robust and efficient portfolio with a diversified combination of assets. These two statements bring the key concepts of investing to the fore. This chapter will elaborate on these common statements about return concepts, risk concepts and ways to steer your portfolio. Specifically, we discuss:

1. *Investment goals*;
2. *Return concepts*. The calculation of return, and return expectations;
3. *Risk concepts*. What risk is and what it is not; the difference between risk and volatility; which risk measure to choose; and how to incorporate risk behavior;
4. *Steering the portfolio*. Benchmarks, the essence of diversification, the role of conventional vs. alternative assets within diversification, and active vs. passive investing.

INVESTMENT GOALS

In order to be able to pay pensions in the future, a fund has to generate a certain (minimum) return from its investment portfolio. This is the investment objective. The premiums paid in today will be paid out as pensions long afterwards, often 30–40 years later. This is why pension investing is a long-horizon problem. All else being equal, the more definite the promise, the less room there is for error on the investment side. There is a trade-off between certainty and premium (on expected outcome). The price for certainty usually varies from high to extremely high. When designing or redesigning a pension fund this should be looked at very carefully.

The pension promise is often stated in real terms, which means that it should be index-linked to wages or inflation. So what are sensible investment goals to set?[1]

- The investment goal should allow flexibility in indexation of pension payouts without changing the investment portfolio mix;
- The investment goal should not jeopardize perpetual operation of the pension fund, for example by current overspending at the expense of the future;
- The investment goal should not trigger procyclical behavior;
- The investment goal should not be tweaked towards exploiting or hiding regulatory loopholes.
- The realization of the investment goal should be congruent with sound investment principles (for example, the period required to earn equity risk premium);
- The investment goal should be simple and easy to understand;

These principles form a sound basis for establishing a formula to guide the pension fund in the future and are well grounded in decision-making literature. Decision-makers tend to focus on the short term and give a disproportionately high weighting to the short-term consequences of their actions. From a human point of view, this makes sense. A trustee can control and oversee the actions that he has initiated during his board terms. The pension fund, however, will exist for decades to come. As a result, there is the risk of delaying the difficult decisions that could be staring the pension fund in the face, such as dealing with the impact of dwindling return expectations.

UNDERSTANDING RETURN CONCEPTS

Generating sufficient return is the ultimate goal of the pension fund. What or how much sufficient is differs among funds. This section lays the foundation for a shared understanding of return concepts. Not all literature on return concepts is discussed; this section only provides the knowledge to understand all topics discussed in this book, as well as the foundation to have a fruitful discussion about return essentials.

Return

A return is the gain or loss on a pension fund's portfolio or investment value in a particular period. The return consists of the income from the investment such as coupons paid, dividend and rent; and the change in price. This sum is also referred to as the "total return." In investment management theory and practice, returns are viewed as "mark-to-market" returns, meaning that the return is based on the market price of the investment at the beginning and the end of the measurement period. The reliability of this market pricing can vary enormously from investment to investment. In very liquid markets, such as the large cap stock market, this provides a good indication. In many other markets, however, such as in corporate credits, a price will often simply be set because there is no recent transaction. Essentially, in illiquid assets, there is no pricing information between the points at which the investment is made and realized. It is important to be aware of this when trying to draw conclusions from detailed and short-horizon performance reports. Two points are important:

1. *Net returns.* What matters to your beneficiaries is the net return, the return after all costs;
2. *Real returns.* Real returns are the returns after deducting inflation. Pensions are meant to provide people with decent living standards during their retirement. Real return takes the cost of living into account, thereby providing a metric that returns real capital increase/decrease. This is important because inflation decreases the real value of money. For example, a continuous inflation of 5% for 10 years reduces the purchasing power by 40%.

Expectations

An investment solution or portfolio is always constructed by looking ahead. Therefore, in board and committee meetings about investing, the orientation should always be forward-looking, with the right horizon. This seems easy, but in practice it is difficult. The past provides a nice collection of very exact facts and data. These can be wonderful tools for accountants and performance measurers. But the future is risky at best and, more often than not, uncertain. In investing, what has happened in the past—even in the recent past—is usually an extremely poor guide as to what will happen in the future. For example, at the time of writing, there has been a continuous decline in both interest rates and bond yields. In many parts of the world, they have moved close to zero. It would be very dangerous to extrapolate the past in order to predict the future.

Similarly, for example, the historical performance of managers is a very poor guide to their future performance. This does not mean that we cannot learn from history. There are always patterns, and there are always lessons to be learned.

Looking ahead at expected returns, the average investment consultant will present you with an expectation that is based on one or more of the following points:

1. The concept of "risk premiums." The differential in returns between equities and bonds is calculated over long periods, and on the grounds that there is no reason to assume that returns in the future will be any different than in the past, this is then projected into future risk premiums;
2. An assessment of the current valuation of an investment plus a long-term "reasonable" valuation. The underlying investment belief is that values revert to a long-term average. It would be more profitable to buy undervalued assets and the board should hesitate to buy overvalued assets, as these might over time converge to their long-term "reasonable" valuation. This is not an uncontested approach. Between 1998 and 2018, consultants and strategists consistently predicted that the interest rate level would revert to its higher long-term average. It did not, and the resulting bad hedging decisions clearly cost funds worldwide;
3. Understanding the components of the underlying economic processes that generate the returns, such as expected profit, profit growth, rent, etc. This approach expands on the current valuation approach and assumes that asset returns are driven in the long term by fundamental long-term economic factors.

What helps in working out expectations is the use of aggregation. If you look at an individual company, it is almost impossible to know whether it will still be around 10 years from now, let alone what its returns will be. If you look at the aggregate stock market, you can make statements with a lot less uncertainty, much in the same way as it is easier to predict the average height of everyone in a certain country than the height of a single individual. So, predictions should be based on the major asset classes at an aggregated level.

Forecasts make for interesting reading and discussion for a board, but many boards interpret and use forecasts wrongly. Most predictions will fail to materialize, time and time again. There is abundant evidence that, at best, they predict the short-term trend, but fail consistently when it comes to major changes in financial markets or economies. Therefore, the board should not spend too much time on a detailed discussion or tweaking of these expectations. The way to use them is by comparison: if we compare changes in the return/risk expectation for equities versus corporate bonds, are we compensated sufficiently for the relative differences in return/risk, and how does this translate into portfolio construction?

A common misconception is that total return is proportional to risk. For example, that an investment with an expected 10% annual standard deviation should have twice the total expected return of an investment with an expected 5% annual standard deviation.[2] While it is true that there is an upward slope in returns that correlates with risk, this is far from a mechanistic relationship. Exhibit 3.1 demonstrates this relationship.

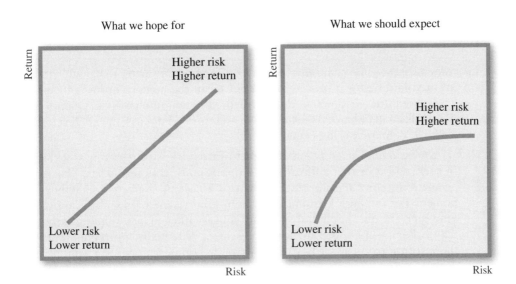

EXHIBIT 3.1 The trade-off between risk and return.

Just because investors generally get paid to carry risk does not mean that the pension fund will want to do so. The difference can be substantial. If one assumes a cash return of 4% in the above-mentioned example, the investment with a 5% annual standard deviation would have an expected return of 6% and the investment with a 10% annual standard deviation would have an expected return of 8%, not 12%. Another question for a trustee is then: which risk premiums are out there and which ones are relevant for them?

UNDERSTANDING RISK CONCEPTS

There is no consensus on a formal definition of risk. Mostly, risk is related to human expectations. It signals a potential negative effect on an asset derived from a given process or future events. Many would, for example, argue that the world has become a riskier place. Politicians would single out 9/11. Economists would probably point to the interdependency of economies, which left no safe haven during the credit crisis of 2008. Dealing with uncertainty and risks are essential parts of doing business for a trustee. Effective monitoring of risks is one of the board's key responsibilities. Board members must protect profitable activities in the face of both routine risks, and improbable disasters.[3]

Risk management is the reaction to risk by investors and pension funds as they attempt to ensure that the risks to which they think they are exposed and want to be exposed are the risks to which they really are exposed. Before developing a framework for managing risks prudently, the following basic fallacies/beliefs should be avoided:[4]

Everyone has the same concept of risk. For a seasoned investor, risk could simply mean volatility; for a trustee, risk could mean the permanent loss of capital. These are different views, with potentially different implications. Quantifying these risks will only partly help; having an informed discussion and developing a shared definition is important.

Risk is always bad. The common attitude towards risk is to regard it as a threat. In itself, risk is neither a threat nor an opportunity. It simply exists. Risk management author Culp illustrates this with a cast of characters including the homeowner in South Carolina for whom a hurricane represents a large risk. However, for the supplier of sandbags and weather radios, this is clearly different. For insurers, the hurricane presents a potentially insurable event; for the institutional investor buying catastrophe bonds, it presents a genuine risk diversification opportunity.

Some risks are so bad that they must be eliminated at all costs. Rather, the reverse is true: there is no risk so great that it has to be eliminated at all costs. Culp drives home two messages. First, risks must be evaluated in terms of probability of occurrence, not only in terms of consequences. Second, risks are about costs and benefits. A pension fund can hedge its inflation risk fully, but also partially, by weighing costs of unexpected inflation against the benefits of lower insurance costs. In other words, risks must be managed, not eliminated.

Playing it safe is really the safest thing to do. Trustees and investors are only human, and thus prone to knee-jerk behavioral reactions. Which investor has not considered a radical switch from equities to bonds when the stock markets took a severe hit? However, this risk-averse behavior, though seemingly safe, might have worse consequences in the long term.

Having a shared understanding of risk concepts helps to avoid fallacies. To help formulate a collective perspective of risk, we discuss several other aspects of risk; namely, that risk is not the same concept as volatility, how risk relates to the risk premium, choosing the right risk measure, and being aware of how risk influences investment decision-making.

Risk Is not Volatility

Risk is the possibility of loss: the chance that the return on a portfolio or an investment will be lower than the expected or targeted return. In everyday investment language, "high risk" often means "high (short-term) volatility." However, risk and volatility are different things, and it is actually dangerous to reduce risk to volatility. In pension investments, we feel there are two central meanings of "risk." The most important one in our view is: can the pension fund reasonably expect to deliver the benefits explicitly or implicitly promised over the relevant horizon? The probability of delivering less than this is called the shortfall risk. The other risk is the shorter-term degree of variability that occurs while working towards the long-term objective. This is the daily meaning that trustees and regulators tend to give to risk. The two concepts can lead to very different conclusions. For example: government bonds are commonly seen as "risk free," meaning they will pay what they promised. At the moment of writing, the expected return on a 20-year German government bond is around 1% nominal. You can be very sure that this promise will be realized, hence, low risk. Meanwhile, expected inflation over the next 20 years is in the order of magnitude of at least 1.5%, but it might end up a lot higher. In other words, you would be buying something that certainly will not contribute to generating a reasonable pension—a very high-risk asset in terms of shortfall risk.

Risk Premium

A risk premium is the return that an investment is expected to yield in excess of the risk-free rate; an asset's risk premium is a form of compensation for investors for tolerating the extra risk in a given investment, as compared to a risk-free asset. For example, high-quality corporate bonds issued by established corporations earning large profits carry very little risk of default. Therefore, such bonds pay a lower interest rate than bonds issued by less-established companies with uncertain profitability and relatively higher debt levels. Investment consultants and researchers are keen to identify new risk premiums.

In Exhibit 3.2 you will find the most widely accepted risk premiums, as well as an idea of the currently accepted order of magnitude. Usually, cash or short-term liquidity at a high-quality debtor (the state or central bank) is seen as the lowest risk asset, and therefore constitutes the basis for comparison.

Risk premium	What is it?	How much?	Asset class
Term premium	Long-term government bonds vs. short-term government bills	1 to 2% over cash	(Government) bonds
Credit premium	Premium for lower quality (BBB) vs. highest quality debt (treasuries)	Credit: 0.5 to 1% High yield: 1.5 to 2.5%	Credits, high yield
Equity premium	Expected return of equities over government bonds	3 to 4%	Equities
Illiquidity premium	Expected return of illiquid assets over their liquid counterparts	2 to 3%	Private assets such as private equity, real estate and infrastructure

EXHIBIT 3.2   Top five risk premiums and accompanying asset classes.

The risk premiums in Exhibit 3.2 provide the bulk of the rationale for constructing portfolios. If the board understands these risk premiums, then 80% of the expected long-term return/risk outcome of the portfolio is covered.

The risk premiums are based on the assumption that risk and return are proportional, i.e. that an additional unit of expected risk results in an additional unit of expected return. More specifically, we assume that "excess return" is proportional to risk. Excess return is the return in excess of a risk-free return such as a return on cash. The measure of risk is the annual standard deviation of returns. So if an investment with an expected 5% annual standard deviation would be expected to return, for instance, 2% more than cash, an investment with an expected 10% annual standard deviation would be expected to return 4% more than cash.

A misconception is that risk-taking is automatically rewarded. Taking risk is not in itself a rewarding activity, which is why it needs a risk premium as a reward—it actually works the other way around. The real questions are: Which risks are on average rewarded, and which are not? Second, is the expected rewarded risk in proportion to the expected extra return, and if not, can the risk be avoided altogether? This leads to strategic choices in investment plans, for example to mitigate currency or interest rate risks.

Getting Risk Measures Right

The goal for trustees is to find applicable measures for the different risks. Aggregating the risks into a few handy, comparable measures with which trustees can influence the outcome would be very helpful. *Stochastic* risk analysis is widely used for estimating errors and small probabilities when the observables are averages of a large quantity of independently acting agents or extremes of such observations. Risk measures have been developed and applied successfully in actuary science and management analysis.

Typical measures of risk are the standard deviation, Value at Risk (VaR), or drawdown frequencies. In reports and risk management systems, these are often measured retrospectively, but purporting to describe the situation looking ahead. A trustee should be aware of this, because the assumption to be challenged is that the information from the past period provides guidance for the future period. In fact, if the current volatility of the stock market is low, for example, this does not say anything about its future volatility.

A bigger problem than whether the data are correct is that trustees are not trained to deal with stochastic measures and probability. Kritzman[5] provides a painful example of how "loss" depends on how you frame the question. Suppose that the investment committee has to decide on the strategic asset allocation, and it has the following information: the expected average yearly return is 10%, and the standard deviation is 20%. How safe is the portfolio? Based on this information, Kritzman comes up with five variants for calculating the likelihood of loss:

- Likelihood single year loss: 14%
- Likelihood average annual loss: 0.03%
- Likelihood cumulative loss: 3%

- Likelihood loss in >1 year: 77%
- Likelihood cumulative loss at some point: 54%

Which number will you use in a discussion with trustees? At this point, trustees may increasingly be feeling that they are at a loss to know what to do. They may be given all the information, in neat tables with percentages, but how can they determine whether the likelihood of a 4% loss is worse than a 2% loss, and if it is, should it be assumed that 4% is twice as bad?[6] Without a firm grounding in statistics, trustees will give widely differing answers, which is not helpful and in some cases downright misleading for decision-making.

The message is clear: it pays for a committee or board to agree on one or more risk measures that guide the investment process and implement them throughout the monitoring and evaluation. Trustees should not work with abstract figures alone, but instead should be trained to cope with real life situations—especially the bad ones. In other words, how can risk measures be put into practice?

There may be underlying or additional beliefs that have to be made explicit, such as the emotional loss-aversion characteristic of trustees, alongside the rational loss-avoiding function of a pension fund embodied in Asset-Liability Management (ALM). What will your actions be when the cover ratio is 150%, 105% or 90%? How will stakeholders react? Will you still rebalance, or not? These are the kind of situations trustees should become familiar with. This type of mental training with scenarios will help a fund cope with future crises and is especially helpful in an unstable environment where the time span between financial and economic crises keeps decreasing.[7] Preparation and training is not new. "We expect firemen and ambulance crews to practice regularly for unexpected situations, so why not the trustees to whom participants have delegated the task of providing for their income once they reach 65?," the prospective pensioner could justifiably ask.

Having determined how to interpret the risk measures, it is also important to consider where to use which risk measure in the investment process. This is visualized in Exhibit 3.3.

Risk Is about Behavior

Trustees have little difficulty making hundreds of decisions every day. This is because the best course of action is often obvious, and because many decisions are not worth spending much time on as the potential outcome has little impact. For pension funds, however, many potential decision paths diverge in outcome, and the correct path may be unclear. There is ample research that provides insights into the psychology of the decision maker or trustee. A central theme is that the natural manner of reacting and thinking, if not tackled effectively, can regularly and unintentionally lead to decisions with unintended and even undesirable outcomes. Portfolio theory and management are based on the following "rational" basic principles:

- The sum is different from the parts;
- Diversification in risky investments can increase the stability of the overall portfolio;

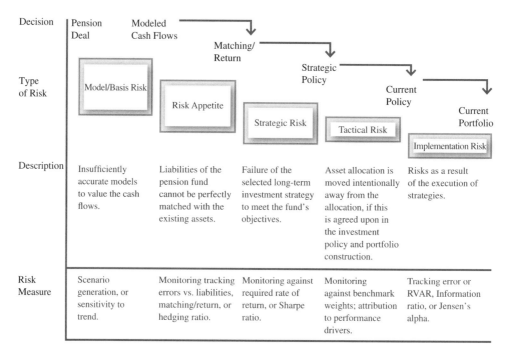

Decision	Pension Deal	Modeled Cash Flows	Matching/ Return	Strategic Policy	Current Policy / Current Portfolio
Type of Risk	Model/Basis Risk	Risk Appetite	Strategic Risk	Tactical Risk	Implementation Risk
Description	Insufficiently accurate models to value the cash flows.	Liabilities of the pension fund cannot be perfectly matched with the existing assets.	Failure of the selected long-term investment strategy to meet the fund's objectives.	Asset allocation is moved intentionally away from the allocation, if this is agreed upon in the investment policy and portfolio construction.	Risks as a result of the execution of strategies.
Risk Measure	Scenario generation, or sensitivity to trend.	Monitoring tracking errors vs. liabilities, matching/return, or hedging ratio.	Monitoring against required rate of return, or Sharpe ratio.	Monitoring against benchmark weights; attribution to performance drivers.	Tracking error or RVAR, Information ratio, or Jensen's alpha.

EXHIBIT 3.3   Monitoring of performance and risk along the investment process.

- Returns are not the only thing that matter—risk and obligation aspects must also be taken into consideration;
- Long-term trends can be overshadowed in the short term by temporary things like market dips, exchange rate issues, and uncertainties that cloud the horizon;
- The desire for short-term certainty and stability of return can significantly harm long-term aims, for example in protecting capital against inflation.

Trustees, investment committees and advisors must therefore avoid three pitfalls: oversimplifying problems, ignoring personal preferences when forming judgments, and short-cut information processing. It is worthwhile training the investment committee to recognize and avoid behavioral pitfalls. The trick is to make sure that, when deciding, you are collectively in "thinking slow" mode; that is, slow, rational and well-thought-out, and not in "thinking fast," intuitive, emotional, "let's make a mental shortcut" mode.[8] Chapter 14 elaborates on these behavioral biases.

STEERING YOUR PORTFOLIO

The final section of this chapter delves deeper into the matter of how to steer your portfolio. This means that given your knowledge of the previous sections, you are able grasp the basics of risk and return. But investing is also about making choices regarding coherence, goals, and managing when trying to reach a goal. This section elaborates more on benchmarks, diversification, asset selection and managing a portfolio.

Benchmarks

In an investment plan, a benchmark often represents an asset class on which the pension fund wants to earn its risk premium. So, for example, if a fund wants to earn the risk premium on equities, it will make an allocation to one or more equity benchmarks, such as the S&P 500-index or the MSCI-All World Index. At the same time, a benchmark is a standard against which the performance of a security, mutual fund or investment manager can be measured. Generally, broad market and market-segment stock and bond indexes are used for this purpose. So what is a sensible benchmark to set? We can think of the following desirable features:[9]

- The combination of benchmarks should aggregate to the overall benchmark that the pension fund has set;
- The benchmark and resulting investment style should not trigger procyclical behavior;
- The benchmark should not be tweaked towards exploiting or concealing regulatory loopholes;
- The investment style and benchmark should be congruent with sound investment principles (such as the period required to earn equity risk premium, etc.);
- The composition and maintenance of the benchmark should be simple and easy to understand.

Trustees choose a market index, or a combination of indexes, to serve as the portfolio benchmark. An index tracks the performance of a broad asset class. Because indexes track returns on a buy-and-hold basis and make no attempt to determine which securities are the most attractive, they represent a "passive" investment approach and can provide a good benchmark against which to compare the performance of a portfolio that is actively managed.

When implementation is delegated to an asset manager or investment management organization, the investment management agreement will describe the choice of and deviation around the benchmark in great detail. The amount of "room" that an investment manager is entitled to between the performance, or investment return, of an individual mandate and its benchmark is known as the relative risk budget. This is often specified as a (annualized) standard deviation percentage of the realized returns versus the benchmark returns, in this context called the "tracking error." The lower the tracking error, the more the outcome of the mandate will resemble that of the benchmark, in other words, the more "passive" the investment style. When a portfolio is actively managed, the tracking error may reflect the investment choices made by the active manager in an attempt to improve performance. Exhibit 3.4 shows different risk budgets accompanied with their characteristics. Important here are the reasons behind these investment choices: the investment style and investment beliefs of the manager. However, this is information that cannot be obtained from a benchmark, but requires a quality conversation.

Tracking error (annualized)	Name	Typical strategies	Normal bandwidth of annual out/ underperformance
< 0,5%	Passive	Passive large cap equity mandates	Between 0% and 1%
0,5% - 2%	Enhanced	Disciplined, often model-based mandates	Between 1% and 4%
2% - 6%	Active	Mandates in less liquid, skill-based markets such as mid and small cap, high yield	Between 4% and 10%

EXHIBIT 3.4   Risk budgets and characteristics.

Diversification

Diversification is a risk management technique that mixes a variety of investments to minimize the potential downfall in adverse times within a portfolio. The rationale behind this technique is that a portfolio constructed out of different kinds of investments will, on average, yield higher returns and pose a lower risk than any individual investment found within the portfolio.

Diversification aims to smooth out unsystematic risk events in a portfolio such that the positive performance of some investments offsets the negative performance of others. Diversification, therefore, only works—on average—if the assets in the portfolio are not perfectly correlated. However, during crises the correlation between assets increases dramatically, eroding the value of diversification—perhaps the sole exception being the lack of correlation between equities and bonds.[10] In other words, diversification 'works' best when it is not needed, but works poorly when financial markets are in crisis. Trustees should allow for these different circumstances (regular business, crisis) in their investment policy. The existence or absence of correlation is the driving force behind diversification. Investment theory teaches that diversifying over different assets makes sense when there is low correlation among asset classes. An investment portfolio with multiple asset classes that have low or negative correlations can deliver a portfolio with more attractive risk/reward characteristics than any one of the asset classes alone.

In recent years, more insights have been gained into why assets are imperfectly correlated. Securities returns could move together by chance, or they might be correlated with a single common factor, such as oil. The financial crisis in 2008–2009 showed that many assets and securities have more in common than previously assumed. When the crisis is serious enough, just about anything is sold in the short term. So, when trustees discuss diversification, they should ask themselves whether the pension fund's goals will still be met when diversification works only partially during stress, or whether other measures—such as a solvency strategy—might be needed to manage the amount and type of risks on the balance sheets, which change when the solvency ratio of the pension fund changes.

Conventional vs. Alternative Assets

Diversification does not tell a trustee which assets to include in the diversification. What is the investment universe that the trustees would like to consider? Trustees can basically make a choice from two options, which will mainly reflect their appetite for complexity and innovative new instruments. The first is to select traditional assets such as bonds and equities to construct a portfolio. These are perfectly adequate for realizing a pension fund's goals, but do not leverage their potential long-term strengths. At the other extreme, trustees could add alternative assets such as private equity and infrastructure, which leverage a pension fund's strengths, but come with a "product warning:" complexity and higher costs that might detract from long-term goals.

The first approach constructs a portfolio with the minimum number of different asset classes to achieve the return/risk objectives. Conventional investment classes such as equities, bonds and cash could fill the bill. The asset allocation of the Norway Fund consists of just that—bonds and equities. However, if the board feels that further diversification benefits could be gained, they can consider alternative investments. Funds with more extensive assets under management and those that feel they have an experienced board and/or staff tend to consider adding alternative assets. Alternative assets are those that are not among the conventional classes of equities, bonds and cash. They include private equity, hedge funds, infrastructure, real estate, commodities and derivatives. Alternative investments also include highly specialized exotica, such as wine, stamps, antiques and art. However, for most funds this is beyond their scope, and very few in fact invest in these areas; these markets are not that well developed and questions may be raised by regulators and participants. Alternative investments share certain characteristics:

- *Low liquidity.* Difficult to buy or sell quickly or at certain, possibly critical, times. As they are not listed on exchanges, it may be difficult or impossible to find a buyer when you want to terminate the investment;
- *Difficult to value.* Sometimes the theoretical price is vastly different from the price (if any) offered by the market. This is otherwise known as the difference between the "mark to model" and "mark to market" prices;
- *Higher degree of due diligence needed.* The regulatory environment for alternative investments is not as strong as for traditional investments. Therefore, a deeper and broader range of enquiry is needed as to by whom, how and where the investment is being managed. Transparency is not something the alternative classes are usually known for.

Alternative investments also claim a large portion of the governance budget of trustees. Transparency is limited, and trustees have to think through the consequences of limited liquidity. These assets cannot be sold in periods of strong market movements, so the other core assets must provide all the liquidity needed for pension payments, derivatives, etc. Furthermore, for many alternative investments the academic debate on diversification is far from settled. For example, does private equity really provide a complementary risk premium compared to equities, or is the investor paying a hefty fee for returns that are similar to, but lagging behind equities?

Active vs. Passive Investing

Trustees are by far the most important principals awarding active managed mandates worldwide in the investment industry, and they therefore support the income model of asset managers to a large extent. The debate on active management started in the late 1960s, when investors started to incorporate the latest ideas about portfolio management into actual investment practices, and benchmarks were developed to measure the relative results of managers. While actively managed investments contribute a small portion of the overall realized performance of the pension fund portfolio, fees for active management form a large slice of the income of the asset management industry that is providing strategies and services to the pension funds.

Active management is a broad brush. Any investment decision that intentionally or unintentionally creates a portfolio that deviates from an agreed reference framework is a form of active management. The aim is to generate returns exceeding those of the reference framework, on a risk-adjusted basis. So, the idea of active management is a strange one from the outset. Most service providers would be content if they delivered what they had promised. Active managers start out by promising that they will over-deliver.

Basically, most studies confirm that managers have a difficult time beating benchmarks, raising questions about the worth of active management for a pension fund. The reasons for this could be summed up as follows:

a) Fees have a high impact, in absolute and relative terms;
b) There are too many smart investment managers chasing the same strategy, collectively lowering returns;
c) Managers have their ups and downs—it is difficult to predict when these will be;
d) Extra returns are not based on skill, but on expensively leveraging cheap benchmark returns.

We will now provide the reader with some more detailed explanations of these reasons:

Reason (a). Trustees are increasingly taking a second look at the one variable that, for a long time, most assumed was too small to matter: fees. The logic is simple: higher costs lower any form of returns, and for the better part of the 1990s and 2000s, costs have been rising, either directly or indirectly. Fees for active management are usually described as "only" as in "only 1%." But that really means 1% of the assets that the investor already has. So what the manager offers to deliver is a return on those assets. If equity returns average 7% going forward, that 1% fee is really—if correctly calculated—much higher: roughly 15% of returns. But since index funds deliver the market return at no more than the market level of risk, any economist would say the true fee for active management is the incremental fee over and above the very low fee for indexing, as a percentage of the incremental risk-adjusted returns. Defined in this rational way, fees for active management are not low. They are actually very high and, surprisingly—until examined closely—average over 100% of the potential additional active returns. The combination of repeated disappointing results and the gradual recognition of the very high incremental cost of active management is prompting an increasing number of investors to shift increasing proportions of their assets into low-cost index funds and exchange-traded funds.

Reason (b). The number of players has increased dramatically. According to the renowned investment writer Charles Ellis, active management is not failing because of bad managers, but because too many similarly trained good managers enter the market,[11] searching for similar strategies and, therefore, on aggregate, reducing the chances of making a decent living.

Reason (c). There is evidence that managers themselves are mean-reverting over a longer period. This is investment jargon for stating that no investment manager is always good. He or she tends to have up and downs.

Reason (d). The final reason for the overall disappointing results is a technical one. If we take a closer look at the extra return, research tends to show that it is highly correlated with the underlying benchmark, which gives rise to another suspicion: alpha is not so much correlated with the skill that the manager has in identifying market-independent opportunities, but rather with the risk of the underlying benchmark. In other words, managers leverage their own positions. Is this all bad news for active management? No. There are studies showing potential for outperformance. For example, recent studies suggest that highly concentrated portfolios deliver better results. This means choosing a limited number of stocks, in contrast to investing in all the stock of the benchmark and only changing its weightings a bit. However, it must be kept in mind that these are academically driven studies, in the sense that they identify corner solutions that require a very specific breed of investors. Either the investment horizon must be very long, or the type of securities must have a specific characteristic that requires some stamina (deeply undervalued securities, for example).

Overall, the previously mentioned reasons still do not explain why current day active management persists. A possible explanation could be the marketing budget of the financial industry, in addition to a matter of perception—the idea that if these managers are highly paid, they must be successful. Alternatively, while investment managers retain their job for decades, trustees only last for a couple of years. This introduces a sort of managerial call-option: "I know that active management fails overall, but if it does, I am not alone. If on the other hand it succeeds, it will be something that I can add to my achievements." Shefrin[12] identifies another possible downside element: investment committees may be perfectly well aware that active management is a zero-sum game. However, when the fund has a lot of active mandates, if they fail, management can fire these mandates, demonstrating resolute action. With only passive mandates and asset allocation choices to show, the investment committee would be far more accountable—and vulnerable. Finally, investment committees tend to choose external advisors perceived to have been successful in investment management. These generally tend to be in the field of active management.

Better Beta: Styles and Factors

Over the past decade, there has been a strong take-up of "smart beta," style and factor investing within public equity markets. This form of implementation lies somewhere between passive and active investing. In investment lingo, "beta" is the part of the return that is to be ascribed to the market or benchmark invested in, and "alpha" is the part that is gained or lost by taking specific positions vis-à-vis the benchmark, or in other words, active management. So, in a passive strategy, beta is one and alpha is—by definition—zero. You can also look at it like this: the beta returns are earned because of the policy and strategy of the plan; the alpha is the part where the degrees of freedom that are allowed to the investment manager contribute.

Typically, at the fund level and for most funds, beta will contribute at least 90% of the net return over time ... and too often more than 100%, if the alpha after cost turns out to be negative. So, for trustees it makes sense to concentrate on generating strong beta returns.

Within the returns of portfolios, specific characteristics can be found, which in the longer term can earn a "systematic" additional risk premium as compared to the market, which may pay out as a higher return or as a lower risk in times of trouble. These are called "styles" or "factors." To mention the most prominent ones: Value (overweight cheap stocks) and Small Cap (overweight small companies) have been around for a long time, and Momentum (overweight stocks that have done well recently) was an important third. Typically, three more will be taken into consideration nowadays: Quality (overweight companies with strong and resilient earnings and growth potential), High income (overweight companies which generate high dividend yields), and Low Volatility (overweight stocks with a low market volatility). For most of these factors, there is a good to reasonably good storyline underpinning the logic of their existence and at least some empirical evidence that they may produce added value over the longer term, such as the course of an investment cycle, although slippage in the form of implementation cost may be high.

These styles and factors explain a large part of the returns that were used to call alpha historically. This is why some people say "alpha is beta waiting to be discovered." The big advantage is that the returns to these factors can be systematically packed into benchmarks and strategy, thereby replacing the artisanal character of alpha by something that is more systematic and controllable by the board, and typically also cheaper than active management. This approach often goes by the term "smart beta investing" or, preferably, "better beta." This approach typically is becoming part of the standard building blocks of equity investing for pension funds. Nowadays, funds will often allocate 20%–40% of their public equity market investments to better beta strategies.

Responsible Investing

Responsible Investing or environmental, social, and governance (ESG) investing is built on two thoughts. First, risk and return on investments are impacted by more than just the financial factors that come into play when evaluating them; more specifically by ESG factors. Thus, investors have a clear interest in taking these into account.

Second, investors and asset owners do have an influence on their investments, which goes further than just being financially literate. This potentially makes for better outcomes with regards to governance, the environment, and the society.

ESG has a strong global presence, especially since the launch of the Principles for Responsible Investment (PRI) by the UN in 2006. The PRI, which is signed by 1,800 asset owners and asset managers, represents some $60 trillion of investments. It is made up of six principles, the first two of which are the most important. Principle 1: We will incorporate ESG issues into investment analysis and decision-making processes; and Principle 2: We will be active owners and incorporate ESG issues into our ownership policies and practices. The genius of these principles is in the fact that they are so generically formulated that investors with very different motives and backgrounds fit in.

Motives or Mission

The motives for asset owners to take ESG issues into account vary from purely financial reasons, to having or taking on a certain responsibility for the outcomes their investments produce. We list potential motives here:

- *Financial.* If there is a material impact from ESG on investment outcomes, it is part of fiduciary duty to incorporate those into the investment process.
- *Potential cost.* Many investments generate external effects in the form of negative outcomes on society, such as carbon emissions. By owning these investments, implicitly you also generate this effect, which, in the longer term, may cost you.
- *Enlightened self-interest.* In the longer term, it is in the interest of asset owners (certainly collectively) to operate in a world in which the environment and governance are well taken care off, because they are crucial ingredients for producing long-term returns.
- *License to operate.* Beneficiaries and broader stakeholders will have changing demands from the asset owners that they entrust their pension savings to. Shouldn't the asset owner reflect the values of the beneficiary in the way it invests? Is the asset owner part of the solution, or part of the problem? If the fund is out of sync with its beneficiaries, its license to operate will come under pressure.
- *Mission.* It can be the mission of the asset owner or the wish of the beneficiaries to enhance ESG issues.

In practice, many pension funds will have a blend of the motives listed above. Investors and sometimes also boards start from the reasoning that taking care of ESG comes at a cost when it comes to investing; in other words, by investing more responsibly, you will earn lower returns, usually because the universe from which you can select your investments becomes smaller. However, this is a false belief, as, on average, this is not actually the case. There now is a large and growing body of evidence[13] that by and large concludes that responsible investing as a bare minimum does not hurt in terms of return and risk, and even may enhance these. So, sound investing and responsible investing can come hand in hand. In other words, there is significant room to act, and given fiduciary duties around the world it may even become compulsory to take ESG issues into account. A word of caution, however. The generic evidence does not say "any responsible investment will pay off," just as investment theory does not say "because diversification is good, including this stock in your portfolio will pay off."

When formulating your mission, it is important to reflect on the pension fund's views on this, because it can have deep consequences for the way it presents itself to its participants and the other stakeholders, and in addition it lays the foundation for investment behavior.

Instruments

The set of instruments available for acting on responsible investing has rapidly evolved over the past decades. A first, rather blunt, instrument is exclusion, with which certain investments are excluded from investment portfolios because they do not live up to minimum standards. Often, human rights or controversial weapons will be subject to exclusions. More recent topics of exclusions are in the field of coal (unsustainable contribution to climate change in the longer term) and tobacco. A second instrument is voting on corporate issues, which is broadly implemented. It is often outsourced. A big advantage of voting is that is does not have to impact your portfolio composition. A third instrument is engagement, with which there will be a dialogue, oftentimes on a specific topic between investors and a company. For example, on carbon emissions or labor conditions. Often, this is done in the form of a cooperation or a coalition between investors, because this is more effective than acting alone.

Over the past few years, certainly in Europe, there has been a strong movement towards trying to have an impact on the real world or having a portfolio that reflects the mission and identity of the pension funds. There is a movement towards inclusion, meaning that funds only want to own companies and investments that reflect the qualities and behavior that fit into their mission and values. There also is a movement towards impact investing, in which asset owners are steering investments into areas and companies that will positively impact one or more topics or themes that are close to their mission, such as improving health care and food security, or avoiding global warming.

Recently, investors have started to think about how they can integrate the 17 Social Development Goals (SDGs) of the United Nations into their investment approach. In the next few years, it may prove to be the case that these will provide an effective common framework that helps classify investments, which makes it easier to allocate to them, delegate investment decision-making towards internal and external managers, and report on sustainability issues.

ENDNOTES

1. See Ennis and Williamson (1976).
2. See Polbennikov et al. (2010).
3. See Andersen et al. (2014).
4. See Culp (2002).
5. See Kritzman (2002).

6. A 4% loss cannot be considered worse than a 2% loss. This depends on another statistical measure: the uncertainty level. If this level is high for both numbers, then they might as well be indistinguishable.
7. See Reinhart and Rogoff (2009).
8. See also Reinhart and Rogoff (2009).
9. See Ennis and Williamson (1976).
10. See for example Ilmanen (2003).
11. See Ellis (2003).
12. See Shefrin (2002).
13. For an overview see, for example, Friede, Busch and Bassen (2015).

TAKING OWNERSHIP OF AND REBUILDING INVESTMENT PRINCIPLES AFTER THE GREAT FINANCIAL CRISIS

Background

PFZW is the compulsory industry pension fund for employees in the Dutch Health Care Industry. It is the second largest pension fund in the Netherlands, with 2.4 million participants, targeting indexation of pension payments with wage inflation. Assets under management are $197.2 billion at the end of 2017. Since 2008, there has been a split between PFZW (the pension fund) and PGGM (its Pension Delivery Organization), which advises on and implements the investments, amongst other things. The board of PFZW includes representatives of employers and employees, with an independent chair.

The challenge

After the financial crisis of 2008–2009, PFZW faced a number of questions that essentially said: the world has changed in a significant way, does our investment thinking reflect these changes? For example, the paradigm of "efficient markets" did not help to prevent large losses. The license to operate for Defined Benefit (DB) pension funds was no longer self-evident. Trust in pension funds by society was at a very low ebb. And PFZW felt the need to integrate sustainability in a more profound way. Last, but not least, after becoming separate entities, PFZW began developing its own identity at a certain distance from its service provider PGGM. Being the asset owner, PFZW felt it should formulate and own the principles for investing. PFZW felt that having a strong set of principles would be of great value in getting everybody in the chain moving in the same direction and speaking the same language.

The process

The preparation for the project began in late 2011, and was called the "White Sheet of Paper." Within the PFZW board, there was broad support for the project. All board members were willing to spend a considerable amount of time on the project, which lasted for 18 months. In particular, six board members, most of them also members of the investment committee and including the chairman, were able and willing to devote one day per week or more. They proved to be the driving force behind the project, both inspiring the PFZW board and directing the PGGM organization.

In order to provoke fresh thinking, the approach was defined as "outside in." The committed board members took it upon themselves to obtain access to the best investment thinking globally. The process, leading to the new Investment Framework, consisted of a pyramid of questions on three pillars: "how can we invest in a way that (i) fits in with our financial ambitions, (ii) in which sustainability is fully integrated, and (iii) which is intelligible and controllable?"

During the process, PFZW's six involved board members interviewed over 30 industry experts from all over the world, ranging from peers such as Angelien Kemna from APG, to consultants such as Keith Ambachtsheer, and researchers like Antti Ilmanen. Furthermore, a number of contrarian thinkers were invited to appear before the full PFZW board and asked to be very explicit on the questions of "What should PFZW keep doing?" "What should PFZW change?" "What should PFZW stop doing?" from their special topics. This led to a very intense and thought-provoking discussion.

During the process, great care was taken to document all the outcomes. Thus, the results of the interviews were written up, and each of the board sessions led to a document in which the statements of the board were summarized. Each of the three pillars led to a "pillar document" that would form the input for the final document.

The outcome

The outcome of the process is PFZW's Investment Framework 2013–2020. This 12-page document briefly describes the identity and the ambition of PFZW, the changed context in which the fund operates and the 16 resulting convictions and principles that will govern the investments going forward. Here we highlight some aspects of the resulting principles.

- *Sustainability.* These principles lay the foundation for a deep commitment to sustainability, from two perspectives: (i) the logic that PFZW assumes responsibility for making a tangible contribution to a sustainable world, and (ii) that at the same time a sustainable world is a necessary condition for adequate return generation over a long horizon. In other words, in the long term, PFZW can't afford to see a system that generates sustainability as an externality. The notion of sustainability also includes the health of the financial system. The principles assume that PFZW can have a serious impact, which is also referred to as "the steering power of money."
- The principles also address principal–agent issues between the fund and its investment managers. The fund asks for long-term relationships and it acknowledges that there's "many a slip twixt cup and lip"—leakage, in the form of agency costs, short termism, and actual costs that has to be addressed in the relationship with the investment managers. Also, a direct link is sought between realization of ambitions and the actual investment management that goes beyond the notion that: "If I beat my benchmark I'm doing a great job as an asset manager." Needless to say, developing a long-term perspective and integrating other goals than just beating a financial benchmark takes some time to achieve.

■ *Simplicity and control.* Additionally, the principles deal with the question "How can the board have total oversight over both policy and implementation" vs. "How complex does the investment solution have to be in order to realize the ambition." The clear call is again for parsimoniousness: keeping the solution as simple as possible, and being very clear about the expected value-added either from adding investment categories or from adding complexity.

The Investment Framework was adopted by the board in June 2013. In order to achieve consistency between the framework and the actual investments, a Strategic Investment Plan 2014–2020 was adopted. This plan translates the framework into 11 workstreams and draws a roadmap for the period up to 2020. This plan provides a framework for incorporating the transformational change in a controlled way, and at the same time argues for "learning by doing," in order to avoid analysis paralysis.

Lessons for Achieving Investment Excellence

■ It takes serious time and collective effort to build shared investment principles.
■ The board should own its investment principles. If it does not, there will always be friction between board and asset manager.
■ An outside-in perspective stimulates fresh thinking and avoids a superficial writing down of the principles behind current practice.
■ The principles should drive implementation. In the actual investment solution you should be able to ask the question: is this rooted in and consistent with our principles?

ENDNOTE

1. This case leans heavily on van Dam (2014).

CHAPTER 4

Investment Beliefs as Guiding Tools

Key Take Aways

- Investment beliefs are an effective tool to facilitate the governance of the investments made by the board or investment committee. Beliefs guide and discipline investment decisions.

- A good set of beliefs is firmly rooted in theory and experience, but at the same should have a good and practical fit with the fund that adopts them.

- In our view, beliefs should be owned by the board and shared between the board and the investment organization.

- Beliefs guide choices for years to come, and thus should not be decided on in an afternoon. They allow trustees to take ownership of the investment process.

- Some beliefs are more evidence-based than others. This is not a problem, but it needs to be made explicit.

- A simple set of beliefs can help to avoid a lot of pitfalls.

With the purpose, mission and goals in place, a board is ready to take the next step and focus on the design of the investment management process: developing investment beliefs. Investment beliefs are important because they create a context for value-creating investing. What are the core competencies of an investment organization that is aiming for success in the capital markets? How does and how should an institutional investor view capital markets? This is a strategic issue that seems obvious but has seldom to date been addressed in the literature.[1] Research by Clark and Urwin[2] shows that best practice funds treat investments as a strategic core element, based on investment beliefs that can stand the tests of logic, informed debate, and occasional revision when new evidence comes to light.

In this chapter[3] we define what investment beliefs are; we argue that these are extremely useful for a board. Next, we consider how to use them and we delve into the question of how to develop them.

WHY INVESTMENT BELIEFS MATTER

Investment beliefs matter more than you know, or that you would like them to. Every investment approach is based, at least implicitly, on a set of beliefs. If thoughtfully developed and diligently implemented, investment beliefs are an essential step towards investment excellence, as well as to funds' long-term survival in the financial markets. In financial markets, pension trustees who ponder the "why" as much as the "how" find themselves at an advantage. Well-thought-out investment beliefs, as well as their implementation and organization are instrumental. Investment beliefs address the "why" question by developing views on how financial markets work and what the consequences are for the investment strategy and the organization of a fund. Investment beliefs are implicit in every investment decision or strategy, but it is not common for them to be made explicit.[4]

It is not difficult to find investment beliefs. In fact, investors and trustees pronounce, act on or ignore investment beliefs on a daily basis. This can sometimes be at their own peril. Consider the following (hypothetical) statements made by trustees:

- *Trustee 1.* "This is such an exceptional situation that the best thing is to do nothing;"
- *Trustee 2.* "Stocks have plunged so dramatically, we should consider postponing rebalancing of the strategic portfolio for the time being;"
- *Trustee 3.* "We should keep faith in the long-term prospects of equities;"
- *Trustee 4.* "We delegate this sort of question to the investment managers because they are able to seize market opportunities;"
- *Trustee 5.* "Sustainability improves the return/risk trade-off of an investment."

All these statements represent different possible beliefs about how financial markets operate. Trustees #1 and #2 assume that the past provides no guidance for future events, while trustee #3 might have a strong belief that equities rebound, even under difficult circumstances. Trustee #4, with his remark on delegation, assumes that specialization and being close to the financial markets generates additional information and investment opportunities that other investors cannot see. Finally, trustee #5 believes that the incorporation of non-financial information will help the investor to develop a better picture of the investment, leading to a better investment decision. These examples show that whatever you do as an investor, beliefs underpin your line of reasoning and acting. Before zooming in on the use of investment beliefs, we need to zoom out and ask why there is such a huge variation in beliefs. This question matters, because investors and consultants tend to present a lot of research as evidence, and this influences boards immensely in their choices on strategic asset allocation, investment styles or risk appetite. Indeed, who is the board to question the investment research? However, investment beliefs matter because we are not dealing with a conventional field of science and realizing this has some major consequences: pragmatic beliefs rather than hard theories guide us in our investment decisions.

Investment theory and practice have developed dramatically over the past five decades, but there is still no objective or universal framework for viewing capital markets and applying these insights for investment purposes.[5] In the 1950s, investment philosophy boiled down to a simple approach: stock selection determined which securities were included in the portfolio, based on a careful analysis of a company's income statement and balance sheet. To founding fathers Graham and Dodd,[6] developing financial ratios from the companies' accounting records was a key element in investment decisions.

A paradigm shift took place from the 1960s onwards with the work of Markowitz,[7] which focused on assembling stocks into portfolios to minimize risk at an acceptable level of return—the "don't put all your eggs in one basket" principle. His main conclusion: portfolio construction is more important than picking individual stocks or timing markets.

The 1970s established the concept of systematic risk. Active management—aimed at earning excess returns relative to benchmarks—met its mirror image in the 1980s in passive management, cleverly combining exposure to different markets to give investors the systematic risk and return they wanted. In the 1990s, new investment strategies were developed at an astronomical pace, based on derivatives markets that had only been in existence for 25 years. Concepts then evolved even further. Since the turn of the century, active management has increasingly come to mean earning absolute returns while leaving benchmarks out of the equation, with investment managers proclaiming they have forged a felicitous union between exploiting inefficiencies in the financial markets (active management) and clever financial engineering to achieve the right degree of systematic risk. This can be seen, for example, in the form of factor investing. All the above-mentioned views of capital markets still coexist, sometimes in harmony and sometimes at odds with one another.

Yet not one can be pinpointed as the right one. Theories in investments and finance simply do not provide the same degree of confidence as theories in natural sciences, for three reasons.[8]

First, finance is a relatively young discipline. Modern finance is roughly 50 years old, whereas other disciplines have been shaped over several hundreds of years. The main theories have not been road tested; basic premises are not (yet) conclusive. For example, for over 30 years, economists have hotly debated whether financial market pricing is efficient or not, and a conclusion is not in sight.

Such a debate has far-reaching consequences for boards. Who to believe? Those who believe that markets are efficient will advocate indexing and other passive strategies such as buy-and-hold, weathering the peaks and troughs of price cycles. Believers in inefficient markets usually invest in what they perceive as undervalued stocks, sectors or assets, and do not shy away from market-timing investment.[9]

Financial data are very "noisy." It requires a lot of effort to extract relevant information from price signals, and the predictive power of models for future returns is generally low. Investment management is essentially a social science, in that markets are driven by people. A truly scientific investment theory would be based on an equation derived from proven laws of nature that specify how we get from point A to point B in the future.[10] Based on such laws, we have, for instance, a pretty clear idea of when Halley's Comet comes close to Earth, and we can accurately predict how long it takes for a car to come to a complete standstill after hitting the brakes at 120 km per hour. Models are based on characteristics such as mass, gravity and velocity, elements that can be clearly defined and precisely measured, and this enables precise predictions to be made.[11] Scientific theories and forecasts for economies and financial markets are impossible for this very reason: there are no proven natural laws underlying the behavior of social systems. Economists therefore opt for a second-best approach, constructing yardsticks such as utility or risk tolerance to *emulate* hard science. Analysts do make predictions based on theories, but such theories are not laws of nature and are not comparable to the scientific methods available in the natural sciences. Analysts' models have limited applicability because the yardsticks are inherently unstable and difficult to establish objectively: risk tolerance varies immensely per person, or before and after a financial crisis, for example.

The second factor setting investment management and economics apart from the hard sciences is that while physics, for example, can test hypotheses through controlled experiments, this is very difficult to do in the case of economics and investments.[12] Economists are creative in circumventing this restriction by gathering as many data as possible and looking for common denominators (when equities go up, bonds do not *on average* increase as much in value). Alternatively, we focus on the actor who sets it all in motion—hence the surge in the study of behavioral finance. While general theories are nearly impossible to construct, modeling structural regularities and irregularities in human behavior is a promising avenue, since human behavior has a tendency to endure for very long periods. However, this allows partial insights at best. With human behavior, we have a pretty clear picture of why markets overreact. This brings us nowhere near to answering the question of how much or for how long stock markets will overreact, which is an answer investment managers are craving.

The bottom line remains: we still cannot conduct experiments in a controlled environment and draw general conclusions. At best, our general theories result in forecasts that are little more reliable than mere naïve guesses.[13] This sobering view should resonate in a wide range of trustee debates on investment management. That is why so many debates never really reach a firm conclusion and keep coming back to haunt both investors and trustees. Proponents of active management – with the ultimate aim of earning more than a benchmark – have just as much ammunition in the form of anecdotal evidence or research to try to prove their case vis-à-vis sympathizers of passive management as the other way around.

This leads to the final reason that tears investment science apart from the natural sciences: certain individuals have the capacity to influence the course of economics and finance in fundamental ways.[14] *Policymakers* have shaped economic growth, inflation and, as a side effect, competitiveness through monetary policy, while on a micro level ambitious investment managers have the capability to arbitrage away any inefficiency that exists. As we progress, our knowledge accumulates, changing the design of the models. A positive consequence of this is that investors and policymakers may take a more adaptive approach to events. For example, regulators and governments acted swiftly when the severity of the credit crisis in 2008 became clear. While one could debate the effectiveness of the measures, there is no doubt that decision-makers had definitely learned lessons from previous crises. The financial markets and the actors in these markets are learning and adapting all the time. Hence, the modern view that the financial markets form an adaptive, living eco-system. But if investors influence the course of finance and investment, this also implies that we cannot simply take it for granted that the financial markets can be described by the same set of static beliefs. Every generation has a different mental framework for macroeconomic policymaking and for investor attitudes and has also accumulated knowledge from earlier events, which makes it risky or even irrational to assume that history will repeat itself.

Investment beliefs accept the reality that economics and finance cannot be encapsulated in hard, predictive models. Instead, they reflect a *view* on how market participants learn or fail to learn on the capital market. We argue that an investment belief system or philosophy is made up of four main elements: basic beliefs, beliefs in relation to theory, beliefs in relation to strategy, and beliefs in relation to organization.

BASICS OF AN INVESTMENT BELIEF

Investment beliefs are not meant to be a contest to rewrite the Declaration of Independence. Their purpose is more mundane: formulating the belief behind important choices in the investment process, agreeing on the theory or the assumptions that support the beliefs, and deciding on what the consequences for implementation within the investment process are. For example, how does your pension fund view diversification? Is the true purpose of diversification to protect against unexpected financial shocks, downward scenarios, or inflation? Even with a relatively simple concept like diversification, the well-prepared trustee should develop a view of what diversification means to their fund, and translate this into a policy or strategy. Exhibit 4.1 shows the framework for formulating and implementing investment beliefs.

Basic investment beliefs are generally formulated as observations of the mechanisms of human behavior in the financial market place. The idea that "diversification is a free lunch, but not all the time" is an example. Investment beliefs accept the reality that, as a discipline, economics and finance cannot be expressed in solid predictive models.

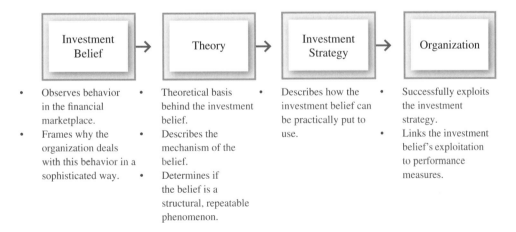

EXHIBIT 4.1 Framework for formulating and implementing investment beliefs.

The term "belief" reflects the fact that investors can choose to interpret observations or mechanisms in different ways.

Next, the **theory** and fundamentals behind the belief need to be sound. Is the belief a lasting phenomenon that could reoccur in the near or distant future? Is there a sound reason why the phenomenon exists? Can we identify performance measures that are directly linked to this investment belief beforehand? If a mechanism is observed in the financial markets but a theoretical basis cannot be found, the pension fund should be reluctant to apply it in its strategy.

There has to be an **investment strategy** in place, describing how the investment belief can be put to use. Such a strategy will specify (i) the investment rules, (ii) the parameters to be applied with the investment rules, (iii) the investment instruments that can be used, and (iv) the time horizon that applies to the rules. Investment rules can be straightforward and are usually formulated in an "*if* …, *then* …" syntax. For example, *if* an asset class appears undervalued, *then* the asset should be over-weighted in the portfolio. Once this is done, there has to be an **organization** to implement the strategy or select and monitor the right managers to do so.

So, an investment belief is workable if it is based on a theory with arguments to defend it, a strategy to exploit it and an organization to support it. But what is there to gain for the trustee? Developing beliefs is firstly about self-discipline, which is worth a lot in terms of governance budget. It saves a lot of time during meetings and leads to subjecting any complex new strategy proposal to some simple questions such as "Does it fit?" and "Does it enhance the investment beliefs?" Investment beliefs are not meant to be overhauled every year, but financial markets and research are dynamic and changing. For investment beliefs to flourish, the pension fund or investment organization needs to allow room for critical debate so that new research and insights can be discussed, when necessary leading to the adaptation of existing beliefs.

An example of this is the Canadian Alberta-based Local Authorities Pension Plan (LAPP), which runs a defined benefit pension plan for employees of local authorities and takes a practical approach. LAPP draws up a table in which each investment belief is followed by its translation into investment policy.[15] One investment belief of LAPP is that "asset mix policy will be a key determinant in the funding risk/return trade-off or asset/liability mismatch accepted to fund the plan." To apply this investment belief, the "asset mix will continue to be the primary tool for the Board to achieve its investment objectives. The asset mix will be established through an approach that integrates both asset and liability projections."

DEVELOPING A SET OF INVESTMENT BELIEFS

Developing a sound set of investment beliefs is crucial, as is having an organization to implement and monitor these beliefs. If risk management is a central investment belief, your organization should have a risk budgeting procedure in place to measure and manage all steps of the investment process. This is a no-brainer. Similarly, diversification as a belief only makes sense if you are willing to make the effort to investigate what really drives diversification and understand how adding new strategies can improve diversification. There are several no-brainers in investment management when shaping an investment philosophy—including investment beliefs with a sound footing in practice and in academic literature.

Any scheme needs to suit its investment strategy to its governance resources. Rather than everyone trying to include the newest alternative strategies around, some schemes should stick to buying or tracking market indices in familiar asset classes. It is important to select the most appropriate level of sophistication, not the highest possible level. Switching from active to passive mandates does not only recognize that the index will beat the majority of active managers over the long term; it is also the right approach for funds that are unable to delve deeply enough into the selection and monitoring of active managers to obtain the best available, as is the case with many smaller funds.

In this paragraph, we summarize the aforementioned investment beliefs as a starter kit: if I am a new trustee, or am managing a fund, I need to be aware of how my fund approaches these beliefs. If my fund does not have explicit views, then what is the basic scenario to start with? We will describe eight investment beliefs; these should be the starting point for all strategic asset allocation reviews and discussions.

Exhibit 4.2 presents eight investment beliefs that more or less sum up the discussions that many pension fund boards have held, where the investment belief is supported by one or more arguments why this belief is relevant to the fund and what evidence there is to back it up. In addition, we list the consequences for portfolio management when the investment belief is adopted.

The intention should be to review these on an annual basis, although major changes should not be expected from year to year—in that case you may as well simply return to writing down your investment plan or program for the coming year. These investment beliefs should provide a basis for reasoned debate, not just words to decorate the website. This entails becoming a confident participant in the financial markets, with investment beliefs—strategies—organization fully aligned. Better yet, can sometimes be rejecting some investment beliefs or adapting them to suit your own view of the financial markets.

WHEN, IF EVER, IS THE TIME TO CHANGE INVESTMENT BELIEFS?

A frequently recurring debate in the boardroom is how it can be sure that the investment beliefs developed are robust and will stand the test of time.

Judgments about evidence and recommendations in investments are complex. Investment evidence and subsequent recommendations leave investors and trustees with varying degrees of confidence. Sources of evidence can range from studies based on small data samples or case reports to well-designed studies with large data sets that have been repeated many times to minimize bias; or simply sound reasoning if there is not much evidence to base the belief on.

When discussing investment beliefs and deciding how much faith (and assets) to place in them, an analogy with the medical profession is useful.[16] There, a system was

Belief	The Argument
Belief 1: Strategic Asset Allocation is the most important choice in the investment process.	**The Argument:** This may be investment theory 101, but needs to be cherished and understood anyway: the asset allocation decision is by far the most important determinant of the fund's risk/return allocation. This insight was developed back in the 1980s, and still stands today. Trustees and investment committees should therefore concentrate on the strategic asset allocation, examine whether it is robust enough for different scenarios, and question whether a new strategy would really improve it. These are simple questions that add more to the long-term health of a fund than anything else. Possible consequences/how it is applied: • Define what strategic asset allocation means, formulate rebalancing, create governance for monitoring, but do not change the allocation frequently. • Focus on the small set of important risk premiums.
Belief 2: Active management does not pay off.	**The Argument:** The main message here is that by default, we use passive strategies for investment. It is dull for the pension fund and disappointing for the asset manager, but highly rewarding for our participants. We only pursue active strategies if we know the source of anomalies, and are very confident that the (selected) manager will be able to exploit them repeatedly in the future and is also willing to agree on a performance schedule that reflects his own confidence. But even then, if external managers are involved, we need to be aware of the soberingly low probability of choosing winners. We resist the temptation to award active mandates simply because we invest in a specific region or asset. Possible consequences/how it is applied: • Use only passive strategies unless you have a deep reason to expect that there is an active source of return to be earned. • In that case, choose a manager that has an extremely disciplined investment approach. Prefer such a manager over the manager with the highest results.
Belief 3: Costs determine net return.	**The Argument:** The basic intuition is that, other things being equal, lower costs mean a higher net return. Costs are certain, returns are not. Many studies investigating the core drivers for future returns point out that costs are a critical factor in determining returns. If a pension fund has to choose between two similar investments, the advice would be to opt for the lower-cost alternative. However, in practice such clear choices are not usually available to trustees. One thing is for sure though: higher costs are never a guarantee of better performance; rather, the opposite can be true. Therefore, pension fund managers should always seek to unearth all the costs attached to the investment (and especially the hidden ones), and avoid transaction costs wherever possible. Possible consequences/how it is applied: • Use only passive strategies unless you have a clear reason to expect that there is an active source of return to be harvested. • When trading off cost to expected added value, the expected added value of the strategy has to cover the cost by a factor of three: an investment strategy costing 40 basis points should reasonably earn the fund 120 basis points. If that is not the case, do not bother as a fund.

EXHIBIT 4.2   Eight investment beliefs and arguments.

Belief 4: There are only a select number of risk premiums worth pursuing.	The Argument: Not all risk premiums are created equal. Some risks we have to bear (inflation, interest rates, longevity); others we choose to bear (equity, illiquidity). We are aware that earning risk premiums is not a certainty over a longer horizon, and therefore do not blindly accept mean reversion as a fundamental. We therefore have to assess which risks we can bear, and what we should at minimum expect in return for the risk on which horizon. For example, we may decide we are especially well-placed to earn the equity risk and liquidity risk premium, but we believe that we are less well-placed to win the foreign exchange risk premium. Possible consequences/how it is applied: • We only invest in risk premiums that we think will be rewarded on the horizon relevant for us. • We avoid, as much as possible, being exposed to risks that in our view will not be rewarded. We will hedge those unrewarded risks at reasonable cost.
Belief 5: Simplicity pays off: we match governance and strategies.	The Argument: Pension funds invest other people's money. We are a financial institution, and our existence is based on the long-term trust of participants. No matter how complex, innovative or attractive a particular investment is, we have to be 100% accountable. If we know beforehand that we cannot live up to this accountability, we should not invest in something, however enticing the investment proposal. Possible consequences/how it is applied: • We have a strong preference for simple over complex when it comes to strategies, instruments, forms of implementation. • When adding complexity to the strategy, it should be significantly rewarded. • No element of the strategy, the instruments or the forms of implementation should be so complex that it cannot be understood or controlled by the board investment committee.
Belief 6: We only invest if we agree on when to exit.	The Argument: We are aware of behavioral biases in financial markets, and within ourselves. We resist the temptation to repeat our mistakes in the future by specifying beforehand what we expect from an investment, how it reinforces our investment beliefs, how and when we will evaluate the results, and especially under what conditions we will exit. This is an integral part of our governance process; we do this to learn from our mistakes, improve our processes and avoid human error. Possible consequences/how it is applied: • For each investment, before we invest we specify under which conditions we will exit it; this gives a strong, disciplined set of decision rules that exist from the outside. • We have a healthy fear of temptation. We can only depart from those rules when there are very, very strong arguments. In practice, this should not happen more often than in 1 out of 100 investment decisions. Similar to the Greek hero Odysseus, the boards ties itself firmly to the ship's mast.

EXHIBIT 4.2 *(Continued)*

| Belief 7: Sustainability is an opportunity, not a necessity. | The Argument: We believe that substantial attention should be devoted to the incorporation of social, ethical and environmental standards in our investments, if participants attach importance to these standards. In doing so, we are driven by common-sense risk management. We are able to minimize future risks (of holding investments for a long-time period) and, consequently, to increase long-term value for the fund and by extension to its participants and stakeholders. We will use both negative screening and positive screening to select the most sustainable investment strategies. For example, well-governed markets and companies drive good returns.

Possible consequences/how it is applied:
• We avoid investments with low governance quality.
• Within constraints, we prefer higher ESG-scores over lower ones.
• We avoid investments where there are material ESG risks. |
| Belief 8: Checking against procyclical behavior pays. | The Argument: Checking against procyclical investment behavior via rebalancing, portfolio construction, or even proactive de-risking under extraordinary circumstances poses the biggest challenge to long-term asset owners. For example, earning the risk premiums envisaged by the strategic asset allocation requires regular rebalancing to sell the assets that have increased in value (resulting in a low expected risk premium), and buy assets that have decreased in value (resulting in a higher risk premium). This rebalancing only pays off if procyclical behavior is avoided. Simultaneously, checking against procyclical behavior helps to identify investment opportunities that can be found where the market displays an inordinate amount of pessimism.

Possible consequences/how it is applied:
• We have a disciplined investment process backed by simulations, and a shared insight on how the board will execute its policies.
• We regularly conduct so called pre-mortems, identifying when we run the danger of acquiring procyclical behavior, and identify measures to counter this. |

EXHIBIT 4.2   (*Continued*)

developed and implemented as a common, transparent and sensible approach to grading the quality of the evidence (also known as "certainty in evidence" or "confidence in effect estimates") and the strength of the recommendations underpinning the investment belief. The approach distinguishes recommendations depending on the evaluation of the evidence as strong or weak. A recommendation to adopt or not to adopt an investment belief should be based on the balance between desirable and undesirable expected consequences of following a recommendation. The degree of uncertainty associated with this balance will determine the strength of the recommendation. The criteria for this are listed in Exhibit 4.3.

So the question here is, how do you scale the investment beliefs? A simple rule of thumb can guide the board.[17] The higher the quality of the evidence underpinning the investment belief, the more the board can allocate strategies and assets to it. And vice versa, the lower the quality of the evidence underpinning the investment belief, the fewer strategies and assets the board should allocate. This is a useful starting point for a review and evaluation. In the review, the board or investment committee can

Level of quality	The Argument	Examples
High	We are very confident about the evidence presented; new research will not provide new insights; we can assume that the true effect lies close to the estimated the effect.	Role of strategic asset allocation, role of costs, return/risk trade-off. Active/passive.
Moderate	We are moderately confident in the evidence presented; the true effect is likely to be close to the estimated effect, but there is a possibility that it could be substantially different.	Factor-investing research Risk premiums Risk averseness
Low	We have limited confidence in the evidence presented: more studies or different methodology might well change the outcome.	Impact Investing
Very low	We have very little confidence in evidence presented: any new research is very likely to change the outcome.	A lot of smaller factors, simple alpha seeking strategies, investors claiming to have skill.

EXHIBIT 4.3 Quality and evidence underpinning investment beliefs.[18]

"downgrade" the quality of the belief when serious risks of biases emerge, when the outcome increasingly deviates from the expected effect, or when a publication bias is expected. On the other hand, when the data sets increase, or the effect seems to be more persistent than predicted, this might suggest an upgrade in the quality of the investment belief.

HOW (NOT) TO USE INVESTMENT BELIEFS

Beliefs are useful from an investment governance point of view, for sorting out the major relevant decisions for the pension funds, and for guiding the investment process. But investment beliefs can also challenge the design and performance of the organization in a negative way. An organization runs into trouble when its beliefs and investment process fit into one or more of the following categories:

- Beliefs that are merely copied from industry leaders without a real grasp of why these beliefs matter. This can be a smart move in many sectors, but not necessarily in the investment industry. Josh Lerner investigated the success of Yale University's endowment and found that a lot of it had to do with the special quality of the staff and resources, as well as their "first mover" advantage in adopting new assets and strategies. Any other funds copying the Yale model tended to have an average quality of staff, and a "second mover" disadvantage in adopting new assets and strategies. This could in some ways sum up the situation of many pension funds that diversified into alternative strategies and hedge funds in the late 1990s, only to wind down these investments a decade later after the financial crisis, due to disappointing results.

- Beliefs based on results. It is possible that an idea might have been bad to start with, but that if the results are all right, then trustees and investment managers gradually warm to the notion that the idea was probably good after all. This is known to statisticians as type I (false negative) and type II (false positive) errors. For example, a pension fund has allocated 15% to commodities without much thought. This is a high proportion, which might not be deemed to be prudent. The price of commodities rises, apparently proving them right, and triggering the debate as to whether the board should not allocate more to commodities. The dilemma here is that a good result is misinterpreted as a good idea. If the board cannot make its assumptions clear, it is rudderless when the investment returns move the other way.
- Beliefs without acting on them. This creates a reputational risk. This is nothing new for Dutch pension funds. In 2007, they were chastised for stating their commitment to sustainability while journalists quite easily found non-sustainable funds. Either you have beliefs and act on them, or you don't act on them, in which case they cannot be very strong beliefs.
- Simplification is the enemy. One cannot validly simply conclude that they are for or against active or passive management. It depends on its place in the investment process, the markets, and the skills required, to name just a few factors. In the search for returns, Europe and the United States have been labeled the old countries, and emerging markets the new—and more attractive—ones. Emerging markets do indeed play an important role. However, there is also a large amount of literature on financial structure, the quality of governance of a country, and economic growth that contains unpleasant information for emerging markets believers. Yet, that people still view emergent markets as more attractive is evidence that they like to discard information in their simplification process. This makes simplification dangerous.
- "I strongly believe in..." There is a quote from Yeats that includes the following lines: "The best lack all conviction, while the worst are full of passionate intensity."[19] With weaker convictions, research and arguments can become centered on what the outcome should be, rather than on challenging the assumptions in the first place. Conversely, beliefs without sensible assumptions or clear evidence should also be treated with suspicion. A lot of money rides on these investment beliefs, so it is important to establish a process to discuss and evaluate them as objectively as possible.

ENDNOTES

1. See Ambachtsheer (2004), Ambachtsheer and Ezra (1998), Ang (2014) or Damodaran (2013).
2. See Clark and Urwin (2008b).

3. This chapter is partly based on Koedijk and Slager (2011), chapter 3.
4. See Raymond (2008).
5. See Lo (2005).
6. See Graham et al. (1951).
7. See Markowitz (1952).
8. See Raymond (2008).
9. See Brav et al. (2004).
10. See Sherden (1998).
11. See Gray (1997).
12. See also Gray (1997).
13. See Sherden (1998).
14. See Gray (1997).
15. See LAPP's Statement Of Investment Policy And Goals (2018).
16. See http://www.gradeworkinggroup.org.
17. See Guyatt et al. (2008).
18. Also based on extending the Grading of Recommendations Assessment, Development and Evaluation (GRADE) approach to investments, see http://www.gradeworkinggroup.org.
19. From the poem "The Second Coming" by William Butler Yeats.

Case Study—New Zealand Superannuation Fund[1]

BUILDING A GLOBAL INVESTMENT FUND FROM SCRATCH WITH THE MISSION TO MAXIMIZE THE FUND'S LONG-TERM RETURN, AND INTEGRATE CLIMATE CHANGE IN A DEEP WAY CONSISTENT WITH THE LONG-HORIZON NATURE OF THE FUND

Background

The New Zealand Superannuation Fund—NZSF was created from scratch in 2001. It started investing in 2003. The fund is a way for New Zealand to save now in order to make future pension costs more affordable. From the beginning, the fund has focused on global best practices in order to learn from them. The size of the fund, in March 2018, was NZ$38 billion[2] (US$25 billion). Although it is a government vehicle to save future tax, it is managed by a fully independent Crown entity with clear separation between the New Zealand Government and the fund. This means that the fund can make independent, long-horizon investment decisions. The fund has a true long-term character: its size will not peak before 2080. Since its creation, the performance of the fund is well ahead of its benchmarks. One of these benchmarks is a passive Reference Portfolio consisting of 80% equities and 20% fixed income. The board delegates responsibility for all investment decision-making to the investments team, except for the choice of the Reference Portfolio. The board makes decisions about the composition of the Reference Portfolio. The fund has to operate in a way that it will not damage New Zealand's reputation as a responsible member of the world community.

The challenge

A big question for the fund over the past few years has been whether it should integrate climate change into the investments of the fund and, if so, how. By doing this in a deep, fundamental way that fits into its beliefs, the fund has succeeded in creating an approach that is fully consistent with its long-term nature and its financial mission.

The process

The integration of climate change into the process was not an overnight exercise. The climate change investment strategy has been a long time in the making. It took the fund back to fundamentals, by asking itself where the risks posed by climate change would fit into the investment beliefs, and its mandate as an investor. It also had to consider how best to approach the strategy; whether to incorporate it into their passive Reference Portfolio and benchmark, or to configure it as an active investment decision.

As the investments team was of the view that climate change created risks and opportunities for the fund, it was apparent that the actual portfolio (making active investment decisions) would be changed as a result. However, the team was also of the view that climate change was such a significant, long-term risk, that it would be wrong to set a Reference Portfolio that would not reflect this risk, given that it acts as a benchmark and default allocation for the fund. As the passive equities portfolio also contained by far the largest concentration of risk, it was a natural first to change the reference portfolio in that respect. In the equity portfolio it is also possible to make large changes at a low cost.

In order to change the Reference Portfolio there needed to be alignment at the board level because doing so, in a sense, made the board directly responsible for the return impact.

From the board's perspective, it took time to become comfortable with making what was a material and very long-term decision. Part of the difficulty was the uncertainty, because the risk was so long-term that the fund was putting together a strategy and starting to implement it without knowing all of the answers. To allay this uncertainty, the investment management organization spent time getting the board up to speed and comfortable with the significance of arriving at a decision to act. In total, the investment team presented to the board five times, from concept to final implementation.

In creating this common understanding the fund used a decision tree. It shows the beliefs regarding climate risks and how to deal with them, and the consequences for the investment approach. The decision tree had statements such as: "You believe that climate change poses a risk to investors" and "You believe that markets properly price the risk." This approach also helped guide the conversation internally and with the board.

Eventually, the fund arrived at an explicit goal: to make the portfolio more resilient to climate-related risks. It agreed on a set of targets for the strategy: to reduce the carbon emissions intensity, which is tons of carbon emissions per dollars of sales, by 20%, and to reduce the carbon reserves held in the portfolio by 40%, both by 2020. Importantly, the fund thinks about this at the whole of portfolio level, meaning it does not have carbon budgets at an individual asset class level.

The outcome

The strategy to make the portfolio more resilient to climate-related risks has four work-streams:

- *Reduce*. Reduce exposure to reserves and emissions.
- *Analyze*. Incorporate climate change into the investment hurdles and investment decision-making process.

- *Engage.* Integrate climate change into the considerations, both in the voting and engagement policy. Engage with companies, particularly disclosing the impact of climate change on them.
- *Search.* Search for attractive investment opportunities as we transition to a low-carbon world.

The fund started implementing the reduce work-stream straight away. In June 2017, it shifted to a lower carbon passive equities portfolio, reallocating approximately $670 million away from companies with high exposure to carbon emissions and reserves into lower risk companies.

It did this while continuing to search for answers on how to best implement the remaining three components of its strategy. The climate change strategy will evolve over time as the fund uncovers more information about the pace of global warming, policy change and market pricing reactions, and as the data and tools available to measure and manage risk improve.

Lessons for Achieving Investment Excellence

- It takes serious time and collective effort to build an approach to climate change that is consistent with the mission and beliefs of the fund.
- The board should be totally aligned with the climate change strategy and the way it is integrated into the reference portfolio and the investment chain.
- Even when there is uncertainty around the long-term development of big forces such as climate change, it is possible to formulate a strategy which is owned by the board and informs and guides the investment decision-making process of the fund. By creating explicit goals, the progress of the strategy can be monitored well.

ENDNOTES

1. Parts of this case study are quoted with kind permission of NZSF, see Working Group on Climate Change (2018).
2. See https://www.nzsuperfund.nz.

CHAPTER 5

Designing the Investment Management Process

Key Take Aways

- The investment management process follows a structured approach from planning, to executing and organizing feedback. It translates the investment objective into investment policy and its execution.

- The investment management process builds on—and should be consistent with—the mission, investment beliefs and strategy formulated by the board.

- The board should have a clear overview of the investment process and its key components. The board's challenge is to not get lost in details, but instead to assess whether the choices made in the investment management process best serve the fund's investment goals.

- The investment policy statement (IPS) is an important document that lays out the investment policy and its inputs. It helps the board and fund to be disciplined and to think ahead. In addition, it facilitates clear communication with participants, investors and broader stakeholders, and fosters the right circumstances for excellent implementation.

The investment management process is the process by which the pension fund intends to achieve its investment objectives, which follow from the fund's mission. Over the longer term, pension funds aim to generate at least the net returns needed to realize the pension's promise, often within a certain risk budget. Often, there is a distinction between a hard, nominal liability and an often less hard ambition to index the liability with price- or wage-inflation. Four key ingredients tend to drive investment decision-making[1]: matching assets and liabilities, generating investment returns over and above the matching return, risk management through portfolio diversification, and cost management. The way in which these ingredients are combined can be called the investment process.

This process varies greatly in shape and size. Two funds that seem similar from the outside might generate different investments returns from the inside. However, despite investment processes differing widely, they all have a number of specific building blocks in common. The process can be viewed as an implementation of the objectives, the investment beliefs, and the governance budget of the fund. There will almost always be constraints, for example on the maximum amount of risk or regarding unacceptable outcomes.

For a trustee, it is important to understand these building blocks, how they work together, and what the underlying assumptions are. It helps to understand how the returns are being made, what investment governance is needed for this (Chapter 6), and how to manage and nurture the success factors in day-to-day operations (Chapters 7–9).

This chapter describes the main steps of the investment management process. The portfolio management process starts with planning, then goes to execution, and finally to feedback. The next part of this chapter gives an overview of the portfolio management process. We then delve deeper into the main decisions of the investment process, namely setting the objectives, formulating the capital market expectations (CMEs), and portfolio construction. Next, implementation and monitoring are considered. The chapter ends with a discussion about the document that helps the board focus and streamline the important choices in the investment process: the Investment Policy Statement (IPS).

At the planning stage, investment objectives and policies are formulated, CMEs are set out and, often, a strategic asset allocation or policy as well as a risk budget are established. At the execution stage, the portfolio manager actually constructs and implements the portfolio. In the feedback stage, the output is reported, monitored, and evaluated by means of comparison to the plan. The feedback can lead to changes in objectives, portfolio or process. There will be a heavy involvement from the board during the planning process and the feedback loop; conversely, the execution will be in the hands of the investment management organization. The level of delegation and the way in which the board specifies the investment objective and mandate to the investment manager vary widely among different investment models, for example as seen in the Canadian (extensive delegation) and the Dutch (little delegation) models.

THE INVESTMENT PROCESS

There are three reasons why trustees should have a well-thought-out investment process:[2] (i) it describes all the necessary steps between the goals and realizing actual returns to achieve those goals; (ii) it makes the assumptions behind these steps clear, allowing them to be challenged and improved; and (iii) it provides the board with insights about which choices do and do not work, helping it to evaluate effectiveness and adapt or change elements where necessary. Let us now further expand on these points.

Point 1. The investment process describes the steps between the clients' objectives and the delivery of investment returns to achieve them. These steps are taken in a specific order and form the main choices that are made. These steps will usually include the formulation of investment objectives, the forming of expectations or assumptions about the future returns and risks in the financial markets, strategic asset allocation, a number of mandates for different asset classes or parts of the portfolio, tactical/dynamic asset allocation, rebalancing and risk management. Risk management is embedded throughout the process to provide the necessary scope for rewarded investment risks, and to avoid, mitigate or sell off additional risks that arise when the asset transformation takes place, and where the investment organization does not expect to be rewarded.

Point 2. The investment process also helps to clarify and challenge the assumptions and beliefs behind all of these choices and provide an argument as to why the board makes particular choices out of the many types of strategies that are available. The choices depend to a large extent on the investment beliefs of the fund (Chapter 4).

Some steps in the investment process are more important than others. For example, the strategic asset allocation is considered to be much more important than tactical asset allocation or implementation choices such as the hire of specific managers for mandates.

Making the assumptions clear, and assessing what the expected contribution of each of the components is in relation to the whole helps a board to deal with the question of information asymmetry: investment managers tend to know more about financial markets and their processes than trustees, and might consciously or unconsciously promote strategies and assets that are in the best interests of the investment managers rather than the fund. A board that knows the assumptions behind the different steps, knows the degree of confidence and the evidence that can be attached to these, and is able to make a more informed decision as to whether such a strategy contributes to meeting the fund's goals.

Point 3. The process provides the pension fund with a learning perspective, giving insights into which steps work and which don't. Investment processes are not static. Financial markets and their participants are adaptive in nature because they continuously interact, learn, and react. What today constitutes a good investment strategy or asset class might be less suited for portfolio construction in five years' time. A decision may have been good at the time it was made, but circumstances could have changed in the meantime, in which case the board should adapt accordingly. It is not easy to decide which decisions hold up for a relatively long time, compared to others that have a shorter life span. Here, the feedback loop plays an important role. When information about the realized results is channeled back to the board and its committees, it provides feedback about the choices that were made, which enables self-correction if limits or boundaries have been breached. It also allows for the learning and adjustment of the investment management process if this can improve potential outcomes. The investment process is visualized in Exhibit 5.1.

SETTING OBJECTIVES: ALIGNING GOALS AND RISK APPETITE

The process begins with the aims that follow from the pension scheme. How can these be translated into financial goals and how much risk can and should be taken in order to achieve them? These goals and restrictions for both the short and long-term for return and risk are then translated into a set of inputs for the portfolio decision process.

The investment objectives and risk appetite must be decided on by the board. The starting point for this is developing the returns objectives, and the investment risk participants can and are willing to incur in achieving investment goals. However, determining risk appetite is not the only risk factor that must be taken into account. One must also

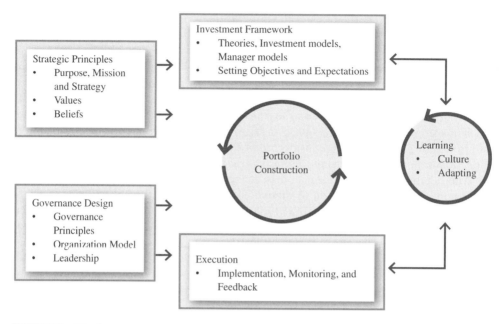

EXHIBIT 5.1   The investment management process.

ask whether the pension fund can afford to incur the investment risk? Or, can it afford *not* take the investment risk? Taking on the appropriate amount of risk on behalf of the participants and subsequent management of risk is a key success factor for pension funds, but it is also a balancing act between short and long-term trade-offs. Taking on risk, for example by increasing the allocation to equities, might on the one hand earn the pension fund a decent return for its participants. But on the other hand, it exposes the pension fund to the risk of the financial markets, which might in the short term hamper progress towards its long-term return goals. In other words, the risk profile not only specifies the amount of investment risk the fund will take in pursuit of its goals, but also describes how the amount of risk varies in different economic circumstances or with the financial health of the pension fund, as well as the trade-off between short-term and long-term risk. These choices are deeply influenced by the availability of a strong sponsor, the maturity of the fund, and the nature of the liabilities.

The risk profile can be (and usually is) established in a quantitative way. Many investment committees are involved in carrying out the asset liability management study. The justification of quantitative assumptions, the choice of (deterministic) scenarios and risk benchmarks, and the creation of asset allocations are the important elements in this context, and committee members will have a controlling role to ensure the assumptions and outcomes are acceptable. A board of trustees has to consider more than just stakeholders, and more than solely financial aspects. A risk profile is therefore quite broad, consisting of three dimensions. First, the financial dimension addresses how much financial risk is needed and how much the fund can absorb. Then, the participants' dimension takes a broader view than just financial risk and determines whether the risk profile fits

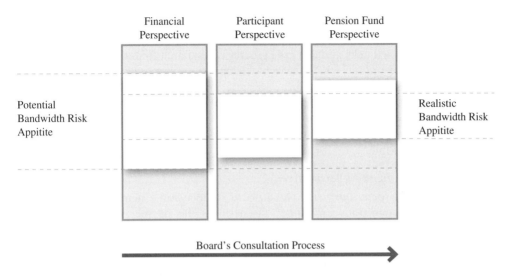

EXHIBIT 5.2 Common denominators in the amount of risk.

the characteristics of the participants. Finally, the pension fund's perspective looks at whether the organization is able, permitted and equipped to take on the amount of risk determined by the financial and participant perspectives. These risk profile dimensions are presented in Exhibit 5.2.[3]

For each of the three dimensions, the board has to consider the following elements:

Financial perspective:

- *Clarity on who accepts how much of the investment risk*, as a consequence of the pension plan. This involves identifying and quantifying investment risk shock absorbers, which potentially are elements such as buffers, premium, sponsors, and a long horizon. As a rule of thumb, the fewer shock absorbers are available, the lower the investment risk that can be taken or the more the promise will have to be flexible;
- *The degree of financial health*, measured by cover ratio or solvency. A higher cover ratio provides a buffer and, therefore, more scope to take risks than a lower cover ratio. The board has to consider different levels of cover ratios; would the fund take the same amount of investment risk regardless of the cover ratio? For example, if the cover ratio increases, this could mean investment risk can be reduced. This provides the framework for a dynamic risk appetite statement;
- *The premium.* The actual premium can be higher/lower than the purely cost-covering premium, meaning that more/less risk can be taken. In young funds with a relatively high premium flowing in, the premium can be a strong steering instrument. However, currently funds around the world are maturing rapidly and premiums are already high, which makes this an instrument of limited value;
- *The sponsor.* A strong sponsor standing behind a fund, such as a state or a strong company, can help to absorb shocks. An example is Royal Dutch Shell, which injected money into the Shell Pension Fund after the great financial crisis.

Participant perspective:

- *The pension fund life-phases.* A young fund requires a longer period to recover from financial setbacks and can take greater risks than a fund that is already in the payment phase and has fewer active participants;
- *Participants' profile.* How flexibly can participants accommodate any mishaps in terms of pension payment within their private situation? For example, a pension fund for poorly educated, low-wage employees cannot assume that participants have any supplementary wealth and can, after retiring, use other assets to ensure the desired income.

Pension fund organization perspective:

- *The desires of social partners.* The aims of the pension scheme are set out when employment conditions are under discussion. The degree of certainty that is required leads to a specific level of risk;
- *Laws and regulations.* The risk profile must "fit" within the existing regulatory framework, and the "prudent person" rule. It should not be aimed at "arbitraging" away regulation;
- *The exclusion of assets*, socially responsible investment, and guidelines in consultation with the sponsor, such as their business principles for example;
- *The board.* A board with more expertise and experience can (but does not necessarily have to) take more complex risks than a board with less experience and expertise;
- *The level of risk preparedness of the board.* The board and board members are personally liable for the fund policy. The board may therefore wish to bear lower risks than are (theoretically) possible as a result.

The role of the board in determining and maintaining the risk appetite cannot be underestimated. "While risk management is the [. . .] first priority, this most definitely does not mean overly conservative "caution."[4] In this setting, alongside monitoring and managing short-term risks, the board must also avoid unnecessary long-term risks by on the one hand tempering the risk appetite in good periods, and on the other hand avoiding opportunity loss by sustaining the risk appetite in periods when risk aversion increases.

Developing a detailed risk profile is becoming more common among funds, but it is not easy for boards to do. An important reason for detailing the risk profile is that it not only disciplines trustees with respect to the risk to be taken, but it also helps them discipline the board in this area.

There are two points at which boards can cause problems for the achievement of the fund's aims.[5] The first is when it is excessively cautious, for example after a period of falling coverage and increasing volatility in financial markets. Capital retention then has precedence. The greater the impact on the pension fund, the longer the risk aversion and caution will be maintained; this may result in the long-term aims not being realized. The second point is that the opposite is also true. A pension fund can build up a large risk appetite and assume greater risks than are really necessary in order to achieve the fund aims. This mainly occurs during periods of expanding markets in which excessive optimism prevails. Developing a disciplined decision-making process to operate within the risk profile is therefore a key element for long-term success. This will be discussed in Chapter 12, in which we explore the dynamics at play between the board and the investment committee, and decision-making under stress.

Investment Objectives

Four groups of investment goals appear during the formulation of the return objectives, where the relevant question for the board is which group or combination best reflects its investment goals. These goals are as follows:

- *Absolute return (or inflation + a specified absolute return)*. The fund aims at a specific percentage investment return, regardless of the liabilities. This goal is suitable for pension funds with a relatively low degree of liabilities or undetermined liabilities such as sovereign wealth funds, or those with a financially strong sponsor who will vouch for pension payments and step in the potential event of pension payout deficits;
- *Investment return derived from the stream of benefits it has to pay*. The fund aims for the continuation of the payments with a specific probability;
- *Investment return on the surplus (also known as liability adjusted returns)*. The fund actively manages the surplus of the pension fund. The assumption here is that part of the assets is designated to match the liabilities and is therefore constrained. Assets and liabilities are managed on the same balance sheet, and are not physically separated. This goal is suitable for pension funds with high liabilities, where compensation of the accrual of liabilities becomes an important part of the objectives;
- *Separate investment returns for the liabilities and the surplus*. Liabilities and surplus are managed separately, such that the investment portfolio for the liabilities matches these liabilities, while the surplus portfolio has to generate returns. The board can define a set of rules under which part of the surplus is transferred to the liabilities portfolio, or could leave this decision to the participants, who invest in the liabilities and surplus portfolios. For example, if the surplus of the fund reaches more than 10%, then a certain percentage is transferred to the liabilities portfolio.

Whichever combination of objectives is chosen, the board must also set the horizon in which the goals apply, and determine the rules for evaluation beforehand. If an absolute return averaging 6% has not been met over a five-year period, how should this be evaluated?

Pension funds usually run a scheme based on a matrix of objectives that combine return and risk measures: the actuarial return should be met or exceeded for the overall portfolio; within the portfolio, the risk-adjusted returns should be above a certain threshold, and when the fund actively aims for the preservation of capital, there are risk limits to protect the liabilities. Exhibit 5.3 presents an example from the pension fund of CERN (the European Organization for Nuclear Research).

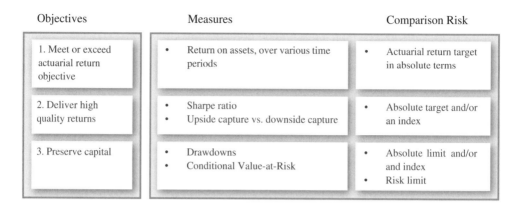

EXHIBIT 5.3   CERN's matrix of objectives, measures and benchmarks.[6]

FORMULATING EXPECTATIONS

Another input in the investment process is CMEs: expectations concerning the risk and return prospects of asset classes, and how they interact. These help to formulate a strategic asset allocation. Defining a CME requires determining short-term and long-term return and risk expectations for the major asset classes in the portfolio, expectations for important variables such as inflation and the interest rate structure, as well as for the correlation matrix for the assets.

Trustees should approve the CMEs, if only to be aware of their sensitivity and the impact that they have on the resulting portfolio and the outcomes of the investment process. The more impact they have on the outcome, the more important it is that the board understand them and consciously approve them. Usually, assumptions about interest rates, inflation, and equity returns determine 80% of the proposed asset allocation, and should thus thoroughly be discussed by the board.

As mentioned previously, CMEs are a key input in formulating a strategic asset allocation. For example, if an investor's IPS specifies and defines eight permissible asset classes, the investor will need to have formulated long-term expectations concerning those asset classes in order to develop a strategic asset allocation. The investor may also act on short-term expectations. In practice, this means that the board at least sets the risk premiums for the main asset categories in the portfolio, i.e.:

- Risk premium for bonds: expected rewards for term spread and inflation;
- Risk premium for equities;
- Risk premium for credit risk;
- Risk premium for illiquid assets, mainly real estate.

Other assumptions about risk premiums related to subcategories, investment styles, etc., should be left to the investment consultant or investment management organization. The trustees' task is not to predict future values of these assets. The investment strategist and staff are better equipped to do this. The main purpose is to achieve an optimal set of assumptions that are internally consistent and reflect all currently available information and future assumptions that might affect the investment outcomes.

However, it is downright naïve for a board to choose just one set of assumptions and build a long-term strategy around this. The board's task may not be to predict the future, but certainly its job is to be prepared for different futures and adapt to them when they emerge. A frequently used approach is for trustees to draw up several sets of assumptions and label these "scenarios." This reflects the understanding that radically different outcomes are possible in the medium and long term, for example an inflationary or a deflationary world (Chapter 4).

PORTFOLIO CONSTRUCTION

Having explored the preferences of the investors in developing a risk profile and setting investment objectives, and having developed a set of inputs in the form of expectations of returns and risks available in the financial markets, it is time to turn to portfolio construction. The investor's return objectives, risk tolerance, and investment constraints are integrated with long-run CMEs to establish exposures to permissible asset classes. Portfolio construction produces four outcomes[7] that the board needs to approve, either as separate policies or integrated into one (the strategic plan for the coming years for example): the policy portfolio or strategic asset allocation, the strategic benchmark portfolio, the benchmark choice of the asset classes, and the rebalancing policy.

The *policy portfolio* or strategic asset allocation is a set of portfolio weights for asset classes. It is the result of strategic asset allocation, which allows investors to choose their portfolio's long-term profile. The assumption is that this high-level portfolio captures a large degree of variation in returns. It is an essential part of portfolio construction, and reflects the acceptable risk level, and thus to a large extent determines the portfolio future performance.

The *strategic benchmark portfolio* represents a set of weights within the asset classes of the policy portfolio, detailing various building blocks of the asset classes, such as the key investment styles or credit portfolios with different rating classes. Each asset class comprises a broad variety of sub-asset classes. For example, sub-asset classes within equities might include large companies, smaller companies, growth funds, income funds, and global equities. Within these sub-asset classes, a manager's approach to investment analysis and security selection can differ widely. To cluster this diversity, the concept of investment style is introduced. We can define an investment style (such as an emphasis on growth stocks or value stocks) as a natural grouping of investment disciplines that has some predictive power concerning the future dispersion in returns across portfolios.[8]

The *benchmark* choice of the asset classes should reflect the desired risk/return exposure in the financial markets for the specific asset class, as well as its investment style. There are three forms of benchmark construction: market-capitalization weightings, static tilts, and factor investing:

- Market-cap-weighted index benchmarks give broad exposure to traditional asset classes. With a high degree of liquidity, transparency, and relative risk control, broad market-capital-weighted indexes can efficiently provide the weighted-average experience of owning all (or virtually all) available securities at the market-clearing price. These diversified investment pools with significant capacity are a valuable starting point for trustees. Market-cap-weighted index funds provide a central point of return and volatility because they reflect the aggregate holdings of all market participants and because within the context of Modern Portfolio Theory, it can be argued that they are optimal, providing all investors with the best possible expected risk/return combination.

- Investors may choose to take on a larger exposure to a portion of the market that they believe offers the opportunity to outperform over the long term. These decisions are often made at the sub-asset-class level. Equity tilts are often made by size, style, sector or location; and fixed income tilts are frequently based on credit quality, duration or location.

- Investors may steer their portfolios away from the global market cap because they have different risk priorities. A prime example of this is liability-driven investing, in which the priority is claims-paying ability, not return maximization. The target duration of such a bond portfolio might well differ from that of a broad market-cap-weighted bond index.

Besides formulating the strategic portfolio and determining its benchmarks, a *rebalancing policy* needs to be in place: a policy on how these portfolio weights are adjusted in line with the risk appetite. This policy details how the policy portfolio is to be adjusted to changes in the cover ratio or financial markets, how to adjust the assets to the weights of the strategic benchmark portfolio, and whether the rebalancing is carried out regularly or based on triggers.

At its simplest, this is a process of regularly rebalancing to constant policy weightings. For example, suppose the policy allocation calls for an initial portfolio with a 70% weighting in stocks and a 30% weighting in bonds. Then suppose the value of the stock holdings grows by 40%, while the value of the bond holdings grows by 10%. The new weighting is roughly 75% in stocks and 25% in bonds. To bring the portfolio back into compliance with the investment policy, it has to be rebalanced back to the long-term policy weights. The rebalancing decision must then take into account many execution factors, such as transaction costs and taxes. Disciplined rebalancing will have a positive impact on the attainment of investment objectives.

Rebalancing on the basis of constant policy weights represents one pole. At the other extreme, the fund could have a solvency program in place. Such a program adjusts the policy weightings depending on the amount of downside risk the fund is willing to take given the funding ratio and financial market conditions. Similarly, the solvency program could adjust the level of policy weightings depending on how close the fund is to achieving its long-term goals. Sometimes, funds allocate part of the bandwidth around policy weightings to tactical asset allocation, which involves making short-term adjustments to asset-class weights based on the expected short-term relative performance among asset classes. The assumption is that investors can avail of short-term opportunities with the aim of achieving the best performance for the portfolio, bearing in mind the defined level of risk.

At times, a portfolio's actual asset allocation may deliberately be allowed to diverge temporarily from the strategic asset allocation. For example, the asset allocation might change to reflect a pension fund's current circumstances if these are different from normal. The temporary allocation may remain in place until circumstances return to those described in the investment policy and reflected in the original strategic asset allocation. If the changed circumstances become permanent, the manager will need to update the IPS, and the temporary asset allocation plan will effectively become the new strategic asset allocation. A strategy known as tactical asset allocation also results in divergences from the strategic asset allocation. Tactical asset allocation responds to changes in short-term CMEs rather than to investor circumstances.

IMPLEMENTATION AND MONITORING

The next element of the investment process is the actual implementation, the evaluation of the results achieved, and the possible modification of choices made in the investment process if the results suggest this. Portfolio management, risk monitoring, and information provision are all carried out by the concerned organization or outside of the pension fund. This involves the creation of the actual investment portfolio and mandates for the asset managers who manage them. Moreover, it also includes due diligence (in this case, a structured method for examining the organization and the manager's investment record before a mandate is issued), and contracting and monitoring the parties that actually implement the investment policy. Implementation is the execution of investment strategies, done by selecting managers and strategies for the portfolio, and allowing managers to initiate transactions on behalf of the fund. To manage this operation, the fund should have a monitoring process in place.

Implementation

Implementation is the process of executing the strategic benchmark portfolio and rebalancing policy. Assets and investment styles are translated into investment instruments and products that are then traded on behalf of the fund. This step introduces—and exposes—trustees to a new arena of organizations and people involved in the day-to-day operations of the fund. Portfolio managers initiate portfolio decisions based on analysts' inputs, and trading desks then implement these decisions (portfolio implementation decision). After that, the portfolio is revised as investor circumstances or expectations change; thus, the execution step interacts constantly with the feedback step. The implementation of the investment management process is further discussed in Chapter 8.

Monitoring

Monitoring involves the use of feedback to manage ongoing exposure to available investment opportunities so that the fund's objectives and constraints continue to be satisfied. Different aspects are monitored by the board, as listed below:

- Monitoring a change in the pension fund and its risk profile and objectives, and whether this is implicit or explicit.

- An assessment of the economic and market input assumptions and if they still hold.
- The rebalancing of the current portfolio within the guidelines.
- An analysis to monitor if the managers who were chosen still reflect the investment styles consistent with the expected return/risk profile, investment beliefs, and other key aspects outlined in the strategic plan.

The board has to decide to whom it will delegate these monitoring questions, for example, to the investment management organization, executive staff or investment committee, and must be clear about how the monitoring process should evolve. Which choices should the board make, and what elements are best left to the other bodies of the pension fund? For trustees, it is important that monitoring signals any potential negative side effects that can be avoided or mitigated. For example, monitoring signals cover the total amount of costs, the utilization of the risk budget, and the level of transparency in the accountability of the different steps in the implementation process.

Portfolio evaluation may also be conducted with respect to specific risk models, such as multifactor models, which seek to explain asset returns in terms of exposure to a set of risk factors. Considering that monitoring is a vital part of the investment management process, this topic is more elaborately discussed in Chapter 9.

The backbone for monitoring and evaluation is provided by performance evaluation. Performance evaluation analyzes the portfolio's results in the context of the investment management process.[9] It answers the following questions: how was performance, how was excess performance realized, and what does it tell us about the added value of our decisions? Performance attribution decomposes returns into all the components that are consistent with the steps in the decision-making process. Performance attribution explains the active choices that made the portfolio overperform (or underperform) its benchmark. For example, what other assets or securities could the portfolio have held in order to obtain a better return? Was the portfolio tilted too far towards a specific type of asset or risk? Performance attribution is based on the assumption that the investment process contains both top-down and bottom-up processes, as listed below:

- The top-down process consists of risk allocation, where the fund attempts to determine the total amount of investment risk compared to, or in excess of, the investment risk of the pension liabilities;
- Next, the strategic asset allocation choice benchmarks the choice of asset categories to maximize return, given the amount of investment risk the fund can take;
- Within each of the assets, the fund can tilt the portfolio towards specific currencies, regions and investment styles;
- From a bottom-up perspective, once the investment styles and mandates have been determined, the manager can be asked to generate outperformance compared to a benchmark, or to stay close to a benchmark.

All of these steps can be compared to a benchmark, and performance attribution determines the additional return (called alpha or outperformance) relative to the additional risk for the over- and underweight choices for each of these steps. If the board has defined clear steps and decisions in the investment management process, and it is able to attribute performance and risk to it, the board can then have an informed discussion on whether each of these steps add value to the fund's goals, and determine whether (i) there is a clear rationale for why this decision adds value, (ii) this added value is proportional to the additional transaction costs that have to be made, and (iii) whether the added value does not consume a disproportionate amount of the board's or investment committee's time spent monitoring and managing.

Different approaches to defining steps in the investment process or attributing performance can produce very different results. It is important for a board to be aware of these differences and why they occur. Here are some key points to consider when interpreting an attribution report:[10]

- The most relevant attribution report is one that is in line with the investment process. An attribution report on sector-level is not useful, if the fund does not use sector allocation decisions;
- The ability to drill down from the top to individual managers is the most useful tool in making sense of the results;
- Performance measurement involves some degree of approximation. The order of magnitude matters more than the actual number;
- Frequency matters. A quarterly report will reveal more volatility and might spur unnecessary reactions or choice, compared to a yearly report;
- Consistency in the performance attribution measures must be imposed, so stick to the standard deviation, tracking error vs. benchmark or liabilities as much as possible;
- Performance evaluation requires multiple key measures during the evaluation, not the monitoring. Evaluation has a lower frequency, once a year or every three years. Monitoring ranges from daily to quarterly.

THE INVESTMENT POLICY STATEMENT

Broad investment policy is the domain of the board of trustees. An investment policy documents the issues that the board must address, concentrating on the desired outcomes.

The key choices in the investment management process, especially those on a strategic level and those guiding the implementation, are often formalized in an IPS. This is an important document. Writing down these choices might seem bureaucratic, but it is vital for there to be any chance of long-term success. It is a visible demonstration that the board has interpreted the wishes of its participants in a prudent, workable manner. The documentation also provides guidance for all the parties involved in carrying out the various activities for fulfilling the fund's goals. At times, the policy statement provides much-needed consistency in the board's decision-making. New and existing board members alike have to work within these boundaries, allowing the fund to commit itself to difficult choices beforehand, thereby avoiding behavioral biases. The IPS not only provides to the investment committee the strategic outline for achieving the fund's long-term goals; it also helps the fund deal with the various parties who are concerned with the investment returns: participants, sponsors, regulators, and other non-committee trustees of the fund.

The IPS describes the investor's risk tolerance, return objectives and expectations, liquidity needs, and other constraints. It may be drafted in relation to a fund's entire financial position or only to the portfolio under consideration. Traditionally, an important part of the IPS has been the strategic benchmark portfolio: what asset classes are to be included and in what proportions. Increasingly, the reasoning behind the choices of benchmarks, investment restrictions, and rebalancing policy has been included. Such an integral statement provides the investment management organization with a practical and useful guideline for setting long-term exposure to systematic risk and making decisions on manager hiring, tactical (i.e. shorter-term) asset allocation changes, and other investment implementation choices.

Developing and maintaining an IPS is a requirement in many countries. Under the Pension Act in the UK, pension schemes are required to have a statement of investment principles (SIPs),[11] which is essentially an IPS. In the EU, institutional investors are required to have a SIP under the European Investment Directive. In the United States, however, there are no nationwide requirements for adopting SIPs. Pension funds in the United States are usually subject to state legislation, so regulations may vary across states. In recent years, pension funds have in any case adopted SIPs/IPS, in line with the trend in other regions.

An IPS includes:[12]

- The purpose of establishing policies and guidelines;
- The duties and investment responsibilities of parties involved, particularly those relating to fiduciary duties, communication, operational efficiency, and accountability. Parties involved include the board of trustees, any investment committee, the investment manager responsible for implementation, and the custodian;
- The strategic mission of the investments: goals, objectives, and constraints. Funds' objectives are usually formulated in terms of required or expected return;
- The level of risk tolerance and investment risk that may be incurred to realize the return, and the investment horizon required;
- The core investment beliefs, and the resulting investment "philosophy" codify guidance as to how the portfolio will be managed;[13]
- Any considerations in connection with portfolio construction to be taken into account in developing the strategic asset allocation;
- The asset mix of the portfolio's various asset classes;
- The asset classes to be included, described at a more general level than investment strategies and investment style(s);
- The vision for manager selection;
- Guidelines and methodology for rebalancing the portfolio based on feedback;
- Performance measures and benchmarks to be used in performance evaluation;
- The schedule for review of investment performance as well as of the IPS itself.

The IPS should be reviewed on a regular basis to ensure that it remains consistent with a fund's circumstances. An IPS is generally reviewed every three years, and in between when material changes occur in objectives, time horizon, or other fund characteristics.

The drafting of the IPS should be tailor-made for the fund, and is actually not as complex as it may sound. Just by looking at the current portfolio, you will be able to distill the implicit beliefs. Writing them down prompts the next step: do you agree with these beliefs? Does your fund have the resources, skills, and risk appetite required to implement them? Equally important, are they actually your beliefs, or do they in fact just reflect what your asset manager says? A goal for an asset manager might just be a means to an end for the fund. For example, pension funds do not necessarily crave "alpha" returns, just as most of us do not really crave a hammer and a nail. The hammer and nail are just unavoidable tools for putting a picture on the wall, which is what you really want. So the questions for the investment policy are what you really want (higher stable returns), what tools you need, and what tools you can do without.

It is the investment manager's role to convince you of the new investment strategy or instrument. And most of the time, this is a good thing. We manage portfolios in a far more informed way and with much better tools than we did 10 years ago. But once again, the investment manager's interests are not identical to those of the fund. So ask yourself, if you cut the expected rewards by half, would you still hire the new external manager? When they project 0.6% excess return per annum, would you settle for 0.3% and still hire them? In other words, manage your own manager's expectations. Which oftentimes means toning them down.

Although the investment policy is reviewed every year, changes tend to—and should—be incremental. Behavioral finance shows that investors' decision-making is subject to biases. In a return-seeking setting, investors are highly vulnerable to herding behavior because, when making decisions, they tend to place the greatest weight on their most recent experiences. Without a framework for making asset allocation decisions, investors will find themselves adrift and more susceptible to getting caught up in the herd.

Trustees and investment committees are therefore well served by relying heavily on the IPS to guide their long-term investment decisions, thus avoiding some major pitfalls in behavioral finance. Many investors have quite a short-term investment horizon, especially in turbulent investment environments in which many react to losses by selling risky assets and moving to cash near the bottom of the market. The IPS counteracts this by providing guidance for the investment philosophy and rebalancing.

Finally, writing an IPS does not in itself prevent such herding behavior and extrapolations when the time horizon is not chosen correctly. If portfolio assumptions are adjusted on a frequent basis, trustees may become part of the herd in a subtle way. In the early 2000s, when the technology bubble burst, many institutional investors found themselves overexposed to equity allocations. This made sense based on what the funds had formulated in their IPS: when the goal is to maximize a portfolio's expected return and future capital market projections for equity are rosy, equities will tend to be over-allocated. A number of high-profile investment managers and funds actually increased their equity exposure just before the stock market downturn.[14]

ENDNOTES

1. See Clark (2000).
2. See Damodaran (2007).
3. Based on Oerlemans et al. (2013).
4. See Ellis (2011a).
5. See Ellis (2011a).
6. See Economou et al. (2013).
7. See Maginn et al. (2010).
8. See Brown et al. (1997).
9. See Brinson et al. (1986, 1991).
10. See for example Damien Laker (2001).
11. See http://www.thepensionsregulator.gov.uk/guidance/guidance-for-trustees.aspx for the pension regulation on SIPs.
12. See Anson (2004).
13. See Terhaar (2010).
14. See Terhaar (2010).

CHAPTER 6

Organizing the Investment Function

Key Take Aways

- The investment process is not unique to any individual fund: every pension fund in the world goes through comparable steps. Rather, it is the combination of goals, investment beliefs, methods of implementation, and organizational culture that can be unique. We call these combinations "investment models."

- The choice of a model is influenced by the nature and the horizon of the fund's objectives, its investment beliefs, and the regulator. But there also is a large cultural influence, such as in the way the board views the pension fund organization.

- There are a limited number of available investment models, no more than approximately half a dozen. Merely copying a successful model may work for a short while, but not over the long term.

- Each model generates a set of questions for trustees, which they should consider before moving in a particular strategic direction.

- Creating a successful model requires time, determination and, above all, an understanding of the pension fund's DNA. There is no clearcut recipe for adopting a particular model; funds tend to combine different elements.

- Choosing a model has consequences for the governance of the fund and the focus of the trustees.

Putting thought into the design of the investment function and organization pays off. In 2004, Keith Ambachtsheer[1] analyzed the investment organizations of Harvard Management Company (HMC) and Ontario Teachers' Pension Plan Board (OTPP), both organizations renowned for their innovative investment policies and strong returns. HMC, which manages Harvard University's endowment, worth $37 billion in June 2017,[2] has surpassed the university's total return target and its internal benchmark, realizing an annualized rate of return of more than 10% over the previous 20 years. The Canadian pension fund OTPP, with $175.6 billion in assets at the end of 2016, realized an average annual rate of return of 10.1% since its inception in 1989,[3] generating $19 billion more than its market benchmarks—almost one-quarter of the fund's growth. Ambachtsheer[4] concluded that the success of these funds has key elements in common: a legal foundation that clarifies stakeholders' interests and minimizes the potential for agency conflicts, and a governance process that crystallizes the organizations' mission and is based on an understanding of the critical elements needed to achieve it. This gives both funds clear mandates and a well-thought-out governance process, two keys to success.

In a broader setting, public pension funds benefit from low operating costs because they enjoy economies of scale and avoid high marketing costs. However, if investment performance lags behind, this important advantage is dissipated. A weak governance structure, a lack of independence from government interference, and a low level of transparency and public accountability can all contribute to poor investment performance.

INVENTORIZING INVESTMENT MODELS

An investment model is formed from a unique combination of goals, risk appetite, investment beliefs and governance of investment implementation. For trustees, it is important not to forget that there are multiple possible models to choose from. Trustees often find themselves already following an existing model, which makes it difficult to achieve an "outside-in" perspective, or asking questions such as "Could we do this differently and better?" The two most visible models today are the Canadian Model and the Norway Model, but a number of other models also exist, such as the tailor-made approaches many funds have created for themselves.[5] We can group the main approaches in the following fashion:

- *Traditional asset allocation model.* This is a model used by most pension funds worldwide, especially in the United States. The strategic asset allocation determines the overall risk appetite, which the board keeps more or less constant. Portfolio construction is carried out with straightforward assets and investment strategies;
- *Endowment model.* This model is used by American endowments and foundations, but larger European pension funds tend to borrow many of these ideas as well. Investing long term, illiquid strategies that earn an illiquidity premium, and/or selecting innovative active management styles are the most characteristic adopted strategies. The idea is that the pension fund leverages its horizon and intellectual resources optimally;
- *Factor allocation model.* This model was pioneered by Washington State Investment Board and Danish Arbejdsmarkedets TillaegsPension (ATP). Diversification centers around spreading risks, rather than spreading of assets. Portfolio construction and the resulting portfolio weights diverge markedly from the traditional asset allocation model, as does the method of rebalancing;
- *Opportunity cost model.* This is a model adopted by Canadian pension funds. Attempting to integrate the endowment model into the traditional asset allocation model, a replicable and investable reference portfolio is established, investments outside of the reference portfolio are "funded" from proxies of the reference portfolio, and adjusted for leverage and illiquidity;
- *Dual strategic/operational benchmark model.* This model was pioneered by the Norway Fund, and applied by many European pension funds. The board sets an

overall benchmark to reflect the risk appetite, while further refinements to reflect the breadth of investable assets and the skill of the investment managers are delegated to the investment management organization;

■ *Risk parity model.* More than any other models, this model embraces uncertainty. We cannot be certain about capital market expectations; hence, the assets are spread equally over different scenario outcomes, based on their contribution to the total portfolio risk.

Each model presented in Exhibit 6.1 can be described by a number of elements that a board should consider. For instance: Is the primary focus on liabilities/risk or on return generation? Does the board have a primary focus on generating benchmark related returns ("passive") or on value creation ("active")? What is the level of delegation to the investment manager by the board? We will now discuss these models in more detail.

Model	Liabilities/ Return focus	Board delegation	Portfolio Construction	Implementation	Examples	Issues for Decision Makers
Traditional Asset Allocation Model	Return, or return/ liabilities focus.	Depends.	ALM process-driven strategic benchmark is translated to mandates.	External/internal and many mandates.	Smaller and traditional funds.	Alpha, cost and oversight.
Endowment Model	Return focus.	Very high.	Return objective or simple reference portfolio.	External/internal, deep relationships, and long-term relationships.	Yale, Harvard, and MIT.	Overconfidence, dominance by one or small group of people.
Factor Allocation	Risk/return focus.	High.	Allocate to factors, not to asset classes.	Usually occurs with a high derivative content.	ATP.	Understanding both the conceptual and operational sides of the process.
Opportunity Cost	Risk/return focus.	Delegation to IMO.	ALM process-driven strategic benchmark is based on best implementable portfolio.	Opportunity-based, investments are "funded" from the policy portfolio.	Canada Pension Plan.	Understanding the conceptual side of the process.
Risk Parity	Return focus.	Delegation to IMO.	Risk weightings are spread evenly over scenarios. The asset allocation is the result of that process.	Very disciplined and scenario-based.	Bridgewater and AQR.	Leverage needed to allocate risk evenly.

EXHIBIT 6.1 Overview of the most common investment models.

MODEL 1: TRADITIONAL ASSET ALLOCATION MODEL

What trustees should be aware of

- Centered on a quasi-static policy portfolio ("policy beta") controlled by trustees with modest value-add ("alpha") within each asset class.
- Longer time horizon needed to harvest equity and liquidity risk premiums while a tight link between policy and actual portfolios imposes rigidity.
- Lack of transparency regarding underlying risk drivers and sources of skill-based value creation, especially for privately traded assets.
- Easy to implement and to outsource in separate sequential steps. Limited delegation by the board. Easy to monitor.

We qualify this model as the middle of the road, the "let's do what the neighbor does" model: it is light on beliefs, and is often implemented via external managers who always promise but hardly ever deliver outperformance. Costs can be relatively low given efficient implementation, while higher costs generally signal a governance problem. This would suggest pension funds with average qualified trustees, a very small investment management organization, and/or overly active investment consultants.

The traditional asset allocation model is one of the processes through which a pension fund aims to realize the returns targeted by the fund. Pension funds usually aim to generate a specified net return over liabilities at the lowest possible risk. Therefore, four ingredients tend to drive investment decision-making:[6] (i) matching assets and liabilities, (ii) risk management through portfolio diversification; (iii) generating investment returns on top of the matching return, and (iv) cost management. The sequence of actions is usually implemented in a decision-making hierarchy.

The choice of strategic asset allocation is paramount here: the underlying assumption is that the choice of policy portfolio (asset allocation and resulting benchmarks) accounts for the bulk of the variability in returns,[7] although this is not undisputed.[8]

Important in determining the strategic asset allocation is firstly the share of risky vs. low-risk assets. The board has to describe the preferences of its participants, and translate their risk aversion into a risk appetite statement; how much risk are they willing to take, and under which circumstances? The outcome of this discussion is reflected in the share of matching versus return, or bonds versus equities. Next, the translation of risk appetite into quantifiable measures forms the framework for the strategic asset allocation, which is in turn further specified in terms of investment styles, and made explicit into a number of mandates that can be handed out to internal or external investment managers. Generally, the board of trustees of a pension fund, endowment or foundation establishes the strategic asset allocation across major asset classes. Strategic asset allocation then represents the institutional investor's investment policy.[9]

MODEL 2: ENDOWMENT MODEL

What trustees should be aware of

- Centered on a simple policy portfolio allocated to a limited number of core asset classes.

- Often has an extreme focus on returns.
- Entrepreneurial, human centered and skill based.
- The quality of the governance and the investment committee seems to be a factor contributing to the success of endowments.
- Extensive delegation to and investment management organization by the board. A highly skilled investment committee is necessary to keep the investment management organization reined in.
- Core belief—liquidity comes at a price, in the shape of lower returns. This leads to a relatively heavy exposure to alternative, illiquid asset classes such as private equity.
- Superior endowment performance may be due not just to asset class allocation, but also to the selection of assets within each class, as well as deal orientation.[10]
- Alternative investments require a staff with considerable skill and experience, engaging in early sourcing of strategies and rigorous self-evaluation.
- Typical size is $10–$25 billion: large enough for a very highly qualified staff, small enough to be flexible and have room to maneuver in markets and deals.

The Endowment Model can be characterized roughly as an investment model where the natural advantages of a long term investor are leveraged. This model was developed in the 1980s by Yale Endowment,[11] with pension funds drawing inspiration from the different approaches that endowments took towards portfolio construction and implementation. Endowments are important institutions in the academic world and in investment society. In the former, they play a role in funding, thereby maintaining academic research and excellence among universities. Regarding investment society, endowment funds operate under less regulatory restrictions than pension funds, allowing them to pioneer and adopt new insights in investment management at an earlier stage than pension funds. Endowments have received much attention recently for their superior investment returns compared with other institutional investors;[12] it has also been observed that these superior investment returns are difficult for other institutional investors to duplicate. We will now briefly review a few reasons for the endowment's superior investment returns.

Similarly to the traditional asset allocation model, much of the endowment's performance is achieved through allocation decisions between asset classes that have different risk and return characteristics. Investment can be separated into five major asset classes: equities, fixed income, real estate, alternatives (which include hedge funds, commodities such as oil and timber, as well as private equity funds), and cash. While the 1970s and 1980s saw a gradual move away from fixed income securities and cash and into equities by endowments, the 1990s and 2000s in turn witnessed a shift away from equities and fixed income towards sophisticated, often illiquid alternative assets.

Secondly, the superior endowment performance may be due not solely to asset class allocation, but also to the selection of assets within each class. The skills and experience of investment managers appear to play a substantial role in the success of endowment investments, with the staff able to identify and source strategies and asset classes at an early stage. The staff of successful academic endowments have considerable experience and have often worked together for many years. Finally, the staff of successful university and college endowments have an academic orientation, which leads to a process of periodic self-evaluation. The staff of many of these funds occasionally stop to consider the processes that led them to make investments that proved particularly successful or problematic, and also engage in an active dialogue with their peers.

A third distinguishing element with regard to the superior endowment performance is investment governance. Top-performing endowments have active investment committees, generally drawn from the ranks of alumni. These bodies see their role not as micromanaging the decisions of the investment staff, but rather as setting broad policy and serving as an informed sounding board. The contrast with public pension funds is particularly stark here.

Riding on the success of Yale Endowment and Harvard Management Company, many boards have been advised by consultants to adopt elements of the endowment model and make major commitments to "alternative" investments in hedge funds of various types, private equity, real estate, venture capital, etc. The long-term record achieved at leading endowments may seem compelling. However, pension funds have at best struggled to emulate this success, and in some cases have even lagged behind compared to traditional bond/equity asset allocation benchmarks.

Mimicking the asset allocation strategies of the best endowments may not lead to the same stellar results, for the simple reason that markets are adaptive and the rewards of mimicking are steadily eroded.[13] The alternative investment markets on which successful endowments have relied are particularly sensitive to inflows of capital. A new or niche alternative investment market often has a limited number of opportunities, so additional capital tends to result in the purchase of securities at higher prices and, therefore, ultimately lower returns. This effect is particularly relevant because the strategies of the elite endowments are being scrutinized and imitated as never before. Investing in alternative asset classes may prove to be risky, because these classes are often opaque and harder to understand. The recent struggle for performance of the endowment model can also be explained by the correlation of an endowment's portfolio with stock markets. When a financial crisis occurs, the performance of endowment funds deteriorates; for example, endowment funds were hit hard during the 2008 crisis. Finally, the scale of the fund could affect returns as well. Ninety-one percent of the funds under $1 billion in assets performed worse than a simple 60/40 holding strategy in every period since records were maintained.[14] Vanguard offers an explanation for this by stating that the larger endowments have better relationships and leverage for negotiating fees.[15] The endowment model is a long-term model. Institutions and investment committees that are not well prepared to maintain a long-term perspective would do well to study the endowment model carefully and adopt the model only to the extent that they have the necessary staff capabilities, financial disciplines, and internal understanding.

MODEL 3: FACTOR ALLOCATION MODEL

What trustees should be aware of
- Premised on the belief that asset returns can largely be explained by a parsimonious set of common factors, e.g. real interest rate, growth, inflation, credit spreads and volatility.

- By design, factor models provide higher transparency on systematic risks, but suffer from investability and stability issues.
- Because of the complexity, it is only suitable for boards with very high skill levels.
- The use of factors also complicates communication with stakeholders, hence its slow adoption rate—even among the converted.
- There is no fund that we know of that seriously puts this into practice across the whole asset mix except, perhaps, ATP.

Traditionally, portfolio diversification was an intuitive, sensible choice for an investor to make, and researchers have steadily added important theoretical ideas, including Mean Variance Optimization, Capital Asset Pricing Model (CAPM) and Asset Pricing Theory (APT), which have shaped our understanding of the meaning of diversification. Investment portfolios today may look quite different from portfolios of a decade ago, but they still share diversification as a central tenet. The factor allocation model takes a different approach to one of the central tenets of the traditional asset allocation model, namely diversification. It is far more important to diversify over a number of risk factors that the assets may have in common than to diversify over assets.

Institutional investors warmed to new forms of diversification in the 1990s, when advanced tools such as Asset Liability Management (ALM) and new innovative concepts in risk management allowed investors to expand the scope of possible investments. Asset categories, hitherto only available to a few savvy investors, slowly entered the portfolios but only really made headway from the 2000s onwards. Investors increasingly became aware that an overreliance on the traditional asset allocation to equities and bonds was vulnerable to high volatility and a lack of sufficient diversification, particularly during periods of crisis. After the 2001–2002 financial meltdown, there was an accelerated shift in asset allocation towards alternative asset classes such as private equity, hedge funds and commodities. These new allocations, however, provided only part of the expected diversification. Alternative asset classes have turned out to be more correlated with traditional equities and bonds than previously thought. Private equity provides diversification if it consists of high-alpha funds, but much of the return is structurally dependent on equities and bonds. Similarly, the majority of long–short equity hedge funds produce returns that are highly correlated with the equity market.[16]

In hindsight, many new alternative investment strategies incorporated in portfolio construction by boards that were inspired by the successes of the endowment model suffered from two problems. First, the success of many new alternative strategies was boosted by the same factors: low interest rates and robust economic growth. Some alternative investments share more factors; private equity gives investors exposure to the same kind of risk as publicly traded equity, albeit with added leverage. When prospects deteriorated, investors with liquidity constraints were forced to sell those alternative asset classes simultaneously. Secondly, some of the asset classes are rather small. For some investors, illiquidity can be attractive, given that it can offer higher returns. As more investors get involved, however, the market becomes more liquid, and the higher return is eroded. But when everyone tries to sell, illiquidity again rears its ugly head—there are no buyers to be found, and prices tumble. This is especially unpleasant when pension funds have to value their investment at mark-to-market.

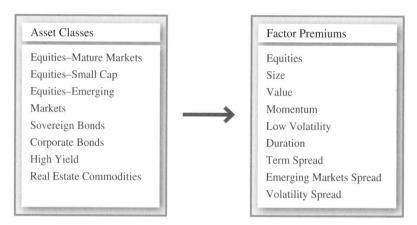

Asset Classes		Factor Premiums
Equities–Mature Markets		Equities
Equities–Small Cap		Size
Equities–Emerging		Value
Markets	→	Momentum
Sovereign Bonds		Low Volatility
Corporate Bonds		Duration
High Yield		Term Spread
Real Estate Commodities		Emerging Markets Spread
		Volatility Spread

EXHIBIT 6.2   Asset classes compared to factor premiums.[17]

Armed with this sobering knowledge, institutions began to reconsider what purpose diversification serves within the investment process and what the most important factors should be to drive portfolio returns.[18] Exhibit 6.2 presents a list of what the drivers of some asset classes are. Within this framework, which is rooted in the APT developed in the late 1970s, any asset can be viewed as a bundle of factors that reflect different risks and rewards. Therefore, it makes perfect sense to focus on these factors, allowing investors to identify them and understand what really drives asset returns. These insights help to develop portfolios that realize the required risk profile not only before, but also during volatile periods.

The novel proposition is that investors should consider redesigning the investment process by directly allocating to factor premiums within the strategic asset allocation as a way forward. A traditional portfolio would first be diversified across asset classes, followed by allocation, for instance to regions and sectors and then to (external) fund managers. A factor-based portfolio is diversified across premiums, such as low-volatility, small-cap, value and momentum premiums. Investment management practice has developed methods of incorporating one or more of these premiums, either by developing investment strategies solely to capture one of the premiums, or by embedding them as tilts in the overall strategic asset allocation. The Norway Pension Fund views this as "harvesting risk premia from multiple sources [which] can be seen as broadly consistent with risk parity investing, which should result in more effective diversification and avoid a heavy reliance on the equity premium."[19]

MODEL 4: OPPORTUNITY COST OR REFERENCE PORTFOLIO MODEL

What trustees should be aware of

- Reference portfolio comprising liquid assets acts as a realistic, cheap-to-replicate passive alternative.

- Investments outside of the reference portfolio (such as real estate, private equity and infrastructure) are funded from best proxies ("projections") of reference betas, which enhance risk and return transparency after adjusting for leverage and illiquidity.
- Residual risks are controlled by the active risk budget and provide a raison d'être for investing in alternatives.
- The investment management organization has the goal of generating a certain excess return over and above the return to the reference portfolio, usually on a rolling three-to-five-year horizon.
- Depending on the size of the risk budget, quite a wide degree of freedom is delegated by the board. In the Canadian pension funds, the modus operandi will typically be quite entrepreneurial, and there will be a substantial allocation to private asset classes such as private equity, real estate and infrastructure.
- In order to control the risk effectively, excellent risk budgeting and monitoring should be in place. This should be a point of attention for the board.

The Reference Portfolio of Opportunity Cost Model was developed by Canada Pension Plan Investment Board (CPPIB) in 2006. The main elements of this governance model, with some variations reflecting specific circumstances, have been adopted by GIC Private Limited (GIC), one of the sovereign wealth funds of Singapore, the New Zealand Superannuation Fund, and a number of other funds. When developing a strategic benchmark, a board could encounter a few dilemmas. If the board were to refine the benchmark into all sorts of sub-asset classes or investment styles, it would be in control, but run the risk of "over-engineering" and losing sight of what the benchmark should do, i.e. optimally reflect the risk/return trade-off needed to achieve the goals. Moreover, no matter how detailed and complete, there would always be investments that are not included but might fit the overall profile of the fund, and the investment management is well placed to identify such opportunities. Therefore, the starting point is that the board decides on a passive investment strategy or reference portfolio that, given the contributions to the fund, can reasonably be expected to meet the liabilities of the fund.

The Opportunity Cost Model does not specify asset classes. Portfolio construction starts with the specification of a Reference Portfolio, which reflects the desired or necessary level of systematic risk required to achieve the fund's objectives in a clear and simple way. The investment manager then considers each investment in the context of its exposure to the underlying factor drivers captured in the Reference Portfolio. The board also specifies an "active risk" appetite, which is the degree to which the fund can diverge from the composition of the Reference Portfolio, through means such as limits on deviations taken from benchmark (conventional "tracking error"), rebalancing requirements, and other risk measures. The asset manager is then responsible for determining asset allocation and approving investment programs within the defined risk appetite constraints. In practice, the fund manager would likely define a Policy Portfolio to reflect its asset allocation decisions and corresponding approvals for investment programs.

A hallmark of the Opportunity Cost Model is that the fund manager is free to invest in assets that are not included in the Reference Portfolio, but all investments are benchmarked against it. The Reference Portfolio could be implemented by a small team of 10–12 people, at almost no cost. The fund manager is deemed to have added value if it covers its own costs and beats the Reference Portfolio. For example, CPPIB's Reference Portfolio consists of 85% global equities and 15% Canadian bonds,[20] with further breakdowns for domestic and international assets. GIC's Reference Portfolio is also a 65% equities and 35% fixed income portfolio. These portfolios are simple, highly scalable, and can be implemented very cheaply.

An underlying principle is that the risk and return attributes of individual assets can be represented by some distinct combination of the factors in the Reference Portfolio (equity and bond exposures). The nature and degree of certainty of the cash flows, as well as the capital structure of each asset determine the mix of asset exposures used to fund that asset. Investments such as real estate, private equity, high-yield bonds and infrastructure can have idiosyncratic characteristics not necessarily captured in the funding assets, which may in turn provide beneficial risk-adjusted returns for the portfolio.[21]

Perhaps the most attractive feature of the Opportunity Cost Model is the clear delineation of accountability. The asset owner makes the most important decisions concerning return objectives and the required level of systematic risk by approving the composition of the Reference Portfolio and specifying other risk appetite parameters. The board ensures that the manager has the requisite capabilities in place before commencing investment programs, monitors the execution and results of those programs, and approves appropriate internal benchmarks. The fund manager then has the latitude to make investment decisions and shape the actual composition of the portfolio subject to the active risk limit determined by the asset owner. It can be argued that this places accountability with the party best able and positioned to make informed decisions. It is the fund manager's responsibility to justify costs of active management and to outperform the Reference Portfolio. Thus, the opportunity cost of the Reference Portfolio can be used for all alternative assets as their benchmarks, rather than having to specify separate benchmarks for each alternative asset class. This also provides more flexibility for the fund manager to take into account the time-varying nature of risk premiums by not having fixed allocations to asset classes. The manager has appropriate incentives to make the investments with the best marginal contribution to risk and return for the overall portfolio, rather than the best available investment within each asset class.

The Opportunity Cost Model is only suitable for long-horizon investors. Inevitably there will be performance differences in any short time period between a real estate asset, for instance, and the mix of equity and bonds used to fund it. Indeed, in the case of real estate for example it could take as long as 7–10 years for the Total Portfolio investment thesis to be realized.

A final governance challenge is that the board—or similar governing body of the investment manager—needs to have the skills to oversee, evaluate, and monitor the systems created by the investment manager in order to implement the Total Portfolio Approach. The board must also be conversant with the construction of—and the concepts behind—the Reference Portfolio.

MODEL 5: DUAL STRATEGIC/OPERATIONAL BENCHMARK MODEL

What trustees should be aware of

- A generic, strategic benchmark is provided by the asset owner, the fund. This strategic benchmark captures the overall risk appetite, adequately reflecting the risks in the pension agreement.
- A policy benchmark is then made more specific by the investment management organization in order to increase diversification and to benefit from a number of systematic sources of return such as value and small cap. The difference between the strategic and policy benchmark reflects the value of the strategic advice from the investment management organization.
- An operational benchmark is then made, refining the policy benchmark into investable mandates. The difference between the policy and the operational benchmark reflects the value of the selection and monitoring of the mandates, including the value of internally managed mandates.
- The ownership of the strategic benchmark lies with the board. Policy and operational benchmarks should also be approved or set by the board.

The Operational Reference Portfolio (ORP) is an approach to improving diversification without losing the reference to broadly accepted standard benchmarks. The ORP was introduced in 2011 and is an internal benchmark constructed by the Norwegian Fund. It is a tailored benchmark with non-market capitalization weights, and takes as its starting point the benchmarks set by the Norwegian Ministry of Finance. The ORP takes advantage of the characteristics of the fund: a large investor with no fixed liabilities and no immediate liquidity requirements, and unconstrained by domestic currency considerations.[22]

The Norwegian Fund uses the ORP for three purposes, to:

1. Diversify more widely than standard benchmarks;
2. Take on systematic factor risk exposure;
3. Implement smart rebalancing.

We discuss each of these in turn, and explain how each component requires a different verification horizon for risk management. The ORP is internally owned by Norges Bank Investment Management (NBIM) and only takes on a limited set of risk factors that have been specified by the Ministry of Finance. A part of NBIM's mandate regarding fiscal strength in the sovereign bond portfolio is not, however, quantitatively expressed in an off-the-shelf benchmark. This mandate is incorporated by NBIM in the ORP.

Alternative investments may have become the mainstream, but not in the ORP of the Norway Fund. Here, the Government Pension Fund Global keeps 60% of its assets in publicly traded equity, 35% in bonds and up to 5% in real estate. Hedge funds, private equity and venture capital have failed to gain a foothold. In other words, it is a clean-cut portfolio that focuses on the main asset allocation choices, with a limited amount of active management.

There is a pragmatic reason for this approach. The Norway Fund is simply too large to invest in alternative types of strategies. It would be too cumbersome and costly to build up a portfolio of illiquid assets that would amount to anything meaningful. Additionally, the Fund operates very much under the public eye. The investment policy is therefore articulated and clear, with limited maneuvering scope for grasping "exciting" new investment opportunities. And yet, the Norwegian fund has fared quite well over the past years. As might be expected, its apparent simplicity could be misinterpreted as an "anyone can do it" approach, i.e. simply by shedding active management and alternative investments. However, trustees should be aware that investment "rules" become important in order to discipline decision-making and combat behavioral biases. The Fund is disciplined in its asset allocation. When stocks decline, the Fund buys enough to get the 60% equity target back; conversely, it buys bonds when that proportion falls below 40%. The Fund rebalances in this way to eliminate emotion from its decisions, compelling it to buy assets with a low valuation and higher expected compensation for the risk premium and vice versa.

"Liquid" is still long term. Therefore, the choice and construction of the indices to achieve the right exposure becomes a big deal. Which risk premiums can reasonably be earned in liquid markets with a long-term horizon? Norway takes on smaller stocks and value stocks, which may be trading at lower prices in the short term, but this is setting them up for higher performance in the long term—which research interprets as decades, not a matter of a few years.

MODEL 6: RISK PARITY MODEL

What trustees should be aware of

- In a risk parity model, different sources of return, such as the equity risk premium, the credit risk premium, and the term premium, are all scaled in such a way that they contribute the same amount of risk to the portfolio.
- This is done by applying leverage to the less-risky return sources.
- The expected return per unit of volatility risk increases as a result, because the diversification over the different sources of return is much better than in traditional portfolios.
- The successful implementation of risk parity requires continuous rebalancing of the different positions. This is operationally challenging and demands deep and liquid markets.
- In practice, few—if any—asset owners use risk parity as their governance model.

The idea behind risk parity is that a portfolio based on traditional asset allocation techniques may look roughly balanced, but from a capital allocation standpoint rather than from a risk perspective. For example, equities have contributed far more to total portfolio volatility than the equity allocation would suggest: between January 1997 and July 2017, 93% of the volatility in a 60% equity + 40% bonds portfolio could be attributed to equities.[23] The solution to this disproportionate risk allocation to stocks is to reduce the weight of stocks according to risk parity and increase the weight of bonds, so that equities and bonds have a similar volatility impact on the portfolio. However, the overall volatility of the portfolio will drop. If the investor is comfortable with the initial volatility of the 60/40 portfolio, proponents of risk parity suggest that leverage should be used to achieve the required risk level. Overall, average returns would have increased with decreased risk. The risk parity–based portfolio construction process is agnostic in the sense that it balances the portfolio so that each asset class contributes the same potential for losses, so-called "risk parity."

The assumption of this risk parity is that an investor will always be rewarded over the long term for taking risks rather than holding cash. Pension funds can develop risk parity, or an "all-weather portfolio," in a two-step process. First, the risk budget is allocated into four compartments (low or high economic growth and low or high inflation). Second, within each risk budget compartment, asset classes are suballocated (also on an even basis), based on the exposure to the growth–inflation dimension. Here, the "purer" the asset class or strategy, preferably based on one factor premium, the more effective this approach is.

Pension funds are increasingly adopting a matching-return approach. This investment model divides the portfolio into a matching portfolio based on fixed income instruments that either partially or fully replicate the cash flows resulting from the pension liabilities. The return portfolio, on the other hand, takes investment risk to build up regulatory reserves and funds for indexation. Theoretically, the risk parity model could also be applicable in a matching-return approach.[24]

The best-known pioneer of this approach is Ray Dalio's Bridgewater hedge fund, which is based on the idea that a portfolio built on the allocation of risk should be more resistant to market downturns than a traditional portfolio. This is an appealing concept for pension funds and their trustees. Ben Inker, director of asset allocation at GMO, singles out three points of criticisms[25] for this approach. His main objection is that volatility and risk are not the same things. For example, leverage allows investors to boost returns, but also introduces path dependency. While an unleveraged investor can wait for a process to converge certain valuations, a leveraged investor may not have this luxury. Leveraged investors cannot expect to maintain the same amount of leverage during high periods of volatility, but rather are forced to reduce leverage and sell securities—at the risk of forgoing positive future returns due to overreaction and mean-reversion after periods of financial distress. Another issue relates to the selection of factors. While risk parity may suggest a valuation-neutral approach, in reality it is not neutral and investors might end up leveraging risks without associated positive returns. For example, the term-structure premium is a factor behind fixed income. A risk parity approach would significantly increase exposure to this factor, but does this make sense in today's monetary environment? Looking at a risk distribution pie chart does not give the investor information as to whether the portfolio is optimally diversified. For example, while country risk might be dealt with in the risk distribution, it still matters *which* country's default risk is included. In other words, for pension funds considering looking into the risk parity approach, one consideration could be that risk parity improves the insight of the investor into the portfolio's risks and sensitivity to scenarios. On the other hand, in-depth insight into the portfolio is still needed, alongside knowledge of the intended or unintended interaction between leverage and risk appetite.

DEVELOPING YOUR OWN INVESTMENT APPROACH

Trustees almost never have the opportunity to start from scratch and design an investment model that is optimally equipped to achieve the fund's goals. Funds that do have this opportunity have a comparative advantage because they can—and should—learn from others. Cases like NEST and Future Fund[26] show that this actually happens. If your fund does not have the luxury of this position, there will often still be opportunity for gradual change.

We think that "choosing your model" is a strategic choice that is easily sidestepped, or only addressed during crises, when maneuvering space is limited. A board of trustees reviews the investment model, without the investment management organization, and asks the right questions: what is the pension fund's context, what ambition is needed for the fund, and what part of the ambition is desired by the board? In addition, what are the underlying assumptions and beliefs supporting this course? Every model has consequences; for example, for governance, sponsors, possible outcomes, and participant communication. Finally, models have "requirements" in terms of size, governance budget, intellectual property of the board, and of the investment organization. This translates into a set of granular questions:

1. The nature of the liabilities and the investment horizon. Are the liabilities clearly defined? How "certain" is the investment horizon to develop long-term strategies?
2. The investment beliefs of the fund. Are they defined? Are the consequences clear, and what is required to implement them successfully?
3. The available governance budget, which is a matter both of scale and of choice. How much do you want to put in a board? Does it limit or expand your choice of investment models?
4. The level of investment knowledge and experience, both of the trustees and the asset management staff. How do you want to deploy it?
5. The regulatory environment often plays an important role. This limits choices, but given these limits, which opportunities are there to leverage the beliefs within the regulatory framework?

At one extreme, for a relatively small fund (let's say, up to $2 billion) with a limited governance budget, knowledge, and resources on the board, the investment model should be very simple: we would suggest "model 1," with an extreme focus on cost and a "passive unless" strategy. To a large extent, it will have to outsource. Even if it does believe in "active" in theory, it will probably not have the time or skills to distinguish good from bad managers. Therefore, a fund such as this one should strive for operational excellence, extremely low cost, and a "no regret" investment model, which simply by avoiding costly mistakes (caused by the board's overestimation of its own intellectual abilities) will turn out to be better than many of its comparators.

At the other extreme, if a fund that is really big (let's say $100 billion) and therefore—in theory—has an ample governance budget, decides that it is willing to invest 10 basis points of the assets in its own governance budget, this budget will be \$100 million, enough to have a very serious investment operation of 100–400 well-paid investment professionals.

Still, in this case, the nature of the liabilities and the investment horizon have a substantial influence on the choices: the heavier the liabilities and the shorter the horizon, the more the investment solution is prescribed, so there will not be a large degree of freedom of which to avail.

ENDNOTES

1. See Ambachtsheer (2004).
2. See annual report of Harvard Endowment Fund. Accessed on: http://www.hmc.harvard.edu/docs/Final_Annual_Report_2017.pdf.
3. For OTTP's performance, see https://www.otpp.com/investments/performance.
4. See Ambachtsheer (2004).
5. See Cheng Chih (2014).
6. See Clark (2000).
7. See Brinson et al. (1986, 1991).
8. See Kritzman and Page (2003).
9. See Anson (2005).
10. See Lerner et al. (2008).
11. See Swensen (2009).
12. See Lerner et al. (2008).
13. See Lerner et al. (2008).
14. See Stewart (2012).
15. See the article by Vanguard Group (2018).
16. See Bender et al. (2010).
17. See Koedijk et al. (2016).
18. See Ilmanen and Kizer (2012).
19. See Chambers et al. (2011).
20. See http://www.cppib.com/en/how-we-invest/our-investment-strategy/investment-framework.
21. The economic theory behind the Total Portfolio Approach is essentially a restatement of the CAPM, and the Arbitrage Pricing Theory of Ross (2013) for multiple factors.
22. See Ang et al. (2009).
23. See Uijting (2017). The MSCI World Equity index (annual volatility 14.65%) is used as proxy for equity and the Bank of America Merrill Lynch Global Bond index as proxy for bonds (annual volatility 5.37%).
24. See the example by Peters (2011), who argues that risk-parity yields better results for pension funds, even if liabilities are not taken into account when the portfolio is constructed.
25. See Inker (2010).
26. NEST and Future Fund are comparatively new pension schemes. The National Employment Savings Trust (NEST) is a defined contribution workplace pension scheme, set up in 2008 to facilitate automatic enrolment as part of the government's workplace pension reforms. The Australian Government Future Fund is an independently managed sovereign fund founded in 2006, to meet liabilities for the payment of superannuation to retired public employees.

Case Study – GPFG

BUILDING A LONG-TERM, RESPONSIBLE FUND ON SOLID ACADEMIC AND EVIDENCE-BASED PRINCIPLES

Background

The Government Pension Fund Global (GPFG) is commonly known as Norges.[1] It is managed by Norges Bank Investment Management[2] and funded from the revenues of the Norwegian oil fields. The investment policy of the fund is designed by the Norwegian Ministry of Finance and approved by parliament. In February 2017, the fund has an approximate value of $900 billion (NOK 7.379 billion). Due to the fund's size, it has on average a 1.3% ownership of all listed companies outside of Europe and 2.3% ownership of all listed companies in Europe. The primary goal of the oil fund is to save for future generations in Norway: "One day the oil will run out, but the return on the fund will continue to benefit the Norwegian population."

GPFG is highly prudent and transparent in sharing the research that underpins its strategy. Ang et al. (2014)[3] found that 99% of the fund's return was the result of policy-driven decisions; furthermore all policy changes and investments can be found on GPFG's website. GPFG has realized an annualized rate of return of 5.6% since 1998. After correction for inflation and management fees, the annualized real return was 3.7%.[4] GPFG thoroughly considers the long term and how investment decisions will work out in the future. In general, GPFG applies a passive investment strategy. In the light of low expected return environment, the equity allocation has been increased at the cost of the allocation to bonds in 2017. The strategy is implemented in an extremely cost-effective way, with total costs amounting to 0.05% in 2016.

The challenge

GPFG has to deal with two major challenges: (i) How to maintain and improve diversification benefits and limit market impact when the fund already has on average a 1%–2% ownership in listed companies worldwide; and (ii), how to incorporate the commonly shared values of the Norwegian people into the investment strategy? Hence, in "The Norway model," Chambers et al. (2011) argue: "The fund is a professional financial investor, and it cannot uphold all of Norway's ethical commitments. Yet the assets belong to the people of Norway, and so the fund has to take account of important, commonly shared ethical values."

The process

For a long period of time, the fund only invested in listed equities and bonds. Recently it started to develop investments in real estate. The strategic asset allocation is now listed equities 65%, bonds 30% and real estate 5%. The scope for deviating from this strategy is extremely small. Therefore, over 99% of the results of the fund reflect the returns on the benchmarks. In this sense, the fund can be seen as a true policy-driven investor, avoiding in a rational way the pitfalls that can arise with active investing and ensuring that each strategic decision is supported by in-depth academic insights. On the one hand, this makes for a very slow-moving, and boring-but-sound strategy. On the other hand, and more importantly, the slow moving, rational, academic, and evidence-based approach to fix the strategy and the implementation has two major advantages:

1. It provides a strong foundation for the accountability that the fund has to its owners, the Norwegian people; and
2. Given the very long horizon of the fund, it makes the transfer of leadership from person to person within the fund relatively risk-free.

Both are probably necessary conditions for the fund to be able to survive relatively easily in the long term and to keep out of public and political turmoil.

GPFG is at a point where additional economies of scale are very hard to realize. On the one hand, allocating 5% to real estate for instance yields a value of approximately $45 billion. This enormous size makes it very difficult to move money around, with acceptable market impact and transaction costs. Diversification through real estate is therefore only possible to a limited degree. Based on multiple academic reports, the focus is more on the effect of a higher allocation to, for instance, diversification benefits, profitability, liquidity, and volatility.[5]

On the other hand, the constraints of size are also visible through the academic approach to investing. Despite the fact that these studies elaborate on factor investing, the essence of the story is that active management is not suitable due to the fund's size—alternatively, GPFG has to seek other ways to enhance diversification benefits. In January 2018, Dahlquist and Odegaard (2018) investigated the active management style of GPFG and advised sticking with the current setup rather than changing to an even more passive management style. In a related study, Stomberg and Doskeland (2018) advised that the fund should open up to investments in private equity.

The outcome

The fund has a strong, long-horizon objective to be a responsible investor. It considers itself a universal owner, meaning that essentially it has a stake in all listed companies. Therefore, the fund aims to contribute to the development of market practices that will benefit its own long-term interests. These include standards for corporate governance, sustainable business practices and the functioning of financial markets. For example, the fund is an active shareholder and uses its voting rights to safeguard its investments. This includes voting to promote sustainable development and good corporate governance.

As a large, long-term investor, the fund engages directly with companies' board and management.

Regarding commonly shared ethical values, GPFG introduced guidelines to the fund's ethical foundations in 2004. The first transcript stated: "The Government Pension Fund Global should not make investments which constitute an unacceptable risk that the Fund may contribute to unethical acts or omissions, such as violations of fundamental humanitarian principles, serious violations of human rights, gross corruption or severe environmental damages."[6]

As a consequence, GPFG can either exclude companies from its investment portfolio or put them on an observation list. Companies on the observation list face the possibility of being excluded in the future. Since 1 January 2015, exclusions have been decided by GPFG Executive Board; this was previously done by the Ministry of Finance. Each decision is based on a recommendation made by the Council on Ethics. Product-based criteria are based on recommendations from GPFG's Investment Management. Examples of product-based exclusions are (i) companies that produce coal or coal-based energy, (ii) companies that produce nuclear weapons, and (iii) companies that produce tobacco. In addition, conduct-based exclusions involve (i) companies that violate human rights, (ii) companies that cause severe environmental damage, (iii) companies with gross corruption, (iv) companies that violate individual human rights in situations of war or conflict, and (v) other serious violations of fundamental ethical norms.[7]

Lessons for Achieving Investment Excellence

- The fund's long-horizon view, size, and responsibilities to future generations puts a natural focus to stewardship and sustainability.
- The policy of the fund was designed by the Ministry of Finance, far removed from both political forces and the implementation of the strategy. This ensures a rational, top-down view of the strategy. The strategy and its results are therefore independent of the person who is at the helm of the fund.
- The deep and very thorough academic underpinning of the strategy and the implementation of the fund facilitate accountability to its owners, the Norwegian people.
- The size of the fund limits its room to maneuver and diversify. Other likely opportunity losses arise from the fact that the fund is set up in this solid, extremely policy-based way; these costs have to be weighed against the positive aspects of the transparency and the sound academic underpinnings.

ENDNOTES

1. See https://www.nbim.no/en/the-fund.
2. See https://www.nbim.no/en/the-fund/governance-model.
3. See also Ang and Kjaer (2012), and Ang et al. (2009).
4. See https://www.nbim.no/en/the-fund/return-on-the-fund.
5. See for example *"The Diversification potential of Real Estate"* by NBIM (2017).
6. See GPFG's Ethical Guidelines (2004).
7. See https://www.nbim.no/en/responsibility/exclusion-of-companies.

Three

Implementing the Investments

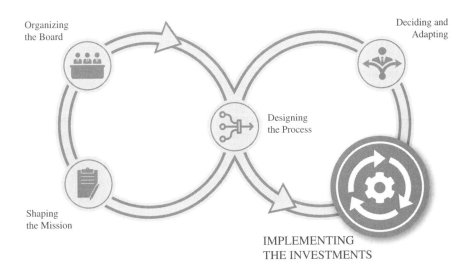

Organizing
the Board

Deciding and
Adapting

Designing
the Process

Shaping
the Mission

IMPLEMENTING
THE INVESTMENTS

Part III concerns the implementation of the investment cycle. Parts I and II have laid the groundwork, defining the purpose, mission and strategy of a pension plan and how this leads to a risk and return framework to achieve the strategy. This part focuses firmly on the implementation of the strategy, which goes through a regular cycle for trustees. The investment plan is created on a yearly basis, and includes the asset allocation, investment styles and benchmarks. The plan is also reviewed—"Are we doing the right thing?" During the year, implementation of the investment plan is monitored on a quarterly, monthly or even weekly basis, as part of continuous execution-and-monitoring, focusing on "Are we doing things right?"

The design of Part III follows the implementation of the investment cycle, and as with the other chapters, stays true to the trustee's perspective: what do you need to do to set out the strategy, to be in control, and to focus on what really matters in order to achieve the fund's goals? As in the earlier parts of the book, we distinguish between the limited choices that produce 80% of the returns, and potential add-ons that might get you above 80%, but which will require a lot of skill and energy.

Part III Topics Include:
- How to formulate and judge capital market expectations;
- How to build an asset allocation and investment plan on the basis of the objective and the expectations;
- How to decide on active versus passive management;
- Effective selection, and avoiding pitfalls with mandates and managers;
- The importance of managing costs;
- Being aware of implementation shortfall;
- Reporting on the results in the right way, i.e. in a way that serves the monitoring process effectively;
- Focusing on the things that matter during the monitoring of the outcomes of the process;
- How to ignore the noise and read the right signal from the outcomes, and use this to make improvements and learn for the future.

CONTRIBUTION OF THIS PART TO INVESTMENT EXCELLENCE

In Part III, the focus shifts from thinking to acting. Central in this part is the execution of the plan. During execution, many very expensive mistakes can be made, ranging from a naïve belief in active management to lax cost management, the lack of disciplined rebalancing and an overdose of hiring and firing of managers. Each badly thought-through or poorly executed decision might have a minor negative impact, but together they can really derail the board's plans to realize decent investment returns for their participants. When the execution does not live up to the goals or expectations, there is shortfall. Shortfall is typically caused by a lack of knowledge and by failing to control human behavioral mistakes, both by boards and investors. The contribution to excellence of this part is clear: shortfall can be dramatically reduced by pragmatic, evidence-based choices, made by disciplined boards.

CHAPTER 7

Implementing the Investment Strategy

Key Take Aways

- Implementation is the process of putting plans and strategies into action in order to reach goals.

- In implementation, shortfall is defined as the gap between planned and realized outcomes. An idea that might be good on paper is not necessarily a good idea in practice. This gap should be minimized.

- The board should have the knowledge and skills to understand and manage the gap. In particular, the interests of the many advisory parties may differ from those of the board and the beneficiaries, potentially adding cost and complexity.

- Effective cost management can materially improve net returns.

- Active management often disappoints and may lead to the costly replacement of external managers as well as to a high manager turnover.

- Implementation shortfall can be reduced by having a clear implementation plan, by identifying potential pitfalls beforehand, and by having clear benchmarks and monitoring systems in place to track the implementation.

Implementation puts plans and strategies in action in order to reach goals. Without implementation, a plan will sit forgotten; implementation means making the pension fund's plans happen.[1] Implementation follows after drafting the investment policy, where objectives for changes in asset categories, investment styles, managers, and the manner of oversight are further specified. This involves a budget that covers the operating time horizon, which is often between one and three years. How implementation takes place is critical to a fund's success, addressing the "who," "where," "when," and "how" of operating in order to reach the desired goals and objectives. Implementing the investment strategy is a matter of assessing resources, quantifying objectives and then combining them into a flexible plan.

ORGANIZING THE IMPLEMENTATION

For a board of trustees, implementation is a key area of policymaking and its importance is obvious: if the board has a clear idea of what needs to be done but the organization charged with implementing the investment plan lacks the will or capacity to actually do it, little will be accomplished. In order to assess progress towards achieving your goals, you need to be clear about what you are trying to achieve and how you are trying to achieve it; that is, your objectives and the activities planned for attaining these. It is helpful to start by clarifying the aims and objectives in the investment policy statement, and to then plan the activities that the board and other actors will carry out to achieve them.

The implementation gap is the difference between the policy laid out in the investment policy statement and how the activities are carried out in practice.

A board's ambition should therefore be to minimize the implementation gap. The board has three resources at its disposal: ownership rights, cost budget, and governance budget.

Ownership rights. The pension fund has the ownership of the assets, but delegates their management to specialized parties, or asset managers. The fund divides the assets up into larger and smaller parcels and assigns mandates to asset managers for each of these parcels. In essence, these mandates are decision rights: the asset manager does not own the assets but can initiate transactions as he or she sees fit—within the framework of the mandate, of course. The board must ensure that all the necessary mandates are awarded, and nothing is left out. The mandates should be MECE—Mutually Exclusive and Collectively Exhaustive. In practice, this is not easy and may lead to coordination problems. For example, in two mandates the managers may operate within their risk limits, but added together, their positions lead to a concentration of risk. In addition, the board has to decide whom to delegate implementation to, a matter that affects the investment portfolio as a whole. For example, with regard to tactical asset allocation, rebalancing or hedging decisions, should this be the investment management organization, the executive staff, or the investment committee? The board should also be clear about how the implementation process should evolve: which choices should the board make, and what elements are best left to the pension fund's other bodies? Boards clarify these fiduciary responsibilities by developing detailed reviews of their decision rights framework, with a focus on investment and risk management decisions. A formal approach, such as the RACI framework (Responsible, Accountable, Consult, and Inform) is very helpful, not only in clarifying roles and responsibilities, but also in allowing for a debate on and review of these decision rights.[2] Exhibit 7.1 presents a RACI framework.

Managing costs. Successful implementation requires effective management of costs from the outset. The Swedish AP3 Fund demonstrates this by pointing out that the fund's annual management fees amount to 0.03% of the fund, or 1% of the fresh pension premium. In other words, pensioners retain 99% of the value of their pensions after all costs have been subtracted. This can be compared to a cost of 0.3%, which reduces the pension premium by 9%; the pensioner would retain only 91% of his or her pension assets after fees. Were a pension saver to buy a pension in a fund where a management fee of 1% a year was charged, his or her pot would fall to 72% of its

	Trustees	Executive Trustee	Investment Committee	Investment Management Organization	Investment Consultant/ Actuary
Goals					
Investment Philosophy	A	I	I	I	C
Investment Beliefs	A	I	I	I	C
Definition of SAA Classes	A	I	C	C	C
Portfolio Construction	A	I	C	C	C
Selection of Mandates	A	R	C	R	
Implementation	A	R	C	R	
Monitoring of Mandates	A	R	C	R	
Evaluation	A	R	C	R	C
Monitoring of Investment Management	A	R	C	R	C

R: Responsible   A: Accountable   I: Informed   C: Consulted

EXHIBIT 7.1   RACI framework.

full value. In this case, costs would eat up more than a quarter of the capital. These figures from AP3 reflect the importance of low asset management and administration costs in the implementation.[3] These examples make clear that adding cost to the investment solution should be done carefully and on the basis of a strong conviction that the higher cost will actually result in higher net returns.

Trustees and administrators have an important role to play in the management of investment costs. In evaluating public pension practices, five approaches that assist in managing costs during implementation[4] can be identified. First, trustees can specify cost management as a high priority in their investment policy. The board can include statements on limiting transaction costs (e.g. brokerage costs or formal measures of manager performance net of fees), and make sure that limiting transaction costs is an integral component of the selection of mandates.

Second, passive management provides important cost advantages, particularly for smaller pension systems that cannot achieve the economies of scale available to larger pensions. Passive management gains a cost advantage stemming from lower investment research costs and less frequent securities trading, among other factors. We will discuss the active versus passive cost considerations in more detail later in this chapter.

Third, the board can also decide to carry out investment management activities internally. For larger pension funds, this can have real cost advantages. However, the cost differential between external and internal management has fallen over the years, especially for the liquid investment categories such as equities and fixed income. For illiquid investments, a reason to continue insourcing could be to improve alignment and to get closer to the fund's assets, thereby improving risk management standards and avoiding opportunity costs.

Fourth, because internal staff usually negotiate contracts with third parties and then administer them on a day-to-day basis, these staff can play a key oversight role in ensuring costs are held in check. Staff can negotiate contracts that reduce investment costs (expressed in basis points) along a sliding scale with investment managers, so that these costs (in basis points) decrease as assets under management increase.

For all of these cost measures, one way for the board to make an informed decision on whether the cost measures are being effectively implemented is to carry out studies to benchmark these costs relative to similar "peer" pension funds.

The governance budget of the board is decisive for the implementation that the fund will choose to pursue. The governance budget represents the combination of time, expertise, and organizational effectiveness of the decision makers. For most funds this includes the board as well as the staff. It is up to the board to decide how it wants to spend its governance budget. One approach could be to "set" this budget as compatible with the lowest possible governance resources, and as a set of arrangements that "manages down" all costs and focus on easily attainable investment returns. What does this mean in effect? For implementation, the board could, for instance, agree on as few as possible different assets as necessary to diversify effectively; only one investment style per asset, preferably passive; and a static, rules-based approach to rebalancing. This set-up would require an extremely low level of governance budget for implementation, an efficient starting point. Reasoning from this starting point, boards could ask themselves: if we added to the governance budget, what would be the expected contribution to the objectives of the fund? Would it be worthwhile?

THE RATIONALE FOR MANAGING COSTS

Where implementation is concerned, the question of costs warrants a more extended discussion. Many pension funds worldwide are regulated in one way or another, and large pension funds are occupationally based or sector-wide. It is then mandatory for participants to join, giving them no real alternative for investing. This mandatory approach has many benefits. The downside, however, is that boards are exposed to market discipline only to a limited extent—or not at all. If they provide pensions at a higher cost, participants have no option to switch to a pension fund with lower costs. Higher costs eat into future pension income and can also be a sign that the board is running the pension fund inefficiently. While relatively little is known about the investment costs of pension funds, there is a large body of literature on the costs incurred by mutual funds. The investment operations of pension funds are similar to those of mutual funds, and many pension funds invest part of their funds through mutual funds. Therefore, this literature can also provide useful insights on the investment operations of pension funds. Empirical evidence suggests substantial economies of scale related to costs in the mutual fund industry.[5]

However, these scale economies turn out to decrease as the fund size increases further, and become zero as soon as the optimal size has been reached.[6]

Of course, mutual funds may incur higher costs because they are hunting for higher returns. However, a growing body of studies shows that higher costs are not correlated to a superior performance in terms of the risk-adjusted rate of return.[7] Thus, the evidence suggests that, in general, higher costs incurred by mutual funds do not lead to higher returns. Since the investment operations of pension funds and mutual funds are similar, it seems reasonable to expect that this result would also hold for pension funds. In other words, participants are likely to be best served by pension funds with low investment costs, and boards should use this as their guideline for decision-making.

There are of course some counterarguments voiced by the investment industry. Costs are important, but lowering or focusing on them should not be taken too far. One could argue that it might come back to hit the trustees like a boomerang; they would miss out on important investment opportunities. An alternative argument is that "if you pay peanuts, you get monkeys": the focus on costs means that overall quality deteriorates, and a decreasing amount can be spent on the research that forms the basis and ensures the quality of many investment strategies. In other words, pension funds are cutting into their own flesh. You should be aware that a permanent focus on costs drives out the best managers, and deprives your pension fund of real alpha potential. After all, according to the investment industry, it's not the costs that matter, but the net return.

If we aggregate the research on active management, ex-post results are mostly disappointing, something we'll discuss in depth further on in this chapter. An idea that may seem good on paper is not necessarily a good idea in practice. Costs and implementation issues can be hindrances.

Is it possible to contain costs through performance-related fees? To answer, we can once again quote what was mentioned previously: "After all, what really matters is the net return." What participant would be concerned about the costs being 5% if the manager was delivering 15%? In other words, if managers could be incentivized to earn more than they cost, then things would balance out. This is a great idea, but in practice it is flawed, for three reasons. First, research[8] suggests that a modest performance fee might work, but that a large one certainly does not. And in the investment industry, most contracts are not modest. Second, the investment manager, when considering the potential rewards, could try to take on more risk so as to earn their performance fee. We pay the investment managers for their "skill" in equities, to select the best performing ones; but the manager may at times think, "Do I feel lucky?" and simply increase the number of equities without being too concerned about the quality of the underlying equities. Trustees can combat this by asking for elaborate quantitative reports to help them decide whether managers have earned their performance fee through skill, or whether they should be denied it because they simply took on more risk. The truth here is sobering: we have no way of distinguishing between skill and luck, except over a very long period. This reaffirms our earlier conclusion, namely that participants are likely to be best served by pension funds with low investment costs, and boards should use this as their guideline for decision-making.

SELECTION OF MANAGERS

Hiring and firing managers is part of the implementation process for pension funds. A whole investment consultancy industry has developed to assist funds in this process, providing a selection process, databases to keep track of the investment management organization and style, and assisting in the negotiation of the contracts. A standard selection process is organized as follows:

1. Setting goals and objectives
2. Drawing up a long list
3. Sending out a Request for Information
4. Drawing up a short list and sending out a Request for Proposal
5. Selection of the Mandate
6. Contracting the Mandate

From a trustee's perspective, getting the first step right is important for an execution that lives up to the board's expectation as well as providing a clear framework for monitoring and evaluation at later stages the process. Selecting and monitoring active management mandates generates a substantial amount of work for investment consultants and staff. Over the past decades, the turnover rate in mandates has increased and the holding period of mandates has decreased. Switching managers is a costly affair, creating sizeable opportunity costs for a fund.

Selecting investment managers is an important responsibility for trustees. Trustees can be involved in several steps of the selection process, preparing the selection in consultation with an advisor mandate search, or deciding on the selection criteria. This involvement depends on the time and resources that a trustee has to dedicate to the process. At the very minimum, trustees set the goals and objectives for the selection process and leave the other steps to the advisor and the pension staff. The goals and objectives are in line with the investment beliefs that the fund sets. For example, if one of the investment beliefs of the fund is that active management pays off, it makes sense to translate this to setting up a selection process that revolves around selecting the best-in-class managers available. The managers who are going through the selection process will stress their ability to beat the benchmark; trustees can then communicate to their participants that the manager with the highest potential for beating the benchmark has been selected.

If selection is considered to be a core implementation function of pension funds for mandates, surprisingly little empirical evidence has been built up to demonstrate its effectiveness. Institutional investors increasingly shorten the period for evaluating external managers, which in turn steps up the pressure to produce good short-term results. At the end of the chain, this puts pressure on the fund to focus on short-term results as well. As stated, the duration of external mandates tends to shorten, while the number of mandates within the same asset category increases. This results in managers being selected and fired more often, which lends support to the view that investment managers are under more pressure to perform. A large study analyzed[9] the selection and monitoring processes for 3,400 institutional investors between 1994 and 2003. The study found that managers for new external mandates were hired after a period during which they had realized substantial outperformance compared with the incumbent manager. However, when the manager was hired, this outperformance dwindled. Instead, the fired manager produced a 1% outperformance on average. If we combine the costs of the search and selection, of switching managers, and the opportunity costs due to differences in performance, the authors estimate a loss in performance of 5–10%. When institutional investors base their hiring and firing decisions primarily on past performance, the lost performance gap increases further. This research raises the question of whether the current selection and monitoring process has introduced incentives for mandates that are actually counterproductive for the clients' goals. Guyatt and Lukomnik[10] interviewed consultants who indicated they were aware that excessive turnover was potentially harmful to their clients, but were reluctant to change things. Among the main reasons for their actions, they cited factors outside their control, such as volatile markets, hedge fund activity, signals from clients, and short-term incentives. Thus, it seems that trying to agree on mandates with a longer horizon in combination with agreeing on caps for transaction turnover might be a sensible approach here.

The selection and monitoring of mandates is more heavily influenced by behavioral aspects than trustees would like to believe, negatively affecting implementation if ignored. Consider, for example, the situation where the assets are managed outside of the pension fund, which is the case for many funds. The incentive for the manager of the external mandate is outperformance relative to the benchmark, and they can choose between securities A and B. Security A has an expected return in line with the market, and a relatively lower risk than the market. Security B, on the other hand, has a higher expected return than the market, but with considerably more risk. Chances are that the external manager opts for B, as it increases the chance of outperformance and a performance fee, even though the fund would actually be better off with Security A. As a result, all the mandates combined might not add up to the total return/risk goals of the fund. Therefore, this interplay between mandates needs to be designed and monitored carefully.

Similarly to individual investors, the pension fund's attitudes towards risk concerning gains may be quite different from their attitudes towards risk concerning losses.[11] When choosing between several profit opportunities, people tend to be risk averse. On the other hand, when confronted with loss-making alternatives, people often choose the risky alternative, a kind of "double or nothing." Although prospect theory already is a few decades old, a lot of ground still remains to be covered regarding pension fund and institutional investors. We suggest some hypotheses that are based on prospect theory that need to be explored:

- An active manager with positive alpha will become risk averse, locking in their profits, while the opposite is true with negative alpha.[12] In the selection and monitoring of active management, this should be a key element to bear in mind.
- In a similar manner, pension fund trustees, when confronted with underfunding, will increase their risk instead of downscaling it. It would therefore make sense to make the risk budget for a pension fund board rule-based, with an inverse relationship between cover ratio and risk budget. This, however, is still the exception, rather than the rule.

■ In some cases, selecting active mandates might even have a less reputable ulterior motive. By selecting active mandates, investment committees have the opportunity to shift the blame to external managers when results disappoint, diverting attention from the choices that are primarily the remit of the investment committees, such as the strategic asset allocation. Conversely, the investment committee can attribute positive results of external managers to the committee's wise selection skills.[13]

ACTIVE VS. PASSIVE MANAGEMENT

Trustees often depend heavily on external managers for the implementation of their investment plans and are by far the most important principals in the investment industry, awarding active managed mandates worldwide. Moreover, pension funds support the income model of asset managers to a large extent. For the implementation of the investment plan, the choice of active vs. passive management matters for several reasons. First, higher costs of active management potentially are a drawdown from the net return of the fund; in addition, the net returns of active management are difficult to predict, and have disappointed in recent decades; and, finally, high costs suggest a different problem in the implementation: the pension fund does not have the skill or bargaining power to reduce the cost to a level that properly reflects the added value. That is why the active versus passive management decision for implementation is a board decision and should be written down in advance in the investment plan.

The purpose of active management is to generate returns that would exceed those of the reference framework or benchmark, on a risk-adjusted basis. Within the context of implementation, this actually makes the idea of active management fascinating. Most service providers would be content if they delivered what they had promised. In contrast, active managers start out by promising that they will over-deliver.

Trustees have increasingly recognized that, overall, active investment managers are failing to deliver on their oft-repeated "mission" of "beating the market."[14] Basically, most studies confirm that managers have a difficult time beating benchmarks consistently, raising questions about the value of active management for a pension fund. The reasons for this suboptimal performance can be summed up as follows:

a) Fees have a high impact, both in absolute and in relative terms;
b) There are too many smart investment managers who are chasing the same strategy, thus collectively lowering returns;
c) Managers fluctuate in consistency of investment style and performance, but it is not realistically possible to predict when these fluctuations occur.

We will now expand on the aforementioned reasons on the underperformance of active managers.

Reason (a) Trustees are increasingly taking a fresh look at the one variable most have long assumed was too small to matter: fees. The logic is brutal; higher costs lower any form of returns, and for the better part of the 1990s and 2000s, costs have been rising, either directly or indirectly. Fees for active management are usually described as "only," as in "only 1%," for example. But this really means 1% of the assets that the investor already has. So, what the manager offers to deliver is a return on those assets. If equity returns average 7% going forward, that 1% fee is really—if correctly calculated—much higher: roughly 15% of returns. But since index funds deliver the market return at no more than the market level of risk, any economist would say that the true fee for active management is really the incremental fee over and above the very low fee for indexing as a percentage of the incremental risk-adjusted returns.[15] Defined in this rational way, fees for active management are in reality not low. They are actually very high and, surprisingly, until examined closely, average over 100% of the potential additional active returns. The combination of repeatedly disappointing results and the gradual recognition of the very high incremental cost of active management is causing an increasing number of investors to shift larger proportions of their assets to low-cost index funds and exchange-traded funds (ETFs).

Reason (b) The number of players is increasing dramatically. According to the renowned investment author Charles Ellis, active management is not failing because of bad managers, but because too many good managers enter the market. These managers are trained similarly, are searching for similar strategies and, therefore, in aggregate, are reducing the chances of realizing consistent and positive outperformance relative to a benchmark.

Reason (c) There is evidence indicating that managers are mean-reverting over a longer period. This is investment jargon for saying that no investment manager can be good all the time, and that they tend to have ups and downs.

So, is it all bad news for active management? We think not. There are studies that find potential for outperformance. For example, recent studies suggest that highly concentrated portfolios where the investor chooses a limited number of stocks deliver better results as compared to a strategy where the investor invests in all the benchmark stock but slightly changes its weighting. However, it must be kept in mind that these are academically driven studies, in the sense that they identify solutions that require a very specific breed of investors. Either the investment horizon must be very long, or the type of securities needs to have a specific characteristic that requires some stamina (strongly undervalued securities for example).

So, overall, this still does not explain why the choice for active management persists. However, there is a strong movement towards passive investing, which is estimated to constitute 15–20% of investments in the S&P500 and expected to rise significantly in the years ahead. At the same time, the demand for active managers and active investment strategies will clearly not disappear any time soon, nor will the active versus passive debate. This is strange, considering the academic evidence piling up against the former. If active management were a medicine, the federal agency responsible for health and safety would have withdrawn it from the market at an early stage, or at the very least would have asked some very tough questions to the producers of this medicine. Why has this not been done for active management and why is it still a prevalent management choice? We can think of the following reasons:

- Trustees may simply be unaware of this debate. Compared with the investment manager, they lag behind in the buildup of knowledge. When trustees seek training, active management is a standard part of the curriculum, which easily gives the impression that it should be part of the investment process in order to satisfy concepts like prudent investing.
- Willful ignorance. While active management might not produce the required results for other pension funds, the staff and external advisors feel that for their specific fund, all the conditions are met to make it a success. This can be compared to the case of car drivers—surveyed drivers consider themselves to be better than the average driver.[16]
- It's not part of the sales pitch employed on trustees. Investment managers and consultants advising pension funds are reluctant to put forward passive strategies for the simple reason that active strategies allow them to display the full breadth of their knowledge, suggesting that they are on top of things, which in turn comforts trustees. On the other hand, passive strategies are covertly framed as a poor man's choice; "beating the index" is presented as an impossibility, so only trustees with "no vision" would succumb to this option. And the stream of fees towards active management of investments is of course a lot bigger than to passive management.
- Human nature. Maybe trustees are knowledgeable about the whole active management debate, but they still just cannot help themselves. This leans on economic psychology, in which we find the following explanation: investors who try to reduce uncertainty about the decisions they have to make tend to prefer more transactions, increasing the feeling of control. This is a behavioral bias that favors active management.
- Fun and entertainment. Passive investing is considered to be boring; trustees might even consider it detrimental for further steps in their trustee careers. After all, active management is intuitively associated with proactive, intelligible, savvy investors, while it is quite the opposite for passive management investors.

INTERNAL VS. EXTERNAL MANAGEMENT

Smaller pension funds outsource a substantial part of their activities out of necessity, namely, costs, scale, and scope advantages. When a large part of the implementation takes place outside of the pension fund, this involves a key decision for trustees—which parts should be managed externally to the fund, and how does a board make this decision? Given that external investment managers are likely to bring superior professional experience and skills to the pension plan investment decisions, outsourcing asset management should improve investment returns. Moreover, outsourcing offers flexibility by allowing pension funds to change their investment managers more easily in response to poor performance, reducing the chances of an implementation gap. A pension fund is likely to find it more difficult to oust internal managers who produced weak results than to dismiss an external firm for similar shortcomings. Finally, external managers are likely to be better shielded against political pressures to pick state and local companies for investment. A comparison of internally managed pension funds with mutual funds during the late 1970s and early 1980s revealed lower risk-adjusted returns among the former, suggesting that external management has yielded superior results in the past.[17]

Pension funds can outsource their investments while still maintaining control of strategic policymaking by directing the staff of the pension fund. The main advantage of this approach is that the board stays close to the development, monitoring and evaluation of the strategy; the implementation is coordinated by the staff, and delegated to individual asset management. If strategic policymaking also is outsourced, the term *fiduciary management* is used. The asset manager takes over implementation, including at a strategic level, leaving only the underlying policymaking to trustees. While this may seem like a good outsourcing bargain, it is not taking off as spectacularly as asset managers had hoped. This is partly due to the fact that trustees fear that they will be unable to maintain control over the pension fund. Moreover, given that a second layer that needs to be paid is created between the investment manager and the board fees tend to increase. On top of these issues, principal–agent problems can arise, and the formulation of investment beliefs matters more than ever for the governance process. For instance, it is crucial to question whether the external manager can implement the investment beliefs that the trustees hold but are unable to execute internally. Another question could be whether the manager may hold investment beliefs that are in stark contrast with the ones held by the fund.

Larger pension funds tend to internalize investment strategies and build proprietary teams. Their scale often makes this a cost-efficient decision. Scale leads to a governance budget, which makes it possible to effectively build up and control the internal teams, so that hiring and firing can be partially replaced by a continuous improvement process, and that strategies that are more tailor-made to the pension fund's goals can be developed. Research indicates that funds with a higher percentage of assets managed internally do better on an after-cost basis. The cost reduction is the predominant driver of this improvement, more important than the improvement of value added before cost. However, pension funds with large internal organizations suffer other potential drawdowns. They might hold on to failing strategies longer because the board is aware of what the repercussions for employees are when the strategy is terminated. In addition, if the internal investment management organization becomes too large, the board eventually runs the risk of being managed by the investment management organization instead of the other way around.

RELATIONSHIP WITH SUPPLIERS

An often overlooked factor that is important for success in implementing the portfolio is what a board expects from the investment manager beyond merely implementing the investment strategy. Is the board inclined to develop strategic partnerships, or is the board leaning more towards a customer-supplier model? In a strategic partnership model (as shown in Exhibit 7.2), the board holds the view that for the specific mandate,

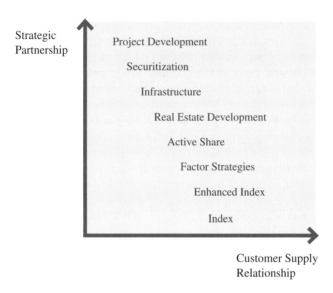

Strategic
Partnership

Project Development

Securitization

Infrastructure

Real Estate Development

Active Share

Factor Strategies

Enhanced Index

Index

Customer Supply
Relationship

EXHIBIT 7.2   Strategic partnership versus customer supply
relationship in the selection process.

the specifications cannot be determined definitively at the beginning, and that shaping
the mandate calls for a collaboration process that is beneficial for the outcome. This
means that the objectives and restrictions for the mandates are more open-ended, and
the selection process is less standardized. When a pension fund ventures into innovative
investment or long-term illiquid strategies, or has an investment solution in mind but
concludes that it can see no optimal implementable strategy, these are typical incentives
for opting for a partnership model.

The customer–supplier relationship lies at the other extreme. There, the pension
fund views the investment strategy as a commodity. Its characteristics are known,
the implementation form is easy to achieve, and the market for these strategies is
mature, keeping down the fees. Equally important, according to this point of view
asset managers are interchangeable, themselves almost becoming a form of commodity.
Pension funds that focus their investment beliefs on the strategic asset allocation rather
than the execution, or that adopt the view that harvesting risk premiums is done best in
a cheap and efficient way, tend to favor a customer-supplier model: a clear defined set
of goals and restrictions, with a uniform selection process. Deciding if the outsourcing
relationship is a partnership or a contract is an evolving process. Boards of pension
funds that are small in size, or have a relatively easy to manage investment process,
will gravitate towards the customer-supplier relationship (choice A in Exhibit 7.3).
This is the most effective utilization of their governance budget. Funds with more
assets, or a more extended investment chain, will spend more time deliberating on
which parts of the investment process should be outsourced, and why. Which choices
add value, and can this value be increased if the step is internalized (choice B in

Approach	Description	Pension Fund
Customer /Supplier	Buying-in investment services "as a commodity."	Defines and uses standardized "building blocks" that are considered market practice. Outcome and process are known.
Coordination/ Outsourcing	Transfer to external suppliers of in-house activities.	Board has framework to assess what/when should be internalized or externalized; focus on SLA Management.
Strategic Partnership	Pooling of facilities to profit from complementary expertise.	Co-creation, board set overall goal, a joint product development/R&D program is set. Process is known, outcome not.

EXHIBIT 7.3 Choices for the fund to make in the relationship with suppliers.

Exhibit 7.3)? Finally, funds that have the size and horizon to consider and tune into developments in the investment industry can take the view that certain developments will lead to new asset classes or strategies, for example regarding climate change or impact investing. Because these strategies have to be developed, the board sets the parameters for this development, and sources partners with whom it can work on their development (choice C in Exhibit 7.3).

BRIDGING THE IMPLEMENTATION GAP

Brilliant investment policies may be plentiful, but getting the good ones implemented can be difficult. Why are some pension funds able to achieve this task better than others? Here, we offer some explanations as to why some funds fare better than others.

- There is a plan. This point is obvious, yet crucial. Implementation often has a clear map, which identifies and maps out the key ingredients that will direct performance. Such ingredients include finances, markets, work environment, operations, people, and partners. The plan has clear deliverables, which the board needs to track implementation.
- There is commitment. A successful implementation plan will have a very visible leader, such as the Chief Executive Officer (CEO), given that they communicate the vision, excitement and behaviors that are necessary for achievement. Everyone in the organization should be engaged in the plan. Performance measurement tools are helpful in providing motivation and allow for follow-up.

- There are resources. To successfully implement a strategy, the right people must be ready to assist with their unique skills and abilities. The structure of management must be communicative and open, with scheduled meetings for updates. Management and technology systems must be in place to track the implementation, and the environment in the workplace must be such that everyone feels comfortable and motivated.
- There is learning from and benchmarking against peers. The board is aware of the best practice for comparable funds, and reviews on a regular basis what it could do to improve its own implementation.
- Pitfalls that occur regularly are addressed in advance. The role and management of costs and internal vs. external management should be discussed in advance by a board, preferably at as high a level as investment beliefs. This should be part of the fund's policy. If these issues have to be discussed at a lower level, it will drain resources and lead to unsatisfying discussion outcomes.
- The board takes, or delegates, clear ownership of the implementation process. Often, a strategic implementation plan is too fuzzy, with little concrete meaning and potential. Boards will often only address the implementation annually, allowing management and employees to become caught up in day-to-day operations and neglect the long-term goals. Another pitfall is not making employees accountable for various aspects of the plan, or powerful enough to make changes authoritatively when necessary.
- Resource-draining activities are minimized, avoided or simply outsourced. The selection of mandates is important, but they can involve huge expenses for the staff; potential investment managers are time-consuming and exhausting to judge. Investment consultants specialize in this process. For any fund, the process is rather agonizing. The hurdle for firing managers should, therefore, be more than just one case of underperformance.

ENDNOTES

1. See for example http://smallbusiness.chron.com/strategic-implementation-5044.html on strategic implementation.
2. See Ghai et al. (2011).
3. APs Third Swedish National Pension Fund, accessed on http://www.ap3.se/en/about-ap3/kostnadseffektiv-forvaltning.
4. See Greifer (2012).
5. See Malhotra and McLeod (1997).
6. See Indro et al. (1999); Collins and Mack (1997).
7. See Jensen (1968); Malkiel (1995); Malhotra and McLeod (1997).
8. See Pfeffer (1998).
9. See Busse et al. (2010).
10. See Guyatt and Lukomnik (2010).
11. See Tversky and Kahneman (1992).
12. See Elton et al. (2003).

13. See Shefrin (2002).
14. While the ex-ante probabilities for funds to beat the market might be low, aggregate active management might add value for financial markets. See for example Pedersen (2018), who argues that active managers in aggregate are able to compensate fees because new shares are issued, repurchased or indices are reconstituted, helping to allocate resources in an economy efficiently.
15. See Ellis (2014).
16. Also known as the better than average effect. See for example Brown (2012).
17. See Berkowitz et al. (1988).

CREATING SCOPE FOR INVESTMENT SOPHISTICATION THROUGH CLARITY OF OBJECTIVES AND STRONG AND TRANSPARENT RISK MANAGEMENT

Background

Arbejdsmarkedets Tillaegspension (ATP), also known as the labor market supplementary pension fund, is a supplementary pension plan of the state-funded first pillar old age pension in Denmark, which was established in 1964. The objective of ATP is to deliver a guaranteed nominal pension. On top of this, it aims to raise pensions in line with inflation by utilizing the returns from its relatively small return-oriented portfolio.

ATP is the largest pension fund in Denmark. As of December 2017, net assets under management were approximately DKK 768 billion ($118 billion),[1] with an annualized rate of return of 8.8% since 1997. The number of members exceeds five million. By 2050, it is estimated that over 50% of Danish pension payments will come from ATP and the state pension. The fund focuses on keeping costs as low as possible. In 2016, total costs amounted to 0.18% of assets.

Challenge

In their 2010 paper, Lars Rohde, at that time Chief Executive Officer (CEO) of ATP, and Chresten Dengsøe, Chief Actuary, discussed several challenges and reforms. They pointed out the pressure being put on the pension fund by (i) increasing life expectancy, (ii) overly high risk levels, (iii) diminishing financial performance as a result of poor financial markets, and (iv) declining interest rates. New financial regulations from the Danish Financial Supervisory Authority (FSA) in 2001 had changed the investment landscape significantly. Mandatory fair value reporting for pension fund liabilities was the hallmark of ATP's reform. Additional reforms involved raising a number of standards for transparency and risk-assessment and management.

The key issue was that ATP had a risk level that was too high to survive a financial crisis, given its solvency. As a consequence, the challenge was "to improve the fund's risk management."

The process

As a response to the new financial regulations imposed by the government, ATP reassessed its investment strategy. This process took several years, and basically encompassed both the investment side and the liability side.

At the heart of each area lies the improvement of risk assessment and the creation of more value. As a result of the FSA regulation in 2001, ATP was at risk of failing the Danish stress test for financial institutions. In essence, this would imply that ATP was too fragile to handle extreme market shocks: "There was a 30% risk on a five-year horizon that ATP would lose its entire reserves."[2]

This is why risk was the most important aspect for ATP to focus on. As a first step, ATP reformulated its objectives, on the one hand by guaranteeing a nominal pension and, on the other, by focusing on maximizing returns. As a consequence, ATP split its asset portfolio into a hedging portfolio, and a return-seeking investment portfolio. The former is designed to deliver a guaranteed nominal pension, while the latter is focused on generating supplementary returns that can provide for inflation linking. Of the premiums paid to the fund, 80% is invested in the liability hedging portfolio and 20% in the return-seeking portfolio.

Secondly, ATP decided to enhance short-term risk management in the return-seeking portfolio by means of a "dynamic risk budget." This approach was intended to address the risk of losses. Essentially, ATP operates in a predefined risk tolerance range ("traffic light system") that is dependent on its solvency. When ATP reaches the lower barrier of risk tolerance, it will increase risk, while at the upper barrier it will reduce risk until it is at a responsible and bearable level for the members of the fund. Alongside generating returns, ATP hedges tail risks. This is necessary because ATP has no sponsor.[3] The fund's focus on risk elimination consequently helped ATP during the financial crisis. The main reason was that ATP had purchased insurance against extreme tail events cheaply, thereby limiting risk and portfolio loss.

Furthermore, ATP's investment strategy in its return-seeking portfolio is based on a risk factor approach: "The idea is that all investments consist of a number of basic building blocks—factors—which can be combined in various ways to achieve an investment portfolio with the desired risk profile."[4] The strategic asset allocation of the return portfolio in 2016 was listed as 49% based on the equity factor, 22% based on the interest rate factor, 11% inflation and the remaining 18% on other factors. By looking at all investments—both private and public—through the same factor approach, ATP is able to allocate risk where it is rewarded the most.

The outcome

By creating very strong mission and objectives and a strong process and risk management orientation, both in a very transparent and controlled way, ATP has built a sustainable long-term framework. Because the risk is so well and transparently contained, the Investment Management Organization can develop and maintain a highly sophisticated investment strategy within its boundaries. This helps build and maintain a competitive advantage, both because of the sophistication (no need for the board to understand all the details) and the agility that this provides.

Lessons for Achieving Investment Excellence

- ATP dared to be radically different from other pension funds, based on a changing regulatory context and disappointing results. This resulted in a strong, marked-to-market liability-oriented and risk-management-oriented investment framework.

■ ATP has an extremely clear mission and objectives. In combination with a transparent short-term oriented risk framework, a highly sustainable setup is created.

■ The combination of clear objectives and strong risk management makes it possible for the supervisory board to delegate the design and implementation of the investment policy to the Investment Management Organization.

■ And this in its turn makes it possible for the investment management organization to create and maintain a highly sophisticated investment approach.

ENDNOTES

1. See ATP's annual report of 2017.
2. See Rohde and Dengsøe (2010).
3. See Rajkumar and Dorfman (2011).
4. See ATP's annual report of 2016.

CHAPTER 8

Building the Investment Portfolio

Key Take Aways

- Building the investment portfolio presents a structured approach to organizing and allocating investment and investment strategies for the pensions fund's whole balance sheet.

- The trustees' approach to portfolio construction should be as unbiased as possible:
  - Start analyses with the least amount of diversification, creating portfolios with just a few main assets to capture the essence of diversification so as not to be distracted by the characteristics of the many different categories. Equities, bonds and real estate are sufficient.
  - Analyze under which economic and financial scenarios this portfolio does or does not hold up.
  - Decide whether you are comfortable with the extreme scenarios in which diversification breaks down, and if not, whether additional measures are needed.
  - Commit to rebalancing discipline to combat the behavioral biases in the board when the going gets tough.

- Portfolio construction hinges on a few key assumptions: capital market assumptions, the method of portfolio construction, and how diversification is shaped. Boards should avoid wasting energy trying to come up with "better" capital market assumptions.

This chapter will guide the reader through the process of building an investment portfolio. The investment portfolio represents the translation of the pension fund's financial objectives into an investable solution for the coming period that can realistically be implemented. While investment managers and strategists may present this process as highly sophisticated, complicated, and requiring unique expertise, from the viewpoint of a trustee the process can be broken down into a limited number of steps, allowing the board to focus on the questions that matter.

This chapter discusses the nature of a good investment portfolio, what the roles of the stakeholders are in determining the portfolio, how to choose a portfolio that achieves the fund's goals, and the main assumptions to be aware of.

Creating the investment portfolio involves seven steps, the starting point being: (i) the investment objective itself, and ensuring it is clearly formulated and realizable. Next, determining the investable universe and how it is implemented and evaluated, namely: (ii) the allocation to a number of asset classes, (iii) a description of the way the asset classes should be implemented (subcategories and investment styles are determined here), and (iv) a set of benchmarks to guide implementation and provide a basis for evaluation. The next steps shape the implementation of the portfolio: (v) a rebalancing procedure between the assets is determined, (vi) a specification of the objectives for the fiduciary or investment manager is drawn up, often in the form of an outperformance target, and (vii) a risk budget determined, specifying the degrees of freedom that the investment manager has around the benchmark. The board writes down the steps in a strategic investment plan. This, in turn, forms the basis for the formal mandate that is given by the board to the investment management organization.

We will start with a brief paragraph on the question of who has ownership of which decision. This is important, because in this part of this investment process there is an intensive interaction between the board investment committee and the organization taking the responsibility for implementing the plan.

FRAMEWORK FOR THE INVESTMENT PORTFOLIO

Portfolio construction can only take place within the frame of the choices that the board has previously made. Chapter 6 discussed the investment policy statement (IPS) as an important document for trustees for shaping and directing the investment management process. Recalling the main elements of an IPS, we can distinguish those that form the framework for the investment portfolio—any portfolio should be in line with, and adhere to, the beliefs, risk appetite and strategy; and objectives that the board has established.

- *Purpose, mission, strategy, objectives.* The strategic mission of the investments: goals, objectives, and constraints. The fund's objectives are usually formulated in terms of required or expected return (see Chapter 3);
- *Risk appetite.* The level of risk tolerance and investment risk that may be incurred in realizing the return and the investment horizon required (see Chapter 4);
- *Beliefs.* The core investment beliefs and the resulting investment "philosophy" codify guidance as to how the portfolio will be managed[1] (see Chapter 5).

If the board has not made these choices beforehand, or if these choices are only more or less implicit, then portfolio construction and implementation will lead to suboptimal results, and will generally leave a board rudderless. Without clear objectives, the board might be more interested in comparing results with other pension funds than discussing whether its own goals are being realized. Without a clear, well-thought-out and communicated risk appetite, the board is doomed to make detrimental choices during financial crises. Without a strong set of beliefs, the choice of investment styles will be based on the preferences of the asset managers and not necessarily on those of the participants.

Within the framework of strategy, objectives, risk appetite and beliefs, portfolio construction then consists of a number of well-defined steps:

- *Definition and review of the investment objective.* From an implementation perspective, is the objective sufficiently clear, and can it be translated into investment mandates? From a policy perspective, have circumstances changed in such a way that the objectives have to be revised?
- *Number of asset classes.* The asset-mix ranges of the portfolio's various asset classes.
- *Implementation.* The asset classes for inclusion, described at a more granular level as investment strategies and investment style(s). For example, "equities" is a broad brush. In this example, you would specify: developed market equities, United States, passive.
- *Objective.* A specification of the objective for the fiduciary or investment manager, often in the form of an outperformance target.
- *Benchmarks.* A set of benchmarks that guide the implementation and will also be used as a basis for judging the outcomes.
- *Risk budget.* These detail the degrees of freedom that the (fiduciary) manager has around the benchmark.
- *Rebalancing.* Guidelines and methodology for rebalancing the portfolio.
- *Evaluation.* Performance measures and benchmarks to be used in performance evaluation.
- *Schedule for monitoring and evaluation.* The schedule for the monitoring and review of investment performance as well as the IPS itself. The IPS should be reviewed on a regular basis to ensure that it remains consistent with the fund's circumstances. An IPS is usually reviewed every three years, with interim reviews added when material changes occur in objective, time horizon, or other fund characteristics.

The process of building the investment portfolio is usually spread out throughout the year, with three milestones that are relevant for the board:

Milestone 1: Evaluation and exploration. A scan of the external environment is carried out to check whether the major assumptions behind the portfolio construction still hold. Any investment portfolio is based on a limited set of assumptions. For example, at the time of writing, they might be: interest rates are nudging towards a higher average rate, equities risk will be rewarded, and due to economic circumstances, default rates in the real economy remain low, suggesting a stable credit spread. The scan questions whether these assumptions still hold, and whether the board can identify new risks or developments that would dramatically alter the validity of these assumptions. In common practice, several economic scenarios are generated to challenge the current assumptions. These scenarios need not be quantitative in nature. Reading up on the literature and sharing experiences on how assets performed in stagflation, depression, or growth periods form a valuable basis for discussion. These analyses lead to a set of recommendations, for example how to reduce excessive exposure to one asset class, or when to consider adding a new asset class. The board collectively decides which recommendation to follow.

In parallel, the internal performance of the investment portfolio is evaluated. Using longer data series, trends can be identified. Investment strategies and asset classes of which the performances are below expectations are singled out. For the investment strategies, the analysis first considers the selection within the asset classes. If the poor results are attributed to this, one must ask whether the investment style still make sense, whether the drivers are still in place, and whether the manager simply is not performing or whether it is the investment style itself that is losing its rationale and attraction. On a broader level, the asset classes themselves are evaluated. Do the capital market expectations for the different asset classes still justify keeping them within the portfolio, or are new asset types becoming more attractive and should they be included in the portfolio? These analyses lead to a set of recommendations to maintain or change the number of asset classes and their form of implementation. Here too, the board ultimately decides which recommendations to follow.

Milestone 2: Analyses. Given the new set of asset classes and investment styles, various portfolios are generated, all of which fit within the framework of the fund in terms of objectives, risk appetite and goals. The analyses therefore focus on the difference in expected return and risk compared to the current portfolio. If the difference is too small, then these portfolios are eliminated from the choice set. The remaining portfolios are scrutinized for other factors. First, does the expected improvement in return and risk outweigh the transition costs? Second, which portfolios disproportionally increase the claim on the time and resources of the board (the so-called governance budget)? Finally, the board may consider further factors. For example, do the potential portfolios improve the environmental, social and governance (ESG) goals of the fund?

Milestone 3: Decision and implementation. The board decides on the definitive portfolio. Several options exist for doing so, depending on the board's preferences:

Approach 1: Create a new portfolio from the ground up. Suppose the fund had the assets invested solely in cash, what would the portfolio look like if the board had the opportunity to create a new portfolio without having to consider existing assets? The board states its preferences and, based on these, the optimal portfolio is created by the investment management organization. Next, the board does take the existing portfolio into account, and works out a transition path from the current to the optimal one. Illiquid and alternative assets cannot be bought or sold easily, so the fund develops a multiyear transition path to smooth costs.

Approach 2: Treat the existing portfolio as the best one available, unless a better alternative presents itself. The relevant potential portfolios are compared to the current one, and the board decides whether the incremental changes are worth the effort. This makes for a straightforward and expeditious decision process: the board should state its preferences beforehand, i.e. which factors it considers most important, and a preferred portfolio can then be agreed upon. But there are a few pitfalls to consider. First, the focus is on incremental differences. The current portfolio serves as the baseline, and it is easy to forget to take a critical look at the baseline itself: are viable alternatives being ignored because we are too comfortable with the choices in the current portfolio? In line with this, the board is naturally inclined to prefer and choose the asset allocation it is familiar with. Adding a new asset category has a big obstacle to overcome, namely, the attitude dictating that if the current mix works fine, there is no need to change it.

Approach 3: Blind-test new portfolios. The third approach overcomes several behavioral pitfalls, increasing objectivity. Why not make the possible portfolios anonymous, not listing the assets, but only the expected return, risk and other key measures? In this approach, the staff develops a number of portfolios that all fit within the framework of the fund in terms of objectives, risk appetite and goals. The discussion is then framed in an alternative way: should we, given the current cover ratio and expected financial environment, choose a portfolio with more or less investment risk? And zooming in on investment risk, should we choose a portfolio with less volatility in normal periods but more shortfalls in extreme periods, or vice versa? Once the number of portfolios is narrowed down by this discussion, the underlying asset allocation is shown, allowing the board to consider implementation issues (costs, complexity) before making the final decision. The main advantage of this strategy is that the decisions are based on a relevant measure: the amount of investment. Preferences and decisions are not biased due to personal likes or dislikes in terms of asset classes. However, it requires a board that knows how to interpret statistical measures such as volatility. Chapter 4 argued that this is a challenge, even for seasoned trustees. Such approaches need to be well prepared in advance.

Whichever approach the board chooses to determine the portfolio, it is best for it to discuss the choice in advance, including identifying pitfalls and suggesting measures to avoid them. Finally, the board decides on the definitive portfolio, adding the requirement of assurances that implementation will be consistent, and that potential return/risk losses due to an implementation gap will be mitigated. This is then written down in the IPS, which can be used to amend the mandate for the investment management organization.

THE BOARD'S ROLE IN PORTFOLIO CONSTRUCTION

The board is responsible for developing the investment policy. The task for the board is to maintain an overview of the different steps, how they interact, and what the role of the board members should be. Board members can easily succumb to the temptation of forming pet theories about asset classes, interest rates, or investment opportunities. It may be true to say that this shows involvement in the subjects that the board has to deal

Framework for the Investment Portfolio	Board's Focus for the Investment Policy
Purpose, mission, strategy, objectives. The strategic mission of the investments: goals, objectives, and constraints. The fund's objectives are usually formulated in terms of required or expected return.	Not up for discussion when developing the investment policy.
Risk appetite. The level of risk tolerance and investment risk that may be incurred to realize the return, and the investment horizon required.	
Beliefs. The core investment beliefs, and the resulting investment "philosophy" codify guidance as to how the portfolio will be managed.	Is the (changes in) investment policy in line with the investment beliefs?
Portfolio construction. Any considerations to be taken into account in developing the strategic asset allocation.	How does the board decide on a portfolio (for example, blind testing versus the existing portfolio)?

EXHIBIT 8.1   Framework for the investment portfolio and the board's focus.

with. But it is not the role of a board to outsmart the financial analysts or investment strategists. What the board can do, however, is challenge their assumptions to test the robustness of the analysis and subsequent recommendations. Below we again review the steps in the IPS, but now with the addition of the specific question: what is the focus for the trustee? Exhibit 8.1 below shows the factors on which the framework of the investment portfolio rests, along with the focus for the trustees.

Building an investment portfolio requires some decisions and steps. What these steps are and what the focus for the trustee should be are shown in Exhibit 8.2.

What Is a Good Investment Portfolio?

A board of trustees is responsible for developing an investment plan that is the best possible option for realizing the fund's goals, given constraints on the amount of risk, horizon, liquidity, and any other constraints. The previous discussion has focused on the steps needed for portfolio construction, which run the risk of overshadowing the real purpose of the process for a board. What exactly, then, is the best possible investment portfolio? We provide you with a list of criteria (also shown in Exhibit 8.3) for judging the quality of a portfolio and for comparing, scoring, or ranking the quality of different portfolios.

Building the Investment Portfolio	Trustees' Focus for the Investment Policy
Number of Asset Classes. The asset mix range of the portfolio's various asset classes.	• Do any proposed changes in asset classes really add to return/risk profile and goals of the fund? • Do we have governance budget available for the proposed changes in asset classes?
Implementation. The asset classes to be included, defined on a more specific level as investment strategies and investment style(s).	• Do we strike the right balance? • What level of specifying assets and instruments will provide a clear picture of the expected diversification?
Objective. A specification of the objective for the fiduciary or investment manager, often in the form of an outperformance target.	• Are the objectives challenging enough? • Are they in line with existing evidence on manager selection and are we avoiding awarding mandates that have a slim chance of succeeding?
Benchmarks. A set of benchmarks that guide the implementation and will also be used as a starting point for judging the outcomes.	• Are the benchmarks transparent – set by the fund, and not by the manager? • Are they challenging enough for active managers? • Does the aggregate of benchmarks adequately represent the overall expected return/risk trade-off?
Risk budget, detailing the degrees of freedom that the (fiduciary) manager has around the benchmark.	• Does the aggregate of risk budgets adequately represent the overall (active) risk of the fund? • Is the risk budget adequate enough for each investment style?
Rebalancing. Guidelines and methodology for rebalancing the portfolio.	• Is the board aware of the discipline needed to execute rebalancing? • Have we thought through under which circumstances rebalancing will be most challenging, and how we should act?
Evaluation. Performance measures and benchmarks to be used in performance evaluation.	• Can the performance measures be broken down in such a way that we can monitor the main drivers and choices of the investment plan?
Schedule for monitoring and evaluation. The schedule for review of investment performance as well as the IPS itself.	• Do we review the IPS on a regular basis to ensure that it remains consistent with the fund's circumstances? • Do we have a shared understanding of what material changes might occur that would lead the board to commission a review of objective, time horizon, or other fund characteristics?

EXHIBIT 8.2 Building the investment portfolio and the board's focus.

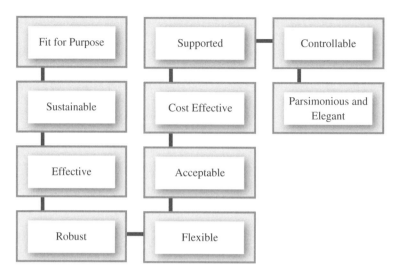

EXHIBIT 8.3 Criteria for scoring the quality of a portfolio.

A good portfolio will help the board:

- Realize the primary investment objective over the relevant horizon with a high level of probability (*fit for purpose*). Is there a high level of probability that the portfolio will realize the primary investment objective over the relevant horizon? Is it fit for purpose? If this is not the case, it is time to rethink either the objective or the portfolio. This, for example, led the Norwegian Fund to increase its equity exposure in order to generate the long-term returns it targets.
- Realize potential secondary objectives such as environmental, societal, or governance goals (*sustainable*). There may or may not be other investment objectives. For example, the South African pension fund Government Employees Pension Fund (GEPF) has the dual objective of realizing return as well as contributing to the economic growth of the local economy.
- Do all of this at the lowest possible initial investment (*effective*). Is the return as high as possible within the set risk appetite; is the risk budget fully utilized? If the risk budget is not fully utilized, the fund might be setting an ineffective premium rate, i.e. charging a higher amount than necessary.
- Be robust in as many circumstances as possible (*robust*). Will the portfolio be robust in different economic and financial scenarios? Many risk premiums simply need time to be earned. It does not make sense to have an investment plan with a high allocation to equities, requiring a long period to earn the premiums, and then change the asset allocation in just a few years. So from the start, the number of assets and resulting asset allocation in the investment plan should be based not on one, but on a number of different scenarios.

- Have as much flexibility as possible for adapting when needed (*flexible*). Is the investment plan flexible over a relatively short term? If an investment plan advises changes in equities and bonds, these are usually easily implementable within a few months. But if a large part of the plan is based on shifts to illiquid assets over a longer period, then the board really needs to discuss how to commit itself to such future investment plans.
- Be based on a shared understanding of the drivers (*acceptable*). Is the investment plan clear about the main drivers and choices in the investment plan? What are the risk premiums, the amount of risk that is accepted to earn those premiums, the investment styles, and the horizon? If the board does not have a shared understanding of the main drivers, new board and committee members will challenge and rethink these drivers over and over again, especially in case of disappointing results. This reduces the horizon of the investment plan considerably.
- Involve the lowest possible cost (*cost effective*). Costs (meaning all costs, visible and less invisible) are always hotly debated. One school of thought argues that it is the net result that counts. Another school argues that costs are a factor that can be managed, and you should always work on cost efficiency because higher-than-necessary cost could be considered misspending the participants' premiums. This is the school we are in. There is quite a lot of evidence to substantiate the view that managing for lower cost is one of the most effective ways to increase the long-term return.[2]
- Have the continued support of the board and any other critical stakeholders to stay the course when things don't work out as planned in the short term (*supported*). Will the board uphold the investment plan even when things go sour? Suppose there is a period of financial turmoil: diversification between equities and bonds will probably work (equities go down, bonds go up) but all the other assets will move more or less in the same direction—downwards. In other words, every now and then, in practice, the quantitative assumptions about correlation, diversification and investment styles fail. Would a board still consider the investment plan to be robust, even if these assumptions fail?
- Be set out in the most transparent, most understandable, and most controlled way possible (*controllable*). Is the board able to monitor the main choices in the investment plan? The drivers of the investment plan should be attributable and visible in monitoring and reporting. If the potential success of the investment plan hinges on the credit spread and this is not reported, trustees cannot monitor or evaluate their own choices.
- Take the simplest, most elegant form in the most transparent, most understandable, and most controlled way possible ("*parsimonious and elegant*"). Is the portfolio as simple as possible, given the objective? Can it be made simpler? Often, complexity comes at a great cost, reducing transparency, oversight and understanding. *Ceteris paribus*, simple is better than complex.

When actually scoring the quality of a portfolio, it is a good idea to assign a weight to each of the criteria, thus helping the board to develop the portfolio that best meets its expectations, as well as providing a framework for a disciplined evaluation of it. For example, for some boards the ease of controlling a portfolio may have a high weighting, whereas other boards might give maximum weight to realizing the primary investment objective.

Among the criteria, there are definitely a lot of trade-offs that a board must consider. For example, trustees might expect to be able to generate another 0.5% annual expected returns at the "cost" of carrying out a number of complex and hard-to-control investments.

CAPITAL MARKET ASSUMPTIONS

Boards are not in the business of predicting financial markets or economies. Yet portfolio construction hinges largely on a small set of assumptions, particularly capital market expectations. Questions ensue such as "What will we earn on equities in the coming period, and is it enough to compensate for the investment risk that we have to incur? And what will interest rates do?" These questions are at the core of the fundamental assumption in financial theory on the trade-off between risk and return (see Chapter 4). Capital Market Assumptions (CMAs) are used by investors and advisors around the world to guide their strategic asset allocation and set realistic risk and return expectations over different time frames. These assumptions help investors formulate solutions aligned with their specific investment needs. They cover expected (excess) return, risk, and correlation over different horizons. A coherent set of CMAs is an economic scenario. It is crucial to generate different scenarios that challenge the achievement of the goals or force trustees to think of the unthinkable.

Determining the CMAs for a broad group of asset classes thus involves analyzing the interaction of risk, return, and correlation. In order to capture these interactions, we use what economists call an "equilibrium model." Equilibrium describes a situation in which all expected asset returns are a fair reflection of their risk and correlations and does not refer to any specific time horizon. What it means in practice is that for asset classes that are reasonably correlated with one another, expected returns in excess of cash are approximately proportional to risk, but for asset classes that exhibit low correlations, expected returns can be a bit lower than from the proportional application of risk.

CMAs can be developed in different ways. The most frequently used approach is to break the CMA down into different components. For example:[3]

$$\text{Equity} = \text{risk free rate} + \text{real earnings growth} + \text{dividend growth}$$
$$+ \text{break-even inflation} + \text{repricing}$$

Similarly, a bond is broken down into its components:

$$\text{Bond} = \text{risk free rate} + \text{term premium} + \text{break-even inflation}$$
$$+ \text{credit spread} + \text{liquidity}$$

Capital market expectations may seem like a pretty objective exercise, but we should not be fooled. If we estimate the expected risk-free rate and the term premium, we are building up insights into expected returns. However, we also know that the level, or level of change, of the risk-free rate is correlated to the level, or level of change, of the term premium. Developing CMAs requires an intertwined choice: determining the economic and financial scenario on which the CMA is based, and the horizon that is required. Estimation with a high risk-free rate and low term premium is historically consistent with a period in which central banks have been active in raising interest rates to slow down expected inflation.

Diversification

Diversification is a much-used term within pension funds. Two questions are of importance for trustees. First, do the trustees share the same notion as to what diversification means for the fund? Secondly, do the assets chosen for diversification stand the test of time, are some of them perhaps only temporarily attractive, or are they truly new and do they diversify risk premiums?

Pension funds are clearly fond of diversification. Since 2002, they have ventured into credits, emerging markets equity, infrastructure, hedge funds, and private equity, while in recent years factor investing or impact investments have experienced an upswing in investment portfolios. Diversification, discussed in Chapter 4, can have different meanings to different people. Trustees should raise the question of which purpose or combination of purposes is relevant to their fund, as each approach leads to a different portfolio:

Diversify to reduce overall portfolio risk. Whenever two imperfectly correlated assets are placed in a portfolio, there is an opportunity to earn a greater return at the same risk, or earn the same return at a lower risk. The correlation between the new asset and the assets in the portfolio should reflect a sufficiently different pattern of returns; and the allocation of the new asset should be sizeable enough to matter.

Diversify to hedge against adverse asset pricing shocks. If there are extreme price movements in the financial markets, will the new asset's lack of correlation disappear and is diversification then be suspended? Or does the new asset provide a really new, independent economic source of return that is ex-ante unlikely to move in step with the other assets? This seems like a simple question, but it is actually hard to answer. For example, research shows that country equity markets offer less diversification in times of falling markets than in times of rising markets. The same is true for global industry returns, individual stocks, hedge fund returns, international bonds, etc. Similarly, international diversification seems to work during good times, when it is least needed, but to disappear during falling markets, when it is most needed. Maybe the only light beacon here is that asset correlation within countries decreases during periods of market turbulence.[4]

Diversify to achieve high absolute and risk-adjusted returns. Is the new combination of assets able to increase outcome relative to the major asset classes in the portfolio? The appropriate measure to use is the Sharpe ratio, measuring the excess return above the risk-free rate per unit of risk.[5]

Diversify to hedge against unexpected inflation or deflation. Conventional wisdom has held that assets such as real estate and long-term bonds hedge against inflation. However, with the exception of inflation-linked bonds, many assets have a complicated relationship with inflation. Inflation elicits differing responses; real estate contracts can have a standard clause in which rents are corrected for inflation, creating an adequate inflation hedge. Many assets by definition provide a partial inflation hedge; inflation may raise future cash flows, but this is partially offset, as inflation also raises the nominal interest rate to discount the cash flows, eroding the overall valuation. In addition, the fact that there is a historical correlation with inflation is not sufficient reason to extrapolate into the future. Unforeseen consequences can always affect the future. For example, thanks to the enormous success of Wal-Mart, few retail chains were able to pass on increased inflation to customers; Wal-Mart alone is credited with reducing inflation in the United States by one percentage point per year in the 1990s.[6]

Reflect the overall investment universe. A portfolio with 50% equities and 50% bonds might be called a balanced portfolio, but it is definitely not a reflection of the investment universe. This implies—in theory—that any portfolio that does not include private equity for example is making an implicit bet that a portfolio without private equity yields better returns.

Diversify to deliver a stable stream of cash flows to the investor. Pension funds are greatly concerned with liquidity, a major concern being the creation of a stream of cash flows that to a large degree offsets the pension payments to be made. Investments with strong cash flows provide a natural hedge against pension liabilities, which are basically a set of guaranteed future cash payouts.

Diversify to capture the underlying economic and financial factors that drive asset returns. Taking a quantitative approach, equities or bonds are not viewed as issued by companies, but rather as representing a bundle of risk factors. According to this view, "decomposing" these assets into risk factors allows the investor to diversify far more effectively.

How many assets are needed for diversification? Having come to a common understanding of diversification, do the assets chosen for diversification stand the test of time, should the set be expanded, or are just a few assets sufficient for effective diversification? In allocating the assets, regulators expect the trustee to diversify the holdings and to exercise prudence. In other words, trustees should not bet the house on anything too risky in the portfolio.[7] However, views on diversification have changed dramatically in the past decades. Pension funds in the 1970s were content with bonds and real estate, assets that were considered to be "safe." But returns were low, so funds progressively moved into equities, commercial property, foreign securities, and derivatives. New technology made this possible. In the 1990s, the pension fund industry experienced a makeover when the combination of Asset Liability Management (ALM) techniques, deregulation, and portfolio optimization approaches gained ground, widening the scope of assets to invest in. The risks were higher, but so were the rewards. Additionally, higher returns brought down the relative costs of running the fund.

In hindsight, it appears that only a limited number of strategies break through and help to diversify effectively. In other words, trustees should quiz their investment managers and advisors critically, because introducing new strategies does not necessarily achieve diversification. Alternative investment strategies have suffered from two problems. First, the success of many new strategies was boosted by the same factors: low interest rates and robust economic growth. This, in turn, encouraged investors to use leverage to enhance returns. Some alternative investments share more factors; private equity gives investors exposure to the same kind of risk as publicly quoted equity, albeit with added leverage. When prospects deteriorated, investors were forced to sell all those asset classes simultaneously. Secondly, some of the asset classes are rather small. This illiquidity is attractive since it offers higher returns. As more investors get involved, the market becomes more liquid, and the higher return is eroded. However, when everyone tries to sell, illiquidity rears its ugly head again—there are no buyers to be found and prices tumble. This is very unpleasant when pension funds have to value their investment at market value. Still, investment managers increasingly look to add new—alternative—investments to bolster diversification advantages,[8] which can mitigate these risks to a large extent. However, there is no point in adding new strategies if the investment does not offer a genuinely different source of return, or if the asset is already overvalued. In other words, the bar for new investments to count as a true "diversifier" has been raised substantially, and if these investments are true diversifiers, their relative size in the investment portfolio will be limited.

Along with the search for alternative investments as a source of diversification, factor investing has gained traction, viewed by some as a replacement for the current approach to diversification. Interest in factor investing started with the Ang, Goetzmann and Schaeffer study,[9] commissioned to investigate why active returns of the Norwegian Fund were disappointing. A major finding was that a large share of active returns could be attributed to systematic factors; five years later, major pension funds such as the Alaska Endowment Fund, the Dutch PFZW or the Danish Arbejdsmarkedets TillægsPension (ATP) all implemented a form of factor investing. From the outset, it seemed like a sensible development. Asset returns can be attributed to a few distinct underlying factors such as macroeconomic factors, firm attributes or style factors, with these factors representing sources of systematic risk and return. This approach aims at providing a relatively precisely defined exposure to factors that may explain differences in asset returns and, to a large degree, the excess returns of actively managed portfolios. The factor approach creates the opportunity to construct portfolios with asset selection based on the knowledge of underlying factors, or even design portfolios using factors rather than assets.[10] Within this factor framework, which is rooted in the Asset Pricing Theory (APT) developed in the late 1970s, any asset can be viewed as a bundle of factors that reflect different risks and rewards. Therefore, it makes perfect sense to focus on these factors, allowing investors to identify them and understand what really drives asset returns. These insights help to develop portfolios that realize the required risk profile not only before, but also during, volatile periods.

Rebalancing

Rebalancing is regarded as a technical component of implementing an investment portfolio plan, where portfolio weights are adjusted in line with the risk appetite of the fund. This policy details when and how the policy portfolio is adjusted in line with changes in the cover ratio or financial markets, how to adjust the assets to the weights of the strategic benchmark portfolio, and whether the rebalancing is done on a frequent regular basis or based on specific triggers.

Rebalancing on the basis of constant policy weights represents one possibility. At the other extreme, the fund can have a solvency program in place, which adjusts the level of policy weights depending on the amount of downside risk the fund is willing to accept given the funding ratio and financial market volatility. Similarly, the solvency program adjusts the level of policy weights depending on how close the fund is to achieving its long-term goals. Sometimes, funds allocate part of the bandwidth around policy weights to TAA (tactical asset allocation), which involves making short-term adjustments to asset-class weights based on short-term expected relative performance among asset classes. The assumption is that investors can take into account short-term opportunities with the aim of achieving the best performance for the portfolio, bearing in mind the level of risk defined.

At times, a portfolio's actual asset allocation may purposefully and temporarily differ from the strategic asset allocation. For example, the asset allocation might change to reflect a pension fund's current circumstances when these are different from normal. The temporary allocation may remain in place until circumstances return to those described in the investment policy and reflected in the strategic asset allocation. If the changed circumstances become permanent, the manager must update the investor's IPS, and the temporary asset allocation plan will effectively become the new strategic asset allocation. TAA also results in divergence from the strategic asset allocation, and responds to changes in short-term capital market expectations rather than to investor circumstances.

ENDNOTES

1. See Terhaar (2010).
2. See, for example, studies based on the Cost Effectiveness Measurement (CEM) Database.
3. See Illmanen (2011).
4. See Chua et al. (2009).
5. See Sharpe (1994).
6. See Basker (2005).
7. See Ellison and Jolly (2008, p. 25).
8. See Hudson-Wilson et al. (2003).
9. See Ang et al. (2009).
10. See Ilmanen and Kizer (2012).

Case Study—OTPP

ONTARIO TEACHERS' IS THE FUND WITH WHICH THE "CANADIAN MODEL" FOR PENSION FUNDS STARTED. THIS HAS INSPIRED PENSION FUNDS IN CANADA AND GLOBALLY. AT ITS CORE LIES A STRONG GOVERNANCE MODEL AND THE CLEAR CONVICTION THAT A PENSION PLAN SHOULD BE RUN LIKE A BUSINESS

Background

Ontario Teachers' Pension Plan (OTPP) is the pension plan for the teachers in the Ontario province of Canada. It was founded in 1990. Its assets under management amount to CAD$190 billion (equivalent of US$147 billion) in December 2017.[1] It is built on four pillars: a clear mission, a strong and independent governance, the vision to manage the fund like a company and the policy to hire and retain top talent.

In practice, there are a number of key characteristics that to a large extent describe both Ontario Teachers' and more generically a number of other large Canadian pension plans:

- A return orientation, with emphasis on generating high and sustainable returns;
- Active investing with an entrepreneurial mind-set;
- A tendency to internalize the investments;
- A large of allocation to private assets (more than 40%).

Ontario Teachers' is a defined benefit plan. It aims to index its pensions. In recent years, flexibility in the indexation, *conditional indexation*, has been introduced as a way to cope with the reduced flexibility of the fund because of its increasing maturity. A sign of this increasing maturity is that net pension payments of the fund already exceed the premiums with almost a factor of 2:1. As compared to the start of the fund in 1990, the ratio of active members vs. pensioners has shrunk from 4:1 to 1:1 and the expected years on pension increased from 25 to 32. This puts much pressure on the return-generating capacity of the plan.

The challenge

Two challenges are central to Ontario Teachers': creating and maintaining a strong board, and generating the strong investment returns they need to maintain the pension promise.

The board has 11 members who are appointed by the sponsors of the fund, the Ontario Teachers Federation and the government of the Ontario Province. The board oversees the management of the fund, for which Chief Executive Officer (CEO) Ron Mock is responsible. Importantly, board members have strong professional backgrounds in finance and governance. Typically, they come from accounting, actuarial sciences, banking, the corporate sector, economics, education, and investment management. The investment committee consists of all the board members, thereby emphasizing the enormous interest Teachers' attaches to the investment part of the fund.

The process

In terms of delegation by the board to the management, the plan adopted the "OneTeachers Strategy"[2] in 2017. The core of this is that the board specifies a long-term return target, which fits the pension promise and is realistic. This target stands at around a 4% real return. This is the objective the investment management organization adopts. It has to be realized on a four-year rolling horizon within a risk budget. Importantly, the OneTeachers' Strategy specifies an absolute, and not a benchmark relative investment goal. In this way, the fund is agnostic about whether the return comes from harvesting from benchmarks (beta) or from benchmark-relative performance (alpha). This is a crucial part in the delegation process by the board: it creates enormous degrees of freedom and, therefore, responsibility for the management team. At the same time, this means that the board investment committee has to be highly qualified in order to be able to judge and support the management team and the investment strategy. This is all the more true in a bad period, when it would be easy for the board to blame the management and create an unsafe environment in which it would be difficult to stay the course for the long term.

As said, internalization of the investment management is an important ingredient of the approach of Teachers'—both because of cost reduction reasons, especially in the private assets, and of the possibility to closely control the quality. Some 80% of the portfolio is managed internally. The choice for internal or external management is made within the investment organization. External management predominantly exists in hedge funds, public equities, and private equity funds.[3] In private equity, partnerships are the way to get access to markets in a high quality way where Teachers' does not have the network or the know-how to invest directly. Teachers' has these so called "strategic relationships" with many of the leading global private equity firms. In addition, in public equity markets they partner up for the longer with high added value external managers. There is even a specific department for searching and managing partnerships.

The core contributor to the long-term success of the Teachers' is their large and extremely successful allocation to private assets, predominantly real estate, infrastructure, and private equity. In order to be successful on the ground, especially in private assets, Teachers' has opened offices in London and Hong Kong, so as to build strategic relationships and identify investment opportunities.

The outcome

To zoom in on private equity, the Private Capital Group invests directly in private companies, either on its own, with partners, or indirectly through private equity funds. The group generates added value to the companies in the portfolio—and thereby to the plan—by helping with their long-term strategic planning, the creation of high-performing management teams and boards, and the creation of strong governance. Over the 25 years up to 2016 this has resulted in annual returns of 20%, net of all costs of the private equity investments.

Lessons for Achieving Investment Excellence

- In order to run a pension plan as an entrepreneurial company, you need strong governance and a board that has all the relevant competences and experience.
- The investment management organization at Teachers' has many degrees of freedom. This creates both opportunity as to where the returns go, and a potential risk of too many responsibilities being delegated by the board. Every fund should make its own care judgment here. Key ingredients for this judgment are: the quality of the investment management organization, the quality of the board, and the strength of the governance arrangements.
- Not many pension funds around the world have the governance budget, the desire, or the capabilities to build an investment operation as strong as Teachers'. Building this capability is a multi-decade process in which there will be both successes and failures. Therefore, if a board wants to go in this direction, it has to be prepared to stay the course.

ENDNOTES

1. See https://www.otpp.com/investments/performance.
2. See White (2017).
3. See Rundell (2017).

CHAPTER 9

Monitoring and Evaluation

Key Take Aways

- Monitoring and evaluation provide the board with feedback on the implementation of the strategy in order to improve its forward thinking.

- Even though monitoring is considered to be one of the key issues, little time is spent on its purpose or the philosophy.

- Monitoring is an ongoing process, where the board looks only for differences from the budgeted or expected course of events. Evaluation, on the other hand, is discrete and strategic in nature.

- There is a difference between monitoring the policy, which should be part of the policy process, and monitoring the execution.

- Evaluation has a more strategic nature than monitoring: Did the strategy live up to its original goals and expectations? Where can we improve on our strategy? Are there better alternatives to our strategy?

- In monitoring and evaluation alike, the right altitude, distance and horizon are important. Boards and investment committees should differentiate between "being in control" from an organizational perspective, and "being on course" on the investment management side.

An important responsibility of trustees is, for all the parts of the process, to monitor and evaluate the overall strategy and selected investment managers. Once the board has decided on the investment strategy, who will implement the different steps and how these will be implemented (e.g. mandate, risk budget), the implementation is set in motion. At this stage, you will want to track whether your fund is performing as you expected in order to alter the strategy or its implementation if necessary. This is not an easy task, mainly because of the fact that capital market outcomes are noisy in the short term: this makes it easy to mistake bad luck (short-term underperformance) for poor skills, and base costly decisions, such as firing and replacing managers, on this. Many behavioral traps come into play at this stage, from a committee shifting into action bias by firing an external manager when there is an underperformance, to the disappointment of trustees, who spent a great deal of time selecting and hiring a manager who subsequently performed below expectations. A high manager turnover rate is a signal that reflects poorly on an investment committee.

Selecting mandates leads to a substantial amount of work for the investment consultants and staff. Yet, once the mandate is selected, most time is spent on monitoring, evaluation, and deciding when to switch managers. Typically, funds' track records on these choices are dismal. Over time, pension funds have cut the average holding period of mandates, but by switching mandates more often, they run the risk of creating opportunity costs that can depress the long-term results.

Following selection, investment committees tend to view monitoring the investments as their number one priority. The monitoring process is an extension of the selection process; the same issues considered in the selection process will be relevant in the monitoring process. Ongoing review will require the provision of information in order to monitor the key issues on which the selection was based. Even though monitoring is considered to be one of the key issues, little time is spent on considering its purpose or philosophy. In recent years, asset managers have increasingly provided information to boards and investment committees that help answer all kinds of questions in detail, and this should help pension funds in their monitoring process. However, more data can also stand in the way of better monitoring.

This chapter aims to help the board to organize the monitoring and evaluation process in a structured way. We define *monitoring* as the analysis of information about an investment project or mandate, undertaken while the investment is ongoing, i.e. is it doing what it was expected to do? Are there signals that this is not the case? *Evaluation* is the periodic, retrospective assessment of a mandate or investment project that might be conducted either internally, or by external independent evaluators. Evaluation has a more strategic nature than monitoring: Can we improve our strategy? Are there better alternatives to our strategy?

We also discuss the timeline in which a board or committee should switch from monitoring to evaluation. Is this a gradual process, or does is require a distinct decision?

MONITORING

Monitoring is the collection and analysis of information about investments of the pension fund, undertaken while the investments are ongoing. The pension fund can monitor the investments integrally, and even in cases where the trustees appoint an investment manager, in the eyes of the beneficiaries they remain responsible for the investment of the assets of the fund.

Trustees monitor the performance of their appointed investment manager or of the performance of their own organization while they are managing. There is little doubt that a good investment performance enhances the achievability of a pension's promises, while poor performance weakens that goal. Under a defined contribution (DC) scheme, a member's benefits will even be directly determined by the returns earned on the contributions that were paid. It is vital that trustees know that their fund is delivering the necessary investment return within the objectives and restrictions. A pension fund's board, therefore, monitors developments at different levels (see Exhibit 9.1).

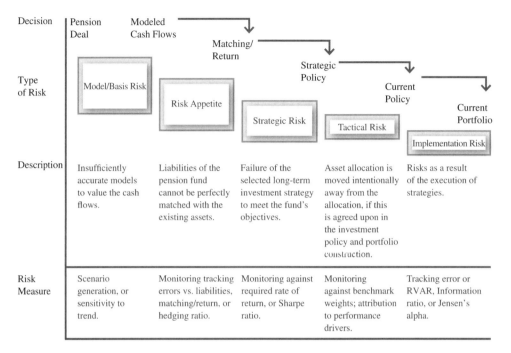

EXHIBIT 9.1   Monitoring of performance and risk along the investment process.

At the balance sheet level, the board considers whether its goals are (still) achievable. Are the investment returns of the total portfolio, as well as the investment returns relative to the returns of the liabilities, within the risk appetite and other bandwidths set by the board? The board monitors the following aspects:

- *Model risk*, resulting from using insufficiently accurate models to value the cash flows that need to be generated to realize the goals of the pension deal. This includes the inability to correctly predict factors that influence the cash flows such as longevity, wrong financial market assumptions like the discount rate, or the uncertainty of the size of cash flows due to complex optionalities and triggers agreed upon within the pension deal.
- *Risk appetite*, which arises when the liabilities of the pension fund cannot be perfectly matched with the existing assets. The board can manage this risk by monitoring deviations and recalibrating where appropriate.
- *Strategic investment risk*, arising from the failure of the selected long-term investment strategy to deliver the level of expected return or risk characteristics necessary to meet the fund's objectives. The board monitors this risk regularly by observing whether the realization of the fund's objectives move within the appropriate long and short-term risk measures and limits defined in the risk appetite.
- *Tactical investment risk*, occurring when the asset allocation is intentionally moved away from the long-term (strategic) allocation, if this is agreed upon in the

investment policy and portfolio construction. This may arise where the manager or team takes the view that, in the short-term, such an allocation can improve the risk-adjusted return of the fund. However, it is possible that these positions may cause losses, or may (because of their scale) distort the strategy of the fund. The board monitors this risk by monitoring the level of risk and performance throughout the period of deviation.

At an operational level, the board monitors the implementation risk as a result of the execution of strategies. Implementation risk comprises:

- *Other risks, which arise due to the mismatching of assets and liabilities.* These include counterparty risk, currency risk, liquidity risk, or concentration risk. The board monitors the level of these risks, and whether they move within the bandwidths set by the board. Mandate compliance risk concerns the individual mandates and strategies in accordance with investment and risk guidelines. When the board appoints a manager, it also sets a performance benchmark, tracking error expectations, alongside other guidelines. The board then monitors its managers against a range of qualitative factors that it believes supports the manager in achieving its goals.
- *Investment management organization.* These are the activities of the investment management organization (or external advisor) that is hired to select and monitor the individual mandates and execute the overall strategic policy in line with the set guidelines.

Monitoring is a forward-looking process. Will the whole set of key decisions deliver the objective over the relevant horizon? The key is to avoid backward-looking bias. Four aspects stand out in monitoring:

1. What to monitor and how to interpret and analyze the data;
2. What scope there is for the committee or board to learn from monitoring;
3. What biases should be avoided by the committee or board;
4. When should the committee or board switch from monitoring to evaluating, i.e. deciding if the mandate is still the best choice for the fund or whether it should be replaced.

What to Monitor?

If monitoring is considered to be one of the key issues for a board, it helps tremendously if the board spends time on the purpose of and its approach to monitoring. Monitoring should be done on the basis of a set of criteria determined in advance. The information provided in the monitoring process reflects these criteria, not irrelevant noise, because that will distract the board from giving proper attention to what matters. If you look at your investment strategy, these criteria should represent a coherent set of design and implementation decisions, probably with a number of layers. For example, top down, you have decided on five steps: your strategic asset allocation, the rebalancing method, investment styles, the benchmarks for the different asset classes, and the implementation of the strategy via a number of mandates. These five decisions should be monitored. In the report, the board should be able to see the changes in portfolio return and cover ratio, decomposed into the steps, as well as the target risk or return bandwidth that the performance of each step should move between. All in all, 10–15 decisions about strategy and implementation will determine more than 95% of the outcomes; and among those, a much smaller handful will determine 80%. It will help the board's monitoring to have all these decisions listed and monitored on a single-page overview document.

The more strategic a decision is (such as the share of equities and bonds), the higher the impact on the risk and return, and therefore on the realization of the objectives of the fund. At the same time, the more strategic a decision is, the longer it will take to get feedback on the strategy. As mentioned previously, we encourage monitoring of the outcomes of the key choices globally in order to maintain oversight. Compare all the strategic choices you have made to a single giant machine that is built to deliver the outcomes that realize your objective. So, the first line in the monitoring report is the overall realization of the objective (e.g. inflation +4%) on a relevant horizon (for example, five years).

This forces you to focus on what matters and avoid wasting your energy on insignificant mandates that will never materially affect the realization of the fund's objective—merely giving you the illusion that you're working very hard.

Monitoring is "management by exception:" only the mandates and strategies that deviate from the defined set of performance and risk criteria or from the expected behavior for an investment manager should be discussed and need to be dealt with in a swift manner. When deciding on a component of the strategy and its implementation, essentially what you always do is form an expectation about its contribution to the realization of the fund's objective. At the same time, you will have ideas about the characteristics of an asset, for example, on a certain horizon. If it veers outside of these boundaries, questions arise about whether you really have bought what you expected and, therefore, whether this part of your strategy will make the expected contribution to your objective. Making these boundaries explicit ex-ante is key to a high-quality monitoring process, because (i) it forces you to think about the key issues, and (ii) once you have decided on the key issues, you can monitor these and forget about an enormous number of trivial issues that might distract from what really matters.

Monitoring as a Multidimensional Process

Monitoring should be multidimensional. Generally, the main focus tends to be on realized performance. But performance is only the output of the process, and largely coincidental—especially over a short horizon. Therefore, it is easy to draw the wrong conclusions from performance. This will potentially lead to "false negative" and "false positive" errors. In the case of a false negative, you incorrectly judge a strategy as being bad (e.g. based on disappointing short-term results). In a "false positive" you incorrectly judge a strategy as being good, e.g. based on historical results. Academic research shows that these errors have many repercussions: "false negatives" lead to excessive firing, and the subsequently hired managers have typically been doing well recently, which is why they were shortlisted by consultants. Remember that decision-making should always be forward-looking and that historical outcomes form a bad guide to the future. This is where the "multidimensional" side of the monitoring process comes into play. Once you know that realized outcomes have very limited meaning, you should concentrate on the inputs, the process and the people creating the output to look for clues about the viability of your strategic decision going forward: a great cappuccino is the product of the ingredients, the coffee machine and the person making the cappuccino!

Monitoring the Policy

Policy Monitoring *ex ante* should focus on the question "Are we doing the right thing?" In other words, what can go wrong? Will this impair the mission of the fund? Can these risks be mitigated or can the fund adapt? How can it do so? How will it react when the risk hits? Proper preparation prevents poor performance. So, the key drivers of the mission must be monitored. In order to do this, we need to use forward-looking scenarios and avoid looking in the mirror of history. It makes sense to distinguish short-term and long-term risks. Short-term risks will typically stem from short financial market movements and will pose a threat to the solvency or liquidity of the fund. But if you don't survive the short term, the long term is not relevant anymore. Long-term risks are slow-moving killers that can lead to shortfall: Are the premium and the long-term expected returns high enough to deliver the pension's promises? What if that promise is wage indexed and wage inflation turns out to be 2% higher per year than expected ... for a 10-year period? Typically, short-term risks will get more attention than long-term risks, because that's the way humans are wired behaviorally. In the following paragraphs, both short-term and long-term monitoring will be worked out. In both cases of monitoring, the key questions to be answered by the board are: Are the risks acceptable? Can they (at least partly) be mitigated? How will we react if they materialize? How do we expect the outside world to react? And how will we communicate to the outside world? Be aware that you have to insure the house before it is on fire; often, when a risk hits it is too late to act and you will pay a high price for doing so. In addition, the bigger you are, the less room there is to maneuver.

For the short-term policy monitoring *solvency and liquidity* are the most important topics. Many trustees have vivid memories of the financial crises of 2008–2009, and perhaps of earlier crises such as the dot-com crisis in the early 2000s. The next crisis will certainly be different. However, we know that financial market crises, independently of their root course or the event that acts as a tipping point, will form a combination of rapidly collapsing prices of equities and related assets, as well as the temporary drying up of liquidity. Correlations between assets will typically increase, so funds can forget about short-term diversification. In the last few crises we saw decreasing interest rates, as central banks have been accommodative. Therefore, going forward it might make sense to also look at rising interest rates and bond yields. Liquidity will disappear (at least for some time) and the future will seem to be hidden in a in a cloud of uncertainty; it takes time to figure out what has happened and what will happen. So, the key to monitoring is this: build a number of scenarios for what could happen on a one-year horizon, and whether the resulting solvency and liquidity are within acceptable bands. Or, conversely, what needs to happen on financial markets to get to the lower border of acceptable solvency or liquidity, and how does that compare to historical movements of markets. These stress tests are helpful. Avoid using probabilities for this type of monitoring, as they will always provide information like, for instance, that there is a 1 in 20 probability that you will end up with a solvency lower than X. When markets are in crisis mode, probabilities mean nothing.

For the long-term monitoring process, *shortfall* is the most important source of attention. Monitoring the risk of not being able to meet the long-term promise is an important part of the policy process and should be a part of the Asset Liability framework. We would suggest monitoring this with a horizon of 5–15 years. This horizon is long enough to steer with available instruments to earn the expected premiums and should be long enough to dampen short-term fluctuations of capital markets. On the other hand, if the horizon of the analysis is too long, people tend to either not care, or expect that some sort of magic will happen. A good analysis will uncover the critical variables, which tend to be generic on a global scale. These can lead to questions such as: What if returns turn out to be significantly lower than expected? What if the discount rate falls even further? What if there is a significant inflationary shock? What if people live longer than what we currently expect?

Only one out of four of these questions is investment related; the other three are liability related. There is a tendency to hope, or even expect, that the investment returns will solve the problem. This can lead to boards postponing other available measures; these can take two forms or a combination of those. First, raising the premium that goes into the fund, or second, lowering the promise—by, for example, increasing the pension age, making indexation more flexible, closing down defined benefit (DB) funds and turning them into DC funds, etc. Because of the slow-moving nature of pensions, the earlier you identify potential risks, the easier it is to gently steer it back in the right direction.

In terms of frequency, we suggest that you monitor both the short and long-term risks in a formal way at least annually. On top of the annual monitoring, the investment management organization could provide you with a "management by exception" monitoring framework, a type of red flag system: only if something significant happens is there a reason to revisit the outcomes. In such a system, it is important to explicitly predefine what these flags may be, for example, "If the stock market declines by more than 15%, we will revisit the solvency risk."

The Position of Monitoring on the Investment Committee's Agenda

In many funds, monitoring and evaluation are delegated to the investment committee. The investment committee should have a thorough understanding of the strategy that has been approved, and make sure that it has a realistic view of what to expect, in which circumstances, and on which horizon. The investment committee should monitor not only outcomes, but also the critical inputs and the process leading to these outcomes.

Given the fact that the board's and investment committee's time is always limited, we propose that strategic issues should come first on the agenda and monitoring, later. Our proposal is to put the ongoing monitoring in the second half of the agenda, it being management by exception aimed at picking up early warning signals. When an exceptional situation pops up (i.e. one of the parts of your investment process shows signs that worry you), this could raise a strategic question that should be put high on the agenda. If calibrated correctly, a handful of those exceptional scenarios should reach the investment committee or the board during the course of a single year.

What Is the Optimal Frequency for Monitoring?

Monitoring follows strategy. One concern is that the "management" horizon of many funds has become increasingly shorter, despite the fact that they are long term in nature and serving the long-term objective of their participants and clients. From this perspective, monitoring frequency should be once per quarter *at most*, definitely not more. You may ask yourself why it should not be done semi-annually. Consider this: If you feel like you cannot wait half a year to look at outcomes, is your strategy actually based on a strong enough foundation? Do you want to micromanage? Do you trust the people to whom you have delegated? Do you trust your own strategic decision-making? It is important that you force yourself into this "thinking slow" mode.

Monitoring Should Be Based on a Sound Approach: It Should Never Be a Mechanical Exercise

A practical way of avoiding biases is for the investment committee in charge of monitoring to stipulate a number of guiding principles for monitoring that can be communicated to the executive office or fiduciary manager, with the requirement that monitoring be performed and reported along those lines. An example set of guiding principles for monitoring is presented in Exhibit 9.2.

David Neal, Chief Executive of the Australian Government Future Fund, promotes an alternative monitoring approach, supporting what he calls "immersed monitoring:" "This model promotes trust and enhances confidence to invest for the long run. It does so by deflecting attention away from short-term performance, toward aspects like decision processes, behaviors and alignment. [...], the Future Fund has intentionally pursued engagement and common understanding of investment decisions. This includes regular reviews to identify and reduce any gaps in understanding around objectives and beliefs, and ongoing opportunities for the Board to review the entire portfolio and be included in its positioning. To build common understanding and ownership across the internal investment team, a 'single portfolio' concept was established. [...] the Fund pursues a relatively smaller number of significant and close relationships which afford greater scope for monitoring via engagement."[1]

WHAT TO LOOK FOR IN MONITORING

Developing a monitoring approach requires the board to know which steps and goals in the investment process need to be monitored, as well as which restrictions or guidelines need to be applied; otherwise the monitoring information is just data, and a monitoring

- We focus on the consistency of the investment philosophy and strategy. These are leading indicators for the performance, not the other way round.

- In order to avoid tunnel vision, we will always monitor all relevant strategic decisions the fund has made top down, recognizing that they are all ultimately owned by the board.

- We will not draw conclusions based on a small set of observations.

- We challenge not the investment manager, but the assumptions behind the investment strategy. We do this on a yearly basis.

- We will assess risk/return in relation to the total balance sheet, not on an individual basis.

- We aim to learn from and continuously improve the monitoring process. We try to deal with root causes, not symptoms.

EXHIBIT 9.2 Set of guiding principles examples for monitoring.

approach. That being said, monitoring is a challenging task. While many boards and committees request the monitoring information, they only spend a small amount of time discussing it.

Good monitoring starts with setting the right expectations. The normal measure of the investment performance monitoring of a fund is a comparison with an equivalent benchmark portfolio or with other pension funds that are of a broadly similar nature. Over time, the performance will develop in line with, above, or below a benchmark. This simply is an observation, and does not actually inform trustees. At the selection phase, the board should have agreed on performance measures relating to the mandate's goals. For example, a mandate investing in so-called value stocks will need between 10 and 20 years to deliver the required return/risk trade-off. Any evaluation horizon shorter than 10 years undersells the potential value of the strategy and might even lead to perverse results: the reported standard deviation could be higher than other strategies and might lead to the conclusion that it does not add value after all. So, for the individual strategies, what to expect from the strategy in terms of risk and return and what horizon was assumed when selecting the strategy should be made clear for effective monitoring. In fact, one could argue that the ideal horizon for a mandate is an infinite one.

The "what to expect" part is also directly linked to performance and risk measures. When a board awards a manager an equities mandate with a tracking error of 2%, it then expects that the results will fluctuate around the benchmark on a yearly basis. The basic statistics tell us, 7 out of 10 times, to expect a performance between −2% and +2%, and 19 out of 20 times they tell us to expect a performance between −4% and +4%. Therefore, when a manager realizes an underperformance in the first years, the board would rather have it be otherwise, but it should not be surprised. The board has to monitor these risk measures and keep the horizon in mind that the board seems fit for the strategy. Patience is a necessary virtue, because positive excess returns are inconsistent, even among managers who outperform over the long-term.[2]

A first challenge is that performance reports are published often, for example, every quarter. If the reports show three subsequent quarters of underperformance, how should the committee react? The temptation will be to extrapolate these quarters and conclude preemptively that the manager will not live up to expectations, possibly ending the mandate early and creating opportunity costs. Therefore, reiterating the investment style, the horizon, and what to expect from the performance and risk measures in the short term is a crucial part of monitoring and monitoring reports, raising the hurdle for taking unnecessary action.

The tracking error example highlights a second challenge in monitoring. When managers or strategies are compared to their benchmarks, the results tend to be positive as well as negative on a monthly or quarterly basis. Trustees' and investors' attitudes towards risks concerning gains may be quite different from their attitudes towards risks concerning losses. Investment committees and asset managers are no exception. When choosing between profit opportunities, risk aversion prevails. On the other hand, when confronted with loss-making alternatives, people often choose the risky alternative. An active manager with positive alpha will become risk averse, locking in his profits, while the opposite is true with negative alpha.[3] So when monitoring the manager, a board should repress its initial reaction to put pressure on the asset manager to improve their results when they are negative. Rather, they could focus on performance measures in the monitoring that provide insight into the consistency of the manager, such as the percentage of outperformance periods, complemented with other measures about the investment style.

A third challenge is the board having to be aware that if monitoring is delegated to investment committees, that the investment committee members are also prone to behavioral biases. For example, investment committee members with an investment background will view a drop in the equities markets as an opportunity to buy equities cheaply, aiming to earn money with cheaply priced equities, subsequently advising the board to do so. On the other hand, pension fund trustees, when confronted with a drop in the cover ratio, might come to a different conclusion, selling more equities to protect the pension rights as much as possible. An investment committee is a delegated monitor on behalf of the board. This means that the board should be clear on what to expect in the monitoring. Having a sound set of investment beliefs, risk appetite, and clear investment guidelines will help the investment committee monitor the market movements from the viewpoint of the board, and provide advice if needed. Thus if the board and committee have done their homework, investment strategies and mandates will be monitored regularly, but changes will be made at a very low frequency. Avoiding turnover is still one of the best performance choices for a board.

It is important that the board or investment committees think about the wider use of the monitoring information. Can it be used for providing feedback, for example? Feedback loops are particularly effective when it comes to monitoring. When people are assigned a goal and given meaningful feedback regarding their performance relative to that goal, they will use the feedback to adjust their actions to better match the goal. A feedback loop involves several distinct stages.[4]

- *Gathering monitoring information.* A behavior must be measured. This consists of three types of information: (i) the performance and risk measures agreed upon in the investment management agreement, (ii) data about the pension fund's investments and balance sheet, and (iii) external sources and opinions regarding the investment style and strategy in general.
- *Linking information to monitoring goals.* The information must be relayed to the investment committee, not in the raw-data form in which it was captured, but in a meaningful context. This is compiled by the investment advisor, the fiduciary manager, or the staff. A monitoring dashboard is compiled to show whether the manager is sticking to the chosen style and working within the preset limits, and whether the investment style is still valid in general.
- *Giving feedback.* The investment committee can give the feedback to the investment manager, give them the opportunity to adjust their behavior, and ensure that the appropriate action is taken by the manager. For example, the committee can see in the monitoring reports that the level of observed or experienced risk is inconsistent with predetermined limits, prompting questions to the investment manager if anything has changed in the investment style or way of operation. If the manager adjusts their behavior, that action is then measured and the monitoring resumes. In other words, the investment committee or board must be able to adjust choices to make sure that things are still done right.

Effective monitoring requires good (factual) reporting. Reporting should provide decision makers with the right key objectives and facilitate them in making the right decision. Every report should be based on facts and verified information. Committees should not have to question or doubt the quality of the data, and the report should be free of errors and redundancies. Finally, every now and then the setup of the report should be discussed. The following factors are of importance:

- A report should contain the key factors that were decided on at the time of the selection of the mandate, namely the investment style, and the key measures of its consistency. If a mandate is considered to be a value mandate, is the book-to-market variable chosen to make this investment style explicit in the monitoring?
- The relevant investment horizon. Going back to our previous example, a value style easily needs 15–20 years to be effective, significantly longer compared to an investment grade mandate that only needs 5–8 years. In order to avoid short-term action bias, it is important to keep in mind the time horizon that was set in the report.
- The most relevant attribution report is one that is in line with the investment process. This type of report provides a breakdown of the type of investment decisions whose risk (ex-ante) and returns (ex-post) trustees should be focusing on in the performance attribution. Ideally, the external manager has indicated in the selection process which of these investment decisions he or she considers to be a competitive

advantage. In this way, it can be monitored as to whether the claims of the manager turn out to be valid.

- A performance attribution that also integrates risk attribution. Absolute vs. relative risk/return measures, where risk information is added to return (attribution) information; as well as downside risk measures (especially stress loss estimates) that could inform trustees of the "worst case" scenarios, the mitigation measures available and how they can be better prepared in the event of another downward market scenario.
- The ability to drill-down from the top down to individual managers, an extremely useful tool in making sense of the results.
- Performance measurement involves some degree of approximation. The order of magnitude matters more than the actual number.
- Deciding on the frequency of reporting. Compared to a yearly report, a quarterly report shows more volatility and might spur unnecessary reactions or choice.

In the minutes of the investment committee or the board, be explicit about the decisions you have made with regard to monitoring. Specifically, be as explicit as possible about the arguments, and evaluate them over a longer period. Is it one factor, such as relative performance, that drives many of the concerns and decisions? And is this consistent with what was agreed upon with the external manager?

WHEN DOES A BOARD MOVE FROM MONITORING TO EVALUATION?

When the mandates and strategies are selected, the monitoring should be based on the idea that mandates are kept indefinitely, and monitoring should be designed accordingly. If nothing had changed since the original selection, there generally would be no need for an evaluation. So periodically, a good question to address in the monitoring process is what (if any) assumptions have changed since the original decision was made. There are three areas where changes might take place:

1. *Needs*. Have the needs of the plan and its participants changed? For instance, changes in plan demographics (e.g. an aging participant population) may necessitate a reconsideration of the plan's risk appetite or strategic asset allocation. A dramatic increase or drop in the size of the plan (plan assets or number of participants) could also necessitate a reconsideration of the types of mandates and its instruments.
2. *Style and strategy*. Has the investment strategy or style changed? Has the investment fund/manager/service provider or its performance changed? Is the manager sticking to the stated investment style? Have managers left? Are quality targets being met? Are performance targets within an acceptable range? Is the investment strategy still sustainable? An active equities strategy that focuses on a specific niche might attract more investors over time, decreasing outperformance potential, at some point perhaps not even covering the costs. A question to ask beforehand would be whether such strategies are worth including in the portfolio, as the monitoring is then more resource intensive and time-consuming.

3. *Market*. Has the market changed? If, for instance, the costs of an investment strategy in the market have gone down on average, then a review of what the plan is paying for these services (compared to the new market conditions) may be in order.

If one or more changes are identified by the investment committee or the board, then it makes sense to plan an evaluation in order to assess whether the strategy is still fit for purpose or whether it should be changed. Before deciding to move from monitoring to evaluation, the board should take into consideration the fact that the cost of hiring and firing is always high. It is useful to have a reliable estimate of the cost of replacing a manager. This can be very substantial, including search cost, market impact, etc.

A seminal study analyzed the selection and monitoring processes for 3400 institutional investors between 1994 and 2003.[5] Managers for new external mandates are hired after a period in which they have realized substantial outperformance compared with the incumbent manager. However, when the manager is hired, this outperformance differential dwindles. Rather, the *fired* manager produces a 1% outperformance on average. If the search and selection costs, costs due to switching managers, and opportunity costs due to differences in performance are combined, then the authors estimate that 5%–10% of performance is lost. When institutional investors base their hiring and firing decisions primarily on past performance, the lost performance gap further increases.

Armed with this knowledge, you now see that you cannot be sure that the new manager will be better than the old one. Therefore, we would argue that, if possible, you should work with existing managers on the continuous improvement of their strategies.

EVALUATION

The previous paragraphs described monitoring as the collection and analysis of information about an investment project or mandate, undertaken while the investment is ongoing. Evaluation, on the other hand, is the assessment of a mandate or investment project. It may be conducted internally or by external independent evaluators, and many investment committees and boards consider evaluation to be part of monitoring. While this might work in practice, it is worthwhile separating these activities, because they actually have different roles. It is helpful to stress the key differences between evaluation and monitoring:

- Evaluation is strategic in nature—monitoring is operational;
- Evaluation looks back and draws lessons geared towards learning to make better decisions in the future—monitoring is a "real time" activity;
- Evaluation has a learning perspective—monitoring has an investment compliance perspective.

Evaluation is the systematic assessment of the mandate or investment project. Evaluation involves assessing whether monitoring has paid off, whether the selected mandates fit within the investment plan, what decisions have turned out to be wrong or right, and whether there are lessons somewhere for the board and the investment committee. Evaluation aims at determining the relevance, impact, effectiveness, efficiency, and sustainability of investment strategy as well as the contributions of the decisions and style to the results achieved.[6]

Evaluation takes place on a number of different levels, depending both on the goals and objectives of the mandate, and the scope of activities and strategies being designed or implemented. For example, evaluation would look different for peer-based comparison; a balance sheet approach where the results are evaluated in relation to the fund's overall goals; a stand-alone basis, compared to the pre-defined benchmark; and an environmental, social and governance perspective. An evaluation should provide evidence-based information that is credible, reliable, and useful. When evaluating managers based on quantitative measures, it is advisable to:[7]

- Consider several different measures, as each provides different information;
- Understand how the various measures interact with one another;
- Compute the measures during different time periods of interest, where longer periods (three to five years) should be dominant in discussion. Avoid short time periods, except for compliance reasons. This induces boards to take unnecessary action;
- Recognize that all measures are by definition backward-looking.

This list of measures is a starting point to include in an evaluation:

- *Information (or Sharpe) ratio.* The manager's excess return above a benchmark, normalized by the standard deviation of relative returns;
- *Sortino ratio.* The manager's excess return above a benchmark, normalized by the standard deviation of downside relative returns;
- *Win–Loss ratio.* The manager's average positive relative return divided by the manager's average negative relative return;
- *Hit ratio.* The percentage of periods where the manager's relative returns were positive (a.k.a. the "batting average");
- *Correlation coefficient.* The correlation of the manager's excess returns with the returns of other existing (or prospective) managers;
- *Correlation between beta and alpha.* Alpha is earned from security selection, tactical asset allocation, or other investment skills. Alpha is scarce and, therefore, should be expensive. Beta, on the other hand, is return that is derived from exposure to a passive index or a risk premium. Beta is abundant and, therefore, should be cheap. It is essential to understand whether an active fund manager's returns are true alpha, or whether they could be replicated through inexpensive beta exposures. A high correlation between beta and alpha is a "red flag," suggesting that the alpha is not skill, but leveraged beta exposures.

The findings, recommendations and lessons of an evaluation should be used to inform the future decision-making processes regarding the mandate. Evaluation should be evidence based, because for any given strategy, there is a lot of data available to compare and learn from. In addition, making it evidence based helps to develop a more objective evaluation process, which is important in the investment sector where strong views and opinions from asset managers might influence decision makers. Surprisingly, very little empirical evidence has been built up regarding the effectiveness of selection and monitoring; in most funds the application of evaluation is still in its infancy.

In many funds, evaluation is delegated to the investment committee. Before starting to evaluate, the investment committee should have a thorough understanding of the strategy that has been approved, and make sure that it has a realistic view of what to expect depending on the circumstances and on the horizon. The investment committee should monitor not only outcomes, but also the critical inputs and process leading to these outcomes. It also helps to be aware of the latest academic insights on hiring and firing and the behavioral biases involved. If the committee determines that the total costs for switching managers amount to 10%–14%, this is a clear hurdle rate to overtake in the decision to evaluate and potentially hire a new manager. Firing managers and blaming others is "managing" symptoms, not effective governance. Evaluation should never be a one-way street. Ideally, the committee includes the investment manager or selected mandate. How would they self-assess the results on the basis of the criteria the board set? In their opinion, how would they attribute the results to the investment beliefs and investment philosophy? Finally, it is important to quiz the manager to understand how he views circumstances in the market, and whether there are any developments that might trigger a change in their investment style.

ENDNOTES

1. See Neal and Warren (2015).
2. See Wallick et al. (2015).
3. See Elton et al. (2003).
4. See Cooper (2012).
5. See Busse et al. (2010).
6. See Gage and Dunn (2009) and Frankel and Gage (2007).
7. International Forum of Sovereign Wealth Funds. IFSWF Subcommittee #2. Case Study #1: Selecting and Monitoring External Fund Managers. Accessed on http://www.ifswf.org/sites/default/files/Publications/oslocs1.pdf.

Four

Organizing the Board

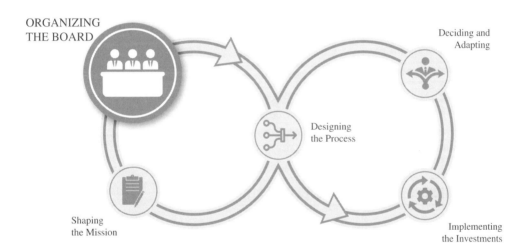

ORGANIZING
THE BOARD

Deciding and
Adapting

Designing
the Process

Shaping
the Mission

Implementing
the Investments

This section looks at the pension fund board from all angles. What are the characteristics of boards and their members, what should pension participants expect from them, how do members operate on boards, what attributes do board members need and how do they organize themselves?

Just as a new trustee would also do, we commence our examination of the pension fund board by reviewing the roles and responsibilities of the board and the characteristics of members, as well as by identifying the characteristics of successful boards and board members. This discussion is centered on maintaining "the right altitude—the right distance—the right horizon" for developing and monitoring the implementation of the strategy.

We examine the roles of boards as collective entities, as well as the parts that individual board members play. The way these members serve on a board, both individually and collectively, makes or breaks the quality of the outcome. Board member competence and knowledge is obviously an asset, but the selection process also highlights managing or representing different stakeholder groups as an important part of the required profile. How do board members balance these different interests?

Next, we move on to the roles and organization of the board staff or executive office, which is close to the board and supports board members in the formulation and evaluation of their strategy. The staff makes sure that the strategy is implementable in a practical way, taking into account the goals and framework set by the board. Reciprocally, the staff aggregates information so as to allow the board to monitor effectively and at the right altitude.

Thirdly, we consider the investment committee, the board's important subcommittee that deals with investment matters.

Lastly, we will have a look at the investment organization (or pension delivery organization) that is responsible for implementing the (strategic) investment plan and is often intimately involved in advising on the investment strategy. The cooperation between the pension fund and the investment management organization requires some forethought to ensure clear roles and responsibilities, as well as mutual trust and smart countervailing powers to maintain the right balance.

Part IV Topics Include:

- What are the key characteristics of an effectively functioning board?;
- What is the "governance budget?;"
- How to identify a board's weaknesses and improve it over time;
- How to prepare for and organize a well-run investment committee;
- How you, as a board member, and the board as a whole, can get a grip on the investment management organization.

CONTRIBUTION OF THIS PART TO INVESTMENT EXCELLENCE

Part IV focuses on the board. The contribution of individual board members, and the board as a whole is often overlooked because discussions and choices tend to be "soft" in nature, while investment theory and advice typically looks at investing as a hard-wired problem that can be solved objectively. Next to that, it can be very challenging to reflect on one's own role when it comes to potentially not realizing excellence. Both the qualities, the knowledge and the competences of the individuals involved and the way the cooperate within the board are important drivers of excellence. A special position is taken by the chairman of the board of the pension fund. Working towards excellence can be done in many ways and starts with understanding the challenges and properly organizing the investment committee meetings. Putting together the right set of individuals may take significant time and planning.

CHAPTER 10

Becoming an Effective Board

Key Take Aways

- An efficient board has a considerably positive influence on long-term outcomes and the fund's license to operate.

- The need to ensure an effectively functioning board may seem obvious, but in order to achieve this it is important to attend to the balance of leadership and structuring of the board. Here, it helps to be explicit about what is expected of the board, board members and chair, and to discuss what sort of board culture and leadership type is best suited for the fund's goals and culture.

- The board should consider in advance what type of decision-making it needs to see on the agenda. Overarching and strategic decision-making and monitoring of implementation should dominate the agenda. Tactical, operational, and adhoc decisions should be delegated.

- In practice, there is often a gap between actual and potential board functioning. Trying to visualize the use of governance budget is a valuable tool for having the relevant discussion.

This chapter focuses on the board. We start by addressing the tasks of the board and then move on to board composition. We expand on a key concept, the so called "governance budget," the combination of time, expertise and organizational effectiveness of the decision makers. To a large extent this "budget" determines whether or not your fund will be able to be excel. Following this, we pinpoint the ingredients of an effectively functioning board, which can help identify the strengths and weaknesses of a board. Here we delve into an already-mentioned key concept of this book, which should help in striking the right balance as a board member: "the right altitude—the right distance—the right horizon." We conclude the chapter by presenting ways to improve the board over time.

RESPONSIBILITIES OF THE BOARD

There are several definitions of a board, but a useful one could be that the board of a pension fund is the instrument to deliver value for its participants[1] by providing the best possible financial outcome for the agreed-upon pension deal. The board's responsibilities are described as fiduciary duties. These responsibilities include policy formulation and foresight, strategic thinking, shaping the governance, supervision of management, and accountability.

Board task 1: Policy formulation and foresight has a long-term, external perspective. It answers the question of why the pension fund exists and what it wants to be. It can take the perspective of the stakeholders. It defines long-term objectives and success. In addition, it monitors the (large) external forces of change and how they may affect the fund.

The framework is the formulation of the mission, goals and objectives, beliefs, and the way they take shape both in the present and in the future. The board should actively own these topics. A mission tends to be timeless and universal: the Dutch health care pension fund PFZW's goal is "to provide a good and affordable pension to all the workers in the health care sector" while the Norway Fund aims "to build and safeguard financial wealth for future generations."[2]

Policy formulation looks many years ahead, with a horizon of 10 years not being unusual given the cycles in the capital markets. This leads to different long-term scenarios. By recognizing the role of uncertainty and exploring the sources of turbulence and uncertainty, the goal is to iteratively and interactively generate new knowledge and insights to help the pension fund assess its circumstances and enable adjustments in strategy.

Board task 2: Strategic thinking shifts the focus of the board from an external to an internal perspective. If the fund knows what success means given its mission and objectives and current and expected future context, how does it become fit for purpose to achieve that success? This translates into a set of strategic questions:

- How will it organize its investment process?
- Which competencies does it need?
- How does it regard its strengths and weaknesses from this perspective and what should it do about them?
- What can it outsource and to whom?
- Is the board itself equipped to take on future challenges?

This exercise looks two to four years ahead and leads to measurable goals. It should be about concrete outcomes (e.g. does passive investing make sense in the current environment) as well as about soft outcome factors (e.g. if there is no learning culture in the investment management organization [IMO] or pension fund, it will never be able to adapt to fast-changing geopolitical developments).

So here, the key question is how to translate the mission and purpose into strategy in an effective and efficient way. This often demands a shared understanding of roles and responsibilities: the board should direct, while the executive should manage. At the same time, it requires a subtle interplay between the board and the IMO: the board needs all the relevant information to be able to make the right strategic choices, while the IMO needs clear guidance from the board in order to translate strategic choices into implementable actions. So, the board should concentrate on the "what" and the executive on the "how."

Board task 3: Shaping the governance. Mission, purpose, and strategy differ from one pension fund to another, making a "one-size-fits all" governance structure challenging for a board of trustees. A key issue for the board is therefore to determine how it will apply strategic principles. Sound corporate governance policies and practices towards staff, investment organization, and other stakeholders should foster shared understanding and a common purpose consisting of achieving the fund's goals.

The investment governance framework should clearly set out the roles and responsibilities of both the board and other fiduciaries such as the investment managers and consultants. It should be explicit about the choices and assumptions made in the investment framework, including key performance indicators (KPIs) for the investment choices so that they can be evaluated, challenged and, where necessary, adapted.

The framework should also identify governance issues that need to be elevated from the subsidiary to the board, or which require the approval of the board. Effective two-way communication between the board and the stakeholders is also important; therefore, the framework should set out how and when issues should be communicated. Finally, the board should periodically revisit its investment governance structures to ensure that they remain appropriate. Changes in operating and regulatory conditions may also necessitate changes.

Board task 4: Supervision of management is the board's monitoring of the total fund and organizational performance—keeping the organization under prudent control. Here lies the essence of the board's supervision of the investment management that is delegated to an IMO. Has it delivered investment outcomes that are good enough, given the circumstances? Is it fit for purpose moving forward? Monitoring involves the use of feedback to manage ongoing exposure to investment opportunities so that the pension fund's objectives and constraints continue to be satisfied and remain achievable looking ahead. Various aspects are monitored by the board:

- Is there an implicit or explicit change in the pension fund's risk profile and objectives?
- Do the assumptions with regard to economic and market input factors still hold?
- Is the current portfolio within the rebalancing guidelines?
- Are the managers chosen to reflect investment styles consistent with the expected return/risk profile, investment beliefs outlined in the strategic plan, and other key factors?

The board has to decide whom to delegate these monitoring questions to, for example to the IMO, executive staff, or investment committee. It also needs to be clear about how the monitoring process should evolve: which choices should the board make, and what elements are best left to the other bodies of the pension fund? Boards clarify these fiduciary responsibilities by developing detailed reviews of their decision rights framework, with a focus on investment and risk management decisions. A formal approach, such as the RACI framework (Recommend, Approve, Consult and Inform) shown in Exhibit 10.1, is extremely helpful not only in clarifying the different roles and responsibilities, but also in allowing for a debate and review of these decision rights.[3]

	Trustees	Executive Trustee	Investment Committee	Investment Management Organization	Investment Consultant/ Actuary
Goals					
Investment Philosophy	A	I	I	I	C
Investment Beliefs	A	I	I	I	C
Definition of SAA Classes	A	I	C	C	C
Portfolio Construction	A	I	C	C	C
Selection of Mandates	A	R	C	R	
Implementation	A	R	C	R	
Monitoring of Mandates	A	R	C	R	
Evaluation	A	R	C	R	C
Monitoring of Investment Management	A	R	C	R	C

R: Responsible   A: Accountable   I: Informed   C: Consulted

EXHIBIT 10.1 Example of a decision right framework for the supervision of investment management.

Another important reason to clarify investment and risk management decisions as part of the investment management framework is that it helps in developing the right reporting, which is key to effective supervision of policy, and monitoring of investment management. Reporting provides the board with the right key objectives in monitoring and aids them in making the right decision. Every report should be factual and based on verified information. The board should not have to question or doubt the quality of the data, and the report should be free from errors and duplication.

An increasingly important part of reporting is the responsibility that the board has to monitor environmental, social and governance (ESG) decisions integrally in the investment management process. Their purview includes topics such as the development and maintenance of proxy voting guidelines. In addition, as ESG integration becomes an increasingly common practice in asset management and pension funds are more often combining activities to address climate change and other environmental and social issues (Climate Action 100+ initiative, Access to Medicine), boards include the monitoring of these activities in their reporting and communication with the beneficiaries.

Board task 5: Accountability. The board has to be accountable to the most important stakeholders and to society at large about everything it does and the results of its actions. The board is accountable to the pension plan members and beneficiaries, its supervisory body (where relevant), and the competent authorities. Accountability to plan members and beneficiaries can be promoted by appointing members of the governing body who are pension plan members, beneficiaries, or members of their representative organizations.

The breadth of accountability varies between the different legal systems and cultures around the world. Accountability will develop over time, and individual institutions can choose between levels of accountability.

Because many different individuals and parties in and around a pension fund contribute in many ways to decisions and policies, it could be difficult to identify who should be accountable for the results. This is known as the problem of many hands.[4] It creates a dilemma over accountability within the pension fund organization. If individuals are held accountable, those who had no role to play in the outcomes of a decision are either unfairly punished, or they "take responsibility" in a symbolic ritual without actually suffering any consequences. For pension funds, the accountability ultimately rests with the board, which has to accept its consequences.

In other words, a board should never undertake any action for which it cannot be accountable. This seems obvious, but it is not necessarily. For example, what if a board agrees to the administration of a pension plan that can only be realized via relatively high investment returns? The board then unwittingly assumes accountability for results caused by factors that are not under their control.

BOARD COMPOSITION

Boards of pension fund plans direct and control implementation, but do not manage it. Boards have the task of defining the purpose of the pension fund and agreeing on a strategy for achieving that purpose. They are responsible for appointing executives to turn strategic plans into action, for supporting and counselling them and, if necessary, for replacing them. Above all, boards are there to provide leadership, and it is in that context that the composition of the board should be considered.[5]

However, the distinction between direction and control (i.e. strategy), and implementation is not always clear, nor is it, for smaller pension funds, a practical one to make. For example, board members can be involved in several steps of the selection process of managers, preparing mandate searches in consultation with an advisor, or deciding on the criteria, for example. Is this strategy, or implementation? At the very minimum, trustees set strategic goals and objectives for the selection process and leave the other steps to the advisor and pension staff.

A single board at the head of a pension fund is the most common board structure. Unitary boards of this type are made up of executive and non-executive board members. Contrastingly, two-tier boards separate these two roles. A pension fund board can have anywhere between 5 and 15 members. A generally accepted view is that boards should not be excessively large; 7 or 8 is often considered to be the ideal number of board members. A pension fund has to strike the right balance. If the number is too low, the board will not have sufficient competency to perform its tasks, nor be considered sufficiently representative by the participants if representation is an important part of the board profile. On the other hand, overly large boards will influence performance negatively, for example by creating inertia when decisive action is needed moments of urgency, such as during financial crises.

A board comprises board members, and individuals supporting the board. Board members are a chairman, and executive and non-executive board members. Their roles can be defined as follows:

- *Chairman.* Their role is to manage the meeting, aiming to distinguish between debate and decision-making, and ensuring that decisions that are consistent and executable are made. The chair can have different styles for fulfilling this role, each with its own influence on decision-making.
- *Executive board members (also called executive director).* Members of the board of the pension fund who also have specific management responsibilities, managing a part or the whole staffed office or IMO.
- *Non-executive board members (also called non-executive director).* Board members without responsibilities for the daily management or operations of the pension fund. The legal duties, responsibilities, and liabilities are the same for both executive and non-executive board members. Both have a fiduciary duty to the pension fund and must act in the best interests of the company. Pension funds can select independent non-executive board members, or non-executive board members who are employed by the sponsor or affiliated to the sponsor companies. Funds make their own choice herein, whereby the background and company culture of the affiliated companies or the sponsor play a role more important than would seem to be the case at first glance. The presence of expert board members from the company or sector is a good, transparent manner of ensuring the company culture is visible. These board members are not only considered to know "what is going on" but can also be addressed directly in the company on the consequences of the decisions and they are aware of this when making decisions. On the other hand, independent (non-expert) non-executive board members bring in outside experience and best practices from other pension funds or industries. Independent non-executive board members, especially if this is their full-time occupation, will be more mindful of reputational risk as this might affect their careers more directly than other board members, focusing on managing risks and creating more stability in outcomes where possible.[6] These different expectations and added values from the non-executive board members should be reflected in the job specification for the selection process.

Roles That Support the Board

- *Secretary.* The secretary supports the chair in setting the agenda and provides documents and materials beforehand to assist the decision-making process. Ensures that complete, timely, relevant, accurate, honest, and accessible information is placed before the board to enable directors to reach an informed decision. Decides with the chair what should be delegated to the staff or executive board members, and checks whether a document supports the right step in the decision-making process. The secretary's task is this to identify the decision needed, generate solutions and alternatives, decide on an alternative, and implement and evaluate the chosen solution). Minutes support the board meeting, providing a consistent record of how decisions have been made, why the board made them, and what arguments supported the decisions.

■ *Board advisors*. They do not have a formal role in decision-making but can certainly influence the discussions. With smaller funds, the actuary is one of the regular attendees, as they are able to cover the pension deal as well as provide expertise in asset liability management. Alternatively, the investment consultant could attend, as they possess knowledge about the investment plan, process, and implementation.

WHAT IS EXPECTED FROM BOARD MEMBERS?

The importance of the competences and knowledge that a board member must have is widely accepted, but what competences and knowledge are actually expected? Huse,[7] a governance researcher, lists seven different elements:

1. Pension fund specific knowledge about the functions, organization, regulation, and pension product. Often, this knowledge has been acquired through board memberships at other pension funds, or previous roles close to the pension fund (staff, consultant). The board member is aware of the strengths and weaknesses of the fund, its strategic challenges, and its bargaining power in the market.
2. A board member may bring in function-oriented competence, such as finance, accounting, strategy, or general management experience. This type of knowledge is particularly important for the advisory tasks of the board. Sought-after skills in pension board members include knowledge of, and experience in, risk management, institutional investments or actual portfolio management, especially if this mirrors the differentiating choices in the pension fund's investment strategy. For example, this might be experience with illiquid assets if the fund has a large allocation to infrastructure, or derivatives if the fund runs an extensive hedging program.
3. Process-oriented competences include knowledge about how a good board functions and how it should be run. Due to the professionalization of boards, there are a growing number of people seeking to make their living from board memberships. These board members have specialized knowledge about the tasks of boards and the way they work.
4. Relational competences shift the focus to the stakeholders of the fund; this kind of competence is related to building relationships with and acquiring influence on important stakeholders outside the pension funds, for example, influence with regulators, political groups, or financial institutions. Communication with internal actors is also very important here.
5. The fifth competence is related to the personalities and personal traits of the pension fund board members. This includes the ability to think creatively, think analytically, think critically, have the courage to address any elephant in the room, and also the ability to generate cohesion.
6. Board members need negotiation skills, as they represent the fund and have to manage and monitor the stakeholders involved in executing the pension plan. Board

members need to influence or shape the decision-making in such a way that it meets the interests of their participants. Negotiation skills therefore have a link with integrity—board members need to be aware of why they are in that position, namely to take care of the interests of the participants. This could lead to a member taking an independent standpoint and not being overly involved and aligned with either the board or the investment organization.

7. Finally, "ownership," or taking personal responsibility for the task, is considered to be the ultimate qualification competence for being a pension fund board member. Board members who ensure that strategy is developed executed and monitored, also ensuring transparency to other stakeholders and embedding the proper checks to make sure that the pension fund develops in a sound way.

What Is Expected of the Chair?

The chair is crucial to the board. The most visible role played by the chair is to govern the workings of the board, including directing its meetings, making sure that decisions are made, and acting as conciliator when elements of the board differ—although the chair is obliged to play this role with moderation and not to bias the outcome of the meetings towards any special agenda.

The core functions of the chair are to provide effective board leadership, be a team leader, and ensure that the characteristics of an effective team are present. These core functions include setting the agenda, presiding at the meeting, and developing the board and board culture, which provides the context for the board functions.[8,9] Better than anyone else, the chair is the person who can and should make sure that the board maintains the right altitude, distance and horizon in relation to the investments.

In most cases, the board will delegate tasks or advisory functions to a number of board committees, one of which will be the investment committee. The chair has an important role in overseeing and, when necessary, improving the functioning of these committees. The core functions of the chair can be broken down as follows:

Setting the Agenda, Presiding Over Meetings

- Setting the ethical tone for the board and the pension fund. The chair embodies and strongly promotes the values that the board aims to develop (see Chapter 3).
- Providing overall leadership for the board.
- Formulating (with the chief executive officer [CEO] of the staff, the investment organization, and the secretary) the yearly work plan for the board based on agreed objectives and playing an active part in setting the agenda for board meetings.
- Upholding rigorous standards of preparation for meetings, ensuring that complete, timely, relevant, accurate, honest, and accessible information is placed before the board to enable members to reach an informed decision.
- Presiding over board meetings and ensuring that time in meetings is used productively.
- Ensuring that decisions made by the board are executed.

Developing the Board and Board Culture

- Participating in the selection of board members (via a nomination committee), and overseeing a formal succession plan for the board, the staff and other senior management appointments within the pension fund.
- Acting as the link between the board and staff, and between the board and the CEO of the IMO.
- Ensuring that good relations are maintained with the fund's major shareholdings (such as the IMO) and its strategic stakeholders (notably the sponsor).
- Making sure that all board members are aware of their responsibilities through a tailored introduction program, and by ensuring that a formal program of continuing professional education is adopted at board level.
- Managing conflicts of interest, making sure that these are made transparent in roles and decision-making, and creating a culture where conflicts of interests can be discussed openly.
- Monitoring how the board works together and how individual board members perform and interact at meetings. Ensuring that members play a full and constructive role in the affairs of the company. The chair also takes a leading role in the process of removing non-performing or unsuitable directors from the board.

It is obvious from this list of tasks that the personality of the chair will play an important role. The board chair not only sets the tone for board meetings, but also for how engaged board members are and how they view the added value or effectiveness of their role. When choosing a chair, the selection committee should be aware of the personality types among board chairs. Many persons embody a combination of types and can easily switch depending on the context, but many do have preferred styles.[10]

Things to keep in mind when choosing a chair are: (i) that one should not expect the chair to be a superhero and (ii) it is worthwhile to carefully describe the traits expected from a chair and select people who come as close to the ideal as possible: the consequences of not selecting the right chair can be very costly and can have long-term implications for the fund.

APPOINTING NEW BOARD MEMBERS[11]

The market for board members is opaque; there is no clear supply and demand. Despite whatever policies are in place, new board members have traditionally been selected from the existing board's professional networks. For pension funds, this means that people regularly switch posts throughout their professional careers, generally from pension fund staff or IMO to the board. For non-executive board members, the network is somewhat wider. Usually, there are limited considerations regarding the qualifications required, and selections often take place without an assessment of the present and future needs of the boards. This is especially true in countries where the remuneration of board members is relatively low given the (legal) liabilities that the board is exposed to compared to similar board roles in other sectors. Therefore, boards are often content with finding a candidate who is actually willing to join. Changes in boards are often incremental, and the selection of a new board member usually takes place after an existing board member withdraws for some reason.

However, more objective and rational selection processes are increasingly taking place. These processes include an assessment of the needs of the pension fund, how these translate to a desired profile for the board member, and an extensive search to consider a larger set of candidates than just in the existing professional network. Creating nomination committees is an increasingly common selection mechanism.

An average pension fund with a board of six to eight members will select one or two new members each year. Given increasing expectations placed upon boards, new board members must be prepared to contribute rapidly. The questions, points of attention, and concerns they have about whether becoming part of the board is a good plan for them fall into different areas:[12]

- Can I commit myself? Given the demands of board term—20–30 days a year for up to nine or more years—it pays to carefully weigh the advantages and disadvantages of a board appointment carefully. The key question is whether joining the board it is mutually beneficial—on the one hand that the prospective trustee finds it engaging and useful as a growth opportunity, and on the other hand that they can also add a valuable perspective to the pension fund board. It is, therefore, important to obtain a good view of the board calendar and activities—not just what the next board meeting will be about, but the key processes of the board over the course of 12 months of board meetings.

- Does it strengthen my network, and can I deploy my own network for the fund? Other considerations may be who else is on the board—in particular, a point of interest is whether the position offers the opportunity to work with a good chair and gain exposure to experienced executives from pension funds from other industries—the strength and diversity of the executive trustees and/or staff, and how well the board works together.

- Getting to understand the fund. As part of your due diligence, read published information about the pension fund. Take a fresh approach; although pension funds seem quite similar due to the pension deal, investment model, and organization, the flow of the fund might be quite different. What many don't appreciate before they've actually done it is just how much pre-reading material there can be, and the amount of time it can take to digest it thoroughly. Focus on the KPIs and lead indicators for the pension fund. What do you as a trustee keep an eye on? Every other question ends up stemming from those KPIs.

- Is the fund aware of its challenges? Understand how the board views sector and pension fund risk. How does management assess, present, and articulate risk? Are assumptions discussed and challenged clearly and freely? New trustees should not be afraid to ask for the process to be tailored to their needs if they want to explore certain areas of the business in greater depth.

- What are my fellow trustees' priorities? One-on-one meetings with as many other trustees as possible prior to the first board meeting can provide a sense of the priorities of the board, as well as the dynamics among trustees and between staff and the board. The time a new trustee may take to meet people upfront definitely pays off in the long run because they get context they otherwise wouldn't have got. Getting a read from other trustees about the board's priorities for example can provide important context, as can do using meeting breaks to follow up on your questions.

- New trustees can and should be involved from the beginning: it will be more helpful to listen than to talk at board meetings, but they should be willing to participate in the discussion, especially in their own area of expertise.
- Raising questions. By definition, a new trustee lacks perspective on the board's history—the sacred cows, the topics that have been debated at length, and other important contexts. This makes knowing when to raise questions or to push for more information all the more difficult. Fresh eyes are good, but one of the worst things a new trustee can do is walk into the boardroom and raise topics that aren't going to be productive and which the board has already discussed at length. That is why it is important at least to have read the board minutes, if not the papers, for the previous year or so, so new trustees can understand some of the key issues and debates.

GOVERNANCE BUDGET OF THE BOARD

The governance budget of the board is crucial for the type of investment model and implementation that the fund is to pursue. Urwin, a researcher and investment advisor, defines the governance budget as the combination of time, expertise and organizational effectiveness of the decision makers.[13] Three types of governance budget can be identified:

- *Cost minimizing budget.* This budget is compatible with the lowest governance resources and is a set of arrangements that manages down all costs and focuses on easily attainable investment returns. Being the least sophisticated investment strategy, it would hold only mutual funds or bonds and equities, and use mainly passive managers and mutual funds.
- *Exploitation budget.* With a greater governance budget available, the fund can pursue more value creation opportunities, but within the existing investment set known to trustees. The focus would be on improving diversity of market exposure outside equities and bonds and adding private market forms of equities and bonds as well as alternative assets like real estate and infrastructure. These assets are considered "tested and proven," and the fund can draw on what is considered common knowledge about these assets. Generally, the portfolio construction will not contain much exposure to active management. Alpha is the hardest part of the investment spectrum to create value with, and also involves more detailed reports and accountability, decomposing the active investment returns.
- *Exploration and Exploitation budget.* The board will further expand resources to enhance diversification but will also include a significant number of resources embedding risk in the overall value chain of the pension fund. There is greater emphasis on selecting manager skills, including when manager skills and market returns are difficult to separate. New strategies and asset classes

are sought out, under the assumption that first mover advantages will translate into a higher return that offsets the extra costs of sourcing, risk management, and pioneering to develop the asset into an investable product.

A question we can then ask, is whether there is a way to quantify the governance budget, compare the actual use of the budget with what is required, and take action as a board to close that gap. Surely, a board that spends only one session per year on investment strategy, evaluating the results and setting out the course for coming years will be deemed to be severely "under-spending" the budget. The board is then much too detached to know what is going on. The governance budget of a board is shown by Exhibit 10.2.

As a simple exercise, consider a board that has allocated its governance budget equally, covering topics such as pension administration, communication, investments, internal organization, and overall accountability. Each topic demands 20% of the time and resources of the board. To continue the exercise, consider your own fund, add 5% for each choice that is more demanding, and subtract 5% for each choice that is less demanding. What is the overall score? For many funds, due to one or more of such choices, the governance budget is overstretched, leading to investments not claiming 20% but between 30% and 40%. The usefulness of this analysis lies in highlighting how the board uses its time and resources, and also in providing an informed basis for addressing this issue: should the board expand the number of meetings (relieving the pressure on the agenda, but not a long-term solution), delegate more to committees and staff (raising the question of what can be effectively delegated without losing one's grip on overall responsibilities), or simplify the investment processes (raising the question of which choices can be altered without affecting the achievement of the fund's goals).

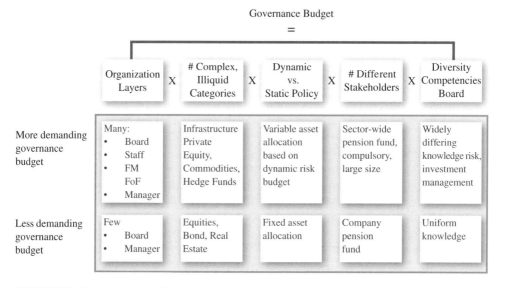

EXHIBIT 10.2   The governance budget of a board.

BOARD DECISION-MAKING CULTURE

The performance of the board is determined by three types of decisions: comprehensive decision-making, strategic decision-making, and ad hoc decision-making.[14] The board avoids tactical decision-making, and delegates operational decision-making, monitoring, and oversight as much as possible. We further explain these three types of decision-making.

- *Comprehensive decision-making.* This is about establishing the purpose, mission, and vision of the pension fund. External stakeholders play an important role here, especially the sponsors and participants of the fund. This type of decision-making is infrequent; reviews or updates will be carried out when the pension deal is renewed, or when circumstances require a critical review of the pension fund's raison d'être. In developing overarching decision-making, the board is challenged to view the pension fund from the ground up, focusing on its functions: what functions are needed to best fulfil the pension deal; is a pension fund actually the best way to realize this; and is this pension fund's approach the best possible one?
- *Strategic decision-making.* Here, the board decides on the investment beliefs and investment model best suited for realizing the financial objectives of the pension deal. Next, the parameters that the investment organization needs to implement this policy are set out in the investment policy (capital market expectations, asset allocation, and investment styles). The asset allocation choice is traditionally considered to be one of the key choices made by a board. For its decision-making, the board needs to use research-based information (which choices have been proven to work, and how robust can this be in the near future), information from peers (similarly, which choices have been proven to work in practice), and information about financial markets (what, if anything, can be said about future risk premiums given the current state of the financial markets).
- *Ad hoc decision-making.* This refers to unanticipated developments in the pension fund and financial markets that fall outside the scope of the strategic framework of the pension fund, alter fundamental assumptions made during strategic decision, and cannot wait to be dealt with in the planning cycle. For example, the investment plan might have included expanding into private equity as a new asset category, but despite previous thorough analysis, new information comes to light suggesting that the expected return will be below the expected hurdle rate set in the investment plan after all. A development could also go in the opposite direction, for example, if the board has established conditions for when to start a particular investment and these conditions are now met, meaning that the investment can go ahead. These types of decisions do not follow the planning cycle of a pension fund as written down in the calendar, but still need to be addressed. Managing through a financial crisis on the other hand is not ad hoc decision-making. As will be discussed in Chapter 14 the choices, impact, and response during a financial crisis can easily be pre-envisaged by a board and should therefore be part of the strategic framework.
- *Oversight decision-making.* The pension fund monitors the implementation of its strategic framework, involving two types of decisions. First, are we doing things

right? The board makes sure that it has an effective mechanism in place to perform these monitoring responsibilities. This will enable it to ensure that all choices have been compliant with the established investment framework. Non-compliant events can be reviewed to see if they have anything in common, and whether this should lead to changes in the monitoring framework. Secondly, the board reviews the monitoring results in order to challenge the goals and assumptions of its own strategic framework: Are we still doing the right things? Are we able to realize our goals? What changes—if any—should be made in order to keep on realizing these goals? If any questions are answered in the negative, how should the board review and adjust its strategic or overarching framework?

In pension governance, a board separates strategic board roles and responsibilities from implementation and execution. Implementation and execution decisions are time-consuming and require specific expertise, and any single decision does not warrant a discussion by the board or alter the outcome in relation to the pension fund's goals. The strategic framework, however, does, and is thus firmly placed on the board agenda. Therefore what is *not* part of the board's decision-making is as follows:

- *Tactical decision-making*. Tactical asset allocations are changes in the portfolio to anticipate changes in financial markets, requiring predictive knowledge and proactive action. Boards are the representatives of asset owners, not asset managers. Setting aside the lackluster results of many tactical choices, boards do not have the knowledge to time the market cycle.
- *Operational decision-making*. This refers to the decisions needed to maintain the pension fund's operational processes, ranging from cash flow management, rebalancing, and collateral management to drawing up reports. These types of decisions are either delegated to an executive board member or to the staff of the pension fund. The board provides resources to facilitate operational decision-making and does not micromanage.
- *Monitoring and oversight*. This is about ensuring compliance with the stated objectives of the pension fund on different levels overall, but also on an individual manager level. This entails reviewing investment management agreements, analyzing performance reports, and setting up an integral compliance framework. The board delegates this to an executive board member or to the staff of the pension fund.

SUPPORTING THE BOARD: EXECUTIVE OFFICE AND STAFF

The board of trustees is supported in its work by a staff or executive office. Larger pension funds are able to set up their own organization and hire staff; smaller pension funds ask an investment consultant, actuary or other professional to provide this support. Giving a clear and decisive mandate to the executive office enables the board of trustees to focus its attention on the strategic challenges that the pension fund faces.

The executive office prepares the basis for the board and the committee's decision-making, is a sparring partner for them, and acts on behalf of the board both as a client of, and a fixed contact point for, the administrative organization. The executive office:

- Supports the board in organizing and servicing meetings of the board and its committees;
- Provides a focal point for the chair of the board to promote controlled, efficient, and effective management;
- Sets priorities and manages internal decision-making;
- Monitors the execution of the board's decisions, and reports back on this to the board and its committees;
- Provides the first point of contact with regulators, participants, journalists, etc.;
- Carries out reviews and analyses of policy issues relating to the plan design.

There is another function that is often not made explicit: the personnel in the executive office will often have been there longer than the individual board members, who in a certain sense are passers-by. This means that they have an important but subtle role in board member education and safeguarding the long-term direction of the fund.

In recent decades, executive offices have increased in importance for several inter-related reasons, often borne out of necessity.[15] A dominant trend in the 1990s was that pension funds spun off their investment activities or pension delivery organization. A strong motivation for doing so was economies of scale: pension funds with internal IMOs found it increasingly difficult to keep up with the increased investments in IT, compliance and risk management, while on the other hand there was constant pressure to reduce costs. Spinning off the investment organizations introduced new opportunities and challenges. First, the board had to develop its own policy and monitor capabilities after spinning off investment organization, introducing the need for a separate staff to support the board in these questions.

Besides the economic rationale for spinning off investment activities, boards were increasingly prompted to adopt insights from other sectors' management theories. A dominant theme was (and still is) to separate policy and implementation and focus on the "core" responsibilities of trustees. Core responsibility is, intuitively, developing the investment framework and realizing the investment returns needed to fulfill the pension promise. Executive offices also play an important role as "interface," monitoring the investment managers and making sure that this implementation is done according to the mandate set. The executive office staff is usually highly specialized and skilled. They understand the investment management side but are able to filter and condense the technical discussions in such a way that the strategic issues are made clear to the board, and that technical details do not overburden the board's agenda. Exhibit 10.3 lists the characteristics of an executive office.

There exists a wide range of executive office organizations. The board can decide on a clear separation of the roles of board chair and CEO. The chair is responsible for leading the board, and the CEO for leading management and the executive office.[16] The board appoints the CEO. Exhibit 10.4 shows the possible configurations, starting with models where the executive office is at most coordinating. The next options show how these offices can be an effective interface between board strategy on the one hand, and

Rationale	Advantages	Disadvantages
• Need to organize countervailing power vis-à-vis the asset manager(s) or fiduciary management organization. • Increased demands on quality of board room knowledge and governance. • Boards need to show that they are in control, adequately managing (outsourcing) risks. • Separation strategy, policy making, execution, and monitoring. • Supporting board members, reducing board time. • Safeguarding long-term continuity of board thinking.	• Improved coordination and supervision of execution. • Better preparation and decision-making. • Freeing up time for board members. • Board that is more "in control." • Supporting the reputation that the pension fund is managed as a professional financial organization.	• Board develops dependency on executive office; policy-making in effect devolved to executive office. • Vulnerability of executive office, limited staff with concentrated functions. • Bloated executive office, hampering decision making and creating a new principal–agent problem for trustees. • Time saving for board member less than expected. • Extra costs in governing the pension fund.

EXHIBIT 10.3 Characteristics of an executive office.[17]

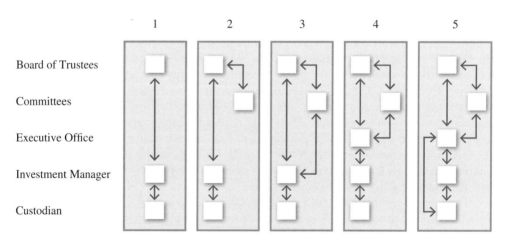

EXHIBIT 10.4 Possible models of a fund's internal organization.

implementation on the other hand. However, the challenge for a board is to ensure that the executive office remains aligned to the fund's goals. That is, there is a risk of the tail wagging the dog. If the office extends too much, the board runs the risk of shifting its countervailing power between the board and the investment organization to the board vs. the executive office. This means it will become too distant and hands-off to have an impact.

INGREDIENTS OF AN EFFECTIVE BOARD[18]

The need to ensure that a board functions effectively may seem obvious, but in order to achieve this, it is important to attend to the balance of leadership and the structure of the board. The structure of the board will also exert the biggest influence on how corporate governance is practiced on an ongoing basis. Creating and maintaining an effective board is hard work. We recapitulate the debates in this section, and end with a list of poor and effective characteristics of boards (Exhibit 10.5).

People and Board Composition

Individually, board members should at least have a working knowledge of all the topics that are handled in this book, so that they are conscious of all the relevant angles. As a group, they should be diverse in terms of competencies. In a good board, the sum is a lot

Signs of Effective Boards	Signs of Poorly Functioning Boards
People— • Listen to each other. • Learn from each other. • Act consistent with earlier decisions or understand why they do not. • Have a strategic mindset. • Think through the lens of the mission, goals, investment beliefs, and principles of the fund. • Build on the insights of investment theory. • Use plain language. • Are not shy to ask questions or name the elephant in the room. • Are well aware of the behavioral pitfalls they may encounter. • Act strictly on behalf of the fund, carefully weighing the long and the short run and the interests of all stakeholders. • There is a clear agenda for each meeting and over the year.	People— • Do not listen to each other. • Do not learn from each other. • One or a few people dominate the decision making. • Technical jargon is used. • Some people are shy to speak. • Decision-making is ad hoc or fear-based emotional decisions. • The short term is dominant. • Not all relevant angles are touched. • There may be wishful thinking. • There's a lot of attention on looking back and looking at details. • Members of the board act more on their own behalf (cover your rear-end, fear of legal issues) than on behalf of the interest of the stakeholders of the fund.

EXHIBIT 10.5 Characteristics of poorly functioning and effective boards.

larger than the individual parts. This means that the individuals also need the necessary skills to work (well) together. Not every personality type is fit for this role. Often we see that one person or a small group of people are dominant in a board, typically the chairman or a group of experts. The role of the chairman is important in building and maintaining a board that functions well. The board also needs to be aware of the main behavioral pitfalls that often lead to poor investment decision-making.

Process

In order to make sure that the board works well on all the relevant angles and topics, it needs an agenda that covers all the topics. To enforce and be well-prepared for this, once again the chairman and the secretary of the board are key. Most board members will have a limited number of hours available, so the board has to make good use of this time. Too often time is not really budgeted for what really matters, with the risk of putting the "urgent" ahead of the "important."

Perspective

The board needs to spend time on policy formulation and foresight, strategic thinking, supervision of management, and accountability. It is essential to have an outside-in perspective, as it is easy for a board to become complacent. Are you really doing the best possible job for your stakeholders? Do you understand them? Does the fund know what its peers are doing and why? These are the questions that need to consistently be asked.

The Right Altitude, Horizon and Distance

There are three perspective issues for the board, namely:

- *Altitude*. Does the board look at the total fund setup and its outcomes from a helicopter perspective? Can it achieve a critical distance towards itself?
- *Horizon*. Has the board organized itself in such a way that it can look forward and backward over a period of at least 5–10 years? Even if that time span is longer than the individual's time span as a member of the board?
- *Distance*. Is the board able to maintain the right distance from the execution of the investment management—is it close enough to be able to fully carry out its responsibility, yet not so close that it is taking operational decisions that should be taken by the executive?

Power and Delegation

The board should take full responsibility for the process and outcomes, and not hide behind experts. Board members cannot hide behind such comments as "apparently, this is the way they do things over here" or "I do not have the power (or expertise) to judge or change things around here." If they feel that way (especially after reading this book!), they should not be a board member. Boards will have to delegate a lot of matters to others such as board committees or external parties—fiduciary and IMOs for example. More and more often there is an executive bureau between the fund and the outside and internal parties. All this delegation can provide specialization and potentially add value in the investment process, but it will also produce principal–agency issues (see Chapter 2) that can increase the implementation gap and drag down results. Boards will hire "experts" or expert organizations, and managing experts is extremely difficult. They tend to have narrow and not holistic expertise, and they are sometimes in love with their own expertise. Therefore, the board should have serious counterbalancing power, and have a clear idea of what this counterbalancing power means in practice (e.g. more checks and monitoring, an executive board member from a similar organization on board, etc.).

Creating the right interaction between the board and the "executive organization" is challenging. Normally, in length of stay, time budget, expertise, sheer number of people, and often in pay check, the IMO is much stronger than the board. In this situation, it is very easy to let the "experts" dominate all the relevant discussions, including the core responsibilities such as the mission, beliefs, and policy. If this is the case, the board is taken hostage by the executive organization. We'll address this important topic in a few chapters.

Learning

Finally, the key difference between an "OK" functioning board and an excellent board is whether or not it is a learning board. In other words, learning becomes part of the day job of boards and is not stacked on top of an already heavy agenda.

ENDNOTES

1. See Huse (2007).
2. Norges Bank Investment Management, Strategy for Norges Bank Investment Management 2017–2019. Accessed on Strategy for Norges Bank Investment Management 2017–2019.
3. See Ghai et al. (2011).
4. See Thompson (2005).
5. See Cadbury (2002).
6. See, for example, Harper (2008).
7. See Huse (2007).
8. See Huse (2007).
9. See Huse (2007).
10. See Furr and Furr (2005).
11. See Huse (2007).
12. Anderson et al. (2017).
13. See Clark and Urwin (2008b).
14. See Clark and Urwin (2008a).
15. See Slager (2012).
16. See Vittas et al. (2008).
17. See Stegeman and Doff (2017); Kamerling and Kramer (2017).
18. See, for example, Ellis (2011a).

Case Study—CalPERS[1]

ONCE DAMAGE HAS BEEN DONE, IT IS VERY HARD TO REPAIR. POOR AND POLITICIZED GOVERNANCE FORMED THE BASIS FOR A HIGH PENSION PROMISE, WHICH COULD NOT BE SUSTAINED BY THE RETURNS FROM THE INVESTMENTS. A LACK OF HIGH QUALITY OVERSIGHT LED TO EXCESSIVELY HIGH COST, A POOR INVESTMENT PROCESS, AND AN INVESTMENT ORGANIZATION THAT WAS NOT FIT FOR THE COMPLEXITY OF THE STRATEGY, RESULTING IN DISASTROUS OUTCOMES DURING AND IN THE AFTERMATH OF THE FINANCIAL CRISIS OF 2008–2009. AFTER THE CRISIS, CHIEF EXECUTIVE OFFICER (CEO) ANNE STAUSBOLL AND CHIEF INVESTMENT OFFICER (CIO) JOE DEAR STARTED A RIGOROUS PROCESS TO STRENGTHEN THE STRATEGY AND THE QUALITY OF THE INVESTMENT MANAGEMENT ORGANIZATION

Background

The California Public Employees' Retirement System (CalPERS) is an American pension fund, founded in 1932 and located in California. The beneficiaries are Californian employees, retirees and their respective families. It is America's largest pension fund with approximately \$347 billion[2] in assets under management in January 2018. The fund has a defined benefit character, and manages the pension, death and health benefits of around 1.8 million participants.[3] In the past, CalPERS was considered a role model due to its transparent communication with its stakeholders, excellent returns[4] and the so-called CalPERS effect, where CalPERS improved returns by focusing on the quality of governance of companies the fund invested in. After the strong 1990s on the financial markets, the funding rate was comfortably high, which led to overgenerous promises to the beneficiaries and unrealistic optimism about future returns. The discount rate forecast was set too high, which meant that the discounted future obligations were less than they should be.

Challenges

The developments within CalPERS during the first decade of the 2000s provides insights into how not to govern a pension fund. In their case study, Ang and Abrams (2012)[5] identified a large number of flaws in the setup, which resulted in a badly run, extremely expensive investment process and huge losses.

Despite its historic reputation, CalPERS was "opaquely transparent" according to Ang and Abrams. They[6] found that although CalPERS provided a lot of documentation, it did not report management expense ratios or the proportion of internally and externally managed funds. When comparing own calculated expense ratios with the fund's peers, they found that CalPERS paid significantly more in expenses. Also, CalPERS lacked a simple benchmark, so it was difficult to identify the added value of choices within the investment process. For example, the cost for real estate was high, but the source of these costs could not be traced. The management steered the fund using the input they received, but when the input is opaque it is very difficult to set the right course.

Furthermore, there was no sound rebalancing process in place, and CalPERS was forced to conduct a fire sale of large portions of its equity portfolio in the midst of the financial crisis due to its liquidity needs. This threatened the sustainability of the fund. The lay board lacked investment knowledge and was highly politicized; it sometimes made investment decisions against the advice of senior management and also sometimes made investment decisions aimed at furthering union interests.

This combination of factors resulted in a period of dramatically failing performances. The funding ratio dropped from around 130% in 1998 to 74% in 2011, and 73% in 2015. This corresponds to an unfunded liability of $85 billion. Even when writing about this case in 2018, the 10-year relative return as compared to the policy benchmark is still suffering from the horrible 2007, 2008, and 2009 years.

The process

CalPERS enforced several changes throughout the years to cope with the challenges. These began in 2009 with the appointment of Anne Stausboll as CEO and the late Joseph Dear as CIO. "My focus was on restoring trust and credibility to the organization, and making it transparent and open," Stausboll says. Both chiefs had a long-term vision and through their experience knew what it meant to be a long-term investor. This focus, together with improved risk management, steered the fund out of the crisis.

The solution for the high costs was to start with reporting transparent and meaningful numbers. Stausboll introduced a financial office. The financial office oversees risk management and is integrated with the actuarial office and investment office. The integration allows for a holistic view of assets and liabilities, thereby making a step towards clearing up the opaque transparency according to the then CEO.

To cope with the investment mistakes, Dear and Stausboll took on a long-horizon focus accompanied by an emphasis on risk management. To enforce the long-term view, fees with external managers were renegotiated to ensure the right incentives and reduce costs. The latter was further reduced by cutting down the number of managers, which resulted in a saving of $135 million not including profit sharing fees in the five years to 2016.[7] To guide the investment choices, investment beliefs were made explicit, along with a sustainability framework.

Stausboll and Dear created a Roadmap for the Investment Office for the years 2012–2014, focusing on three aspects: Performance, Plumbing and People.

- *Performance.* Geared towards achieving the target rate of return without exposing the fund to an undue risk of major drawdown.

- *Plumbing*. Developing and implementing the systems, controls, and processes necessary to ensure the integrity of operations.
- *People*. Ensuring the right number of people with the right skills to achieve investment performance improvement and control of operations.

The outcome

The process is not yet finished, but it is well underway. The hemorrhaging has stopped. Over the past five years, the relative return is around zero. Strong investment beliefs now drive the investment process and reporting. This provides a shared structure between the board and the investment office. The costs and the number of managers have come down. Annual cost savings were already at around $300 million in 2015.[8] In addition, the complexity has been reduced, for example by halting investments in hedge funds.

Probably the biggest potential difficulty is the governance: CalPERS still has a lay board. And given the fund's limitations in the pay structure, it is still difficult to hire the right people. An ongoing conversation is underway about this.

Lessons for Achieving Investment Excellence

- Neither investment policy nor results can compensate for a pension promise that is unsustainably high given the premium levels.
- A lack of critical supervision can lead to a deteriorating organization that is not fit for purpose. This will eventually lead to bad investment outcomes.
- The quality, independence, and knowledge of the board is extremely important for avoiding these situations. This is even more true in an environment where market discipline in the form of competition is lacking.
- Boards should make sure that they achieve proper insight into critical measures and regularly benchmark them against relevant peers.

ENDNOTES

1. Part of this case study is based on the case study by Ang and Abrams (2012). We gratefully thank Andrew Ang for allowing us to quote from that.
2. See www.calpers.ca.gov/page/investments.
3. See www.calpers.ca.gov/docs/forms-publications/facts-at-a-glance.pdf.
4. See Rose-Smith (2016).
5. See White (2012).
6. See White (2012).
7. See White (2016).
8. See www.calpers.ca.gov/docs/board-agendas/201608/invest/item05a-01.pdf.

CHAPTER 11

Establishing the Investment Committee

Key Take Aways

- Boards establish investment committees to provide advice on investment policy, to oversee policy implementation, and monitor the investment management.

- The task of the committee is "more governance than execution," overseeing the operations of the investment management organization. It provides a countervailing force to balance the investment management organization and helps create the atmosphere of trust needed for an effective investment management organization.

- Necessary skills for an investment committee are knowledge of investments and the investment industry, and the ability to assess and foster the quality of the investment management organization.

- Many investment committees fail to achieve the right altitude (too operational), distance (too close to operational decisions) and horizon (overly short-term oriented) and are thus deficient in oversight. This can result in substantial cost and opportunity loss.

The board has a fiduciary obligation to monitor the investments on an ongoing basis to ensure they continue to be prudent and appropriate. It is considered best practice for boards to form an investment committee to oversee the plan's investments. Smaller pension funds sometimes argue against having investment committees, suggesting it is too time-consuming. However, size does not matter here. Under most legislations, the trustees are fiduciaries and, as such, personally liable for their actions. Having a casual approach to the important job of monitoring the investment options being provided for participants would be failing to carry this responsibility. An investment committee should help establish the right quality standards for investment policymaking as well as for implementation and monitoring.

The board can delegate a wide range of responsibilities to the investment committee. In some cases, the committee plays a highly proactive role based on an executive mandate for making investment decisions on behalf of the fund. This is often the case in relatively small funds. In other instances, the duties and responsibilities of the committee may be restricted to more advisory, policy-setting and oversight roles. This is usually when there is a professional and/or proprietary investment management organization attached to the fund. We discuss which of these types of investment committees best serve the specific goals and investment process of particular pension funds. We examine the composition of the investment committee and discuss how its members and the committee's external advisors can operate and collaborate in an effective way. We also identify the potential pitfalls of external advisors. The chapter concludes with a review of the investment committee's agenda, the role of its chairperson, and the interplay between the committee and the board.

ROLES AND RESPONSIBILITIES

The aim of an investment committee is to provide expert advice and assistance to the board on drawing up strategic investment policy and to monitor the execution of the investment policy via internal and external asset managers. To do this, the investment committee establishes a prudent process by which the investment plan (see Chapter 8), strategies, asset managers, advisors and costs are analyzed, monitored and evaluated on a regular basis. The main focus of the committee is on the investment management process (discussed in Chapter 6), which translates goals into investments, and its underlying assumptions. The committee oversees the management of the investments and the investment management process but does not actually manage the investments.

These responsibilities are written down in a charter, approved by the board. Basically, the investment committee is charged with advising on or actually developing the pension fund's long-term investment policy and ensuring that it is carried out on a consistent, effective, and efficient basis. An investment committee can have the following responsibilities,[1] where we distinguish whether the investment committee only advises on the task, or whether it has a mandated role and is therefore responsible for the task:

- Setting the right investment policy: develop, or advise the board on an investment policy statement (IPS);
- Evaluate the managers' performance and take appropriate action;
- Document the investment process and decisions made;
- Review and approve ad hoc operational investment changes that might affect the fund's goals;
- Hold meetings on a regular basis;
- Select the manager(s) to execute the policy, remove investment managers;
- Solicit and monitor the activities of experts (advisors, investment consultants, actuaries);
- Review investment management fees paid by the plan and participants;
- Review its own effectiveness.

The first three responsibilities relate to the board's fiduciary's duties and to the realization of the long-term risk and return of the fund. Advice on the investment policy, evaluation of managers, and documentation of the investment process are key tasks.

Advise the Board on an Investment Policy Statement

The investment committee will advise on four different topics concerning the IPS. First, investment principles or investment beliefs. These are set by the board, but the investment committee can advise on their validity and also be an important party in their creation. External asset managers should not be involved in this process, as they have too large a vested interest in the outcome. Second, the capital market expectations and scenarios that form the basis for asset-liability management (ALM) and the choice of asset classes. Third, ALM, and its translation into a reference policy or portfolio. The investment committee advises on optimizing the investments within the framework of goals and risk appetite. It can challenge the investment management organization as well as the trustees on whether the proposed policies are realistic and can generate the required returns, and whether the risk fits in the profile. Finally, strategic asset allocation and policy. The investment committee assesses the resulting asset allocation for consistency with the board's investment policy, whether it can be implemented, and whether the results can be objectively evaluated.

Evaluate the Managers' Performance and Take Appropriate Actions

This role is often under-appreciated. This is why we devote a whole chapter to it (Chapter 10). Some members of an investment committee are likely to come from the investment management industry, and may be inclined to dwell (too often and in too much detail) on the outcomes of the investment process. It can therefore be helpful for the investment committee to review the quality of the investment management organization based on scorecards with multiple criteria. Performance is not enough. Quality standards should be set, not so much for hiring and firing as for achieving continuous improvement.

Document the Investment Process and Decisions Made

The committee can be responsible for the design and oversight of the investment process (governance) as well as the implementation thereof (management). Within the investment process, it reviews whether there is an effective and practical organizational structure that regulates supervision, authority, responsibility, and execution; whether the correct process is followed with respect to delegation of tasks; and whether the process is carried out efficiently with regard to speed, accuracy, and frequency.

The long-term effectiveness of the committee will be challenged by short-term market events. It is therefore critical for investment committees to understand their role and maintain their discipline. Investment author Charles Ellis argues that "the Investment Committee's primary role is not investment *management*, but *good governance*."[2] For most investment committees, the main task is to help determine the long-term investment policy most appropriate for realizing the fund's goals while optimizing the use of the fund's resources and organization. The challenge is to not get too close to or too involved in the actual investment management process. Rather, the investment committee needs to continually monitor the external short-term and long-term forces that

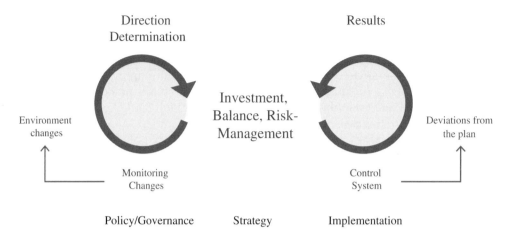

EXHIBIT 11.1   The investment committee's role in the investment process.

impact investment policy to determine whether the policy and governance are still adequate or are in need of change.

Exhibit 11.1 provides a useful picture of how an investment committee can operate in this context. The left cycle indicates the adjustments and the learning behavior based on the external environment. Which changes could affect the fund's aims, and would this effect be long or short term? And what policy can a pension fund develop in order to anticipate this? Organizational adaptiveness is central here. This requires a long-term and broad outlook from the investment committee. Here, we see that the investment committee is pivotal between the strategic and the implementation loops.

In contrast, the second cycle in Exhibit 11.1 focuses on the internal environment. How can the plan be set up as efficiently as possible? Between which steps in the investment process could there be an unnecessary loss of returns, and how can this be prevented? This cycle has a shorter-term focus. The continuous interaction between policy, strategy, and execution leads to a high degree of complexity. To manage this, roles and responsibilities must be well organized and agreed upon.

The board can decide whether the investment committee has a largely advisory role or a mandated role in these shorter-term and longer-term cycles, which in turn determines the governance remit of the investment committee. In an advisory role, the committee focuses on strategic, longer-term oversight. It advises and gives feedback on decisions that the board or investment management organization plans to take. The committee can, however, also be mandated to take decisions within the framework of the IPS and other guidelines of the fund. This reduces the time spent by the board on decision-making, but also changes the role of the committee vis-à-vis of the board: the committee becomes accountable for certain decisions. The advisory or mandated role should be made explicit in the charter.

The choice of a mandated or advisory/oversight role of the investment committee is very much dependent on the interaction of two governance choices. Clearly, it depends on the portion of responsibilities that the board wishes to delegate to the investment committee, but it is also a function of the way in which the execution of the investments is organized: is this fully outsourced or internally managed?

In the case of Ontario Teachers' Pension Plan, the investment committee has the same composition as the board itself. The board is made up of highly qualified people. Board members have extensive experience in a wide range of disciplines and are required to oversee a complex pension plan. They are drawn from the fields of business management, finance, investment management, actuarial science, economics, education, and accounting. Therefore, the board and the investment committee have the qualities to judge and direct the investment management organization. If, for example, board members have a political background, they should be shielded from making or influencing investment decisions to avoid the risk of political influence or bias.[3]

The more the execution of the investments is outsourced (e.g. to a fiduciary manager or an investment management organization), the less operational and the more strategic the work of the investment committee will be, and the stronger the emphasis on oversight. In summary, the responsibilities of the investment committee can vary due to these factors, and should be laid down in a charter or similar document approved by the board.

MEMBERS OF THE INVESTMENT COMMITTEE

Members of an investment committee are frequently chosen because of their position or experiences in benefit administration, accounting, or legal or corporate finance. Given the varying level of skills and experience available, it makes sense to recruit individuals in the investment committee who have an interest or basic understanding of financial markets.[4] The challenge for the chair is to avoid inviting people who do investing or stock picking as a hobby. This may sound obvious, but retail investing really is a very different area of expertise than institutional investments. There may be some overlap in knowledge about the same securities; however, given the discussions on the investment process, stakeholders, horizon, risk appetite, etc., it is clear that a different form of knowledge and competency is required of board members than might have been acquired from retail investing.

An investment committee normally has around five to nine members. An odd number is preferred, to avoid deadlock in voting. The investment committee will consist of board members, external members, and the chair.

Board members are appointed to the committee based on their roles on the board of trustees. The investment committee tends to be perceived as one of the more exciting committees in a pension fund. The chair should avoid appointing trustees as members as a form of reward, and also make sure that the committee does not become too dependent on any one board member.

The external members are appointed based on their expertise. When the board sets the charter for the investment committee, the chair of the investment committee can work out the skills and competences needed to fulfill its tasks and responsibilities. External members bring in complementary skills to those of trustees. External members generally have a background in the financial markets, as portfolio managers, strategists, former chief investment officers (CIOs), or trustees at another fund. The chair should avoid appointing external members solely for their status or reputation, but make sure they can fulfill their roles, fit in, and not dominate the investment committee meeting. Potential external members, on the other hand, should have sufficient knowledge of the fund's most important policy documents, and of the charter of the investment committee in order to understand what is expected of them, whether their role is advisory and whether they also have a vote—which changes their responsibilities and liabilities. The chairman should have a thorough understanding of the fund's characteristics and goals and set the agenda accordingly. As on the board, the chairman has an important role to play.

All the individual investment committee members should have a reasonably active knowledge on investments and financial markets. Collectively, a high level of expertise on the theoretical and practical side of investing is required, as well as expertise on how to judge and evaluate investment management organizations. Individual members need the ability to formulate their views clearly and to be trustworthy. At least collectively, a strategic mindset is necessary. The ability to listen is also important. Members need enough time on their hands to be well prepared, and to be able to reflect on serious questions. Their remuneration reflects the time they need to spend on the job in order to do it properly. The ideal investment committee has a good mix of long-standing and diverse skills, collectively providing all the required knowledge and experience. And as investment advisor and author Ellis says, "All members should have demonstrated good judgment of people, concepts, and organizations—and play well with others."[5]

FORMING AN EFFECTIVE INVESTMENT COMMITTEE

Forming an effective investment committee is, similarly to board governance, about setting the right goals, and is also about avoiding pitfalls in investments and decision-making (see also Chapter 4). For an investment committee, the investment policy, strategic asset allocation, and monitoring whether the implementation is still leading to the realization of the strategic goals constitute the biggest responsibilities—and creating the highest value for the fund means maintaining the right perspective or altitude. Maintaining the right altitude means always start from the big picture and then zoom in, not the other way around. The big picture is the fund's goals, risk appetite, investment beliefs, and strategic policy. Zooming in means observing the financial markets and monitoring whether the fund is still on course, or whether important assumptions are being challenged in such a fundamental way that this should trigger a review or evaluation. As with many choices in the financial markets, the committee has to base its decisions on interpretations and estimations of how financial markets and economies might develop, and the implications for the fund's goals. A core element that distinguishes good from great investment committees is, therefore, whether they have the ability to differentiate between fact and opinion. In fact, an effective investment committee has several distinguishing characteristics, listed in the following paragraph.

An effective investment committee is future-oriented. It should always be forward-looking. This aspect requires serious attention. For example, the tendency is to underestimate risk after a period of calm or positive markets, and to overestimate risk after heavy turbulence or falls. It is really useful that short-term volatility measures such as implied volatility or even historical volatility are often used to describe the "riskiness" of the market.

An effective investment committee refers back to principles and beliefs. There should be complete consistency between principles and the agenda. For example, if the principles are based on the concept of efficient markets, all talk of out- or under-performance should be treated as worrying. Reading the stock market pages of a newspaper should be forbidden!

An effective investment committee avoids jargon. Given that the investment committee is populated by experts, and oftentimes supplemented by people from the investment management organization, there may be a tendency to speak in financial markets jargon. This can sometimes be misleading jargon (such as "bet:" have you hired a gambler to manage your portfolio? or "tracking error:" is it an error to deviate from a benchmark? We hope not!) But this is also confusing for the non-technical members of the committee. Although we are sure many investors do not do it on purpose, the use of jargon creates a sense of expertise that may be overwhelming. Don't accept it!

An effective investment committee is wary of groupthink. Often, with experts in the room, after the expert has spoken, committee members with less expertise might be inclined to agree with the expert, shying away from (or being unable to) challenging the assumptions behind the expert's reasoning, even though this may be sorely needed. An expert is by definition trained in a specific area of expertise and reasons accordingly, while board members have to oversee and balance a wide range of expertise and make decisions on this basis.

An effective investment committee has a clear decision-making process. How are decisions made? By majority? By consensus? What is done with minority points of view? Often, when a decision has to be made, there is time pressure. However, a bad decision, or even a badly formulated decision, will come back to haunt you! The chairman should state the decision and confirm whether this really is the decision either by consensus or by asking individual members. More importantly, the chair also needs to make the consequences of this decision clear. A decision without stipulating consequences leads to procrastination of difficult choices, or ineffective implementation. In addition, decisions and advice by the investment committee will be closely read by the investment management organization for example. Ambiguity will lead to massive wastage of energy.

An effective investment committee sets its own agenda. If there are others involved in the investment committee, be it external experts, asset managers, or people from the fund's own investment management organization, every meeting should be designed and controlled by the investment committee, not by the investment manager. The investment committee sets the agenda and obtains relevant documentation from the external party, and there should also be ample preparation time for the meeting for the members of the investment committee.

Finally, they should understand the probabilistic nature of financial markets. An important aspect is the long horizon nature of decision-making in the pensions industry and the noisy environment that financial markets provide, leading to long and loose feedback loops. The big challenge is the probabilistic nature of markets. Like tossing a coin, you never know for sure what's going to happen next. As a result, the link between process (how an organization makes a decision) and the outcome (the result of that decision) is weak in the short to medium term, and gains substance and even some measure of predictability in the long term. So, the challenge for an investment committee is to focus on the governance of the process, rather than on the short-term results.

Most of these previously listed characteristics concern getting the role of the committee right in terms of making decisions and of the way it advises. The precise structure of a committee is thus regarded as slightly less important; the ultimate structure will depend more on the organizational culture of the sponsor or company branch and can take a formal or informal approach. An effectively functioning investment committee has enough structure to maintain the process, but not so much that debate and discussion are inhibited, and decision-making becomes boxed in or "pre-arranged."[6]

The Role of the Chairman of the Investment Committee

Pension board chairs and investment committee chairs carry greater responsibility than other board or committee members[7] in leading their members in relation to agreed goals and objectives. With their leadership style, they embody the values of the fund, and influence the way their members are involved in decision-making. The chair of the investment committee sets the agenda, decides on the composition of the investment committee, guards the continuity, and makes sure that members come well prepared and aware of their duties. Finally, and most importantly, the chair structures decision-making in such a way that decisions are in line with the fund's goals and can be executed and evaluated. Effective leadership of the chair requires the following attributes:[8]

- Inspiring strong personal respect, derived from industry reputation and commitment to the institution;
- An ability to structure decision-making, particularly to set priorities and establish time devoted to making crucial decisions;
- An ability to articulate and mediate between various decision-making styles on the board;
- Sensitivity to managing stakeholder expectations, with regard for both soft and hard considerations;
- Competency with internal staffing of the fund and the framing and implementation of outside delegations;
- Commitment to a culture and practice of accountability and measurement, both for board operations and the performance of the executive team;
- An ability to build the culture of the organization and promote it to others.

A MODEL FOR AN EFFECTIVE INVESTMENT COMMITTEE MEETING

In this section, we describe how an effective investment committee meeting could be organized. We consider the following aspects: (i) Agenda, (ii) Preparation, (iii) the Meeting itself and the roles of the different people around the table, (iv) the Output—decision-making, and (v) Evaluation and learning.

The Investment Committee Agenda

The typical investment committee will meet six to eight times per annum, for approximately three hours. So, the total time spent annually will be in the range of 18–24 hours. Essentially, this is all the time available per year to direct the investments. This should be used productively. If it is not planned wisely, the investment committee may find itself in a bottleneck in the investment process. Careful preparation of the agenda is therefore very important. What should be on the agenda? The key responsibilities of the investment committee are: (i) Setting the right investment policy; (ii) Hiring the managers to execute the policy; and (iii) Monitoring and evaluating the policy and its execution. It is important to strike the right balance between these three responsibilities during the year. This is best done by actually putting them on the agenda. The natural tendency is to spend more time on urgent, but possibly trivial issues, rather than important matters; and doing things right rather than doing the right things. Therefore, strong agenda management is needed to counterbalance these tendencies.

There will generally be a predictable pattern for the topics of investment committee meetings during a year. For example, the agenda for the first quarter will consider evaluation of outcomes of the strategy, context, and the implementation of the past period, identifying critical issues to look into. In the second quarter, the external environment is considered in depth, and consequences (if any) are formulated for the existing set of return and risk expectations. In the third quarter, the issues raised in the first quarter are discussed further, along with how these affect the current portfolio construction. Alternatives for the portfolio strategy can be considered, based on the new insights on return and risk considerations that the committee discussed in the second quarter. In the fourth quarter, the committee recapitulates the evaluations and discussions, and decides on the next period's policy and plan, with a focus on the effectiveness of implementation.

Strong agenda management is very important. In order to make sure that the investment committee touches on all aspects, the chair and secretary will set up a scheme well ahead of the meetings. It should not be so rigid that it is impossible to adapt if another urgent matter arises. The average investment committee can run the risk of spending too much time on recent "news" and "prices," totally irrelevant and potentially even harmful for strategic decision-making; this is a human weakness to be aware of. Sometimes, this is partly because the responsibility involved with the big questions is so large that committee members prefer to make minor and barely relevant decisions, effectively procrastinating on the difficult questions while still hoping to show that the committee has been decisive. If the investment committee members are savvy, they should be aware of this danger.

Our ideal agenda looks like this (keeping in mind that a meeting should take a maximum of three hours):

1. Opening, agenda, last meeting's notes.
2. Current events: What's new, is it relevant and if so, why? Should it be addressed today, or put on the agenda for a later meeting?
3. Evaluation of past period: has anything happened that is so significant that a red light is flashing? Again, it is important to distinguish between the urgent and the

important. Address urgent issues quickly or put them down for the next meeting, where the urgency will be toned down by management by exception.

4. First strategic issue (at least one hour per issue), with a clear focus on what sort of decision is required. Strategic issues should be highest on the agenda. "If there is always a lot of urgent stuff, there's something wrong."[9]

5. If absolutely needed: second strategic issue; decision.

6. Small formal decisions to be made, allocate half an hour at most.

7. Look forward to the agenda of the next meeting(s).

8. Once or twice per year, spend time scanning the strategic horizon: PEST (political, economic, sociocultural and technological) or DESTEP (demographic, economic, social, technological, environmental, political) … What does it mean for you? What's going on?

Committee Preparation: Quality, Clarity and Timeliness and Extent of Materials

The members of the investment committee should have the tools to prepare themselves well for the meeting. As they tend to be busy, the materials should be available at least a week before the meeting. The necessary details of any topic on the agenda that requires decision-making will need to be available in written form. For discussion topics, this is less strict.

The total set of documents should take no longer to read than the length of the investment committee meeting. So, three hours of meeting equates to a maximum three hours of preparation. At an average reading speed of 30 pages per hour, this comes to a hard maximum of 100 pages of must-read material per meeting for a three-hour meeting. We often see 500+ pages of material, with boards having to struggle to distill the main items. Next to "must-read" material, there may be technical annexes for specialists, etc., but all the relevant information should be in the must-read part.

In order to be relevant, investment committee documents have to be written in clear language and be accessible to all the investment committee members. It is a very good idea to write these documents in "pyramid" style, so that committee members can get a good grasp of the issue at the beginning of the document: (i) What is the issue? (ii) What is the key question? (iii) What alternatives have been generated? (iv) What is the proposed solution and why? (v) How will it be implemented and reported back to the committee?

The investment committee needs a strong gatekeeper demanding this kind of input: this will be the chair, working closely with the secretary. The fiduciary or investment management organization should be explicitly asked to produce this kind of input, and it should be part of the service level agreement. The committee should not be lenient on the relevancy and quality of the documents. If left to their own devices, the people from investment management organizations or consultancies writing these documents may tend to revert to a technical writing style that they are most familiar with, but which is unsuited to decision-making, as it is not easy to strike the right note. Often, they are specialists, writing from a very specific angle. For them it is often challenging to understand where their part of the puzzle fits in the bigger whole, or to understand how to look at their challenges from a board perspective. If they are technical people, e.g. part of the ALM process or part of risk management, they run the risk of becoming stuck "in the box:" they tend to see the world through the lens of their models, and thus restrict their view of it. The investment committee needs to be able to understand the key assumptions underlying the models and their limitations. A good template for documents to be discussed by the investment committee is a great help:

- What is the topic?
- What is the concrete question the committee should answer?
- Why does this issue come up?
- Where does it fit in the investment process?
- What is or are the proposed answers/alternatives and why?
- What are the pros and cons?
- How does it fit in with existing policy?
- How does it fit in with investment beliefs?

It is very easy for people on investment committees—especially those who are not experts in the financial area—to be overwhelmed by the jargon and the apparent precision of reports. Don't be! If you use external people, make sure they are able to convey their message well, clearly, and consistently in written form. The number of pages should be limited. A proposal should be explicit, supported by facts and sound reasoning, and should refer to specific objectives as well as principles and beliefs. There should be consistency in the approach to comparable problems. Also, good proposals consistently build on the historical decision-making by the fund.

Roles

The investment committee is an important junction where fund and the investment management organization meet. Here, creating an effective working relationship is important. On the one hand, there is the strategic plan—execution—accountability axis of the relationship, in which the fund is the client and the investment manager needs to deliver efficiently. On the other hand, the investment management organization should ideally be a trusted and valued partner of the fund, with its inputs and thoughts worth taking very seriously. The following roles need to be clear at the start of the meeting: the CIO; external managers/consultants; and committee peers.

a) The mandate for executing the strategy is given to the investment management organization, in the form of a fiduciary, chief executive officer (CEO) or delegated CIO. The CIO/CEO of the investment management organization can act as the bridge between the pension fund and the investment management organization. The board of the fund is in charge of strategy, governance, and the investment management organization of execution, but they need a good working relationship, and this is fostered through the investment committee. The committee may also need to be aware that the CIO of the investment management organization could have a conflict of interest with the fund, if other clients are being served. So, which role can the CIO best play in these meetings?

- Act as a lookout: given the fact that the investment management organization operates in the financial markets, they have intimate knowledge of what's going on;
- On some topics, the CIO may help to clarify written input by shining a fresh light on it;
- The CIO represents the investment management organization and should therefore be deeply involved in the evaluation of investments and be at the helm of plans to strategically improve the investment management organization, making clear how this helps the pension fund's goals;
- On some questions, the CIO could introduce a reality check, bridging the gap between strategy and implementation: e.g. the board wants element A, but can element A realistically be accomplished?

b) External investment managers/consultants often have different roles and have many agendas, such as the profitability of their firm, serving many clients or having relatively short-lived relationships with the fund, and might therefore be tempted to "double or quit." They might be very dependent on whether you like them, so there is always a risk that they will knowingly or unknowingly say what you would like to hear. Similarly, many external investment managers genuinely have a very difficult time really understanding the perspective of the fund. Where you stand depends on where you sit. Their horizon will be a lot shorter, they are used to thinking in a financial market perspective and not in risk management or fund objective terms. They may also have difficulty in appreciating that they are only a part of the whole.

c) Trustees and managers from other pension funds can bring a very important perspective to the table. For example, every now and then the committee could hold a session in which peers are asked to review a part of the whole setup or strategy. The learning effect of such exercises can be great, provided that participants are open to learning!

The Results of the Meeting

The minutes of the investment committee meetings should be extremely clear and available to all people involved in the investment management process. Like the verdict of a judge, these are the words that will nudge people's future behavior. The minutes thus form a very important part of the history and the DNA of the fund. Strong reasoning will help direct energy effectively in the future. This also means that historical investment committee results should be easily accessible for all people involved.

Evaluation and Learning

After you have attended a couple of investment committee meetings as a board member, observing with a fresh pair of eyes, you will likely have noticed a lot of things along the lines of the above-mentioned points. Write these down and score them! This will provide very useful input later on, for sharing with the chairman or with colleagues on the investment committee. The chair can even decide that committee members take turns to share observations about the effectiveness of the meeting on a regular basis, providing constant feedback.

With health problems, you have to look at the symptoms and work on establishing a diagnosis. In a similar way, you can start to improve the relevant aspects of the investment committee. In order to improve the situation, it is necessary to be aware of how change works. Nobody wants to be a lone wolf howling in the wilderness. It is important to build on evidence that you are not alone in your observations and somehow make them objective and share them. Sharing your insights may be more or less formal: from a casual conversation over coffee to raising an item on the agenda to, for example, ask an independent consultant to make an assessment of how the board functions.

There may be situations where this is very difficult, and it may be a long-horizon process, e.g. when there is a power structure in which the chairman is extremely powerful or dominant. Be aware that the wrong personality types act against their own interests and are not able to look at themselves objectively and learn. This makes it important to think carefully about the personality types you want on the committee.

ENDNOTES

1. See DiBruno (2015).
2. See Ellis (1998).
3. See Andonov et al. (2011).
4. See DiBruno (2015).
5. See Ellis (1998).
6. See Olah and Sturiale (2006)
7. See Clark and Urwin (2008a).
8. See Clark and Urwin (2008a).
9. See Ellis (1998).

CHAPTER 12

Managing the Investment Management Organization

Key Take Aways

- In almost every case, the board delegates significant parts of the investment process to external or internal agents.

- The design is often partially a function of the size of the fund. The smaller the fund, the more it has to buy externally; the larger the fund, the more it can bring parts of the process in-house.

- The board is responsible for the design, the contact, the oversight, and the evaluation of the outsourcing. This is a complex and time-consuming board task. Misunderstanding and agency issues may arise.

- In the relationship between the pension fund and the investment management provider there are elements of "client-provider" but also of "partnership." The first relationship is about the execution of the mandate. The second targets the continuous improvement of the way the investment puzzle is solved in changing circumstances.

- In order to fulfill this task successfully, the board needs a relevant governance budget in terms of time, competences, and resources. The requirements change with the complexity of the fund.

Any pension fund must have an individual or appoint an entity that is responsible for the actual implementation of the investment strategy. In a very small pension fund, this may be a trustee or an administrator who buys a few mutual funds and monitors these investments. A larger pension fund can appoint an external organization to carry out the investment strategy. This can be done in many forms, e.g. the Outsourced chief investment officer (OCIO) or fiduciary manager models. As funds grow in size and complexity, they tend to add their own professional investment staff, developing an internal investment management organization (IMO) or committee. Dedicated investment staff can add value to the investment process at any level of the operation. Funds make their own individual choices, incorporating portfolio construction, selection and monitoring of mandates or even the internal management of mandates. However, the role of the in-house IMO must be clearly defined.

We begin this chapter with a discussion of the different types of IMOs, ranging from fully outsourced to fully insourced. In this section, we also address the important question of the size of the "governance budget" for managing and overseeing the IMO from the perspective of the pension fund, i.e. the budget in terms of allocated time, resources, and knowledge. The board decides on this. In practice, this budget is often seen as a given, so the question becomes "What can we do we given the budget?" In reality, the more relevant question is "What governance budget do we need in order to be fit for purpose?"

Governing the investment management part of the fund is no easy task, regardless of whether this is done internally, partially externally, or fully externally to the pension fund. Therefore, in the later parts of the chapter we zoom in on the critical instruments the board possesses to make this structure, which often has elements key for a partnership to work well, such as delegation, the service level agreement (SLA), monitoring, and evaluation.

THE ROLES OF THE INVESTMENT MANAGEMENT ORGANIZATION

In order to be of most value to the fund, the board has to be clear about the roles and responsibilities of the IMO. The following roles can come into play:

1. To execute the investment strategy or policy set by the board;
2. Optionally, there might be a requirement from the fund to add extra value beyond a reference or benchmark portfolio;
3. The IMO may in turn be in charge of the external agents; i.e. the investment managers it selects and monitors for individual mandates on behalf of the pension fund;
4. The IMO is also likely to have an advisory role for the staff and board of trustees of the fund.

The first and most fundamental role of the IMO is to execute the investment strategy or policy set by the board, within the specified parameters. This often appears in the investment policy statement in the form of a set portfolio with boundaries for asset weights, in combination with a risk budget. The execution should be cost efficient, and operational risks should be managed. The board normally also sets a cost range beforehand, and is aware of when costs could change reflecting performance or growth in assets. Regarding the operational risks, the board is likely to have conducted a risk due diligence, identified the most important risks of outsourcing to the IMO, and discussed with the organization what sort of mitigating measures have been taken.

Secondly, there might be a value-added requirement from the fund that the IMO should, at a specified horizon, realize added value over and above a reference portfolio or strategic benchmark when carrying out the policy portfolio of investments. The board of trustees would quiz the IMO as to why it believes there is an opportunity to create extra added value, usually in the form of discussing the organization's beliefs and set up. The board of trustees needs to make sure that these beliefs at least do not contradict the pension fund's values and beliefs. If possible, they should be fully aligned, which is of course easier when the pension fund controls or owns the IMO. Next, the fund has to make sure the IMO has the skills and resources needed to add value.

Thirdly, the IMO can in turn be expected to be in charge of external agents. Execution of the investment strategy requires the selection and monitoring of mandates and developing hedging strategies for interest rate or currency risk. If the pension fund were to deal directly with the individual parties carrying out these mandates and derivatives transactions, information asymmetry would arise. Among other things, the board would face the high cost of information collection. After their purchase, the board would have to monitor its investments in a timely and complete fashion. Failure to monitor would expose the fund to agency costs, i.e. the risk that the asset managers will take actions contrary to the promises made at the start or as stipulated in the covenants or agreements. This is especially relevant when the manager as party to a financial transaction has information the board does not, and when control and enforcement of contracts is costly. The IMO should therefore play a valuable role in intermediating between the board of trustees and individual asset managers, controlling the outsourced activities and making sure that there are no incentives for the asset managers to manage the investments other than in the interests of the pension fund. Combining internal fund management with external management leads to potential agency issues where the IMO may be biased towards internal management.

Fourthly, the IMO is likely to play an advisory role to the staff and board of trustees of the fund: given the objectives of the fund, it can advise on asset liability management (ALM), strategic asset allocation (SAA), the implementation forms within asset classes, and discussions on investment styles such as active vs. passive. This advisory role is important for a board. Because the search and transaction costs of switching to another IMO are high, it is desirable for a long-term relationship to develop, where the IMO builds up intimate knowledge about how the fund and board works, enabling it to provide tailor-made advice. The IMO will know the risk appetite, preferences in implementation, and particular dislikes that board members might have where investment management is concerned, all very helpful insights for drafting the right proposal. On the other hand, the IMO does have to balance both the goals of the board, and the goals of its own organization. The challenge for the board is to recognize that the IMO has a difficult role to perform. On the one hand, the board expects the advisory role to be aligned with the fund's goals insofar as possible, and not solely reflect its own particular views or investment solutions. On the other hand, the IMO has assets under management and profitability targets, so the advice cannot be entirely disinterested.

Finally, the IMO needs to be alert to developments in financial markets and be adaptive. While the pension fund sets out the long-term strategy and the set of asset classes or investment solutions in its most simple form, to reflect its return objective and risk appetite, the role of the IMO is to critically monitor this set of asset and investment solutions. This includes envisaging how it will evolve and develop, and looking out for better alternatives for achieving the fund's goals. Investment classes that fit well in the portfolio today might not do so in a couple of years, due either to the economic cycle that affects the return/risk assumptions, or to in or outflows in the investment class reflecting increasing or decreasing popularity. To be an effective manager of external agents, the IMO needs to develop insights on how the value chain can best be organized—starting with the fund and ending with external managers—to deal with a changing set of opportunities and threats, and to develop strengths. If the IMO itself has no innovative skills, it will have to monitor developments in the asset management industry and adopt innovations at an early stage.

FUNCTIONS AND TYPICAL EVOLUTION OF THE IMO

The size and development of the IMO is a function of the size and complexity of the pension scheme.[1] As a general rule, when the size of the fund grows, more resources become available to make informed decisions on where to allocate policymaking, execution, and monitoring in the investment management process. During the process, the fund acquires more and more intellectual property on its own. Three types of investment organization models emerge (see Exhibit 12.1), which could be tied in to the governance budget that a board wants to spend.

The first model concerns the smallest pension funds. These are funds with less than $500 million assets under management. Due to the scale, these funds are usually price takers in the investment management industry, having little or no bargaining power to drive down costs, or resources to allocate to investment solutions that create a higher expected return. Cost minimization, focus on the strategy at hand, and eliminating all elements that detract from achieving the goals or where the fund has no influence or bargaining power, such as active management or illiquid investments, are key driving factors for the IMO. These funds will generally employ an external investment manager to recommend and implement both strategy and selection decisions through a few generalist funds or a selection of specialist funds. The investments in this model are all-in funds, comingled with the assets of other institutional investors that have similar objectives. The external manager may use funds from their own organization, where the preference is for mutual funds that combine different assets to diversify effectively, and/or investment strategies that are passive in nature, thus reducing the monitoring pressure on trustees to invest in depth in the monitoring of the funds and focus on the strategic choices instead.

Trustees of such small pension funds may have little investment experience and rely entirely on the judgment of the chosen asset manager. A consultant may help to establish a strategy, recommend an investment manager, and monitor the results. The manager will make tactical asset class decisions. There might be an in-house staff or executive office. But their prime responsibility is administration, and the monitoring of policy and investments is just a part-time role.

The second phase in size and complexity is when the pension fund moves from generalist to specialist management. This process involves adding other funds or managers, either to expand diversification by adding new asset classes, or by gaining investment styles and strategies within the asset classes. Comingled or generalist mutual funds become less important in portfolio construction, as more and more specialized strategies are added. Within the pension fund, the selection and monitoring process as well as the portfolio construction will require more attention. The executive office will have one or more investment officers for the overall coordination, supported by an investment

	Characteristics organization	Governance budget board	Organizational Changes
First Phase	Strategy formulation, implementation, and monitoring fully outsourced.	Cost minimization.	Board: • Hires an investment officer or investment consultant to support the board. External IMO: • Advises, coordinates, implements, and reports on the investment policy.
Second Phase	Strategy formulation (partially) insourced.	Design and monitoring: Policy and strategy formulation, and monitoring.	Board: • Hires small staff on strategy (ALM/Policy/ Portfolio Construction) external manager selection and risk management (focusing on risk management framework and dashboards). IMO: • Specializes in manager selection; e.g., equity, bonds, and alternatives. • Risk management, second line monitoring, and risk management framework. In a later stage, the IMO: • Starts insourcing: treasury/liability management. From this moment on, you need serious systems, back office, etc. • Expand risk management, conducting own in-depth reviews, following up on incidents, increasing maturity level risk management. • Portfolio research, developing and internalizing dynamic asset allocation, and balance sheet management.
Third Phase	Strategy, implementation and monitoring partially or fully insourced.	Design, implementation, and monitoring.	Board: • Expands staff to monitor in depth, alternative strategies. IMO: • Start building internal teams (e.g., credits). • Expand number of teams. From this moment on, culture becomes a very serious element to consider. • Start internalizing individual deals. • Start developing own strategies; in the alternative/illiquid categories. • Build serious capacity on alternative assets: real estate, private equity, and infrastructure.

EXHIBIT 12.1   Investment organization models.

consultant. An investment committee is established, composed of a few board members, and several external members. The committee is charged with monitoring the execution of the investment policy, providing countervailing power to the advice from the IMO and, at times, the committee is used in an advisory capacity on investment issues. If the assets are large enough, the fund will opt for one or more segregated mandates.

What separates the first phase from the second phase is that the fund internalizes strategy formulation, as well as parts of the selection and monitoring policy. In some cases, the fund also internalizes tactical asset allocation decisions. The executive office must be able to aggregate and prepare effective information for the investment committee to be able to make tactical decisions or have enough investment experience to do themselves. The investment committee, on the other hand, must contain sufficient professional experience to make judgments in that area and have enough seniority to remain focused on the long-term goals of the fund, rather than engaging in day-to-day financial markets. The role of the investment consultant also changes. In the first phase, the consultant normally educates as well as directs the board of trustees, laying a large proof of burden on the consultant to give the right advice. In the second stage, the investment consultant encounters financially educated investment staff and the investment committee. Their job is now to convince the staff and committee on specific pieces of advice. In this phase, funds run the danger of receiving and discussing overly technical material, trying to get to grips with it rather than setting the course based on the information.

The third stage is the development of a full in-house capacity. This involves a full time, in-house group of asset managers and portfolio strategists. Pension funds managing $5 billion or more have the suitable scale to start considering this model. The scope and form of the in-house capacity depends on the following decisions:

- Does the board see any value in a full in-house capacity? For example, is there a strong case that the pension scheme's characteristics cannot be served adequately in standard administrative systems; does the board hold distinguishing views towards financial markets, requiring tailor made investment solutions not easily available or does the board hold a view which skills and capacities should be retained within the fund to provide maximum adaptability for future developments?
- Within the investment management process, should the fund manage strategic investment policy and portfolio construction as well as implementation, managing the mandates in-house?
- Should the staff concern itself with setting the strategic policy, the management of the balance sheet on a higher level? Or should the fund be involved in the in-house management of segregated mandates? In other words, where in the value chain could be the most value added by insourcing?
- In terms of business model, should the fund consider a separate investment management company, or consider a separate asset management arm?
- Related to the previous question, should the pension fund incorporate staff and executive office within the asset management arm, or keep it as a function close to the board?

Form	Outsourcing/External Management	Insourcing/Internal Management
Description	Contract for delivery of investment management services, no impact on existing organization, no equity stakes.	Creation of a new legal entity with 100% ownership. Certain existing resources can be transferred to the subsidiary.
Investment required	None	Moderate/Substantial
Control over operation	None	Substantial/Direct
Flexibility of operation	Depends on the Service Level Agreement	Flexible
Resources required from Board	Few: • Specification of outsourcing requirements. • Monitoring and evaluation skills. • Clear framework when to continue or terminate contract.	Few to many • Board skills include managerial as well. • Vision on relationship fund-owned company. • Manage beforehand known issues, such as remuneration, level of investment, etc.
Examples	• Pension funds in a wide range of countries outsource their asset management functions by hiring external managers and outsourcing back- and mid-office operations.	• ATP (1994, 2003-6), creating 11 affiliated companies as independent platforms to implement ATP's investment strategies. • TIAA-CREF (2008), announcing to open office in London.

EXHIBIT 12.2 Outsourcing versus insourcing investment management.[2]

Jumping from an external to an internal IMO is not a forgone conclusion. Pension fund boards have a wide range of organizational forms to execute their investment management function. The relationship can have one of the forms in Exhibit 12.2.

Outsourcing

The board basically outsources investment management. It transfers the investment function from the pension fund to a (commercial) IMO that is not owned. In turn, the IMO can (and often will) outsource a number of functions to third parties, a form of subcontracting.

Outsourcing can provide a number of substantial benefits.[3] For example, it may permit boards to obtain necessary expertise at a lower cost than might be possible by hiring internal staff, and allows boards to focus on their core business: strategy formulation and monitoring.

With outsourcing, the board decides to have services provided by an IMO, without any financial ties other than the stipulated in the contract. The relationship is for a specific period, after which the services can be tendered in the market or renewed with the existing IMO. The board has to draw up an investment management agreement and an SLA.

Outsourcing poses a number of challenges for pension fund boards. Transferring investment functions to an IMO may have a detrimental impact on the board's understanding of how the function is performed, with a consequent loss of control. There is a risk that the inappropriate selection of an IMO may lead to a business disruption, with negative consequences for the pension fund's participants and, in certain instances, the potential for systemic risk to the market as a whole. The external organization will serve more masters and will be a for-profit organization, which may distract from the priority of serving the pension fund. Finally, the board runs the risk that due to inadequate internal process with the IMO, mistakes or gaps in oversight arise, causing reputational damage for the fund.

Outsourcing also creates important challenges for the integrity and effectiveness of the regulator. First, where outsourcing takes place by regulated entities, a firm's control over the people and processes dealing with the outsourced function may decrease. Nonetheless, regulators require that the outsourcing firm, including its board of directors and senior management, remain fully responsible (towards clients and regulatory authorities) for the outsourced function, as if the service was being performed in-house. Second, regulators expect that they will have complete access to books and records concerning an outsourcing firm's activities, even if such documents are in the custody of the firm's service provider. Regulators must also take into account the possible operational and systemic risks that may exist in the event that multiple regulated entities use a common service provider.

The mentioned risks and benefits need to be on the board's mind when entering the outsourcing relationship.

The connection with the external investment manager can range from strictly transactional (client–provider) to relationship- or partnership-based (partner–partner). In the first case, services are clearly defined in terms of deliverable, price, and monitoring; and investment services are predominantly seen as interchangeable components. In the second case, the board views outsourcing mainly based on relationship. The more proprietary information is shared between the pension fund and investment organization, the more tailor-made the investment function can be designed for the pension board. This, is turn, should result in a higher alignment with the board's goals and better outcomes in the short term and in the long run. For the IMO, the relationship-based model has pros, such as a potentially long and deeper relationship with the client, and cons, such as potential higher cost of customization, as is shown in Exhibit 12.3.

Subsidiaries: Majority or Fully Owned by the Pension Fund

The pension fund can also fully control and/or own the investment organization. The fully owned IMO is a legal extension of the pension fund. The IMO is fully owned, but a separately constituted corporation. The reasons for a board to set up a legally separate organization are:

- Strategic focus—the pension fund's organization (board and executive office) focuses on policymaking, the IMO on execution;

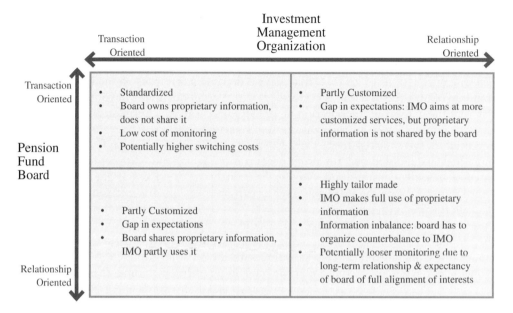

EXHIBIT 12.3   Relationship characteristics between a fund's board and an IMO.

- Remuneration—the IMO has more leeway in attracting staff with higher remuneration than would be possible within a pension fund;
- Professionalism in investment management;
- Culture—the board's task is, due to the very nature of a pension scheme, more conservative, while the IMO is probably tasked with a more entrepreneurial, explorative culture to achieve the long-term investment goals. Separating these two cultures makes strategic sense;
- Licenses—the IMO can operate under a different regulatory regime, requiring different licenses;
- Possibility of acquiring other clients next to the owner-pension fund.

Essentially, the IMO is a company that is run on behalf of the fund. The profitability targets of the IMO are therefore different from a typical commercial investment manager. On the one hand, it should charge a high enough fee and earn enough to maintain the regulatory reserves and keep investing in systems, infrastructure and personnel. On the other hand, the IMO is essentially a not-for-profit organization and, therefore, it makes no sense to raise it to commercial levels. Overall, this structure should lead to cost savings for the fund. Second, the fact that the proprietary IMO is a not-for-profit organization sets it apart from its commercial asset management counterparts, which always serve at least two masters: their clients and the financial bottom line.

Another difference between a proprietary IMO and asset manager is that an asset manager should only be expected to be geared towards the effective and efficient execution of a mandate, whereas the IMO also has the task to advise on strategy. In this case, the board should expect a full alignment of interests in the advice. Thus, the IMO executes and advises at the same time.

Pros and Cons of a Proprietary IMO

Setting up a proprietary investment organization requires a considerable amount of governance budget from the board, as well as long-term commitment and investments. This makes sense if the board of trustees clearly sees the strategic added value of the organization. The proprietary organization should be able to make the fund fulfill its long-term investment mission in the most effective and efficient way possible. So, what are the potential pros and cons of such a set up?

Pros

- Cost reduction over the long term;
- Developing a strategy that exploits long-term benefits in the financial markets, which would not have been possible if the IMO would not have been owned;
- Less agency issues due to the alignment between board and IMO;
- Improved countervailing power against the external commercial financial industry; knowledge of external parties and financial markets that should at least help avoiding big mistakes in deals and strategy selection;
- Manufacturing capacity to further improve existing strategies in-house, or create new ones;
- Having control over the whole value chain of the investment management process, hence being able to fully control the portfolio;
- Controlling and building the culture of the IMO;
- Being able to adapt to changing circumstances.

Cons

- Loss of flexibility and adaptability: when in-house teams have been built up, the organization will find it more difficult to make changes in the portfolio construction, even if the teams perform suboptimally or the asset class becomes less attractive;
- The certainty of assets that the IMO has, lacking the discipline of the market, may make it lazy, inward-looking and ineffective;
- Knowledge issues: the board runs the risk of internalizing agency issues;
- If the IMO grows too much it may turn into a bureaucracy.

ISSUES IN DEALING WITH AN INVESTMENT ORGANIZATION

In dealing with the investment organization (whether external or proprietary), the board has to consider the following issues: delegation, compensation, alignment of interests, and potential differences in culture. We further detail these issues in the following paragraphs.

Delegation. The board assigns specific tasks or authority to the IMO, specifically one or more of the activities described at the beginning of the chapter: execute the investment strategy or policy set by the board, adding value beyond implementation of the policy portfolio, be demonstrably in control and in charge of the mandates and investment managers they select, and monitor on behalf of the pension fund. This delegation is one of the core concepts of board leadership. However, the board remains accountable for the outcome of the delegated work: board responsibility cannot be delegated. In addition, delegation always requires countervailing power, understanding, and probing. If that isn't done right, problems will arise.

Delegation empowers a subordinate to make decisions, i.e. it is a shifting of decision-making authority from one organizational level to a lower one. There is no simple answer to the question of what is the right level of delegation of the fund to the IMO. The following points must be taken into account:

1. A necessary ingredient for delegation is trust. Trust requires maintenance and understanding.
2. Delegation always introduces agency issues. The right level of delegation is a balancing act between the added value of specialization and the cost of delegation.
3. The more material a decision is for the realization of its objectives, the more the board should be involved and own it; therefore, crucial decisions about the SAA should always be owned by the board, and the implementation can be delegated to the investment organization.
4. The more technical knowledge and know-how are required for a task, the more it should be delegated to the part of the chain of the investment process in which this is available. This should be done in such a way that the board sets the policy and the parameters. While the board cannot predict the outcome (nor should it necessarily have the knowledge to predict it), it can determine in advance the acceptable bandwidth of the outcomes. Hiring and firing of individual external asset managers should be within the realm of the IMO. When the strategic parameters on investment style, type of mandate, and horizon are set, the actual selection and monitoring come down to operational decisions and are skill intensive.
5. If the board of trustees wants to build a culture and DNA for the long term, it has to invest a lot of time in developing a shared set of beliefs and a shared culture. It has more control over the IMO when this is done in its close proximity.

Compensation. Another complex issue with which trustees are currently struggling is the manner in which investment organizations are being compensated for their services. Given that trustees are responsible for negotiating fees or salaries, they can exert significant influence on the way people work and collaborate, provided of course that a properly designed compensation framework is in place. However, experience demonstrates that the conventional and widely used model of pay-for-performance is often in conflict with long horizon value creation.

Alignment of interests. There are a number of significant implementation issues regarding the investment organization that currently dominate an industry-wide debate among trustees. "Alignment of interests" is such an issue, because the interaction between the investment committee (representing the interest of the fund) and the IMO is regarded as probably the most important factor in creating investment success. If this discussion is not dealt with from the beginning, a lack of understanding and trust increases between fund and IMO. It is not always clear who is in charge: the pension fund or the IMO. Since by nature the IMO has more resources, experience, and continuity in the investment field than the board, it should help the board in a subtle way to ask the right questions. When asked, both board members and executives state that trust is the most important ingredient between a fund and the IMO.

THE SERVICE LEVEL AGREEMENT

Delegation of responsibilities is the basis for a board to draw up an SLA, setting out in detail the services to be provided and the mutual obligations of the partners and attendant parties. In other words, the expectations of a working relationship between the board and IMO are dealt with. In our view, the SLA is a valuable tool regardless of whether the investment management is outsourced or owned.

A pension fund should be able to rely on the integrity of its IMO manager and on the solidity of their contract to guarantee an effective partnership, but when it comes to the management of specific tasks, a clear, concise, comprehensive and unambiguous SLA is a must. This is without a doubt one of the most important prerequisites for entering an effective, surprise-free, long-term fiduciary relationship. Transparency is the key to an SLA and detail is its best servant: it is better to spend extra time in definition and dialogue up-front than to find out that the partners don't agree on things when an emergency appears.

A fair and effective SLA can only be based on clearly defined mutual obligations between the partners. A pension fund board should also indicate its responsibilities in the SLA so that the fiduciary manager can be confident it will be called upon to deliver its services at the desired level and on a fair playing field.

To monitor the effective delivery of the services described, an SLA should contain guidelines for assessing the performance of a fiduciary manager per service. Each service is then represented by a set of agreed-upon performance indicators, which are a just reflection on the core of the service. Agreeing on fair measurements up-front will help providers stay on top of their game and the pension fund assess its partners' performance.

The SLA is a valuable framework to evaluate the IMO, where the executive office and the board discuss and monitor the progress on a regular basis. This is only part of the story in the long-term relationship. The board should be aware of the elements that are more difficult to capture in SLAs. Assessing how the investment management scores on them and tracking this over time will provide valuable insights on whether the relationship is more transaction-based or relationship-based. A board could also ask the IMO to reflect on these issues and indicate how the board scores on them.

The delegation of responsibilities requires a board to draw up an SLA, setting out the services to be provided and the mutual obligations of the partners and attendant parties in detail. In other words, expectations of a working relationship between the board and the IMO are enshrined therein.

MONITORING AND EVALUATING THE INVESTMENT MANAGEMENT ORGANIZATION

The investment management should be monitored continuously and evaluated regularly—at least once in three to five years—both when it is outsourced to an external or to a proprietary IMO.

The SLA should form the basis for these activities: it should clearly outline what is expected from the investor, in terms of goals and acceptable outcomes, but also in terms of behavior and deliverables such as reporting and communication to the board. Ideally, the SLA contains a multidimensional scorecard that forms the basis for monitoring and evaluation. This should be acceptable and fully understood by both parties beforehand, so that no ambiguity arises during the execution. The more the relationship resembles a partnership, the more the monitoring and evaluation will be two-sided; the board, and especially the board investment committee, are very important parts of the value chain and should therefore be open to monitoring and feedback.

Of course, every now and then there will be very tough conversations between the parties. In a learning system between fund and investment manager, we feel the primary objective should be to learn and improve from the ongoing monitoring and evaluation process. The more long-term the relationship is, the more attention there can and should be paid to the learning part; this is where the collective intellectual property of the fund and the investor will increase.

Whereas the monitoring is an ongoing process, the evaluation should in principle take place on a regular basis, unless there is a specific reason for more immediate action. It may be valuable to have an external party such as a consultant involved in the process. On the basis of the scorecard mechanism in the SLA combined with observations by the parties involved in the process, it should be possible to draw up an agenda for the evaluation. The outcome could be that some of the aspects of the services will have to be upgraded or improved. Often, an evaluation will result in a new version of the SLA containing the new insights resulting from the evaluation process.

ENDNOTES

1. See Russell (2006).
2. See Pecchioli (1983) and Robinson (1972).
3. See IOSCO (2005) on Principles on Outsourcing of Financial Services for Market Intermediaries.

Case Study—Future Fund

LONG-HORIZON FUND, A MASTER IN MANAGING AGENCY ISSUES, WITH FOCUS ON THE WHOLE AND NOT ON THE PARTS

Background

The Australian Government Future Fund is an independently managed sovereign fund founded in 2006, financed with a capital injection of AUD 60 billion by the Australian government.[1] Future Fund had AUD 139 billion (approximately $102 billion) under management at the end of 2017. Its main purpose is to reach AUD 140 billion to meet liabilities for the payment of superannuation to retired public employees.[2] The benchmark is the Consumer Price Index (CPI) plus a percentage range of 4%–5% in 2017. The fund outsources almost all of the assets to external managers. Future Fund has a clear approach on how to manage the assets. It sees its long horizon as a key ingredient for generating high returns, for three reasons: (i) the ability to take on greater levels of market risk, under the assumption that a long-term investor is able to tolerate the shorter-term losses; (ii) the ability to accept capital being locked up in assets or structures that are costly to sell out of within a short period of time; and (iii) the ability to be countercyclical, patient and opportunistic. External managers execute the implementation of the strategy; this is due to the fund's founding legislation.[3]

Challenges

Future Fund has been very active in overcoming agency problems. David Neal, managing director of Future Fund, addresses four common agency problems that occur within a fund that could worsen performance:[4]

1. *Principal agent problem.* Short-term evaluation of performance should not be a common practice. "Good results tend to be taken as confirmation that things are on track and the manager is skilled. Bad results foster doubt, and throw the onus of proof back on demonstrating that the manager is acting appropriately. When a manager senses they are being evaluated on short-term results, then delivering good short-term results is what they will work towards."
2. *Rewarding.* Too many rewards are linked to short-term performance. This creates an issue where short-term-minded managers are incentivized to follow long-term goals. But there is an issue that is subtler and more personal in nature, e.g. career

prospects can be greatly improved by a solid recent performance history, which enhances the scope for being promoted, head-hunted, or for starting up an own fund.

3. *When things don't initially turn out as expected.* Both principal and agent will be trying to judge if a mistake has been made and the manager's position should be terminated, versus whether the payoff has merely been delayed. The risk is that principals then act in ways that undermine the capacity to invest for the long term. They may respond to noise rather than signal, incorrectly blame the manager, and either pressure them to stem the losses or replace them, or withdraw funds.

4. *Long-term commitment.* Success in the long run requires commitment from the principal in the fund and the manager. This, however, creates an agency problem for the manager and the commitment of funding sacrifices liquidity.

The process

Neal and Warren propose solutions to the agency issues they identify in their paper. They come up with four solutions:

Align the Organizational Settings   When everyone's compass in the fund is set in a collective direction, they will think and act in terms of long-term objectives. This can be achieved by explicitly writing down guiding principles such as mission, purpose, and belief statements; but also by working on culture by improving leadership, professionalism, and creating an environment of trust. In addition, "attention should be focused on whether outcomes are on track to achieve long-term goals, rather than period-by-period returns." To cope with myopic loss aversion, Neal and Warren suggest less frequent feedback and fewer opportunities to take action, encouraging team decision-making, and employing the right people who have affinity with long-term investing. Lastly, the above-mentioned solutions should be extended downwards to external managers to build partnerships based around mutual trust and respect. Contracts should be designed in such way in order to maintain long-lived relationships and fulfill the long-term objective.

Build Understanding through Engagement   A key strategy of Future Fund is engaging in a collective understanding among all stakeholders of investment decisions and outcome. This way, principals remain on board and the strategy dilutes the tendency to monitor short-term results. Neal and Warren say: "Engagement means involving principals in decisions, rather than maintaining independence and distance. Engaging over investment decisions sits uncomfortably with the concept that there should be clear separation between governance and management. Engagement is a compromise that recognizes the deficiencies in monitoring by the flow of results when investing for the long term." Rather than having "distant monitoring," where there is distance between the different parts of the chain, the Fund uses what it calls "immersed monitoring," in which there is a deep and shared understanding about the investment decision being made in the different parts of the chain, e.g. between the board and the investment management organization.

Design of incentives   Financial incentives should not distract from the long term. The fund recognizes the problem of remuneration based on long-term rolling periods performance, but opts for a system of three-year rolling performance evaluation to align interest although this might not be in line with the realities of the employment market. An additional subjective component is explicitly used to reward actions that contribute to long-term outcomes, such as collaboration across the portfolio, challenging accepted ideas and orthodoxies, and building productive relationships. In this way, the remuneration structure focuses on portfolio performance, while giving ample consideration for the quality and sustainability of how performance is achieved.

Commit to the long term   "Demonstrating commitment to the manager themselves is a matter of placing faith and trust in them, and resisting holding them to account for short-term performance. The main caveat is that managers should be answerable for behaviors that deviate from the long-term mission and agreed-upon strategies. The aim is to foster the expectation of an extended career or relationship with the organization. Commitment might be demonstrated by not handing out terminations lightly; and giving consideration to the messaging around commitment when doing so."

The outcome

Future Fund is relatively young. It had the advantage of designing itself while taking into consideration how other funds have structured themselves. Future Fund therefore puts much effort in managing the principal–agent problem and aligning interests of the people with the goals of the fund. Over time, the fund has made its beliefs more explicit and expanded the transparency and openness within the organization. Also, "The 'one portfolio' approach is central; and regardless of job function, remuneration for all employees is partly based on the entire portfolio performance, so that the portfolio is boosted by the alignment of everyone's interest."[5]

Since the size of the investment team is deliberately relatively small by design, it has the means to include all relevant people in the investment process, thereby avoiding silos in the organization. The staff of the firm is strongly encouraged to feed ideas; even the manager review committee and asset review committee feed ideas to the investment committee. The main idea is that an idea should enhance the portfolio. The staff is rewarded for supporting ideas that are not their own, thereby eliminating biases such as empire-building and silo-ing.

Lessons for Achieving Investment Excellence

- Future Fund is a master of recognizing and reducing agency issues between all the parties involved in the investment process.
- The tools to do so are predominantly qualitative in nature—creating a shared understanding and culture, and involvement along the whole organization, beginning with the board.

- It addresses long-horizon agency issues between the board and the investment management organization through "immersed monitoring."
- The people within the investment management organization are strongly aligned because of the "total fund perspective" and the fact that they are incentivized to the portfolio as a whole and not to parts of it.

ENDNOTES

1. See White (2015).
2. See www.futurefund.gov.au/about-us/our-funds.
3. See Adamson (2013).
4. See Neal and Warren (2015).
5. See Adamson (2013).

Five

Learning, Adapting and Improving

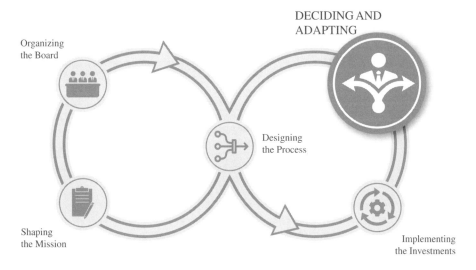

This part of the book focuses on the daily practice of trustees and decision makers. In this part, the focus is placed on building effective boards, assessing the quality of the investment set-up and improving it—be it continuously or with a big leap, like the Dutch PFZW and the California Public Employees' Retirement System (CalPERS) have done and many others do as well. In other words, the emphasis lies on assessment, change, adaptation and learning.

Trustees new to a pension fund board will hardly ever have the luxury of designing its setup from scratch. They are thrown into an environment comprising other people, and an existing fund DNA, culture and structure. Oftentimes, the longer the history of the fund, the stickier or more inflexible the set-up will be. "Culture eats strategy for breakfast", so to speak.

The starting point for change is the individual trustee as change and improvement must necessarily start with an individual. This individual observes and assesses a situation, feels that it can and should be improved, and then has to start working on it. Scaling up from what the individual sees to a collective and shared view; putting this vision into a shared set of observations, or into a shared language is both difficult and fragile, but necessary to start the process of changing.

CONTRIBUTION OF THIS PART TO INVESTMENT EXCELLENCE

Part V helps boards to move towards investment excellence and turn the activities needed to improve and adapt in a continuous rather than a one-off process. By doing this, the fund becomes a learning organization. Thereby it learns to adapt continuously to the rapidly changing environment and to gently replace weaknesses by strengths over time instead of ending up in crisis and having to take drastic measures. Thereby, the fund avoids incurring high costs in terms of losses or opportunity costs, which are often hard or impossible to repair and can be a threat towards the survival of the fund. The learning should be collective in order to avoid making the same mistakes over and over again. This requires a disciplined effort, which has to be supported by the board.

CHAPTER 13

Learning to Decide and to Take Advice

Key Take Aways

- Decision-making is by far the most important task of trustees; identifying the problem, developing alternatives, making a choice, monitoring the follow up, and evaluating the decision to improve future decision-making.

- Decision-making in investments is complex: the future is unknown, the set of available alternatives is large, and the interdependencies are not always clear.

- Effective decision-making involves the right agenda, the right preparation, and a dialogue between board members, external advisors and the investment management organization. This can be organized.

- Successful decision-making depends on the role of the chair, as well as on an agreed path on how to make decisions.

- Boards should prepare regularly for decision-making during financial crises. Financial crises cannot be predicted but occur frequently, and poorly prepared decision-making under stress can cost the fund dearly.

This chapter covers what is required from a board to make decisions. Decision-making turns a group of individuals into a board. Decision-making combines all of the individual contributions into one, collective result. It provides unity of processes and deliberations. The board members might hold different beliefs or viewpoints, but the decision-making process leads to a unified choice that is communicated to the stakeholders.

Within this decision-making process, committee members make choices, future plans, and/or respond to environmental changes. They can demonstrate what they think and believe, and put in the open what they want or doubt. The result of the process provides direction and visibility as to what people can and want to do together, and what they collectively believe and create. They each deliver a contribution to a collective result, for which they receive money, appreciation and recognition. In order to create a collective result from all of the individual contributions, people must not only be able to provide their contribution, they must also be able to accept contributions from others. The collective contributions must somehow be compared with one another, weighed up, and assessed. In the end result, the individual contributions may not be visible but they must all have been considered seriously.

In this chapter, we review the potential behavioral pitfalls in decision-making, and formulate several practical recommendations that a board can put into practice to improve decision-making. Then, we turn our attention to the roles of external advisors in decision-making. Investment consultants, actuaries, external advisors: what should a board be aware of in order to be able to use their input as optimally as possible, but also see to be aware of the caveats that they entail?

Trustees depend heavily on investment consultants, actuaries, and other external advisors for their decision-making. In making investment decisions, trustees are expected to take "proper advice." Failure to comply means that a trustee might be directly answerable to the regulator in his country for any mistakes. For smaller pension funds, it might mean turning to an independent financial advisor, investment consultant, or to the fund's actuary, who generally is also qualified to give financial advice. Although in theory they are optional, investment consultants are usually necessary in larger schemes to advise trustees on the asset side of the balance sheet, in contrast to actuaries, who advise on the liabilities. A trustee needs to have proper expectations of these advisors, whether they are investment consultants, actuaries, external members, or experts in the investment committee.

Finally, this chapter addresses two special types of decision-making: complex decision-making with asset liability management (ALM), and decision-making during periods of stress or crisis.

PSYCHOLOGY OF DECISION-MAKING: BIASES, PREFERENCES, AND HABITS

Boards and committees, as a group, can achieve better results via the decision-making process than would be the case with individuals; this potential, however, is not always utilized. The good intentions of a group process can even lead to undesirable results, particularly if the group dynamics and behavioral biases come to the fore.

In the face of uncertainty, most people cannot and do not systematically describe problems, record all the necessary data, or synthesize information to create rules for making decisions. Instead, most people venture down somewhat more subjective, less ideal paths of reasoning in an attempt to determine the course of action consistent with their basic judgments and preferences. How, then, can decision-making best be organized? Before answering this question, we need to develop more insight about the psychology of trustees when they are making decisions.

There is increasing research on, and insights into, the motivational psychology of the investor or decider, known as behavioral finance. A central theme in behavioral finance is that the natural manner of reacting and thinking, if not tackled effectively, can regularly and unintentionally lead to decisions that, in turn, lead to unintended and even undesirable outcomes. Investment committees and boards must therefore avoid three types of pitfalls: simplifying problems, preferences when forming judgments, and information processing; Exhibit 13.1 elaborates on this.

Description of behavioral effect	

1. Simplification of problems	
Mental accounting	The tendency to focus on parts rather than the "whole." Assets and liabilities are set apart; household budgets are divided into "pots." Decisions are made within the categories, whereby the diversification effect between categories cannot be estimated accurately.
Mister Jones effect	The tendency to see the trend in a few, coincidental cases, or to decide, for one case, that "it can't be a coincidence." After achieving a few good results, committees can, for example, believe that they are really good when it comes to interest-rate hedging, TAA or manager selection when, in reality, it is probably just coincidence.
Availability and representativeness	People estimate the chances of an event occurring on the basis of how easily they remember individual events. An accident with a shark is ascribed greater probability than an accident with an airplane. The chance of a new, repeated financial crisis is therefore evaluated as too high just after a crisis by boards and investment committees.
2. Preferences in forming a judgment	
Prospect theory and endowment effect	Losses cause more pain than comparable gains. Investors are sensitive to descriptions of results such as gains or losses (or under/outperformance) and adapt their behavior accordingly. People avoid risks if they make gains (i.e. they do not want to give up what they have realized), but seek to avoid the risk of losses. External managers can also demonstrate risk-seeking behavior when there is underperformance.
Framing effect	The glass is half full or half empty. The way in which people make decisions is greatly influenced by the way in which it is presented for decision-making. A quarterly report or presentation can, for example, begin with a sobering image of the financial markets, resulting in the fund's results looking more pessimistic.
Myopia	Recent events overshadow. People do not adapt their judgments according to the impact of new information. Investment analysts do not amend their profit forecasts quickly enough, leading to positive profit surprises that are probably followed by more positive surprises (and vice versa).
Molehill effect	There is a tendency to overestimate the impact of events with low probability, and to work to reduce uncertainty as a result. Investors thus lean towards short-term cash and bonds, even if this impacts upon the long-term aims.

EXHIBIT 13.1 Behavioral pitfalls in decision-making.[1]

Othello effect	Increased detailing in explanations and information leads to increased confidence or conviction. Boards and committees confuse precision in ALM or portfolio construction with reliability, and see quantitative information as more reliable than qualitative information. One consequence of this is that there is a quest to "calculate" as much as possible, even though models that deal with the economy and financial markets are highly unreliable as a result of forecasting errors.
Quasi-magical thinking	People tend to take action or pay for information, even if they know that the actions or information actually have no effect. With respect to pension funds, this involves performance fees; this form of payment is often used in the financial sector even though its effectiveness has not really been proven scientifically.
3. Information processing	
Desired vision or selective perception	The tendency to seek only positive information or information that confirms the existing viewpoint, and to ignore other data or not seek it out. Arguments and issues are framed so that the desired facts more often take the foreground. One variant is the hindsight bias, whereby recent facts are presented as a logical sequence of events that could have been predicted in advance.
Overconfidence	Overconfidence refers to the phenomenon that people or organizations sometimes tend to overrate their knowledge. Boards are particularly overconfident when it comes to the results over which they believe they have a degree of control and in which they have a high level of involvement. Interest-rate hedging, tactical asset allocation or selections by managers fulfill this criterion. Trustees choose investment managers for their passion and confidence of management style. Nearly half of the investment teams pension funds work with choose passion as a core value. A story might be conveyed with confidence, whether or not supported by good arguments, and generally pleases the investment committee or trustees (now we really have something to decide about). This is, however a false certainty; we make up stories to explain reality, thereby comforting ourselves. The stories might not be true, however.

EXHIBIT 13.1   *(Continued)*

How do these points influence decision-making in investment committees and boards? One or more of the following elements could play a role in the discussion:

- Boards and investment committees have the tendency to focus on the investments and absolute returns and less on the developments of investments in relation to the pension liabilities. Alternatively, they will opt to deal with part of the portfolio on its own merits, without considering the interactions (such as correlation) with the rest of the portfolio.
- The tendency to reduce risk in the short term, e.g. by not rebalancing if that is necessary, and thus ascribing greater weight to short-term rather than long-term aims (see the discussion on risk appetite in Chapter 4).
- The tendency to believe that bonds and cash are safer than equity.

- The tendency to think that a low-risk portfolio comprises individual solid investments, ignoring the long-term advantage of diversification. Committees and boards respond to the loss-making elements of the portfolio and tackle these but, as a result, risk the intended risk premium not being earned because of the disposal or risk-reduction process. Famous examples are choosing not to rebalance when stocks drop substantially in value, even though this is the agreed upon policy. Risk premiums are, after all, primarily "earned" when investors are risk averse with respect to the investment.
- The tendency to overreact to recent events. Recent events are given a high degree of consideration in the decision-making process. This comes to the fore in a variety of ways. Think, for example, of investing in successful managers or strategies before they level off, investing in growth equities at the end of the 1990s, hiring of managers after a few successful years, or setting up the investment portfolio on a financial crisis in the coming years (see Chapter 12 on the selection of managers).

These tendencies are often ascribed to individual investors, but there is no reason to assume that boards and investment committees might not fall prey to them every now and then. Members think just like ordinary investors, in mental accounts, i.e. separated accounts. This effect is reinforced by external members who, for example, are involved in specific disciplines such as property or derivatives, which reinforce this behavior. An external member with a strong hedge-fund background, for example, will make the committee feel comfortable about being in control of this investment category. A confident share investor will tend to not retrace their footsteps and predict a negative share risk premium. When creating the committee, some funds take this into account, and thus combine "extreme" opinions that correspond to the risk of "mental accounts."

Aside from behavioral effects on an individual level, the interaction between the board and the committee members also creates all sorts of other effects. Easily observed effects are:

- The pressure on uniformity;
- The pressure on conformity;
- Action bias;
- Invincibility;
- Isolation from new information.

Pressure on uniformity. The pressure on uniformity means that committee members are hesitant to express their doubts regarding a shared decision. There is a strong need to be a team player, and a subdued feeling that a lack of unity would jeopardize the board's or committee's effectiveness. Working and deciding in groups can be counterproductive and lead to "groupthink," in which the desire to achieve group unanimity and consensus overrides the motivation to view information realistically and critically asses it within the investment process.[2] As a result of this self-imposed censure, the committee believes that they are more unified than is actually the case; this can lead to tensions if the decisions do not work out as planned. This self-censure can be reinforced by self-appointed "mind guards." Some members of the committee appoint themselves to the role of keeping others within the committee to the so-called consensus. "A decision we have already taken, will not quickly be reversed" is an expression of this.

Pressure on conformity. The pressure on uniformity also encompasses an external component: the tendency for the fund to be set up in a way that it fulfills the image that participants, externals, and supervisors have of the fund. The culture of the fund and the board members are the determining factors in this regard. Is the culture such that the results of good and less-good decisions can be ascribed to the committee's own actions (internalization), or is there a case of results being ascribed to elements outside the control of the fund (externalization)? For an observer of a pension fund, an easy way to get an impression of whether internalization or externalization dominates the culture of the fund is to read the annual report of the board. If the (bad) results were mostly attributed to the financial markets outside the pension fund's sphere of influence, then it is a sure sign of externalization. Conformity can also be the result of career risk. The board and committee might align policy in such a way that it will lead to the least "discussion" with a regulator. Pension fund policy then implicitly corresponds to what is expected by the supervisor even if they have not prescribed this. For some board members this can serve as a rational reason to do nothing deviant, even if the deviant vision in terms of investment policy is well founded and in the interests of the participants.

Action bias. A committee may also lean towards making a decision simply because the issue or proposal is in front of them. If a proposal to employ a specific instrument, such as swap options, is discussed on numerous occasions, it creates a process that is comparable to the selection of active managers. If it seems that swap options could have led to good results and that they have not been used, the committee has to explain this partly because it has been discussed on several occasions. The best alternative is thus to decide to use swap options but at a level that will have little impact on the fund composition. The committee proposes gaining some experience with these. The worst "regret" of the committee members and the board will then only be that they made a good decision but that the scope was too insignificant. Action bias is also evident in times of great uncertainty or crisis. A committee can propose to intervene in the portfolio in the short term (strategy) in order to limit negative consequences. Another part of the proposals, however, serves more as an indicator. The committee and the board thus demonstrate to the outside world that they are working actively, even though the modifications have little or no impact.

The illusion of invincibility. This is often reinforced by earlier successes. The committee believes that a lucky streak is developing as a result of the fact, for example, that they have provided the correct advice regarding modifications to interest-rate hedging, or on the relative weighting of shares and obligations on several, consecutive occasions. A pattern can be derived from single, more or less coincidental observations. This is also known as the law of small numbers. The committee can also, together with the board, justify a completely different path. One variant on this is that the successes are not forthcoming but that the committee has built up the idea that it has "right" on its side, even if the financial markets are not quite there yet. An investment committee thus runs the risk of recommending or maintaining a decision that is not going to do well in the longer term because the committee or the board processes information selectively or is closed to new information.

Isolation from new information. Another group of effects focuses on the "isolation" of the committee from the outside world. Group members can convince themselves that they do not need to venture outside the group for supplementary arguments or information. This is a form of collective rationalization. The committee can even go so far as to declare the outside world more or less irrelevant. A stereotype is formed regarding people outside the group. There is a tendency to think that the group is above average and that the people outside the group are below average, weak, or irrational in their responses.

The more the group takes on the identified characteristics, the more the quality and decision-making process, upon closer inspection, will deteriorate. The behavioral effects we presented could give the impression that this is only the case for investment committees. But nothing could be further from the truth: the effects occur with respect to almost all forms of decision-making. What distinguishes pension fund boards and investment committees in this setting is that the nature of the problem is different. Boards and committees are more susceptible to behavioral effects if there is no clear answer to the issues faced by the group; and there are rarely clear problem definitions and/or obvious answers when it comes to investment issues. Investment committees, however, are hired to resolve exactly this type of issue. More often than not, investment issues involve questions for which there is no consensus on the existing developments or the effect on the future developments or position of the fund. Within this context of uncertainty, a decision must be made when there are many policy alternatives and possible scenarios. Committee members formulate and are often confronted with various opinions on how the portfolio aims can be achieved. Decisions on this subject are often trade-offs between the current situation and the long-term aims.

GROUP PROCESSES ON THE RIGHT TRACK

Now that the pitfalls that are faced by the committee members and the committee as a whole have been described, the next question is which conditions are required in order to make good decisions. Kahneman, one of the pioneers in the subject of investment psychology, developed a list of recommendations that applies to institutional investors. Using his recommendations as a basis, we find the following useful suggestions in decision-making:[3]

- Consider an investment problem integrally, not independently. For example, loans as part of real estate portfolios are rarely offset against loans in the fixed-interest value allocation or included in the "leverage" report of the pension fund's total balance.

- Follow an investment policy that is top-down and applies to all fund elements simultaneously, and avoid a bottom-up process whereby investment aims are set per separate category.
- The risk of loss is important for board members, but loss is a relative concept. Frame the loss by clearly defining the reference point in advance (level of coverage, period of evaluation, assets only or not).
- Remind one another of the importance of maintaining a long-term view and ensure that members do not "talk" long-term but "think" short-term. Make sure that the (long-term) policy is set out sufficiently clearly so that administrators are not tempted to substantially deviate from this if there are unexpected events.
- Be modest about own capabilities. When the fund opts for a strategy that deviates from market standards (such as deviating from a market-weighted index), an answer must be provided to the question of whether the fund is genuinely capable of gathering and using more expertise than the market.
- Keep track of the board's decisions and evaluate them. The fact that boards are more likely to remember successes means that it is useful to maintain a chronological list of all decisions, whether they are successful or not, and the reasons for this. It is common for committee members or investment managers not to remember exactly what their thoughts or reactions were at the time of the decision. Confronted with the realized returns, members develop an explanation that intuitively or comfortably fills in the gaps. Performance attribution should therefore not just be a mechanical exercise. The rationale for all major decisions should be recorded ex ante in the minutes, whether this is a change in asset allocation or the selection of a new manager.
- To expand on keeping track of decisions and evaluating them—be clear in the requirements and selection process for the investment committee or board members entrusted with investments that personal investing experience should not be confused institutional investing. To what extent is the belief influenced by the personal beliefs of trustees and by wishful thinking? This matters, because trustees can for the most part no longer function based on their direct experience of handling investments in their personal portfolios.[4] Instead, they must work hard to learn the unique characteristics of asset classes that are now available to institutional portfolios. It is not unusual for pension funds to hold as many as 15 different asset classes in their portfolios,[5] compared to five as recently as 15 years ago.
- Remind each other about the seeming appearance of certainty with respect to quantification and the uncertainties regarding investment decisions. The decision to choose an investment policy with a slightly higher expected return can, in practice, be wiped out entirely by the corresponding uncertainties.
- Fight against the tendency to be overoptimistic regarding decisions or to take steps and then use the new information to justify them, and focus on the things that can go wrong. Choose realistic departure points and combat the tendency to only see the upside.
- Before a new investment category is purchased, or a new manager is recruited, set out the conditions (return/risk aims, period of evaluation) under which the manager can be dismissed, or the investment choice can be considered unsuccessful and rejected.

LEARNING TO MAKE COMPLEX DECISIONS

Despite the advance of quantitative modeling and tooling, decision-making remains one of the toughest choices for trustees. The previous challenges are those that board members face when dealing with investment choices. However, new assets and strategies not only have to be considered in an asset-context, but also simultaneously in a liability context. In other words, decision-making becomes a complex problem to be solved. "Simple" decision-making supposes that the board can consider a problem is well posed, well formulated regarding the reality involved, and they usually consider the existence of a single objective, evaluation criterion, or point of view that underlies the conducted analysis. In such a case the solution is easy to obtain. In reality, the modeling of financial problems is based on a different kind of logic taking into consideration the following elements:[6]

- The existence of multiple criteria. Which criteria are these, and what is the priority structure of the objectives?
- The conflicting situation among the criteria.
- The complex, subjective, and ill-structured nature of the decision and evaluation process.
- The introduction of financial decision makers in the evaluation process. The different financial decisions are taken by board members or the staffed office and not by the models; the decision makers get more and more deeply involved in the decision-making process. In order to solve problems, it becomes necessary to take into consideration their preferences, experiences, and knowledge.

All decisions on a strategic level—risk appetite, strategic asset allocation—are complex decision processes for a board. One approach to tackle the existence of multiple criteria and structure the decision process has been the development of advanced decision-making systems that support pension fund managers with this, e.g. ALM, that helps boards in developing long-term investment strategies that are attuned to pension liabilities. Pension fund boards use ALM heavily to support their decision-making.

ALM aims to analyze the risks of the pension balance and the impact of policies on this. ALM generates future scenario analyses to chart the dynamics of the balance sheet and show how they translate into retirement (including surcharges and discounts), premium, and solvency. ALM especially supports the board in the relationships between goals, risk appetite, and the investment model. The ALM process is made up of the following steps:

- Defining goals and a framework for the goals to be achieved. What does the fund want to achieve with this process? Is it a regular update, checking whether investment goals are still achievable or the risk appetite needs updating, or is it a more fundamental review?
- Determining sensitivities. Is the balance sheet of the pension fund well understood? Getting to understand what interests or wishes the stakeholders have and translating it into an implicit or explicit choice on the balance sheet goes a long way in framing the problem towards a solution.

■ Understanding the sensitivities of ALM model. How are the choices made and based on what assumptions. If the risk premiums for equities are slightly changed, will the simulations be wildly different?

■ Generate and analyze alternatives: What are the outcomes sensitive to, and what are the main choices for a board to take?

The above-described steps form a consistent framework that can be used in the ALM process to support the board's decision-making process. Practices may often differ. Boards and investment committees, despite training and experience, often struggle to translate abstract and key figures from the ALM study to sound decision-making. We list the most important challenges:

■ ALM can be used to postpone choices. ALM has a long-term focus—the calculations can be projected 10–15 years in time, sometimes longer. Less effective boards, however, suffer from procrastination and time discounting: choices that are just down the road might become less urgent to make. If the ALM analyses show that long-term results turn out to be positive, then this might lead a board to the conclusion that short-term choices are not necessary, even though in reality they are.

■ Knowledge of ALM can negatively influence boardroom dynamics. In recent years, pension funds and committees worldwide who use ALM have been professionalized, gaining investment expertise along the way. Expert members know how the sensitivity of the assumptions tend to influence the outcomes. This knowledge, however, is generally not widely shared in the fund. For example, it helps tremendously for the outcomes if interest rates in the long term are set slightly higher than average. A board member with a positive attitude towards markets can therefore (un)knowingly "tweak" the assumptions so that the results do not hurt too much, and decision-making then becomes easier.

■ Boards confuse frequency with probabilities. This is a big problem. ALM is critical to simulate possible scenarios. For example, when 1,000 scenarios are generated, 10%, or 100 in number, might show a coverage ratio less than 90. The 100 out of 1,000 generated scenarios can be expressed as a frequency of 10%. The board, however, intuitively translates this as the probability that a coverage ratio below 90 will be achieved with this policy is 10%. But this is incorrect. It suggests an accurate prediction about the future, with the bandwidths of the various results known. The best that can be said is that if similar scenarios would occur, 1 out of 10 outcomes on average would show results under 90. This is less appealing to communicate, but does indicate where the crux is: a frequency is not a probability.

■ This confusion leads to further problems. Supposing the board would know the difference between probability and frequency, does this actually help decision-making? If I have a 5% chance of crossing a street to be hit by a biker, would do I do this? By crossing 100 times, I should on average run against a biker about five times. Is that a lot or not? When would I decide to take precautions?

The challenges described here are recognizable for boards. Fortunately, there are relatively simple ways to tackle complex decision-making:

- Decide on how to tackle complex decision-making beforehand. What goals should be prioritized, where does one know beforehand that a trade-off between goals needs to be addressed, and what information does a board need to make this trade-off? Is there a shared understanding about the steps to be taken? What should ALM do, or not do, in decision-making? Will the board apply other models or opinions along the way? Is it also clear when and why these are not applied?
- Have a shared view of the underlying assumptions. Which of these are a personal "belief," supported by a few members instead of the whole board? Agree on the assumptions, and decide that they will not be revisited or tweaked during the decision-making process.
- Make a distinction between factors the board can influence and those it cannot. For example, the board could decide that risk appetite, costs, and the level of the premium are fixed, or have a limited bandwidth, thus reducing the number of outcomes. Determine what policy space there is around these factors and focus on concrete results and agreements.
- Visualize and internalize the results. The board is not deciding about percentages, but deciding about monthly paychecks that participants receive. One could also think in specific scenarios and look at the sensitivities. A change in perspective can help prioritize the results. There are different ways to make this personalized. Think in specific scenarios, look at the sensitivities. Which rules of thumb can be deduced from this?
- Work on unbiasing yourself. The behavioral effects that cause decision-making to be less effective have been discussed earlier. Be aware of these effects on the board-room dynamics; be especially critical on the role of the expert who impresses the board with their statistical knowledge. Do this by evaluating this at the end and, during the process, designate a trustee who can order a "time out" if one of these effects is likely to occur.
- Force yourself to act in the short term. An important step to avoid procrastination or risk averseness in a board is to develop the risk appetite and act on it. Avoid wishful thinking and lethargy in difficult decisions, especially when it comes to possible losses.

Using Expert Opinions

Boards add experts to their own board or investment committees as external advisers or external members. Funds select several advisers. The pension fund considers the expertise profile that the committee must have in order to perform its tasks properly. The idea is that a combination of additional knowledge and competencies that complements the knowledge of the board must be at the table. For example, the advisers often bring knowledge about macroeconomic topics, the functioning of the financial markets, risk management, ALM and, above all, experience with (interest) derivatives. For example, a fund can select its advisors around topics such as interest rate hedging, real estate, and ALM.

Prior to choosing advisers, the question is what the exact role of the advisor should be. The external consultants are explicitly selected on the basis of knowledge and expertise and also implicitly on status and network, but are actually largely free to fulfill their role. The profiles are in fact well described in terms of required knowledge, but might be less specific in what is intended with the role of the external advisor. Possible roles are as follows:

- The external advisor is relatively operational and is there to supplement existing knowledge to set up decision-making as efficiently as possible, for example in monitoring and selection, interest-rate hedging, tactical asset allocation, and shocks in the financial markets.
- The external advisor is there to design countervailing power towards the investment management organization.
- The external advisor plays the role of consultant, providing market information and practical examples of implementation and pitfalls. The consultant's role can also involve initiating; the board then expects initiatives in the area of policy.

Given the importance of the advisor, it is important to consider what "expert" and "expertise" actually mean. An expert has four characteristics: (i) a high degree of education, (ii) qualifications in the field and/or economy, finances, and investments; (iii) training focused on the task; and (iv) extensive experience. The expert must have experienced the problems and their application over a long period of time.

Furthermore, an expert must work in the field. Under this angle, an expert is especially complementary to the knowledge and abilities of the existing board members. This set of competencies can also often been seen in vacancy postings, where an extensive and deep knowledge of the financial markets, instruments, risk management, etc. are required. A word of caution, however: being an expert in an area is not the same as developing expertise. Expertise should be interpreted as the extent to which problems can be addressed or resolved in certain circumstances. A board should look for four distinctive features in expert candidates during the recruitment process:[7]

1. Experts spend more time analyzing the problem and less on solving it, while novices do the opposite;
2. Experts recognize and categorize problems based on underlying trends and principles, while novices remain "on the surface;"
3. Experts are able to process large amounts of information rapidly;
4. Experts have a good memory for information that is relevant to the problem, both in the short and the long term.

The role of the expert is therefore to give their interpretation of situations, often on the basis of (economic) parallels. This can be done using personal experience or based on qualifications and education. For instance, during the sharp fall in equities in the fourth quarter of 2008, experts were asked to provide interpretations (e.g. "Is the major depression of 1933 repeating itself?"), and experience (e.g. "Will shares rebound or not?"). Thus, it is likely that the ability to tell consistent stories when providing interpretations is an important precondition and added value of an expert. Therefore, an underlying principle for an expert is that they are consistent and able to rapidly adapt to changing circumstances.

However, experts can also fall prey to their own convictions. Their extensive experience can introduce behavioral biases such as invincibility, in which previous successful choices support the conviction that they should keep on being correct. This also makes a case for experts to be employed: employment gives them the most incentives to keep reviewing their starting points when new insights and information develop.[8]

A possible trap is that if a committee leads to group thinking, experts reinforce and confirm the opinions of the loudest voices in the groups. Committee members are more or less dependent on the actions and opinions of others, especially experts. This is the paradox of the role of an expert: the expert is employed because of their available knowledge and expertise to improve the decision-making process. However, they can be intimidating to other group members precisely because of their expertise and reputation, making the discussion in the group less open, or causing earlier consensus to be sought without the expert's opinion.

Pension funds are aware of the different roles that experts can have and are increasingly adding different forms of expertise to a committee. A common model is the addition of one external member or advisor with an academic background; and another external member or advisor who has an investment or advising background. However, their form of advice is fundamentally different.

Exhibit 13.2 highlights the differences in characteristics and method of advice between investment professionals and academics. These differences are not always clear-cut. Consider an academic who moved to an asset manager position and provides advice to an investment committee. How can they be classified? Exhibit 13.2 can help a board look for the desired characteristics when forming a committee or board.

For their advice, academic advisors have as starting point a theoretical framework in which it is important that the argumentation is consistent and based on theories. However, the recommendations and conclusions that scientists give to the committee are limited in scope. As in research, hypotheses cannot be confirmed; at best they are not denied. A scientist is always looking for more confirmation and data. In contrast, consultants have applicability as a starting point. The advice must lead to an action and help the board with its problem. The argumentation and theory formation do not have to be watertight; it is more important that the intended approach and solutions have already worked in other situations.

The Investment Consultant

Advisors such as investment consultants are generally trusted advisors of boards, and could be characterized as a happy marriage between the academic and practical advisor. On the one hand, their job is to advice on a practical implementation of the investment management strategy of the fund; on the other hand, they are expected to be sensitive to future developments and new (academic) insights that might change the investment governance.

	Investment Professional Advisor	Academic Advisor
Characteristics	• Doctor role with awareness for the advice process. • Identification with practical questions from the board, takes a multidisciplinary approach. • Open to and critical of the board's values and interests. Focused on working together with the board. Personal approach focused on social values. • Practical and problem-solving leading. Focused on short-term knowledge; theory on current topics. • Experience serves as a source of valid and valuable knowledge. Scientific knowledge is too limited to rely on as the sole source of knowledge.	• Information expert with little awareness of the investment process of the pension fund. • Identification with specialized applied knowledge from economic or financial subdisciplines. • Applied knowledge and advice must comply with scientific values. Distant expert approach. Indifferent to the boards' values and interests. • Theoretical and general knowledge leading. Long-term perspectives to deal with the issues, rather than short-term practical solutions are offered. Committed to generating, accumulating and preserving sustainable knowledge. • Uses positive science ideal. Relevant knowledge is applicable for advice when information research meets scientific standards.
Preferred method of providing advice.	• Concrete or evaluative conclusions and advice. Emphasis on probability and practical reservation. • More breadth in the argumentation: generalist approach. Doing direct and practical positive statements and valuations in advisory reports and committee meetings. • Justification mainly based on "common sense" causality and not on heavy theory. Often reference to values, motives, standards, criteria. • Support based on experience, rough estimate and personal assessment. Results must comply with a "common sense" test. • Presentation: emphasis on advice, conclusions and the argument.	• General and neutral conclusions; no normative advice. Emphasis on uncertainty and theoretical reservation. • More depth in the argumentation, specialist approach. Preference for exact, reliable statements, no valuations. • Justification mainly based on theory embedded in economic disciplines and non-controversial values, motives, standards, criteria. • Support based on scientific method. Little sympathy for "quick-and-dirty" research, experiential knowledge and "common sense." • Presentation: emphasis on scientific support by presenting method, lots of data and theory in the structure of the report.

EXHIBIT 13.2 Stylized differences in character and preferred method of giving advice between investment professionals and academics.[9]

Giving advice on asset classes, portfolio construction, benchmarks, selection and monitoring, and performance is one of the roles of investment consultants. Investment consultants advise on fund manager and investment-style selection, drawing on proprietary databases of managers and, where necessary, the termination of managers. They may assist in the process of selection and subsequently provide a monitoring service.

Consultants are selected for their knowledge, experience, and understanding of the issues of the pension fund. They have built up large databases and developed an extensive process around the selection and monitoring. The expectation should not be that this process generates the best outcome, but rather that it was a thorough process that leads to an adequate result. In a sobering study, researchers analyzed the factors that drive consultants' recommendations in the United States, what impact these recommendations have on flows, and how well the recommended funds perform. They found that investment consultants' recommendations are driven largely by soft factors rather than the funds' past performance, and that their recommendations have a very significant effect on fund flows. However, they find no evidence that the recommendations of the investment consultants add value, suggesting that the search for winners, encouraged and guided by investment consultants, is fruitless.[10] This begs the question why trustees employ this service.

First, trustees might simply value the hand-holding service of consultants. Even though trustees might have derived similar results, they value the relationship, which gives them confidence to make decisions. Second, investment consultants may provide a shield that plan sponsors can use to defend their decisions.[11] Trustees might even disregard their own expectations of fund managers' performance in favor of the recommendations of investment consultants. An investment committee or fund might overemphasize active strategies, even though they are not convinced of its added value. Firing a bad performing active manager reflects on the manager, while the fund seems decisive. With passive managers, disappointing outcomes reflect on the overall asset allocation strategy and, therefore, on the quality of the board of trustees. Third, information asymmetry might be at work here. Trustees may misunderstand the added value of these recommendations. While consultants insist on full transparency in the performance of the fund managers they rate, they do not themselves disclose past recommendations to allow evaluation of their own performance.

Challenges and Dilemmas in Taking Advice

Effective committees and the board value the differences in background and opinions in the board and try to invite different opinions and viewpoints to the table. Discussions will be trickier, and advice will be less likely to be taken on board if:

- The adviser's preferences differ to those of the committee. If, for example, the board is considering a proposal to increase the allocation to equities, considerations will include the fact that an (external) member of the investment committee is a confirmed believer in equities in all circumstances, and that the advice must therefore be taken with a grain of salt.

- The perception is that the adviser is prioritizing his own interests. During the selection process, the background of the investment committee members and staff is checked to ensure that there are no conflicts of interest. Explicit conflicts are an issue if the external member works for an asset manager. There are also implicit conflicts of interest when pension funds have their own investment management organization with in-house assets.
- The adviser is not to be trusted; this relates to the other values and own interests.
- The adviser cannot justify the advice; this occurs with numeric advice. A quantitative recommendation can be more quickly regarded as convincing than a qualitative recommendation.

The outcome of a group discussion, in contrast, will be accepted if the group perceives that the evaluation and decision-making process is honest in terms of steps and procedures. The chairman plays an important role herein. Topics, for example, must not be "capped" as a result of time restrictions. Furthermore, it helps if the participants in the process are considered to be trustworthy. This is expressed via discussing collective values on a regular basis, and departure points and the absence of personal interests in the advisory phase.

Another dilemma is that responsibility and accountability for the advice do not always overlap. Without any reservation, boards (or investment committees) and funds should take full responsibility for their actions. This might seem self-evident; it is what fiduciary duty is all about. People with an investment management background or occupation, however, are usually wired somewhat differently. They are probably likely to take credit for their successes, attributing them to skill; they will dismiss their failures, attributing them to bad luck, other people's mistakes, or adverse markets that hit everyone. This "blame game" is a very subtle process. Researchers illustrated this by way of commentary found in the *Wall Street Journal*.[12] They found that articles about positive returns used active phrases like "the stock climbed upwards," "regained its path," or "turned the corner." These are examples of positive, skill-based terms. With negative returns, they found an abundance of stocks "spiraling downwards," "gravitating downwards," or "negative sentiment." The message here is clear: negative returns are passive—they are due to the market; positive returns are active—they are due to individuals' decisions and skills. This trap has two negative consequences:

- It further contributes to the overconfidence bias, with trustees thinking that they made wonderful decisions;
- It is a powerful incentive for creating a "blame" culture in which people point fingers at others and work to avoid getting blamed themselves.

The blame culture has some unintended repercussions. First, investment philosophy and strategic asset allocation will tend to be based on what the peer group decides to do, not on what is essential for the fund. This is a form of cognitive dissonance: board members disagreeing with decisions, but not wanting to confront them. Second, it will block learning by the board, given that a candid and open-minded performance attribution will not be possible. It would be appropriate discuss the risk of the "blame game" beforehand, and the chair has an important role in facilitating this.

DECISION-MAKING UNDER PRESSURE

A particular aspect of decision-making is that the decisions that really matter to the continuity of the fund regularly have to be made under pressure. Take the worldwide financial crisis in 2008–2009, the Eurozone crisis in 2011, or the fallout after the collapse of Long-Term Capital Management (LTCM) in 1998 for example: the different choices that boards made for interest rate hedge, rebalancing of equities, or counterparty risk substantially influenced the financial results. Boards seem to get used to making decisions under pressure, but are they getting better at it? In policy preparations, increasing consideration is given to the fact that boards and committees must be able to respond to and anticipate rapid changes in the environment and have elaborated action plans regarding how to proceed in order to maintain the fund capital or aims.

A crisis begins with the knowledge of what actually constitutes a crisis. Crises are hard to predict but do encompass common elements. The most visible is a strong fall in the degree of coverage in a short period of time. In the financial markets, exchange rate fluctuations increase, principally in a downward direction. The number of buyers reduces substantially and there is talk of "liquidity drying up" as a result. Spreads increase significantly, and the number of safe havens reduces as many investment categories drop in value and no longer compensate for one another.

Investors as well as board members experience this environment as extremely uncertain. Analysts and commentators will increasingly talk of an "unprecedented" situation. This feeling of uncertainty increases as a result of problems that were more or less evident but seemed to be manageable, causing major, unexpected problems in a short time frame. The fall of hedge fund LTCM led to a worldwide crisis in 1998 because it was caused, among other things, by Russia announcing a moratorium on loans that were provided by foreign countries. The fall of the corporate bank Bear Stearns was predictable and difficult, but the downfall of Lehman caused worldwide panic. Panic is a classic element in the crisis as customers run to the bank to take out their money or financial establishments are unable to attract further cash. Another reaction is unlimited confidence in central bankers or politicians because they have the resources to function as lender of last resort. Given this, what steps can pension fund boards take?

Pension funds' boards, experts and advisors are unable to predict or influence financial crises, neither their timing nor their impact. However, boards can assess the impact that a financial crisis might have on its investments and balance sheet. They can think beforehand what sort of impact is acceptable within the risk appetite of the fund (see Chapter 4), what sort of measures would be needed to achieve this and, most importantly, what this means for decision-making under stress. We summarize 10 actions to create effective decision-making during a crisis, borrowing insights from other disciplines.

1. Create a crisis response team in advance. Delegate responsibilities and make clear who is responsible for what in a given crisis. The response team includes the "face" of the fund (usually the chairman), the one who will be in charge of facing the press. The crisis response team will also need to be bolstered with people who have a comprehensive knowledge of the daily operations of your business, such as the chief financial officer (CFO) and the risk manager.

2. Discuss beforehand when the crisis response team should be deployed. A sudden drop in cover ratio, market prices, or interest rates that acutely threaten the solvency definitely count as valid triggers. The board should determine what constitutes a threat as specifically as possible.
3. Determine beforehand who is in charge: the risk manager or the investment manager? When the crisis is imminent, a number of pension funds held discussions along the following lines:
   a. Trustee: "We need to de-risk in order to preserve capital."
   b. The asset manager: "If you de-risk now, you will not be able to profit from the recovery imminent after a crisis. Also, you forsake the possibility to buy investments at bargain prices. It's your loss!"

      De-risking makes perfect sense during a crisis to preserve capital and is far more important than hunting for investment opportunities. A belief is that the risk manager is in charge during a crisis, and the asset manager advisor on how the measures might be implemented — not the other way around. This is of course incorrect, as neither the risk manager nor the investment manager is in charge. This trade-off should be dealt with when the board draws up the risk appetite of the fund.
4. Know your enemy—develop a thorough understanding of what a crisis is. Crises cannot be predicted, but experience shows that crises tend to exhibit the following elements:
   a. A sudden drop in reserves and/or cover ratio, a more or less downward oscillation, in a very short period of time.
   b. Markets shift: shortfall in liquidity. Spreads increase. Drop in asset prices. Diversification effects become non-existent.
   c. Increased uncertainty in a very short time, increased talk of "unprecedented situations."
   d. Half-expected problems that tend to be followed and worsened by larger, unexpected problems.
   e. Unlimited faith in the healing powers of central bankers, or the deep pockets of politicians, as saviors of last resort.
   f. Psychological difficulty in group and individual decision making to see a "way out."
5. Plan in advance. You should already have a written plan in place to be used as soon as the crisis occurs. Try to determine in advance any type of situation that may arise to affect your pension fund, and confront these situations with the risk appetite that the fund has set up. Make sure the organization can come up with a detailed breakdown of the portfolio, by potential risks (credit, market, liquidity, etc.) This need not be a quarterly report; it should be accurate and swiftly delivered. A detailed assessment of potential risks can mean the difference between responding immediately and responding after it is too late. Be as specific in your actions as possible. It requires far less time to update scenarios then to think of alternatives under (time) pressure. Do not write an elaborate manual, the steps and decision to taken and who is in charge of what suffices. The more complex the fund is, the

easier it is for a board member to overlook details and to err, sometimes at great costs. Hence, the usefulness of a well-thought-out to-do list.[13]

6. Prepare for the obvious, foreseeable problems during a crisis. Pension fund trustees generally face four dangers in any crises, which they need to address, but can prepare for:

   a. Running behind developments, instead of preparing for upcoming ones; the fear that they might become a forced buyer or seller due to the derivatives, outstanding commitments, pension pay-outs, or a stringent application of rebalancing policies.

   b. A decrease in risk appetite, especially if the risk appetite is not formalized in any way.

   c. A sense of regret that certain measures were not taken earlier.

   d. Awareness that any risk-reducing measure (especially in the derivatives sphere) suggested in a late phase of the crisis is too costly to execute, procrastinating sensible actions.

7. Train well in advance in a simulated environment; try to fine-tune the planning for the following issues:

   a. Uncover fundamental differences in how trustees approach a crisis. For example, within a board some trustees might make a compelling case to buy more equities after a sudden drop in prices, while other trustees would prefer the opposite. Address the obvious: a discussion in the board that the circumstances are so exceptional, that well thought-out-policies should be abandoned, instead of doing what was agreed upon.

   b. Challenge the board regularly on its risk appetite. Is it constant throughout, or should it be rescaled when crises occur?

8. Communicate what you know, not what you wish for. Refraining from speculation during the earliest stages of the crisis is imperative. If you don't have solid proof of your facts, don't release them. Try to step in the shoes of the participant of the fund. Presenting factual updates may not be pleasant news, but is a sign that the trustees are on top of things. Trustees should refrain from forward-looking statements.

9. Refocus the management agenda when things heat up or cool down. The start of the financial crisis is usually too late to start putting together a plan for management and response. Differentiate between normal times and abnormal times. In abnormal times, correlation is absent, all assets save short-term government bonds dive downwards. An effective board reallocates time from the "normal times" management in favor of the "abnormal" times period. Planning in advance and training are crucial elements here.

10. Conduct brutally honest post mortems after crises or periods of turmoil. What were the challenges that the fund faced? Set up a chronology. Determine for each event what the reaction was, if it was the right reaction in hindsight, whether it could have been foreseen and prepared, and how the decision process took place. What recommendations can be made? Post them on the fund's website, to share with participants, signaling that the fund is learning and adapting to new realities.

Whatever you do, avoid phrases like "these are exceptional times" as an excuse to do nothing. We have been forewarned by the publications of Nicholas Taleb, and are now living it: the regularity is not in the risk/return distribution, but in the frequency of occurrence of crisis. In that sense, we are probably heading towards a new management style of pension fund trustees that might be closer to the job descriptions of firemen, ambulances, pilot fighters, and athletes. These groups have in common that they train 95% of the time, to excel in 5%, whether it is on the battlefield or the football field. Participants should expect no less from their trustees.

Simulating decision-making under stress is not only helpful for stressful times, it also supports more effective decision-making during "normal times." Pension consultant Paul Trickett and head of pension consultant Watson Wyatt views this as "moving away from the historical practice of making investment decisions around dates in the diary and opt instead for investment processes that can be implemented according to predefined rules, as and when the opportunities arise."[14] Markets are becoming increasingly volatile; a financial crisis every three or four years will not be out of the ordinary. Long-term investing will increasingly mean making changes based on long-term principles. Successful committees adopt more dynamic long-term strategies. The best way is to do the thinking about the market conditions in which you would make a change in advance, and set up a process for acting on a pre-agreed decision, fitting within the right governance framework.

ENDNOTES

1. See Maynard (2012).
2. See SEI Investments (2016). Governance and Groupthink in UK Defined Benefit Pension Schemes. Available at: https://seicdrupalcdn.azureedge.net/cdn/farfuture/31Ek9HflEkEAOPl NPFgIK55BP-9wym5XG8VUqWJ0Cd4/1518212992/sites/default/files/inline-files/SEI-Groupthink-Research-Study.pdf.
3. See Kahneman (1991).
4. See Morrell (2008).
5. In general, portfolios consist of the traditional five asset classes: equities, fixed income, real estate, cash equivalents, and alternatives. Over time, more asset classes have become available. Other possible asset classes, denominated by the alternative asset class, include: real estate, artwork, hedge funds, venture capital, and crowdsourcing.
6. See Roy (2005).
7. See Wagner (2002).
8. See for example Clark (2004).
9. Based on Bouwmeester (2008).
10. See Jenkinson et al. (2016).
11. See Jones and Martinez (2017).
12. See Morris et al. (2007).
13. Based on the Checklist Manifesto, by Gawande and Lloyd (2010).
14. See Watson Wyatt Worldwide (2005).

CHAPTER 14

Achieving Investment Excellence

Key Take Aways

- This chapter deals with moving your pension fund towards investment excellence. Boards have a key role in achieving investment excellence.

- The activities that contribute to excellence are (1) shaping the strategy, (2) designing the process, (3) implementing the investment cycle, (4) organizing the board, and (5) learning to adapt.

- A change process is required to move to higher levels of excellence.

- Both change and learning require a significant governance budget of time and skills committed by the board. If the board has no intrinsic motivation to move towards excellence, success will be temporary.

- It is important to ensure that new key people in the process are immersed in the collective knowledge that has been built up with this learning.

Congratulations! You have almost finished the book. The only thing left is to effectively implement the lessons discussed in the previous five parts. They have provided you with insights about the activities that contribute to excellence. To summarize, the five parts are (i) Pension Funds: Understanding the Role, Shaping the Mission; (ii) Designing the Process; (iii) Implementing the Investments; (iv) Organizing the Board; and (v) Learning, Adapting and Improving.

This chapter is about moving your pension fund towards investment excellence. After reading this book, you will know the activities that contribute to excellence; and you will be able to identify the key differences between the levels of excellence.

What has to be done in order to start moving is essentially quite simple. You have to understand and accept where you stand now as a pension fund, and you have to know where you want to go to best serve the future needs of your participants. Subsequently, you have to define sensible steps to get there and you then have to take them. How to do this successfully is less straightforward. There are hurdles to overcome: How do you make sure the goal is one that participants share, how do you arrange the necessary governance budget of the board in terms of time and skill, and who will actually lead the process? Along the way, how do you overcome resistance to change and how do you, as a board, develop alternatives that allow you to achieve the goals as well? Finally, how do trustees make sure that what is being achieved sticks within the board culture and investment organization, for example when new trustees join the board?

A pension fund faces two demands: it must execute its current activities so as to survive today's challenges, and it must adapt these activities to survive tomorrow's. Today's pension funds have to balance both. Boards that are overly focused on effective execution create high barriers to adaptation for tomorrow. On the other hand, a pension fund board that spends too much time on strategic long-term issues runs the risk of not dealing effectively with the short-term challenges, in turn reducing the chances of being around in the long term. Since execution as well as adaptation requires resources, trustees face an unending competition for money, people and especially time to address the need to perform in the short run and the equally vital need to improve and change in the long run.[1]

This chapter summarizes the key activities required to achieve investment excellence. We present the key characteristics and prerequisites for becoming a learning organization, realizing that the transition towards investment excellence is a multiyear, multistage process. To make this process more practical and manageable for the board, we introduce different levels of excellence coupled with which characteristics and qualities are needed to move one step closer to achieving the long-term investment goals for the participants.

THE FIVE ACTIVITIES DRIVING TOWARDS EXCELLENCE

It is actually not that difficult for an adequate pension fund to achieve excellence if you know where to improve. This requires work but is achievable. There are examples available to copy and learn from. Attaining investment excellence and remaining excellent, however, is difficult for pension funds to achieve.

Going from being a fine pension fund to an excellent pension fund can translate into better structural results. Doing 1%–2% better is a considerable amount in a world in which expected returns for well-diversified portfolios are somewhere in the range of 3%–6% in nominal terms. It involves designing an investment process that helps to achieve your fund's goals, as well as tackling the main governance issues that are out there for everyone to see. We believe that there are five activities that together can achieve "excellent investing." These are visualized by Exhibit 14.1. We feel these are the roughly the same for every fund, even though pension funds come in all shapes and sizes around the world. Our experience is that the same issues pop up around the globe. These five activities correspond with the five parts of this book.

Part I covers how to shape the strategy, thereby setting the framework for the board to design the investment process in Part II. Part III focuses on implementing the investment cycle. Part IV shares the latest insights on how to organize the board. Finally, Part V highlights the learning and adaptation process that is vital for the pension fund's long-term success.

Hereunder we recap the key aspects of these activities. To summarize this in a way that is practical for boards with limited time, we list the desired outcomes for each

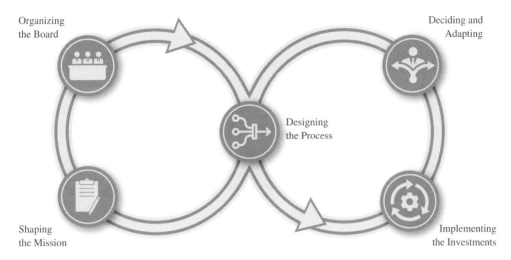

Organizing
the Board

Deciding and
Adapting

Designing
the Process

Shaping
the Mission

Implementing
the Investments

EXHIBIT 14.1   The investment excellence loop.

of these activities. These statements are meant to be food for thought for trustees. If you can affirm that each of these outcomes have been achieved by the board without reservation, then your fund has taken some major steps towards investment excellence. If not, then you get a feeling of the kind of work that remains to be done.

Activity 1: Setting the Strategy (Chapters 1–2)

This activity lays the foundations for the pension fund, defines purpose and translates purpose into strategy. What is the role of the fund, what are the roles and responsibilities of the board? Who are you and what do you want to achieve for your participants? This consists of having clarity about your purpose – why you exist for your participants, what the added value is that trustees want to highlight. Purpose, mission and strategy translate into achievable goals, such as the pension deal that you are you offering.

The output of this activity should be a clear purpose, a clear strategy that fits the changing context, and a clear set of board responsibilities—be they delegated or not. These elements should be laid down in documents easily accessible to the people within the fund and its stakeholders. These documents have to be alive and be written in simple language. The board should use them for everyday practice, regularly review them and update them (Exhibit 14.2).

Activity 2: Designing the Investment Process (Chapters 3–6)

This activity covers the design of the investment activities. Before designing the investment process, the board has a shared understanding of the key concepts of risk and investments. Having a shared starting point helps trustees to distinguish between minor and major details, and the difference between risk and uncertainty. Additionally, developing investment beliefs and/or principles are important tools for the investment set-up.

Key Element Activity 1: Setting the Strategy

1.1 The fund has a document outlining Purpose and Mission.
1.2 The fund has identified strengths and weaknesses, opportunities and threats and its sustainable competitive advantage for its participants, and as an institutional investor.
1.3 The fund has an explicit set of measurable goals and objectives.
1.4 The fund regularly evaluates and (re-)formulates goals and objectives.
1.5 The key stakeholders in the fund have been consulted in the process of developing goals, understand and support these.
1.6 The board spends at least 20% of the available annual time on formulating and evaluating mission, vision or strategy.
1.7 There is a strategic plan with a 3 to 5 year horizon, combining the advantages of being a long-term investor with the adaptability to short-term developments.

EXHIBIT 14.2 Key Elements Activity 1: Setting the strategy.

With a clear purpose and investment beliefs, the next step is choosing, or reaffirming the right investment model that helps you align realistic goals, implementation and governance budget. In other words, how do you organize the investment process in such a way that it leverages the strong point of the pension fund identified in the mission, purpose and investment beliefs discussion?

The output of this activity is a clear and shared investment language and a set of investment beliefs that are owned by the board. The investment beliefs should be used by everyone who plays a role in the investment process of the fund, even—or especially—when it's an external party. The beliefs should be transparent to beneficiaries and stakeholders, and understood and accepted by the trustees and the investors. This activity results in a clear and fit for purpose investment process based on a number of building blocks that realize the investment objective by transforming the premiums of the participants into investment returns for the pension payouts. Finally, a choice for an investment model should be made, in which there are a number of choices that, to a large extent, reflect whether the fund believes in a top-down benchmark-oriented structure or in a more bottom-up, entrepreneurial structure. Size, governance budget and culture all play a role in this choice (Exhibit 14.3).

Key Elements Activity 2: Designing the Investment process

2.1 The fund has an explicit set of investment beliefs or principles owned by the board.
2.2 The investment beliefs are applied consequently and consistently within the investment process and decision making.
2.3 The board is aware of evolving best practices in the investment beliefs and goals formulation field.
2.4 There is a clear and explicit investment process which logically builds on the strengths, weaknesses, competitive advantages and beliefs.
2.5 The investment model which is chosen reflects the beliefs and culture the board is looking for.

EXHIBIT 14.3 Key Elements Activity 2: Designing the investment process.

Activity 3: Implementing the Investments (Chapters 7–9)

This activity is about the effective execution of the investment process. Effective execution combines portfolio construction, implementation and feedback, monitoring and evaluation, and translating the objectives into investment outcomes in the best way possible. There will always be leakage between implementation and plan but this should be minimized. The board will delegate the entire or almost the entire process to an internal or external fiduciary manager who has to be selected and evaluated. Therefore, for pension fund boards and investment committees, execution predominantly translates into the question, how do you organize the investment process in such a way that the different steps build on each other's insights, and how do you make sure that the results are continuously evaluated where the art is to separate random short-term noise from results that affect the fund's long-term goals? Finding and keeping the right distance, horizon and altitude to the parties to which the process is delegated is a key to excellence here. In addition, the board or investment committee commands a serious dose of investment knowledge to be able to delegate, counterbalance and monitor effectively.

The output of this activity is a well-designed portfolio, which is executed in a cost-effective way by fit-for-purpose managers, who are monitored continuously with a management by exception approach. The identification of potential weak areas is done in a structured way (Exhibit 14.4).

Activity 4: Organizing the Board (Chapters 10–12)

This activity focuses on the oversight and governance of the investment process; designing, steering and overseeing the realization of the mission of the pension fund. In the earlier activities, the emphasis was on relatively hard and objective matter: strategy,

---

Key Elements Activity 3. Implementing the Investments

3.1 The resulting portfolio is clearly based on and consistent with purpose, mission & strategy, risk appetite and investment beliefs.
3.2 The board has established criteria to judge the goodness of the portfolio. Based on these criteria, the board has ascertained that the current portfolio is a good portfolio.
3.3 The board or investment committee understands sensitivity of the assumptions or predictions for the portfolio and its potential outcomes.
3.4 The board has clearly and unambiguous delegated roles and decision rights in the investment process.
3.5 There is a clear policy on total investment cost. The board measures and weighs internal as well as external costs from the same perspective.
3.6 The board has determined the governance budget needed to fulfill its fiduciary and management responsibilities. The governance budget of the board is in line with the tasks required of the fund given the set up.
3.7 When a strategic decision is made, the fund specifies ex ante flags (both on performance and on process) that will lead to a deeper look into the strategy.
3.8 The monitoring reports are top down in nature and only reflect relevant details for oversight and decision making.
3.9 The fund takes great care to avoid behavioral and emotional biases in decision making.

EXHIBIT 14.4 Key Elements Activity 3: Implementing the investments.

process, and implementation. The present activity is performed by boards and committees consisting of individuals with different backgrounds, skillsets, and mental make-ups. To turn these into a well-performing orchestra, both in peace and in wartime, is an enormous task. So, in this activity the harder-to-pinpoint human factor plays the main role: How will the board organize itself to realize purpose and mission? What are the board's key tasks; what does it delegate to whom? What should the board be aware of, and organize beforehand when setting up investment committees and executive offices to support their tasks? And what are valuable insights in dealing with the investment management organization (IMO)? The fund needs significant governance budget to have serious countervailing power to the investors. It is a key task of the board to oversee the investment organization and to verify and make sure that it is fit for purpose. Often, the understanding between board members and investors is limited and vulnerable because of the differences in their perspectives. Key concepts that will come up time and again are: the right distance, the right altitude and the right horizon.

The key output of this activity is fourfold: a well-functioning board, a well-functioning board investment committee, a fit-for-purpose investment organization to which the implementation of the investments is delegated, and an effective working relationship with that organization. The board should have the trust and respect of everyone it deals with and be able to both define and execute on the strategy (Exhibit 14.5).

Key Elements Activity 4: Organizing the Board

4.1 The board and its committees have sound knowledge about (best practice) investing and apply that to the relevant investment decision process.

4.2 The board has carefully thought about the right distance, altitude and horizon. The board focuses on the right things: scanning the external environment, setting strategy, managing and overseeing the delegated tasks and reviewing results.

4.3 The board has carefully designed the role of the investment committee, how the committee monitors the investment process, and supports the board in policymaking and oversight.

4.4 Board meetings run smoothly, everybody gets a voice, decisions are made in an orderly fashion and the decisions are well formulated.

4.5 Within the board all relevant competencies are represented. Collectively, the board members understand the key stakeholders' groups well.

4.6 There is a clear annual board agenda covering the formal responsibilities and strategic choices. There is equilibrium between important and urgent topics. Preparatory documents are available in a timely manner, and are clear and well written.

4.7 The board is regularly challenged by an outside-in perspective, e.g., by other pension funds, stakeholders or participants.

4.8 The investment management organization to which the investments have been delegated is fit for purpose —and the criteria for this are transparent.

4.9 There is a regular review of this organization and its relevant parts in order to judge its fit—also under changing circumstances.

EXHIBIT 14.5 Key Elements Activity 4: Organizing the board.

Key Elements Activity 5: Learning to adapt

5.1 The fund adapts well and is proactive to changing circumstances and context.
5.2 The fund learns from its history and has a process for continuous improvement.
5.3 Change and learning are fully integrated in the board process.
5.4 20% or more of the Governance Budget of the Board (time and money) is spent on learning.
5.5 There is a formal board training process in place. New board members are put through this process in their first six months.

EXHIBIT 14.6 Key Elements Activity 5: Learning to adapt

Activity 5: Learning to Adapt (Chapter 13)

This activity focuses its attention on board room dynamics. What does it take to make a good decision and what special challenges does a pension fund board have when it is supported with complex decision tools such as Asset Liability Management? Is the board aware of the special role advisors have, and how they can influence decision-making? In the end, it probably comes down to a down-to-earth board to take all the necessary steps to implement the elements to achieve investment excellence. It requires, on the one hand, an exceptional board to hold on to the strategy and beliefs and financial markets become under stress and, on the other hand, the ability to keep an open mind to adapt insights as new research and developments in the industry come to light that require the board to adjust its principles (Exhibit 14.6).

THE LEARNING BOARD AND THE CHARACTERISTICS OF THE LEVELS OF EXCELLENCE

Learning forms the bridge between the present and the future of the pension fund in a systematic way. The term "learning organization" was coined by management author Robert Senge,[2] who stated that "an organization that is continually expanding its capacity to create its future. For such an organization, it is not enough to merely survive . . . 'Adaptive learning' must be joined by 'generative learning', learning that enhances our capacity to create."

So what is a learning organization? It is an organization that is able to consider the external environment (opportunities and threats) in an open, strategical way; to practice introspection in an open and critical way (strengths and weaknesses); and it has a strong sense of where it is and where it wants to be, and to create the movement in the direction it wants to go.

The board plays a large role in shaping the learning organization. It can encourage and stimulate an open, learning environment, but also easily kill a learning attitude ("waste," blame games, "if you admit that you can improve, why haven't you done better in the past," etc.). It also can play an important part in creating a learning system.

And, last but certainly not least, the board itself has serious collective learning to do. Otherwise, with each change of board membership, important lessons may be lost. There are a number of important prerequisites to create a learning system and a learning board: leadership, resources, mindset and cultures, measure scorecard, maintenance, and education.

Leadership

Often, the spark of the creation of a learning board comes from an individual leader or board member, who dares to step out of the box and say, "Why are we doing this? Are we doing this in the right way? Are we all on the same page in terms of doing this?" They translate these questions into action. For example, in the case of the Dutch healthcare pension fund PFZW, it was the chairman of the Investment Committee, Florent Vlak, who asked these questions. And to answer them, he initiated an annual summer course at PFZW that grew into a mechanism to educate PFZW's board over the past decade.

Resources

It is often surprisingly hard to find the resources, the "governance budget"—essentially, time and money—for learning, both by board and the organization. We feel that learning is an integral part of the cost of doing business and therefore should be budgeted for, both in terms of (board) time and money. We have negative and positive examples for both aspects. In current years, with solvency being low, we have come across boards that have, for instance, cut their travel budgets to close to zero out of fear of public outcry. One could just as well state that it is "forbidden to learn." However, we also see many positive examples, such as the Future Fund from Australia and Railpen from the UK, who spend serious time and money to learn from peers and systematically work towards achieving and maintaining investment excellence. For many boards, time may be an even more precious resource than money. It may feel uncomfortable to dedicate one or two board meetings per year to learning and change.

Mind-Set and Culture

We have come across executives who communicate ideas such as "Change and learning come after you have completed your day time job." This sends a clear message: change and learning are hobbies, and to be dealt with in your own time. In many organizations, being extremely busy is the way to strongly convey that you are important. For many leaders, both in boards and in IMOs, life is about back-to-back meetings. However, this type of message is counterproductive in the face of the observation that financial markets are adaptive, that today's participant is changing, and that the macroeconomic environment—such as low interest—might become more disruptive than we currently expect. In that sense, change and learning are an integral part of fulfilling the fiduciary duty. This is why we advocate spending 20% of board time on learning and achieving excellence—take a step back from the day-to-day execution, and learn and reflect. Of course, 20% is a bit of an arbitrary number, but you get the idea.

A learning organization is about the board and its organization learning, not the individual trustee. A highly individualistic, based on zero-sum game winning (I win—you lose) corporate culture is hard to reconcile with a learning culture. In environments like that, it is not that easy to imagine that the sum is sustainably greater than the parts, because there is some vulnerability in learning, which often starts with being open about the fact that things can be improved, that there are things you do not know and that sharing these things lays the basis for collective improvement.

Also, in many organizational cultures, being certain about things is highly rewarded. Admitting that you have doubts about whether you are doing things in the right way is often seen as being "soft." In cases where uncertainty is deeply ingrained in the problem that you are trying to solve, and feedback loops take time—as is the case with investing—this is outright counterproductive.

That overconfidence (or acting in an overconfident way) may come at a great cost has been documented extensively, for example in the medical world. People who are certain—or have to appear certain—have no need to learn. Therefore, the board has to carefully create settings and a culture in which there is room for a conversation on what can be improved, both individually and collectively. The challenge is to look at the whole pension fund from a bird's eye view, seeing it as a "machine" or integral value chain designed to deliver pensions. This includes the board itself and all activities and decisions we discuss throughout this book. Then, ask the question of where you could improve the machine, or parts of it, to deliver even better output.

Measures and Scorecards

In order to learn and improve, an organization needs to take score of where it is in order to understand collectively where it stands, to be able to measure progress, and to pinpoint in which areas it wants to improve. Often, in the investment industry, we use output measures: risk, return, added value. We do this even on short horizons where we know that the noise overwhelms the signal. To admit where you are now may be painful sometimes, but it is unavoidable in order to become better, to learn and adapt. We take the view that the five activities done well will lead to great outcomes, but the relationship is a long-term one. Therefore, we put the emphasis on assessing the level of excellence of each of the activities, and not on the output measures.

Also, of course, people like to use SMART ways in goal-setting: specific, measurable, attainable, realistic and time-bound. Our point of view is, measure as SMART as you can, but be very aware of the fact that SMART is inherently reductionist in nature. You reduce a complex, often ambiguous reality to a few numbers. There should be room for subjectivity in the way you keep score, for things that do not fall neatly into a measurable box. Otherwise, you will end in "what gets measured gets managed" territory. Interpreting a scorecard as a starting point or a menu for a deep conversation leading to questions such as '"Why have you scored culture so low?" or "Why do you rate the governance so poorly?" is a much richer approach.

Maintenance and Education

Being a learning organization requires maintenance and education. Learning to be a learning organization will almost certainly require education. And, similarly to stopping with smoking, it is easy to fall back into old habits, for example in times of stress. New people should be immersed in the learning culture. If they bring bad habits from old companies they should be gently familiarized with the learning culture of the pension fund before being introduced in the board or in the organization.

The drive to move towards investment excellence emanates from this opinion, not only because it will enhance the current and future capacity to deliver the returns that pension funds need in order to deliver on the promise they made, but also in the form that is required by the current world. So, for example, it might require changing from collective defined benefit (DB) to individual defined contribution (DC). "Enhancing the capacity to create" in our minds means creating options to be fit for purpose under conditions of uncertainty. Creating a proprietary learning capacity is an important strategic consideration when thinking about whether to outsource or not: the learning is often almost free when you're doing things in house, and more difficult to capture externally.

LEVELS OF EXCELLENCE AND THE BOARD LEARNING PERSPECTIVE

Exhibit 14.7 relates the characteristics of the level of excellence to the learning perspective of the board. The way this builds up is the same as the levels of excellence: levels of weak practice and sufficient practice can be described with terms such as reactive, ad hoc, coincidental, individual, local, dogmatic and rigid; and the higher levels with terms like proactive, planned, systematic, collective, holistic, learning and adaptive.

THE BOARD'S JOURNEY TOWARDS ACHIEVING EXCELLENCE

As stated in the introduction to this chapter, there are four steps in the journey towards achieving excellence. First, understand where you stand now based on honest self-reflection. Second, decide where you want to go in the long term. Third, define sensible steps towards the goal. Fourth, execute them.

Step 1: Determine Where You Are Now

In order to learn and improve, an organization needs to take score of where it is in order to understand collectively where it stands, to be able to measure progress, and to pinpoint in which areas it wants to improve. To honestly admit where you are now may be painful sometimes, but it is unavoidable in order to become better, to learn and adapt.

How to do this? There are three different situations that initiate processes leading to achieving excellence: (i) An individual (e.g. a trustee) identifies the wish or need to change or improve; (ii) there is a serious crisis that forces change; and (iii) other, for

Level of Excellence	Board Characteristics	Learning Perspective
Weak Practice	There are serious components missing from a dimension or the quality of the component is unacceptably low. Not well documented. Board has to trust that somebody takes care—or not.	No board learning. Ad hoc, individual board member brings expert knowledge, or the knowledge is missing.
Sufficient Practice	Design, decision-making and or implementation are thought out and documented. Key processes work reasonably well and are mostly independent of specific people. The fund has carefully looked at all required standards and complies.	Ad hoc learning sessions to make board knowledge collective. Documentation for the board available on all key issues.
Strong Practice	Design, decision and implementation are sound and well founded. Comparable pension funds are taking a comparable approach. The board might be aware of the development and research behind it, but has not developed these insights itself. Serious evaluation and improvement is part of the regular process.	All knowledge is collective. Board and investors can give clear answers to many of the questions surrounding the why, how an of the five activities. They have been well documented and are regularly reviewed.
Excellent Practice	The fund consciously builds on its strengths and reduces its weaknesses. The fund aims to be best-practice or even to shape the best practice on a continual basis, not one-off but in a permanent way.	Learning is integrated, planned, collective and continuous. A broad set of stakeholders is intensively involved. New board members are routinely trained and brought up to speed.

EXHIBIT 14.7 Levels of excellence and the learning perspective of the board.

example the regulator raising the quality standard. In the first situation, there often is a new leader. This makes life relatively easy, because a fresh look is expected from new leaders. A much more difficult situation is when an individual trustee gets the insight or the ambition to bring the fund to a higher level. In this case, they have to at least build a small group of people who share the vision or ambition in order to get the clout needed to put the change on the agenda. The second situation, crisis, is much easier, because crisis is easy to recognize collectively and the need for action is unquestionable. But even then, there is the question of whether a fund uses a crisis just to fix what was broken or as a catalyst to become fundamentally better, and move up on the scale of excellence. In addition, this often depends on the ambition or leadership of a small group of people.

In all cases, what we propose is to go through a process in which a set of relevant people asses the level of excellence of the fund on the five activities in two stages. Who are these relevant people? The board could consider involving at least a combination of board and investment committee members, trustees' key personnel of the investment office or IMO, or trustees from respected peers. First, the people involved individually should reflect on a set of questions, identify what they feel is the level of excellence for each of the activities and bring up topics for further reflection and action. Armed with this information, the answers are brought together and a structured conversation is built on this. An issue can be that the people chosen to answer the questions do not have a relevant frame of reference, for example they do not know the best practices or the practices of the relevant peers. In that case, it probably makes sense to retain a party that does have this frame of reference, such as a consultant. At the same time, a board should collectively have this frame of reference. Understanding what the others do and why is, in our eyes, part of their remit.

The outcome of the process should be at least a brief report in which the output of the different ideas and discussions is recorded; where there is a collectively shared supported outcome in terms of level of excellence (weak, sufficient, strong, excellent); and where there is a structured list of agenda issues by activity (order by importance and urgency) that need to be addressed. Effectively, this is the zero measurement of your fund.

Step 2: Define Your Long-Term Ambition

The next step is defining your long-term ambition. Do you want to become and remain an excellent fund? This has consequences is terms of governance budget spent, organizing, and keeping alive the energy needed to move into that direction. Sometimes it may make more sense to strive for "strong practice" for example. The key is to have a collective definition of what level of excellence the fund is aiming for, and understanding what that looks like in terms of the different activities. Our advice would be to create this picture of the desired situation totally independently from the current situation, otherwise is will be hard to see through the inherent limitations of the current situation. If you describe the situation you want to reach on a 5 to 10-year horizon you can make evolutionary steps towards the goal.

Step 3: Define the Roadmap

The connection between the outcomes from step one, in which the current situation is assessed, and step two, where the ambition is formulated, is the roadmap towards achieving your ambition. We estimate that moving up the ladder of excellence by one step, for example from sufficient to strong, can easily take three or even five years. So moving from sufficient to excellent might theoretically take up to 10 years. The amount of time needed is dependent on a number of factors. When you start from a crisis situation, or when you have the luxury of starting from scratch, often you can move relatively fast. When the urgency is not that high, processes tend to take longer. In terms of the roadmap, it probably makes sense not to plan the whole journey towards excellence from the start. If you build a roadmap for three to five years, with clear annual steps, then you are planning for a foreseeable future. An advantage of this horizon is that the board members who initiate and support the transformation will still be there. Examples of roadmaps are the roadmap that CalPERS' Chief Investment Officer Joe

Dear created to improve CalPERS after 2008–2009 and PGGM's Investment Strategy 2020, a five-year plan to realize the strategic goals formulated by PFZW in its investment framework.

Step 4: Execute the Roadmap

Executing on the roadmap requires a strong and explicit team led by a board member and/or reporting to the board. The execution should be done in acceptable steps, so that there will be measurable progress on a short horizon. There will be moments when it will be tempting to aim for lower goals, but this should be avoided.

ENDURING INVESTMENT EXCELLENCE

Organizational learning, staying fit for purpose, is or should be a part of fiduciary duty. Investment excellence requires serious maintenance. Financial markets and consumers are adaptive. If you do not maintain the quality of your investing, it will wear down. Like with cars, an excellent model from 2008 is no longer an excellent model in 2018.

The best IMOs in the world understand this. Australia's Future Fund has a legal obligation to inform itself about global best practice and takes this very seriously. The Norwegian Government Pension Fund Global (GPFG) commits top-notch academics to do deep research into improving its investment strategy. The British pension fund Railpen rates itself annually against a scorecard and very consciously and measurably improves itself. Boards and executives make combined research trips to visit and study the practice of peers.

Becoming a learning board means embracing the fact that change and continuous improvement are facts of life and therefore, should be part of the normal process of the board and the IMO. Exhibit 14.8 shows an execution and adaptation framework. This is opposite to what most organizations are used to; "big" change comes in big shocks, causing a lot of upheaval, once in 5–10 years. It is reactive rather than proactive, and it is stacked on top of everyday practice instead of being part of it. Often, the fund needs a serious crisis before the change happens, as we've seen in multiple cases throughout the book, such as the case of Californian pension fund CalPERS.

In order to be a learning board and operate in a learning system, the board can plan six steps. First, it needs to understand and regularly review the external environment. How will demographics affect the affordability of a pension scheme? What will populism mean for the way society looks at pensions? How will technological disruption affect its investment beliefs? How should it integrate climate change in the way it invests? This is probably most effectively done in a combination of board and representatives of external parties such as the IMO. It can be prepared by the IMO, but make sure that this organization is not—consciously or unconsciously—selective in its interpretation because of certain beliefs and interests it may hold. You might want to involve beneficiaries, non-governmental organizations (NGOs) or other stakeholders. Also, keep in mind that you can be blinded by your own deep beliefs. For example, if you very deeply believe in the superiority of a collective pension system, opening your

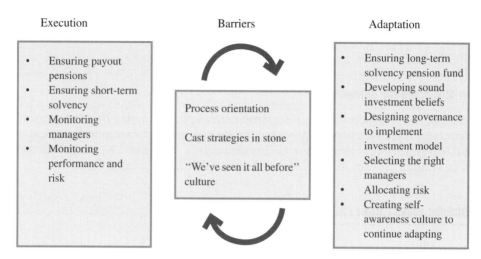

Execution	Barriers	Adaptation
• Ensuring payout pensions • Ensuring short-term solvency • Monitoring managers • Monitoring performance and risk	Process orientation Cast strategies in stone "We've seen it all before" culture	• Ensuring long-term solvency pension fund • Developing sound investment beliefs • Designing governance to implement investment model • Selecting the right managers • Allocating risk • Creating self-awareness culture to continue adapting

EXHIBIT 14.8 Execution versus adaptation decisions for pension investors.

eyes to a societal movement towards DC may be extremely difficult. Therefore, use influential, external sources to open your eyes! Confront the brutal facts.

Second, you need to receive honest input about all the relevant dimensions—which form the content of this book—from multiple angles. The board members should provide their inputs, and we strongly recommend that you also ask a few trusted and respected peers and, for example, a good consultant to provide you with an objective picture of the current state of affairs. Make sure that the people involved have ample room to add their observations to the inputs. Encourage honesty. This will give you a sense of where you stand and a list of topics to think about. Create safety for everybody around this exercise; if anonymity is required, then make sure it is there. It probably doesn't hurt to make this an annual exercise. The board may expect the IMO to be capable of judging its own issues. If it is not, then it is not yet a fully mature organization. At the same time, when you are part of the process, it is hard to get an outside-in view. A board really should open itself up for frank criticism from the outside.

Thirdly, set a realistic target for where you want the board to be three to five years from now. Build programs to improve weak spots (board, governance), or demand programs to improve weak spots from the management of the executive office or IMO supporting the board. Create measures to monitor progress.

Fourth, create a serious amount of time in the annual agenda for the learning process. We feel that 10% of board time is a bare minimum, and we would encourage boards to make this 15%–20% of their total scarce time.

Fifth, make sure the learning is collective between boards, IMO and, as far as possible, a broader set of stakeholders. Document the learning history and the lessons and make sure it is accessible to newcomers joining the board; otherwise they might start from the beginning of the learning curve. There are funds like GPFG and Future Fund that extensively document what they do, how they do it and why they do it on the Internet—this is also collective learning, even on a larger scale! Spending a day on the Internet may be very enlightening.

As a sixth step, enjoy as much diversity as possible, in a broad sense. Often, investment people in senior positions are middle-aged, high-earning, white, finance-trained males. They generally work for segments of the population they hardly know. When thinking of the potential futures of the pension system, some funds also involve historians and sociologists. In addition, if you want to understand the future: involve young people.

In this respect, our aim is to help trustees to identify activities that need to be carried out in order to achieve a good pension fund and, if their ambition reaches higher (which, in our opinion, should), what is needed to achieve an excellent pension fund. While drawing on the authors' own experiences and research and that of generations of trustees and investment professionals, the Self-Reflection Questions section offers trustees a practical set of "how to" questions grasping the fundamentals of creating and operating a pension organization successfully, helping boards to start and integrate the processes towards a higher level of excellence and becoming a learning board.

ENDNOTES

1. See Beinhocker (2006).
2. See Smith (2001).

Self-Reflection Questions

Trustees often implicitly take processes or steps for granted; it is helpful to make these steps or processes explicit. This chapter therefore presents practical self-reflection questions that boards can use for self-reflection. It links the material presented in the previous chapters by asking question designed to help you understand where you are at the moment, or it reminds you of important questions that nobody has asked you, nor have you asked yourself. Furthermore, this chapter will help you to scale your practice level which were discussed in Chapter 14. The exhibit presents the levels of excellence. We strongly encourage you to keep these levels in mind when reading the questions. Try to assess yourself depending on the answer you give to the questions. But do not stop there. Try to answer the questions as if you are at the different levels. We feel that this helps you to think of the steps that can help to increase your level of excellence.

Practice level	Description
Weak Practice	Attention needed. Missing parts in design or implementation. Reactive and ad hoc way of operating, often depending on a few people who happen to be around.
Sufficient Practice	Design, decision-making and or implementation are thought out and documented. The fund complies fully with regulatory requirements. Key processes work well and are independent of specific people.
Strong Practice	Design, decision and implementation are sound and well founded. Comparable pension funds are taking a comparable approach. The board might be aware of the development and research behind it, but has not developed these insights itself. Serious evaluation and improvement are part of the regular process.
Excellent Practice	The fund aims to be best-practice or even to shape the best practice on a continual basis, not one-off but in a permanent way. The choice, design or implementation are recognized by peers as leading and serve as examples. Sometimes, this will mean going into uncharted territory, but always on the back of sound reasoning, well-founded beliefs and adequate skills. Learning and adapting are fully integrated in the processes.

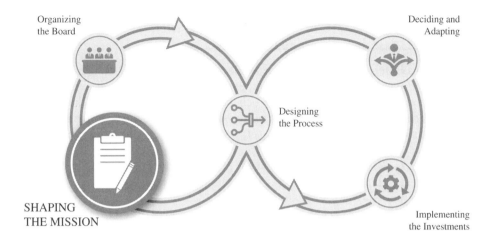

CHAPTER 1: THE ROLE OF PENSION FUNDS, AND THE ROLE OF BOARDS

The primary role of the board is to define the goals, set policy, organize the investment process, and monitor and adjust choices in order to adapt to any changing circumstances.

1. Are there clear and up-to-date documents defining the main duties of the board, focusing on key decisions and functions such as the choice of investment policy, the selection and monitoring of the fund's key executive staff and external service providers, and the monitoring of the fund's performance?
2. Are these documents regularly and explicitly reviewed and brought to the attention of the board?
3. Do board activities comprise everything they should do according to those documents? Do all activities get a balanced amount of attention?
4. Do you have a mechanism ensuring that you pay attention to all tasks?
5. Do you, either as an individual or as the board, collectively have the skills and experience to fulfill all these tasks well?
6. Is the governance design fit for purpose? Are subcommittees (such as an investment committee) well defined and staffed to ensure that key topics receive the required level of consideration?
7. Does the board evaluate its role on a regular basis? Does it use external help to do so?
8. What is your overall opinion of the board?

CHAPTER 2: DEVELOPING PURPOSE, MISSION, VISION, AND GOALS

A key responsibility of the board is to develop, implement and foster mission, goals and strategy. Investment organizations should have a purpose, made explicit in their statement of mission and goals. Based on beliefs, principles and theories, the investment organization and process is then designed to enable pension funds to formulate their strategic course.

1. Does the fund have a clearly defined purpose, mission, vision, and strategic goals?
2. Does the fund have an explicit and shared idea of where it is now (Strengths, Weaknesses) and the relevant changes in the context over the next 5–10 years (Opportunities, Threats)?
3. Are the values of the fund clear to everyone involved and do they have significant meaning in practice?
4. Is there an explicit strategic plan to keep it fit for purpose in the light of the changing context? Does the strategic plan provide direction and focus?
5. Does the board regularly spend time on strategy formulation, i.e. does it have a fresh look at the purpose and the mission, define the strategic objectives, define the competitive strategy, implement strategies, and evaluate progress?
6. Are the employees and stakeholders aware of the fund's objectives, mission, and purpose? Do they understand and share them?
7. Is the board able to effectively implement its strategic plan in order to achieve success? Are there clear action steps for meeting the strategies objectives?

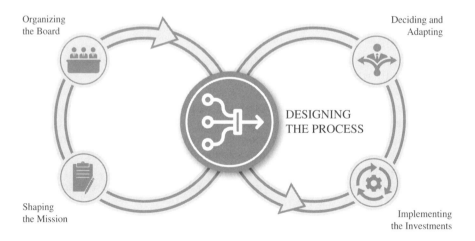

CHAPTER 3: GRASPING THE INVESTMENT ESSENTIALS

For a trustee to become comfortable in the day-to-day implementation of the investment strategy, he or she needs to be relatively fluent in investment terminology, grasping its essence, limitations and application.

1. Is there a shared understanding within the board of the meaning of the most important investment concepts? Is the board trained in this? Is there a manual defining the key concepts?
2. When discussing and reporting on strategic investment issues, are you looking at the right level of the concepts?
3. Is the board aware of and trained in recognizing behavioral traps? Is decision-making organized in a "thinking slow" way?
4. Are you able to describe the investment approach of your fund on a single sheet of paper using the key concepts that we have talked about in this book?
5. Are you honest and brave enough to declare yourself not capable of contributing to the decision-making in a certain area because you lack the relevant knowledge or skill?
6. Do you regularly train and retrain existing and new board members in the key investment concepts and behavioral traps?

CHAPTER 4: INVESTMENT BELIEFS AS GUIDING TOOLS

Investment beliefs can and will differ widely among the various funds and investment organizations. They are part of the fund's DNA and tell you something about the nature and character of the board and its stakeholders. Beliefs are not rigid or cast in stone, rather, they tend to evolve and grow over time. And while some beliefs are obvious, others have proven to be crucial for those choices that determine success or failure.

1. Does your fund have an actively and consciously developed set of investment beliefs? Are they spanning purely the investments, or also the organization of the investment process (e.g. delegation or agency issues)?
2. Are these beliefs coherent and consistent? Do they have tangible impact on the investment process?
3. Is the investment policy based on these investment beliefs? The translation of investment beliefs into investment policy should be straightforward, otherwise the investment beliefs need to be reformulated.
4. Is the setup of your organization consistent with your investment beliefs?
5. Are the beliefs shared broadly internally and externally?
6. Are you able to attach tangible results to the beliefs that are reflected in the organization?
7. Is there a regular process in which the beliefs are reviewed and improved every 5–10 years?

CHAPTER 5: DESIGNING THE INVESTMENT MANAGEMENT PROCESS

The investment process translates the mission, vision, goals and beliefs into actual investment choices and investments. The portfolio management process is an integrated combination of steps that need to be taken in a consistent and coherent manner in order to create and maintain an appropriate portfolio (i.e. a combination of assets) that meets the pension fund's stated goals. The portfolio management process moves from planning, through execution, and then to feedback.

1. Is the investment process in your fund organized in a clear and consistent way? Are the components clear, and is it clear which role the board or the investment committee has in the decision-making during the process?
2. Are the different parts of the process brought to the board (or investment committee) in an understandable way? Is there a clear and logical link between the inputs and the outputs of the components of the process?
3. Is it clear why this process was chosen and not a different one? What would be the viable alternatives?
4. Do you consider the board or investment committee fit for purpose to decide based on the provided information?
5. Is there an Investment Policy Statement (IPS)? When was the last time it was updated?
6. Have all the stakeholders been informed about the IPS?
7. Is it clearly defined which service providers are serving in a fiduciary capacity versus which are not? How are conflicts of interest being resolved in the portfolio's favor?

CHAPTER 6: ORGANIZING THE INVESTMENT FUNCTION

Boards implicitly or explicitly adopt an investment approach model which includes predefined set of assumptions, means of implementation, and requirements for governance.

1. After reading this chapter, do you consider your investment approach fully fit for purpose given your beliefs, DNA, and governance budget?
2. Is there a clear reasoning why this approach has been chosen? Do you subscribe to the pros and cons of it?
3. Are your competitive advantages fully used in the approach? Or, the other way around, does the approach need skills/intellectual property that are currently not available?
4. Do you feel significant improvements could be made to the current approach?
5. Are there exchanges of thoughts with boards or investment committees of funds that have chosen to take a different approach?

6. Is the board or investment committee well equipped to govern the investment approach?
7. Would you like to have a closer look at one of the alternatives for organizing the investment function?

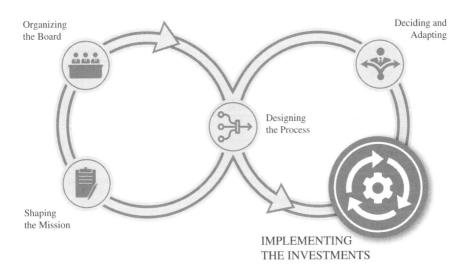

CHAPTER 7: IMPLEMENTING THE INVESTMENT STRATEGY

Implementation is the process that puts the pension fund's plans and strategies into action in order to achieve its goals and objectives. A fund's strategy should address the essential aspects of implementation that will ultimately determine the success (or failure) of an investment strategy. Moreover, the plan should also explain how the fund intends to diversify across opportunities and how it aims to manage the risk of failure in meeting minimum required returns.

1. Is it clear how the roles and decision rights in the investment process are delegated and why delegation is done this way? Is the delegation map complete? Is it Mutually Exclusive and Collectively Exhaustive?
2. Is there a clear policy on total investment cost? Are internal costs (explicit and visible) and external cost (often more implicit) looked at from the same perspective?
3. Is there a clear reasoning which underpins the logic of spending additional marginal cost?
4. The governance budget is the combination of time, expertise, intellectual property, and organizational effectiveness of the decision makers, including the staff. Is the government budget in line with the tasks required of the fund given the set up? Would increasing the budget lead to better outcomes? Are there significant bottle-necks?

5. Is there a well-defined manager selection process? Does it explicitly address the behavioral traps surrounding manager selection and evaluation?
6. Is there sound reasoning behind the choice for passive or active management? Is the implementation fully aligned with the relevant beliefs?
7. Is there clear and strategic reasoning behind the choice for internalizing or externalizing parts of the investment process?
8. Do you have a clear policy on the relationship with external suppliers? Is this a pure and simple client-supplier relationship or do you strive for partnership, in which the supply of a service to the fund is an important part of the relationship?

CHAPTER 8: BUILDING THE INVESTMENT PORTFOLIO

In portfolio construction, trustees have a wide range of choices to make at this stage of the design process, including asset allocation and diversification.

1. Is the resulting portfolio clearly based on and consistent with purpose, mission and strategy, risk appetite, and beliefs? Do you see a gap?
2. Are the nine component steps clearly represented in the portfolio? Is each of them supported and documented by clear reasoning?
3. Is the role of the board/investment committee in the different component steps clearly defined?
4. Do you consider your portfolio to be a good portfolio based on the criteria in Exhibit 8.2? Has the board established criteria to judge the quality of the portfolio?
5. Is the process of the building of the investment portfolio spread out well in the board-year?
6. Are the different component parts reviewed/evaluated regularly by the board/investment committee? Do you use the outside opinions of peers or others to do this?
7. Can the board or investment committee understand and look through the sensitivity of the assumptions or predictions portfolio and its potential outcomes?

CHAPTER 9: MONITORING AND EVALUATION

Ineffective governance of pension funds comes at a significant cost and is thus one of the biggest concerns for board members and those who are involved in the actual execution of the investments. The monitoring and feedback process should be carefully designed in a way that not only includes the outcomes of the process but, more importantly, also considers the quality of the process itself, so that (collective) learning is valid and can lead to improvement.

1. How much of the time of the board or investment committee is spent on monitoring the investment outcomes? Is there a sound and positive relationship between the importance (the contribution to the fund objectives) and the time spent monitoring?

2. How often do you monitor the investment outcomes?
3. When you make a strategic decision, for which horizon do you do that?
4. When you make a strategic decision, do you specify the ex-ante flags (both performance and machine) that will lead to look deeper into the strategy?
5. Do you monitor on the basis of pre-specified criteria?
6. Are the reports you base the monitoring on fit for their purpose? Have they been aligned to match your fund's strategy?
7. Do you monitor both strategy (i.e. are we doing the right things) and implementation (i.e. are we doing things right)?
8. Does the monitoring process lead to action? On which basis? How often? Do you think that you sometimes act on the basis of false negatives?
9. Do you feel this action is based on the right reasons? Could it be that you suffer from action bias?

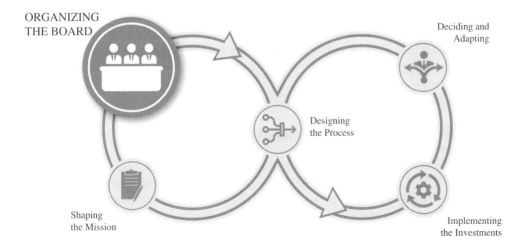

ORGANIZING THE BOARD

Deciding and Adapting

Designing the Process

Shaping the Mission

Implementing the Investments

CHAPTER 10: BECOMING AN EFFECTIVE BOARD

The primary role of the board is defining the goals, organizing the investment process, and monitoring and (re)adjusting choices in order to adapt to any changing circumstances. This may seem straightforward, while actually it seldom is.

1. Do the individual board members have a good working knowledge of all the topics that are handled in this book? Is there a board education program?
2. Does the chairman take their role seriously? Do they make sure that the meeting runs smoothly, everybody gets a voice, decisions are made in an orderly fashion, and the decisions are well formulated?

3. Within the board, are all relevant competencies represented, i.e. internal/external and strategic/operational mindset? Are there board members who have a good understanding of each of the key stakeholders' groups?
4. Are the people in the board working well together? Are they listening, understanding, etc.? Are there dominant individuals or subgroups? Is there explicit attention for the cooperation in the board? Are a few people dominating the conversation?
5. Is there explicit attention in the succession planning of the board to hire the best possible quality and personality when taking on board new board members?
6. Is there a clear annual board agenda covering the formal responsibilities and strategic choices? For every meeting, is there a clear, balanced agenda? Are important topics in equilibrium with urgent topics? Are preparatory documents available in a timely manner, are they clear and well written? Do they have an acceptable length?
7. Is the board challenged by an outside-in perspective? E.g. do you get feedback of peers, stakeholders or participants?
8. Is the board and are the board members acting and fully feeling their responsibility? Do board members hide behind "experts" or arguments such as "apparently, this is the way they do things over here?"
9. Does the board have the countervailing power and knowledge necessary to direct and manage the specialist parties and experts to whom tasks are delegated?
10. Is the board aware of the big behavioral pitfalls that often lead to poor investment decision-making? Is there explicit attention to these pitfalls?

CHAPTER 11: ESTABLISHING THE INVESTMENT COMMITTEE

The Board is highly dependent on the investment committee and the executive office. It is therefore imperative that the board has articulated how they (should) work together. In some cases the committee fulfills a highly proactive role on the basis of the executive mandate that is entrusted to the committee in making investment decisions on behalf of the fund. In other instances, the duties and responsibilities of the committee may be restricted to a purely advisory role, requiring its members to only meet a few times per year.

1. Do you feel the committee has the right altitude? Can you look at the total fund set up and its outcomes from a helicopter perspective?
2. Has the committee organized itself in a way that you can look, analyze, and decide forward and backward at least in a 5–10-year perspective?
3. Does the board keep the right distance from the execution of the investment management operation? Are you close enough to be able to fully bear your responsibility, yet not so close that you are taking operational decisions you really should not be making as a board?
4. Are the committee and members fully feeling and acting on their responsibility?
5. Is the balance between the investment committee and the executive organization right?

The investment committee also shares a number of self-reflection questions discussed with the board in Chapter 10:

6. For every meeting, is there a clear, balanced agenda? Are important topics in equilibrium with urgent topics? Is the structure of the meeting clearly demarcated? How are decisions being made? Are they well documented? Is information on the historical decision-making accessible?
7. Are preparatory documents available timely, are they clear and well written? Do they have an acceptable length?
8. Is the committee challenged by an outside in perspective? Do you get feedback from peers, stakeholders or participants? Does the committee challenge the board's perspectives and assumptions?
9. Do members hide behind "experts" or arguments like "apparently, this is the way they do things over here?"
10. Does the board have the countervailing power and knowledge necessary to direct and manage the specialist parties and experts to whom tasks are delegated?

CHAPTER 12: MANAGING THE INVESTMENT MANAGEMENT ORGANIZATION

The interaction between board, investment committee and investment management organization is regarded as probably the most important factor in creating investment success.

1. How clear and standardized is the mandate that the board has awarded the investment management organization? Is it well defined so that agency issues are adequately managed or minimized?
2. Is the investment management organization aligned with the chosen investment model? How much "governance budget" do you have available?
3. Is the board hands-on or hands-off? How much will it delegate to the investment management organization in practice?
4. Is the compensation aligned with the objectives of the fund? Does the compensation system contribute to agency issues, rigidity in the organization, and selfish or uncooperative behavior? Does the compensation align with the investment management organization's urge to expand?
5. How does the investment management organization monitor and manage the cost effectiveness?
6. How does the investment management organization assess the quality of the building blocks? If building blocks have a lower than acceptable quality, what is done? Improve? Fire? Move from external to internal or vice versa?
7. Are protocols in place when the investment management organization is not functioning properly? Do you know how to deal with this? Is it easy to change? Or is the barrier to change too large for cost-effective change?

8. Do the people in the investment management organization know and align with the objectives and the principles of the fund? In the conversations with people from the investment management organization, do you observe and feel many of the success factors? Which ones are missing?

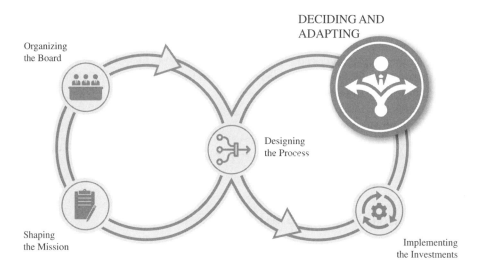

CHAPTER 13: LEARNING TO DECIDE AND TO TAKE ADVICE

Trustees have to make decisions all the time, ranging from trivial investment decisions to decisions that have a substantial impact on the entire organization. Whatever the procedure of decision-making, trustees are expected to solicit and pursue "proper advice" because failure to comply often means that a trustee might be directly (and personally) accountable to the relevant regulator.

1. Do you feel your fund adapts fast enough to changing circumstances and context?
2. Do you feel that your fund learns from its history and has a process for continuous improvement?
3. Would you consider your board to be a learning board?
4. Is the learning collective between board and investment management organization?
5. What would be needed to become a learning board and organization?
6. How much of the governance budget of the board (time and money) do you spend on learning?
7. Is there a formal board learning process in place?
8. Are new board members put through a formal learning process?

CHAPTER 14: ACHIEVING INVESTMENT EXCELLENCE

To attain excellence, a board has to learn and be able to assess their fund's status in terms of achieving sustainable investment excellence. A board should be able to, with the necessary intelligence and practical tools, to transform into a perpetual "learning board."

1. Does your fund have a process in play to promote learning and achieve higher forms of quality?
2. Achieving excellence requires resources; does the board allocate enough governance budget of time and skill to move the fund towards it?
3. Are new people in the organization introduced and schooled in the learnings of the fund? Do they get the proper guidance to achieve the fund's vision of excellence?
4. Are documents regarding strategy, mission, vision, and beliefs regularly reviewed and updated when deemed needed? Does the board make sure this happens in a timely manner?
5. Does the board view excellence as a continuous state of improving? If not, is this for the right reasons?
6. Is there a shared understanding of all concepts used in the fund? Is there a system in place that ensures a collective reasoning?
7. Is effort taken to minimize the effect of behavioral biases and focus on the goals that match the maturity of the fund? Are these effective now, and will they be in the future?
8. Is enough time allocated to learning? How much time is spent on this, and how does this compare to other organizations?

OECD PRINCIPLES

The OECD (Organisation for Economic Co-operation and Development) Principles of Corporate Governance provide guidance on the responsibilities of directors (OECD 2015; amended to pension funds):

1. Board members should act on a fully informed basis, in good faith, with due diligence and care, and in the best interest of the company and the participants.
2. Where board decisions may affect different shareholder groups differently, the board should treat all shareholders fairly.
3. The board should apply high ethical standards. It should take into account the interests of stakeholders.
4. The board should fulfill certain key functions, including:
   a. Reviewing and guiding corporate strategy, major plans of action, risk policy, annual budgets and business plans; setting performance objectives; monitoring implementation and corporate performance; and overseeing major capital expenditures, acquisitions and divestitures.
   b. Monitoring the effectiveness of the company's governance practices and making changes as needed.
   c. Selecting, compensating, monitoring and, when necessary, replacing key executives and overseeing succession planning.
   d. Aligning key executive and board remuneration with the longer term interests of the company and its shareholders.
   e. Ensuring a formal and transparent board nomination and election process.
   f. Monitoring and managing potential conflicts of interest of management, board members and shareholders, including misuse of corporate assets and abuse in related party transactions.
   g. Ensuring the integrity of the corporation's accounting and financial reporting systems, including the independent audit, and that appropriate systems of control are in place, in particular, systems for risk management, financial and operational control, and compliance with the law and relevant standards.
   h. Overseeing the process of disclosure and communications.
5. The board should be able to exercise objective independent judgment on corporate affairs.
   a. Boards should consider assigning a sufficient number of non-executive board members capable of exercising independent judgment to tasks where there is a potential for conflict of interest. Examples of such key responsibilities are

ensuring the integrity of financial and non-financial reporting, the review of related party transactions, nomination of board members and key executives, and board remuneration.

b. When committees of the board are established, their mandate, composition and working procedures should be well defined and disclosed by the board.

c. Board members should be able to commit themselves effectively to their responsibilities.

6. In order to fulfill their responsibilities, board members should have access to accurate, relevant and timely information.

Appendix B

HOW TO DEVELOP STRATEGIC GOALS

Strategy is about delivering the goals that you have established. This requires an evaluation of the *external environment* in which the pension fund operates and a review of the fund's *current position—is it fit for purpose?* The aim of such a review is to enable the board to identify the factors important for success in the market, its own strengths and weaknesses as well as those of the competition (see Exhibit B.1).

In this appendix, we will take you through the steps of the process. As an introduction, we provide you with some do's and don'ts about the way you could organize the process:

1. The board is responsible for setting the strategy. The board can be assisted and facilitated, but strategy formulation cannot be delegated.
2. Depending on the personalities and the history of the board, the strategy formulation process can be very intense. Arranging external help with these boardroom dynamics could therefore be worthwhile.

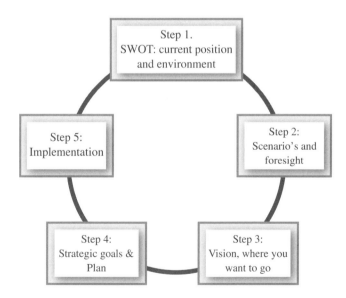

EXHIBIT B.1 Steps for developing strategy.

3. A collective effort has a greater chance of ending up as a collectively supported strategy.
4. Organize outside-in views, and avoid tunnel vision and complacency. You can use all kinds of players to do this, ranging from peers to consultants. It's important not to get stuck in your own box.
5. Involve stakeholders. In order to get a good view of your position, you could involve key stakeholders, such as participants, non-governmental organizations (NGOs), or employees.
6. Make sure that you create an open, honest environment. There will definitely be things you'd rather not hear. But these will come back to haunt you if you don't listen. What about participants who say they don't understand your communication, or NGOs that say that you are insensitive to a changing world?
7. Budget serious time for strategy formulation. The more challenging and dynamic the environment is, the more important the process.
8. Don't try to do strategy formulation in regular board meetings. Strategy requires time. It is likely to be productive to go offsite for a day or for a 24-hour retreat.
9. We suggest that you go through a strategic review at least once every five years. In the years in between, you can watch out for whether significant matters are popping up that need urgent attention. The five-year frequency also helps to involve and immerse new board members on a regular basis.
10. Make sure that the output and the process leading to the output are well documented, so that you can easily communicate your strategic thinking to others.

Step 1: PEST, SWOT and Five Forces: Scanning the Current Position and Environment   A board is in need of a base level to start with, to provide a benchmark for the current organization. Questions to be asked are:

- What are the key relevant characteristics of the pension fund? (i.e. size, solvency, cost level, level of investment excellence, etc.)
- What are the current strengths and weaknesses of the pension fund?
- What will drive change in the next 5–10 years? Which of these changes or combinations of changes could be perceived as stable, and which as turbulent?
- Are there signs of new changes emerging, and how should they be characterized?

The most commonly used tools to support trustees are the PEST analysis, the Five Forces Model, and the SWOT Analysis.

PEST Analysis   PEST (Political, Economic, Sociocultural, Technological) represents a point of entry for a more extensive analysis. PEST can be used to establish an overview or the big picture of the current situation, and to set the course for further investigation. The PEST analysis provides the framework within which the board can pursue its purpose, striking the balance that ensures its continuing existence. The method involves a breakdown of the environment into six segments:

Political	Political issues and forces.
Participant	Understanding your current and future customers.
Environmental	Environmental, habitat and sustainability issues.
Technological	Scientific and technological issues.
Social	Social issues, such as individualism or lack of trust.
Economic	Economic issues such as long bond yields or an inflationary context.

The significance of the individual segments may differ according to the focus and perspectives of the particular pension fund. As an example, Exhibit B.2 shows the PEST Analysis performed by the Tyne and Wear Pension Fund, where the focus lies on economic and political factors.

SWOT Analysis Whereas the PEST Analysis can be viewed as a structured view of the external environment in which the pension fund is operating in, SWOT (Strengths,

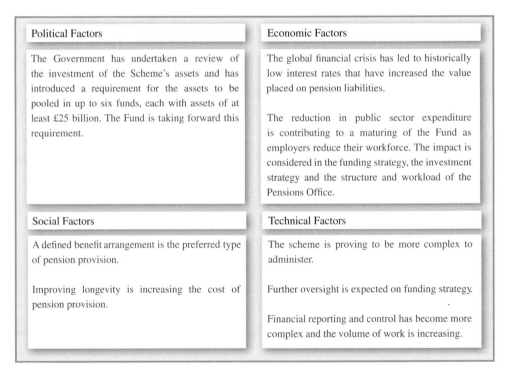

Political Factors	Economic Factors
The Government has undertaken a review of the investment of the Scheme's assets and has introduced a requirement for the assets to be pooled in up to six funds, each with assets of at least £25 billion. The Fund is taking forward this requirement.	The global financial crisis has led to historically low interest rates that have increased the value placed on pension liabilities. The reduction in public sector expenditure is contributing to a maturing of the Fund as employers reduce their workforce. The impact is considered in the funding strategy, the investment strategy and the structure and workload of the Pensions Office.

Social Factors	Technical Factors
A defined benefit arrangement is the preferred type of pension provision. Improving longevity is increasing the cost of pension provision.	The scheme is proving to be more complex to administer. Further oversight is expected on funding strategy. Financial reporting and control has become more complex and the volume of work is increasing.

EXHIBIT B.2 Excerpt from PEST Analysis performed by Tyne and Wear Pension Fund.[1]

Weaknesses, Opportunities, Threats) is an analysis of the internal environment of the pension fund, based on its pension products and services. The components of the SWOT analysis are:

- *Strengths*. Analyzes the company's strengths regarding the product/service and identifies its unique selling propositions. The strengths of a pension fund or product make it stand out in comparison with competitors.
- *Weaknesses*. Analyzes any current weaknesses that the fund may have and how they relate to the product. This should give the board a bird's eye view for seeing which areas are deficient so that it can deal with them.
- *Opportunities* are for the pension fund to gain, master, and derive benefits from. Usually, weaknesses are dealt with here by a strategy of transforming them into opportunities, when the board can work on itself or the pension product.
- *Threats*. This means facing up to the threats that able and potential competitors may pose for the company and its products/services. Barriers to entry and how potential competition can be tackled effectively are also analyzed.

Five Forces Analysis   Porter's five forces analysis is a framework for analyzing the level of competition within an industry and business strategy development. It is created for the analysis of industries that are for-profit, whereas most pension funds are not. At first sight, being a captive institution may seem like an advantage, but in fact, it is not. The absence of short-term market forces actually means that the fund has to put more effort into understanding whether it is really efficient and fit for purpose. If not, sooner or later its existence will be threatened.

Porter's five forces determine the competitive intensity and therefore the attractiveness of an industry. Attractiveness in this context refers to the overall industry profitability. An "unattractive" industry is one in which the combination of these five forces acts to drive down overall profitability or success. A very unattractive industry would be one approaching "pure competition," in which available profits for all firms are driven down to a minimum normal profit.

The five forces also affect pension funds' ability to serve their customers and generate sustainable income and/or make a profit. A change in any of the forces normally requires a business unit to reassess the marketplace given the overall change in industry information. Porter's five forces include three forces from "horizontal" competition: the threat of substitute products or services, the threat of established rivals, and the threat of new entrants; and two forces from "vertical" competition: the bargaining power of suppliers and the bargaining power of customers Exhibit B.3.

- *Competition in the industry*. The importance of this force depends on the number of competitors and their ability to threaten a company. The larger the number of competitors, along with the number of equivalent products and services they offer, the weaker the power of an individual company. Suppliers and buyers can seek out a company's competitor if they are cannot get a good deal.
- *Potential new entrants into an industry*. A company's power is also affected by the force of new entrants into its market. The less money and time it takes for a

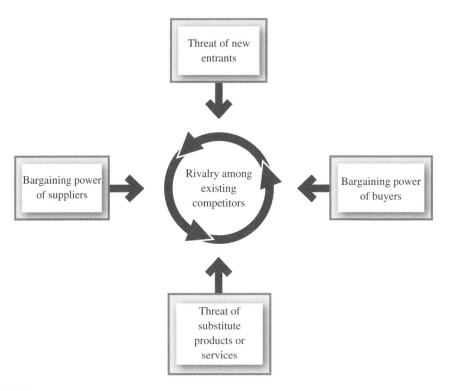

EXHIBIT B.3 The Five Forces identified by Michael Porter that shape industry competition.[2]

competitor to enter a company's market and become an effective competitor, the
more easily a company's position may be significantly weakened.

- *Power of suppliers*. This force reflects how easily suppliers can drive up the price of
  goods and services. It is determined by the number of suppliers of a good or service,
  how unique these are, and how much it would cost a company to switch from one
  supplier to another. The fewer suppliers there are and the more a company depends
  on a single supplier, the more power the supplier holds.
- *Power of customers*. This specifically deals with the ability customers have to drive
  prices down. It is determined by how many buyers, or customers, a company has,
  how significant each customer is, and how much it would cost a customer to switch
  from one company to another. The smaller and more powerful a client base, the
  more power it holds.
- *Threat of substitutes*. Competitor substitutions that can be used instead of a company's products or services pose a threat. For example, if customers rely on a
  company to provide a tool or service that can be substituted by another tool or
  service or by performing the task manually, and this substitution is fairly easy and
  inexpensive, a company's power can be weakened.

Step 2: Structuring and Foresight The board now has a clear understanding of the fund's characteristics, its strengths, weaknesses, and internal and external development. The next challenge is to structure this knowledge and use it to shape strategy development for the future. In the process, the board "memorizes" the future, developing scenarios to visualize where it is heading.[3]

Unless the board operates in a perfect monopoly, the future is inherently uncertain. This makes it necessary to develop many different "futures" and assess how they would affect achieving the fund's goals and how to allow for this within policies. External forces will have a strong influence on the way the mission takes shape in the current and future environment. Where a Defined Benefit system was once the logical solution in European and American pension systems, pension systems in many parts of the world are changing nowadays to collective or individual Defined Contribution (DC) systems. This development has been accelerated by structural trends, such as changing accounting rules, the effects of increasing longevity, increased individualism, changing technology, and the effects of climate change on financial markets. Scenario-based thinking would have allowed boards to pick up on these trends at an early stage. So, the challenge for the board is to identify developments early on, and internalize them by turning them into "uneasy" questions:

- Are we really providing a good pension for our beneficiaries given the premium they pay and the expectations they have?
- What is the measure of success that our key stakeholders will apply to us given the context and will we deliver?
- Is there a role, and if so what, for climate change in our investment policy?

These "foresight" questions are often skipped or overlooked by the board, pressured by time to focus on day-to-day decision-making. Board members should be able to look stakeholders in the eye—both individually and collectively—and say that they have explored all relevant alternatives and possible futures to ensure the objectives can be met as well as possible. The board cannot outsource these questions, although it can be assisted by external parties.

With the use of scenarios, pension funds can anticipate and respond more rapidly to new developments, opportunities, and risks. Scenarios can convey a picture of how the future could unfold and can provide a choice of different, very varied future images. None of these scenarios is good or bad as such. The most important point is that they are plausible and that the board and/or the investment committee can translate them into a relevant policy (investment policy and risk management). Working with scenarios helps both investors and decision makers think outside the existing framework.[4] The theory behind this is that if decision makers are aware of, and prepared for, a number of scenarios, the organization can adapt to any unforeseen or unexpected changes more effectively and rapidly.

Scenarios are inherently different to regular plans and annual budgeting. Plans can extrapolate developments for a number of years and lay down the most logical measures. Thinking in terms of scenarios takes such an overview as the base and develops

Phase	Approach
1. Analyze current situation	Chart the current pension fund situation and identify the most important market 'drivers', using PEST, SWOT and/or Five Forces.
2. Set out the most logical future overview.	Elaborate a future overview on the basis of the current and obvious situation and expectations on how the market will develop.
3. Develop alternative scenarios	On the basis of the most important drivers, develop alternative future scenarios using the future overview.
4. Determine the impact and measures	Work out the consequences of each scenario and set possible preventative measures for the organization.
5. Embed measures in the investment organization	Embed insights, consequences and measures for the most likely scenarios in the internal organization.

EXHIBIT B.4 Phases scenarios.

alternative directions. An abiding tool for the development of scenarios is knowledge of the variables that impact on a pension fund. High and low growth in the financial markets and high or low economic growth and/or inflation are among the most important economic variables.

Many funds, therefore, work with a limited number of scenarios. This could include deflation (meaning pension obligations can't be paid), inflation or stagflation (eroding purchasing power), and also a recovery scenario. An asset allocation is then worked out for each scenario. Economic indicators can be linked to the scenarios so that the investment committee can assess whether the assumptions on which the fund policy is based (the basic scenario) seem to be changing. This allows the pension fund to anticipate such changes at an early stage. This is not the same as forecasting, but rather a matter of perceiving a situation at an early stage. Economic scenarios can be used to elaborate the consequences if a decision does not work out. This is also referred to as the "regret" criterion Exhibit B.4.

Scenarios are not predictions. Forecasts, projections, and extrapolations only work effectively as the basis for strategic planning in a stable world, something from which we are all far removed. Pierre Wack, the founding father of strategic planning at Shell, puts it as follows:

> Forecasts are not always wrong; more often than not, they can be reasonably accurate. And that makes them so dangerous. They are usually constructed on the assumption that tomorrow's world will be much like today's [. . .] forecasts will fail when they are needed most: in anticipating major shifts in the business environment that make whole strategies obsolete. [. . .] The better approach, I believe, is to accept uncertainty, try to understand it, and make it part of our reasoning.

Economic scenarios can be ascribed levels of probability in order to base policy on them. However, ascribing probability to scenarios is a notoriously difficult exercise and suffers from psychological biases. Scenarios that most resemble the recent past are often ascribed the greatest probability; if emotions play a role, the impact is estimated to be higher, and there is the risk of new information being searched for and used to bolster existing ideas.

In most scenario-planning exercises, the scenarios are developed within the pension fund, either by the board or by investment committee. As a starting point, the most "known" scenarios are likely to be elaborated. This limits effectiveness with respect to decision-making, and calls for divergent thinking at an early stage. This can be illustrated by the streetlamp problem. When people have lost their car keys in the street, they intuitively look for them in the light of the streetlamp even though this only covers a small area of the street. In other words, new information and insights can be related to scenarios already developed and used to confirm choices made previously. One method of combating this potential bias is to invite outsiders who represent minority viewpoints on the future to participate. This form of deliberate diversity of opinions will reduce "frame blindness" within an organization. An alternative to organizing a structured debate is to draw up a limited number of scenarios in sub-groups and allow them to be critically discussed by the groups; this will put the spotlight on assumptions, justification and correlations.

Step 3: Vision and Goal Formulation In Step 3, the Vision and Goals are formulated on a 5–10 year horizon. What is especially characteristic of the pension fund? How does the board view the future, and is this reflected in or consistent with the defined purpose and mission? We mentioned this earlier in this Appendix. Given where you are, the external forces, your purpose and mission, and your values, where do you want to be 5–10 years from now? Which weaknesses must be addressed? Do you aspire to become more excellent, or more efficient, or more sustainable than you currently are? If you define this clearly and put it into words, you have your vision. Remember that it should be a realistic vision, but that a certain amount of stretching of the mind in general gives all the parties involved a lot of energy.

Step 4: Strategic Plan Once you know where you are (Step 1) and where you want to go (Step 3) you can make a plan on how to get there: this is the plan. A strategic plan typically has a five-year horizon, and will most often be subdivided in three stages of one to two years. The strategic plan should inform the annual planning cycle, so that you can take concrete annual steps in implementing the plan. The plan should, as far as possible, be formulated in SMART (Specific, Measurable, Achievable, Realistic and Time-bound) form.

Step 5: Implementation Knowledge gained from the analysis is translated into concrete organizational goals, measures, projects, or programs. What concrete measures are to be deployed? How can one become even better prepared for the future?

ENDNOTES

1. See http://www.twpf.info/CHttpHandler.ashx?id=26120&p=0 on the approach Tyne and Wear Pension Fund.
2. See Porter (2008).
3. See Pillkahn (2008).
4. Scenarios can be used in four ways (OECD):
   - Sensitivity analysis, analyzing the effect of other assumptions on pension obligations, cash flows, risks. The sensitivity analysis most closely relates to stress tests that are applied in risk management.
   - "Contingency" plans for unexpected events, in order to determine what must be done in certain circumstances, if there is talk of an unexpected event. Contingency planning has been brought up-to-date as a result of a requirement by De Nederlandsche Bank that pension funds develop plans for extreme situations.
   - Plans for unexpected events, but then applied to fund policy.
   - Scenarios as a research instrument. This is not specifically elaborated as a strategy but rather as "a more exploratory tool so that a scenario is less a strategy and more a coherently structured speculation, of interest for education."

References

Adamson, L. (2013). *Australia's Future Fund Investment Wizardry*. Retrieved from Institutional Investor: http://www.institutionalinvestor.com/Article/3205504/Australias-Future-Fund-Investment-Wizardry.html?ArticleId=3205504&single=true#/.WJg7sfkrLIV

Allen, F. and Santomero, A.M. (1997). The theory of financial intermediation. *Journal of Banking & Finance* 21 (11–12): 1461–1485.

Ambachtsheer, K. (2004). *Cleaning Up the Pensions Mess: Why It Will Take More Than Money*. CD Howe Institute.

Ambachtsheer, K.P. (2016). *The Future of Pension Management: Integrating Design, Governance, and Investing*. New York: Wiley.

Ambachtsheer, K., Capelle, R., and Lum, H. (2006). Pension fund governance today: strengths, weaknesses and opportunities for improvement. *Financial Analysts Journal* 20: 383–403.

Ambachtsheer, K., Capelle, R., and Lum, H. (2007). *The State of Global Pension Fund Governance Today: Board Competency Still a Problem*. Rotman International Centre for Pension Management.

Ambachtsheer, K.P. and Ezra, D.D. (1998). *Pension Fund Excellence: Creating Value for Stakeholders*. New York: Wiley.

Andersen, T.J., Garvey, M., and Roggi, O. (2014). *Managing Risk and Opportunity: The Governance of Strategic Risk-Taking*. Oxford University Press.

Anderson, G., Bamford, T., Baumgarten, J., and Jurd, K. (2017) The Five Most Common New Director Questions. Advice for First-Time Board Directors on Getting a Strong Start. Retrieved from: https://www.spencerstuart.com/research-and-insight/the-five-most-common-new-director-questions

Andonov, A., Bauer, R., and Cremers, M. (2011). Can large pension funds beat the market. *Asset Allocation, Market Timing, Security Selection and the Limits of Liquidity (October 2012)*.

Ang, A. (2014). *Asset Management: A Systematic Approach to Factor Investing*. Oxford University Press.

Ang, A. and Abrams, J. (2012). *California Dreamin': The Mess at CalPERS*. Columbia Business School.

Ang, A. and Kjaer, K. N. (2012). *Investing for the Long Run*. Netspar Discussion Paper No. 11/2011-104.

Ang, A., Goetzmann, W. N., and Schaefer, S. (2009). Evaluation of active management of the Norwegian government pension fund–global. *Report to the Norwegian Ministry of Finance*.

Ang, A., Brandt, M. W. and Denison, D. G. (2014). Review of the Active Management of the Norwegian Government Pension Fund Global. 20 January, 2014. Retrieved from https://www0.gsb.columbia.edu/faculty/aang/papers/AngBrandtDenison.pdf

Anson, M. (2004). Strategic versus tactical asset allocation. *The Journal of Portfolio Management* 30: 8–22.

Anson, M. (2005). Institutional portfolio management. *The Journal of Portfolio Management* (Summer) 31: 33–43.

AP2 (2018). *Our mission*. http://www.ap2.se/en/about-ap2/our-mission (accessed 07-03-2018).

ATP (2016) Annual Report. https://www.atp.dk/sites/default/files/atp_annual-report-2016.pdf (accessed on 15-05-2018).

ATP (2017) Annual Report. https://www.atp.dk/sites/default/files/atp_annual-report-2017.pdf (accessed on 15-05-2018).

Bank for International Settlements. (2003). Incentive Structures in Institutional Asset Management and Their Implications for Financial Markets. Committee on the Global Financial System.

Basker, E. (2005). Selling a cheaper mousetrap: Wal-Mart's effect on retail prices. *Journal of Urban Economics* 58 (2): 203–229.

Beinhocker, E.D. (2006). *The Origin of Wealth: Evolution, Complexity, and the Radical Remaking of Economics*. Harvard Business Press.

Bender, J., Briand, R., Nielsen, F., and Stefek, D. (2010). Portfolio of risk premia: a new approach to diversification. *Journal of Portfolio Management* 36 (2): 17.

Berkowitz, S.A., Finney, L.D., and Logue, D.E. (1988). Pension plans vs. mutual funds: is the client victim or culprit? *California Management Review* 30 (3): 74–91.

Bouwmeester, O. (2008). Advice as Argument: Economic Deliberation in Management Consulting and Academic Contract Research.

Brav, A., Heaton, J.B., and Rosenberg, A. (2004). The rational-behavioral debate in financial economics. *Journal of Economic Methodology* 11 (4): 393–409.

Brinson, G.P., Hood, L.R., and Beebower, G. (1986). Determinants of portfolio performance. *Financial Analysts Journal* 42 (4): 39–44.

Brinson, G.P., Singer, B.D., and Beebower, G.L. (1991). Determinants of portfolio performance II: an update. *Financial Analysts Journal* 47 (3): 40–48.

Brown, J.D. (2012). Understanding the better than average effect: motives (still) matter. *Personality and Social Psychology Bulletin* 38 (2): 209–219.

Brown, S. J., Goetzmann, W. N., and Grinblatt, M. (1997). Positive portfolio factors.

Busse, J.A., Goyal, A., and Wahal, S. (2010). Performance and persistence in institutional investment management. *The Journal of Finance* 65 (2): 765–790.

Cadbury, A. (2002). *Corporate Governance and Chairmanship: A Personal View*. Oxford University Press on Demand.

Chambers, D., Dimson, E., and Ilmanen, A. (2011). The Norway Model.

Cheng Chih, S. (2014). The Why, What and How of Long-Term Investing. Presented at the ABFER 2nd Annual Conference, Singapore.

Chua, D.B., Kritzman, M., and Page, S. (2009). The myth of diversification. *Journal of Portfolio Management* 36 (1): 26.

Clark, G. (2000). *Pension systems: A comparative perspective*.

Clark, G.L. (2004). Pension fund governance: expertise and organizational form. *Journal of Pension Economics & Finance* 3 (2): 233–253.

Clark, G. L. and Urwin, R. (2007). Best-Practice Investment Management: Lessons for Asset Owners from the Oxford-Watson Wyatt Project on Governance. October 2007. In *available at SSRN*: http://ssrn.com/abstract (Vol. 1019212).

Clark, G.L. and Urwin, R. (2008a). Making pension boards work: the critical role of leadership. *Rotman International Journal of Pension Management* 1 (1): 38–45.

Clark, G.L. and Urwin, R. (2008b). Best-practice pension fund governance. *Journal of Asset Management* 9: 9–21.

Clark, G.L. and Urwin, R. (2010). Innovative models of pension fund governance in the context of the global financial crisis. *Pensions: An International Journal* 15 (1): 62–77.

Collins, J. (1996). Aligning action and values. In: *Leader to Leader*, vol. 1, 19–24. https://doi.org/10.1002/ltl.40619960307.

Collins, S. and Mack, P. (1997). The optimal amount of assets under management in the mutual fund industry. *Financial Analysts Journal* 53 (5): 67–73.

Cooper, T. (2012). The Power of Feedback Loops: Attaining and Sustaining a Healthy ERM Program, Enterprise Risk Compliance. Wolters Kluwer Financial Services.

Credit Suisse Research Institute, Zurich (2017). *Global Wealth Report*.

Culp, C.L. (2002). *The Risk Management Process: Business Strategy and Tactics*, vol. 103. Wiley.

Dahlquist, M. and Ødegaard, B. A. (2018). A Review of Norges Bank's Active Management of the Government Pension Fund Global.

Damodaran, A. (2007). Investment Philosophy: The Secret Ingredient in Investment Success. Presentation at New York University School of Business.

Damodaran, A. (2013). Equity risk premiums (ERP): determinants, estimation and implications— the 2012 edition. In: *Managing and Measuring Risk: Emerging Global Standards and Regulations After the Financial Crisis* (ed. O. Roggie and E. Altman), 343–455. New Jersey: World Scientific.

Davies, B. (2000). Equity within and between generations: pension systems and equity. In: *Pensions in the European Union: Adapting to Economic and Social Change* (ed. G. Hughes and J. Stewart), 109–126. Boston, MA: Springer.

Davis, E.P. and Steil, B. (2004). *Institutional Investors*, 450. MIT press.

Department of Labor Employee Benefits Security Administration, U.S. (2017). Meeting Your Fiduciary Responsibilities.

DiBruno, R. (2015). *Best Practices for Investment Committees*, vol. 78. Wiley.

Drucker, P.F. (1976/1995). *The Unseen Revolution/The Pension/The Pension Fund Revolution*. New Brunswick, NJ: Transaction Publishers.

Dufey, G. (1998). The changing role of financial intermediation in Europe. *International Journal of Business* 3 (1): 49–68.

Economou, T., Haenni, G., and Manola-Bonthond, E. (2013). A governance framework designed for dynamic asset allocation: the CERN pension fund model. *The Journal of Investment*.

Edwards, J. and Fischer, K. (1996). *Banks, Finance and Investment in Germany*. Cambridge University Press.

Eisenhardt, K.M. (1989). Agency theory: an assessment and review. *Academy of Management Review* 14 (1): 57–74.

Ellis, C.D. (1998). *Winning the Loser's Game*. New York: Mcgraw-Hill Education.

Ellis, C.D. (2003). The winner's game. *Financial Analysts Journal* 67 (4): 11–17.

Ellis, C.D. (2011a). Best practice investment committees. *The Journal of Portfolio Management, Winter 2011* 37 (2): 139–147.

Ellis, C.D. (2011b). *Capital: The Story of Long-Term Investment Excellence*. Wiley.

Ellis, C.D. (2014). The rise and fall of performance investing. *Financial Analysts Journal* 70 (4): 14–23.

Ellison, R. and Jolly, R.E. (2008). *Pension Trustee's Investment Guide*. Thorogood Publishing.

Elton, E.J., Gruber, M.J., and Blake, C.R. (2003). Incentive fees and mutual funds. *The Journal of Finance* 58 (2): 779–804.

England, A. and Cotterill, J. (2016). PIC considers black consortium for Barclays Africa. Retrieved on 18-02-2016, from https://www.ft.com/content/e0f47544-1e92-11e6-b286-cddde55ca122

Ennis, R.M. and Williamson, J.P. (1976). *Spending Policy for Educational Endowments: A Research and Publication Project of the Common Fund*. Common Fund.

Frankel, N. and Gage, A. (2007). M&E fundamentals: a self-guided minicourse.

Friede, G., Busch, T., and Bassen, A. (2015). ESG and financial performance: aggregated evidence from more than 2000 empirical studies. *Journal of Sustainable Finance & Investment* 5 (4): 210–233.

Furr, R.M. and Furr, L.J. (2005). Is your chairman a leader. *Corporate Board* 26 (154): 11–15.

Gage, A. and Dunn, M. (2009). Monitoring and Evaluating Gender-Based Violence Prevention and Mitigation Programs. *US Agency for International Development, MEASURE Evaluation, Interagency Gender Working Group, Washington DC*.

Garratt, B. (2010). *The Fish Rots From the Head: The Crisis in Our Boardrooms: Developing the Crucial Skills of the Competent Director*. Profile Books.

Gawande, A. and Lloyd, J.B. (2010). *The Checklist Manifesto: How To Get Things Right*, vol. 200. New York: Metropolitan Books.

GEPF. (2014). *Vision, Mission and Values*. www.gepf.gov.za/index.php/about_us/article/vision-and-values (accessed 07-03-2018).

Ghai, S., Tarnowski, M., and Tétrault, J. (2011). *The Best of Times and the Worst of Times for Institutional Investors*. McKinsey & Company.

GPFG (2004). *Guidelines for Observation and Exclusion of Companies from the Government Pension Fund Global*. Government Pension Fund Global. Retrieved from https://etikkradet.no/files/2017/04/Etikkraadet_Guidelines-_eng_2017_web.pdf.

Graham, B., Dodd, D., and Tatham, C. (1951). *Security Analysis. Principles and Technique*. McGraw-Hill Book Company.

Gray, J. (1997). Overquantification. *Financial Analysts Journal* 53: 5–12.

Greifer, N. (2012). *Pension Investing: Fundamentals and Best Practices*. Government Finance Officers Association.

Guyatt, D.J. and Lukomnik, J. (2010). Does portfolio turnover exceed expectations? *Rotman International Journal of Pension Management* 3 (2): 40.

Guyatt, G.H., Oxman, A.D., Vist, G.E. et al. (2008). GRADE: an emerging consensus on rating quality of evidence and strength of recommendations. *BMJ (Clinical Research Ed.)* 336 (7650): 924–926.

Harper, J. (2008). Board of trustee composition and investment performance of US public pension plans. *Rotman International Centre for Pension Management, University of Toronto*.

Hudson-Wilson, S., Fabozzi, F.J., and Gordon, J.N. (2003). Why real estate? *The Journal of Portfolio Management* 29 (5): 12–25.

Huse, M. (2007). *Boards, Governance and Value Creation: The Human Side of Corporate Governance*. Cambridge University Press.

Ilmanen, A. (2003). Stock-bond correlations. *The Journal of Fixed Income* 13 (2): 55–66.

Ilmanen, A. (2011). *Expected Returns: An Investor's Guide to Harvesting Market Rewards*. Wiley.

Ilmanen, A. and Kizer, J. (2012). The death of diversification has been greatly exaggerated. *Journal of Portfolio Management* 38 (3): 15.

Indro, D.C., Jiang, C.X., Hu, M.Y., and Lee, W.Y. (1999). Mutual fund performance: does fund size matter? *Financial Analysts Journal* 55 (3): 74–87.

Inker, B. (2010). The hidden risks of risk parity portfolios. *GMO white paper*.

International Organization of Securities Commissions (IOSCO) (2005). "Principles on Outsourcing of Financial Services for Market Intermediaries," February 2005, Available at: http://www.iosco.org/library/pubdocs/pdf/IOSCOPD187.pdf.

Jenkinson, T., Jones, H., and Martinez, J.V. (2016). Picking winners? Investment consultants' recommendations of fund managers. *The Journal of Finance* 71 (5): 2333–2370.

Jensen, M.C. (1968). The performance of mutual funds in the period 1945–1964. *The Journal of Finance* 23 (2): 389–416.

Jones, H. and Martinez, J.V. (2017). Institutional investor expectations, manager performance, and fund flows. *Journal of Financial and Quantitative Analysis* 52 (6): 2755–2777.

Kahneman, D. (1991). Article commentary: judgment and decision making: a personal view. *Psychological Science* 2 (3): 142–145.

Kamerling, R., Kramer, R. (2017). *Veel beloven, weinig geven*. Nyenrode Tax Academy Press.

Koedijk, K. and Slager, A.M.H. (2011). *Investment Beliefs. A Positive Approach to Institutional Investing*. Palgrave Macmillan: Houndmills, Basingstoke, Hampshire.

Koedijk, K., Slager, A.M.H., and Stork, P.A. (2016). A Trustee guide to factor investing. *The Journal of Portfolio Management* (Special Issue) 42: 1–11.

Kritzman, M.P. (2002). *Puzzles of Finance: Six Practical Problems and Their Remarkable Solutions*, vol. 89. Wiley.

Kritzman, M. and Page, S. (2003). The hierarchy of investment choice. *The Journal of Portfolio Management* 29 (4): 11–23.

Laker, D. (2001). Interpreting performance attribution reports. *JASSA* (3, Spring 2001) 3: 1–27. Retrieved from www.finsia.com.

LAPP. (2018). *Statement of Investment Policy and Goals*. https://www.lapp.ca/assets/lapp/files/publications/funding/lappsipg2018.pdf (accessed 20-03-2018).

Law Commission (2014). Fiduciary duties of investment intermediaries. *Law Com* 350: 2014–2015.

Lencioni, P. (2002). Make your values mean something. *Harvard Business Review* (July 2002) 80: 5–9.

Lerner, J., Schoar, A., and Wang, J. (2008). Secrets of the academy: the drivers of university endowment success. *Journal of Economic Perspectives* 22 (3): 207–222.

Lo, A.W. (2005). Reconciling efficient markets with behavioral finance: the adaptive markets hypothesis. *Journal of Investment Consulting* 7 (2): 21–44.

London Pension Fund Authority (2013). *Strategic Policy Statement 2013 – 16*. www.lpfa.org.uk (accessed 15-05-2018).

Maginn, J.L., Tuttle, D.O., McLeavey, D.W., and Pinto, J.E. (2010). *Managing Investment Portfolios*. Wiley.

Malhotra, D.K. and McLeod, R.W. (1997). An empirical analysis of mutual fund expenses. *Journal of Financial Research* 20 (2): 175–190.

Malkiel, B.G. (1995). Returns from investing in equity mutual funds 1971 to 1991. *The Journal of Finance* 50 (2): 549–572.

Markowitz, H. (1952). Portfolio selection. *The Journal of Finance* 7 (1): 77–91.

Maynard, A. (2012). The powers and pitfalls of payment for performance. *Health Economics* 21 (1): 3–12.

Merton, R.C. (1995). A functional perspective of financial intermediation. *Financial Management* 24: 23–41.

Morrell, K. (2008). The narrative of 'evidence-based' management: a polemic. *Journal of Management Studies* 45 (3): 613–635.

Morris, M.W., Sheldon, O.J., Ames, D.R., and Young, M.J. (2007). Metaphors and the market: consequences and preconditions of agent and object metaphors in stock market commentary. *Organizational Behavior and Human Decision Processes* 102 (2): 174–192.

NBIM. (2017). *Mission and Values*. https://www.nbim.no/en/organisation/career/our-culture/mission-and-values (accessed 07-03-2018).

Neal, D. and Warren, G. (2015). Long-term investing as an agency problem.

OECD (2015). G20/OECD Principles for Corporate Governance. September 2015. Retrieved from https://www.oecd.org/daf/ca/Corporate-Governance-Principles-ENG.pdf

Oerlemans, A.G., van Lieshout, L., van Foreest, P. et al. (2013). *Beleggingsrisicos. Aanpak voor het beheersen van de risico's in het beleggingsbeleid van pensioenfondsen*. FNV Bondgenoten.

Olah, M. and Sturiale, J. (2006). *Building an Effective Investment Committee*, 1–16. Schwab Retirement Plan Services.

Pecchioli, R.M. (1983). *The Internationalisation of Banking: The Policy Issues*. Organization for Economic.

Pedersen, L.H. (2018). Sharpening the arithmetic of active management. *Financial Analysts Journal* 74 (1): 21–36.

Peters, E.E. (2011). Balancing asset growth and liability hedging through risk parity. *The Journal of Investing* 20 (1): 128–136.

Pfeffer, J. (1998). *The Human Equation: Building Profits By Putting People First*. Harvard Business Press.

Pillkahn, U. (2008). *Using Trends and Scenarios as Tools for Strategy Development: Shaping the Future of Your Enterprise*. Wiley.

Polbennikov, S., Desclée, A., and Hyman, J. (2010). Horizon diversification: reducing risk in a portfolio of active strategies. *Journal of Portfolio Management* 36 (2): 26.

Porter, M.E. (2008). The five competitive forces that shape strategy. *Harvard Business Review* (January 2008) 86: 1–17.

PTL (2003). "Distinguishing Features of DC Governance," Available at: http://ptluk.com/files/2013/11/DC-Grid1.pdf

Rajkumar, S. and Dorfman, M.C. (eds.) (2011). *Governance and Investment of Public Pension Assets: Practitioners' Perspectives*. World Bank Publications.

Raymond, D.M. (2008). Chapter 7: Investment beliefs. In: *Handbook of Finance*, vol. 1 (ed. F.J. Fabozzi). New Jersey: Wiley.

Reinhart, C.M. and Rogoff, K. (2009). *This Time Is Different*. Princeton, NJ: Princeton University Press.

Riley, S. (2012). African fund invests for returns and development. Retrieved on 18-02-2017, on http://www.top1000funds.com/profile/2012/03/21/african-fund-invests-for-returns-and-development

Robinson, S.W. (1972). *Multinational Banking: A Study of Certain Legal and Financial Aspects of the Postwar Operations of the US Branch Banks in Western Europe*. Sijthoff.

Rohde, L. and Dengsoe, C. (2010). Higher pensions and less risk: innovation in Denmark's ATP pension plan. *Rotman International Journal of Pension Management* 3 (2): 22–29.

Rose-Smith, I. (2016). How Low Can CalPERS Go? Retrieved from Institutional Investor: http://www.institutionalinvestor.com/article/3605572/investors-pensions/how-low-can-calpers-go.html#/.WJhlOvkrLRZ

Ross, S.A. (2013). The arbitrage theory of capital asset pricing. In: *Handbook of the Fundamentals of Financial Decision Making: Part I* (ed. L.C. MacLean and W.T. Ziemba), 11–30. New Jersey: World Scientific.

Roy, B. (2005). Paradigms and challenges. In: *Multiple Criteria Decision Analysis: State of the Art Surveys*, 3–24. New York, NY: Springer.

Rundell, S. (2017). OTPP's private equity revolution. Retrieved May 06, 2018, from https://www.top1000funds.com/profile/2017/08/03/otpps-private-equity-revolution

Russell, C. (2006). *Trustee Investment Strategy for Endowments and Foundations*. Wiley.

Saklatvala, K. (2014). Local responsibility—ESG evolution at Africa's Largest Pension Fund. Retrieved on 18-02-2017, on https://www.oecd.org/daf/fin/private-pensions/AdrianBertrandOECDEuromoneyLTIRoundtable.pdf

Saunders, A. (1994). Banking and commerce: an overview of the public policy issues. *Journal of Banking & Finance* 18 (2): 231–254.

SEI Investments (2016). Governance and Groupthink in UK Defined Benefit Pension Schemes. January 2016.

Sharpe, W.F. (1994). The Sharpe ratio. *Journal of Portfolio Management* 21 (1): 49–58.

Shefrin, H. (2002). *Beyond Greed and Fear: Understanding Behavioral Finance and the Psychology of Investing*. Oxford University Press on Demand.

Sherden, W.A. (1998). *The Fortune Sellers: The Big Business of Buying and Selling Predictions*. Wiley.

Sirri, E. and Tufano, P. (1995). *The Economics of Pooling*. Boston: Harvard Business School Press.

Slager, A. (2012) Institutional Investor Conference. Executive Offices.

Smith, M. K. (2001). Peter Senge and the learning organization. *The encyclopedia of informal education*.

Stegeman, B. and Doff, R. (2017). Het bestuursbureau; de nieuwe fiduciair?

Stewart, J.B. (2012) University Endowments Face a Hard Landing. The New York Times. https://www.nytimes.com/2012/10/13/business/colleges-and-universities-invest-in-unconventional-ways.html?_r=3 (accessed 12-07-2018).

Stewart, F. and Yermo, J. (2008). Pension fund governance: challenges and potential solutions. *OECD Journal: Financial Market Trends* 2008 (2): 1–42.

Stromberg, P. and Døskeland, T. M. (2018). EVALUATING INVESTMENTS IN UNLISTED EQUITY FOR THE NORWEGIAN GOVERNMENT PENSION FUND GLOBAL (GPFG).

Swensen, D.F. (2009). *Pioneering Portfolio Management: An Unconventional Approach to Institutional Investment, Fully Revised and Updated*. Simon and Schuster.

Sych, R. and Metzger, R. (2014). What the Fiduciary Are you Talking About?. In: CBIA Annual Benefits Survey Report.

Terhaar, K. (2010). CFA: The future of the investment policy statement. Financial Times. London.

The Economist (2009). *The End of Retirement*. https://www.economist.com/node/13900145 (accessed 15-05-2018).

Thompson, D.F. (2005). *Restoring Responsibility: Ethics in Government, Business, and Healthcare*, vol. 575. Cambridge University Press. [5] Cadbury, A. (2002). *Corporate governance and chairmanship: A personal view*. Oxford University Press on Demand.

TIAA-CREF (2014). *Code of Business Conduct*. https://www.tiaa.org/public/TIAA-CREF+Code+of+Business+Conduct (accessed 15-05-2018).

Tversky, A. and Kahneman, D. (1992). Advances in prospect theory: cumulative representation of uncertainty. *Journal of Risk and Uncertainty* 5 (4): 297–323.

Uijting, R.J.M. (2017). *The battle for parity: risk allocation matters too!* (Master thesis). Tilburg University Theses Database.

Van Dam, J. (2014). Rethinking investing from the ground up: how PFZW and PGGM are meeting this challenge. *Rotman International Journal of Pension Management* 7 (1), 6 pages.

Vanguard Group (2018). Is the "endowment model" good for all endowments? (accessed 12-07-2018).

Vittas, D., Impavido, G., and O'Connor, R. (2008). *Upgrading the Investment Policy Framework of Public Pension Funds*, vol. 4499. World Bank Publications.

Viviers, S. (2013). 21 Years of responsible investing in South-Africa: key investment strategies and criteria. *Journal of Economic and Financial Sciences* 7 (3): 737–774.

Wagner, R.K. (2002). Smart people doing dumb things: the case of managerial incompetence. In: *Why Smart People Can Be So Stupid* (ed. R.J. Sternberg), 42–62. Yale: Yale University Press.

Wallick, D. W., Wimmer, B. R., and Balsamo, J. (2015). Keys to improving the odds of active management success.

Watson Wyatt Worldwide (2005). *Global Investment Review*. London.

White, A. (2012). CALPERS: "OPAQUELY TRANSPARENT". Retrieved from top1000funds: https://www.top1000funds.com/news/2012/07/25/calpers-%E2%80%9Copaquely-transparent%E2%80%9D

White, A. (2015). The Future Fund 2.0. Retrieved from Top1000funds: https://www.top1000funds.com/profile/2015/11/11/the-future-fund-2-0

White, A. (2016). CALPERS' CHIEF NAVIGATES "PERFECT STORM." Retrieved from Top1000funds: https://www.top1000funds.com/conversation/2016/05/27/caipers-chief-navigates-perfect-storm

White, A. (2017). OTPP: An innovator's tale. Retrieved May 08, 2018, from https://www.top1000funds.com/profile/2017/06/15/otpp-an-innovators-tale

Willis Towers Watson, UK (2017). *Global Pension Assets Study.*

Willis Towers Watson (2017). *The Search for a Long-Term Premium.* Thinking Ahead Institute.

Working Group on Climate Change (2018). "Climate change for asset owners." June 2018. Toronto: The International Centre for Pension Management (ICPM).

Index